Federico García Lorca
and the Culture of
Male Homosexuality

Federico García Lorca and the Culture of Male Homosexuality

ÁNGEL SAHUQUILLO

Translated by Erica Frouman-Smith
Foreword by Alberto Mira

McFarland & Company, Inc., Publishers
Jefferson, North Carolina, and London

This book was previously published as a doctoral dissertation, *Federico García Lorca y la cultura de la homosexualidad. Lorca, Dalí, Cernuda, Gil-Albert y la voz silenciada del amor homosexual*, by Akademitryck (Stockholm, 1986); and as *Federico García Lorca y la cultura de la homosexualidad masculina*, by Instituto de Cultura "Juan Gil-Albert," (Alicante, Spain, 1991). It has been revised by the author and translated by Erica Frouman-Smith, who also contributed to its revision.

Spanish-language works by Federico García Lorca ©Herederos de Federico García Lorca. From *Obras Completas* (Galaxia Gutenberg, 1996 edition). English-language translations ©Herederos de Federico García Lorca and the various translators. All rights reserved. For information regarding rights and permissions, please contact lorca@artslaw.co.uk or William Peter Kosmas, Esq., 8 Franklin Square, London W14 9UU. Excerpts from *The Public and Play Without a Title*, by Federico García Lorca, copyright translation © 1978 by Herederos de Federico García Lorca, © 1983 by Carlos Bauer. Reprinted by permission of New Directions Publishing Corporation. Excerpts from *Selected Letters* by Federico García Lorca, copyright ©1978 by Herederos de Federico García Lorca, © 1977 by the Estate of Federico García Lorca. Reprinted by permission of New Directions Publishing Corporation. "Yerma" and "Blood Wedding" by Federico García Lorca, translated by James Graham-Lujan and Richard L. O'Connell, from *Three Tragedies*, copyright © 1947 by New Directions Publishing Corp. Reprinted by permission of New Directions Publishing Corporation. "The Love of Don Perlimplín," "Doña Rosita, the Spinster," and "The Butterfly's Evil Spell" by Federico García Lorca, Translated by James Graham and Richard L. O'Connell, from *Five Plays*, copyright © 1983 by New Directions Publishing Corp. Copyright 1941 by Charles Scribner's Sons. Reprinted by permission of New Directions Publishing Corporation. Spanish-language works of Luis Cernuda © Ángel María Yanguas Cernuda. Used by permission. Translations of poems by Luis Cernuda, from *Selected Poems of Luis Cernuda*, published by Sheep Meadow Press, 1999, copyright by Reginald Gibbons. Reprinted by permission of the translator. Poems of Emilio Prados © Paloma Araoz Prados. Used by permission. *Obra poética completa* by Juan Gil-Albert copyright © 1981. Published by la Institució Alfons el Magnànim. Used by permission. Works of Juan Gil-Albert copyright estate of Juan Gil-Albert, Dr. Claudia Simón, representative. Use and translation by permission.

LIBRARY OF CONGRESS CATALOGUING-IN-PUBLICATION DATA

Sahuquillo, Ángel.
   [Federico García Lorca y la cultura de la homosexualidad masculina. English]
   Federico García Lorca and the culture of male homosexuality / Ángel Sahuquillo ; translated by Erica Frouman-Smith ; foreword by Alberto Mira.
      p.   cm.
   Includes bibliographical references and index.
   ISBN-13: 978-0-7864-2897-7
   softcover : 50# alkaline paper ∞

   1. García Lorca, Federico, 1898–1936—Criticism and interpretation.   2. Homosexuality in literature. 3. Homosexuality and literature—Spain.   I. Title.
PQ6613.A763Z878213   2007
868'.6209—dc22   2007002190

British Library cataloguing data are available

©2007 Ángel Sahuquillo. All rights reserved

No part of this book may be reproduced or transmitted in any form or by any means, electronic or mechanical, including photocopying or recording, or by any information storage and retrieval system, without permission in writing from the publisher.

Cover photograph: Federico García Lorca in 1927, Granada, Spain

Manufactured in the United States of America

McFarland & Company, Inc., Publishers
   Box 611, Jefferson, North Carolina 28640
   www.mcfarlandpub.com

Table of Contents

Translator's Note	1
Foreword by Alberto Mira	3
Preface to the English-Language Edition	11

Introduction — 13
    Homosexuality and Lorquian Scholarship. "The Unspeakable." — 13
    Homosexuality and Literary Criticism. The Poetry and
        Sexuality of Emilio Prados. Prados and Lorca. — 14
    Cernuda. Exile, Marginalization and the Critical Reception. — 16
    Juan Gil-Albert. The Marginalization of His Work. Belated and
        Controversial Recognition. The Generation of '27 Members. — 17
    The So-Called "Friendship" of Dalí and Lorca — 19
    Relationships among Lorca, Cernuda,
        Prados and Gil-Albert — 20
    Lorca's Life and Letters: Silences and Secrets — 21
    Clarifications of Homosexual Culture and Homosexuality.
        The Erotic Dimension of Language. — 26
    Overview of the Contents and Methods of This Study — 30

1 Culture, Homosexuality and Lorquian Criticism — 33
    Legal Opposition to Homosexuality — 33
    Homosexuality and Lorquian Criticism — 36
    Reactions to Homosexuality — 38
    Emerging Changes in Lorquian Criticism and Gay Culture — 50
    The Heritage of the "Queer with the Bowtie" — 60
    Summary and Conclusions — 65

2 "The Other Half": Homosexual Purity in the Sewers — 66
    Rage of the Marginalized Towards the Establishment — 66

Lorquian Criticism and "The Other Half"	68
Orality. Flight. Purity and the Pure.	69
Purity and Lorquian Criticism. Lorca and Walt Whitman.	71
Bacchanalian Purification. Homosexual Purity.	73
The Ambiguity of Victorian Purity. Whiteness.	74
The Accursed "Breed" or "Race." Animal Blood. "Sailor's Blood." Those of a "Different Blood."	75
Sailors as Archetypal Figures in the Homosexual World	77
Lorca and Sailors	78
The Symbolism of Death, the "Bitter One," Knives, and the Act of Mounting	84
Heads and Necks. Biting and Beheading. Oscar Wilde's *Salomé* and "Beheading the Baptist."	88
Otherness, Homosexuality and Childhood. Rimbaud. Cernuda. Gide. Green. Ruiz López. Lorca's "Childhood and Death." Rats and Sewers.	93
"Everyone" and the Other	97
Lorca's Doves. The Incompatibility of the Christian Dove and the Lorquian Dove. The Doves of the Sewers.	98
Homosexual Purity in the Sewers and the Messianism of the Other	100
Summary and Conclusions	104

3 "Oppressed Norms": Homosexuality and Class Struggle — 105

The Economic and Determining Factors	106
A Study of "I Know That My Profile Will Be Serene"	108
Different Versions of the Poem	108
Technical Elements. Hernández and the Reading of the "Autoepitaph."	109
The Author's Presence	110
Symbols and Homosexual Intertextuality	110
Norms and Criticism	118
Summary and Conclusions	126

4 The Metamorphoses of the Billy Goat: Hell, Gag, and the Rebellion of Homosexual Love — 128

Introduction: "Book of Poems" and the Critics	130
The Sociopsychological Function of the Scapegoats	133
Popular Fantasies about the Billy Goat. The Religious Connection.	134
The Billy Goat and "Perverse" Sexuality	134

Christianity and Homosexuals	135
Myth and Criticism. The Mythic Reading of "The Billy Goat."	140
Lorca's Billy Goat	142
Fire and Blinding Light	146
Summary and Conclusions	160

5 Shadows and Dreams: "Verlaine," "Bacchus," and Criticism of the Dominant Reality — 162

Lorca, Prados, Cernuda and the Rejection of "Reality"	163
"Reality"	165
Freud and the Generation of '27. Art Against "Reality."	166
"Dream"	169
The Symbolism of Mounting and Blood. *Blood Wedding*.	172
The Horse's Lullaby. Water. Green. Tail. Branches.	174
From "Dream" to "Verlaine"	176
"Verlaine" and the Dream	183
"Bacchus." Shadow of "Verlaine."	185
Lorca's *Unpublished Poetry of Youth*	195
Summary and Conclusions	198

6 "Suicide": A Poem and Its Milieu, a Psyche and Its Circumstances — 199

"Suicide" from the "Back of the World" Section of *Songs*	201
Songs. The Book and Its Critical Reception.	202
The Grouping, Order and Background of the Poems	203
"Back of the World"	205
"Suicide" and Criticism. The Refusal to Reproduce, and Death.	206
Analysis of "Suicide." Preliminaries.	208
Summary and Conclusions	231

Epilogue: The Centenary	235
Chapter Notes	237
Bibliography	247
Index	263

Translator's Note

Where a page number is given with no other information, the reference is to the *Obras completas* of Lorca. When two sets of page numbers separated by a semicolon follow a quotation, the first number will refer to an existing English translation, and unless otherwise noted, the second to *Obras completas*. When only one page number is given for quotations from works in languages other than English, the translation is mine. All titles of works in languages other than English will appear once in their original form and then subsequently in English. The exception is for titles that are obvious cognates of English; they will remain in their original language.

Frequently cited titles are presented in abbreviated form after the first reference; i.e., *Poet in New York* becomes *PNY*. The following abbreviations are used with some frequency in the text: *OC en prosa* for *Obra completa en prosa*, Vol. 2 (Complete Works in Prose), and *OPC* for *Obra poética completa* (Complete Poetic Works) of Juan Gil-Albert; *PC*, for *Poesía completa* (Complete Poetry) of Luis Cernuda and for *Poesías completas* (Complete Poetry, 2 vols.) of Emilio Prados. Included here are two unpublished translations by Christopher Maurer of Lorca's "El macho cabrío" (The Billy Goat) and "Sueño" (Dream), indicated by "trans. Maurer."

I have made repeated references to the following translations whose complete reference can be found in the bibliography. By García Lorca: *Collected Poems* (*CP*), edited by Christopher Maurer, and *Poet in New York* (*PNY*), translated by Greg Simon and Steve F. White. (Belitt *PNY*) refers to miscellaneous prose pieces translated by Ben Belitt in his translation of Lorca's *Poet in New York*. By Luis Cernuda: (*Selected Poems*) translated by Reginald Gibbons; (*Young Sailor*), *The Young Sailor and Other Poems* translated by Rick Lipinski.

I would like to express my gratitude to the following for their invaluable assistance: to Carolyn Cassidy and Carlee Lippman for their help in reviewing the translation; to Steven Daniels, for his patient technical support; to Alberto Mira, for contributing the foreword to this translation; to

Daniel Eisenberg, David William Foster and Ian Gibson for their encouragement to go ahead with the project; to Edmund Miller, who first brought this book to my attention; and to Lou Pisha, at the C.W. Post Library. I wish to extend a special thanks to the C.W. Post Research Committee for their support of this project and to Christopher Maurer, for graciously providing additional translations of Lorca's poems and for his generous help on many issues.

— Erica Frouman-Smith

Foreword
by Alberto Mira
Oxford Brookes University

Federico García Lorca and the Culture of Male Homosexuality by Ángel Sahuquillo appeared in Spain only in 1991, in a limited edition that had almost no repercusion among "Lorquistas" and other authoritive voices on Spanish literature (either reviewers or academics). Before that, no significant work had focused on how homosexuality could affect the works of canonical writers, or indeed, on personalities of Spanish culture and their position towards homosexuality. Literature on the topic included rabidly homophobic treatises such as Mauricio Carlavilla's *Sodomitas* (1954), and a smattering of essays on homosexuality as a social problem in the late seventies. More precisely, the mechanism in which homosexual experience was turned into writing (in terms of literary influence, imagery and stylistic choices) remained undiscussed in academic studies: homosexual experience was not regarded as something creative; it was the passive situation of social and legal opresion that had to be overturned. After this was achieved we would move from silence caused by harsh repression to a (much better, it was suggested) silence reflecting newly found normality of the situation. Of course, after decades of enforced discretion and obstacles, the homosexuality of Lorca and Cernuda was by then acknowledged without resistance and beyond doubt. But such liberal acknowledgment was as far as critics and intellectuals wished to go (with some exceptions, such as Terenci Moix). Once it was frankly admitted, there seemed to be nothing else to say about it: "All right, so Cernuda's poems express desire for a younger man, so what, let's now move on to more serious matters; what about his use of metaphor?"

In spite of such awkward attitudes, so unblinkingly maintained by the cultural establishment, no Spanish intellectual has ever recognized having "a problem" with homosexuality. For Pío Baroja, as stated in his memoirs, the problem was homosexuality itself, and one too disgusting to discuss (he compared it to a physiological disorder such as piles, something that has to be "extirpated"). Other opinions are kinder or more liberal: for Rafael Cansinos Assens, a key intellectual of the first half of the twentieth century, homosexuals could only produce frivolous literature, and he always presented them as ridiculous figures, to be laughed at; Nobel Prize winner Camilo José Cela thought that homosexuals were perfectly fine "as long as they didn't try to stick it up his ass," as he delicately put it, in a notorious television interview. Of course, after the forceful stance for liberalism, brought upon by the political transition, the situation showed signs of change. Now, such opinions were regarded as too blatantly old fashioned, unworthy of the new Spain, the one that left behind the gloom of authoritarian Francoism, of black years of repression and intolerance. Even today, intellectuals continue claiming they don't have a problem; they are not to be labelled as "homophobic," as the word has the wrong connotations in a predominantly liberal landscape. At the same time, they don't see any contradiction in taking issue with, as they would put it, hysterical homosexuals whose outspokenness is always excessive ("what is there to express in such a visible way?"), who are a bit too assertive ("*what* is there to assert?"), who, in short, are obsessed with sex as the centre of life ("Love is, after all, just love, whatever the sexual orientation; and sex is indifferent to sexual identity, isn't it?").

In Spanish literary criticism, homosexuality is either something everybody knows about and accepts and therefore has nothing more to say about it (as in the case of Lorca), or homosexuality belongs to private life and knowledge of sexual identity does not contribute anything to artistic effect and therefore there is nothing more to say about it. Cernuda's poetry is just "love poetry," and there is no need to make much fuss about actual addressees, or the actual sex his imagined objects of desire happen to be.

That's the bottom line, actually: a 1990 edition of Lorca's *El público* managed to devote over forty pages to an analysis of the play without ever coming to engage with the issue of sexual dissidence. Given the play expresses anxiety about the homophobia of audiences, it would be fair to suggest that the editor was paradoxically becoming part of the audience Lorca feared so much.

Pointing out that homosexuality can be relevant in making sense of certain literary works, or, more specifically, attempting to engage with homosexuality as a source of meaning in the artistic work, as Sahuquillo boldly and rigorously does in the present volume, puts one in an awkward position, which accounts for the muted response that greeted his essay. Since intellectuals insist that their silence about homosexuality is based on liberal principles of scrupulous respect for every individual and their sacrosanct privacy (how odd, then that their *heterosexual* privacy seldom seems to deserve such respect), those questioning such principles are, by definition, intolerant or illiberal, only interested in "proselitism." Actually, the horror of homosexual proselitism is a constant source of concern in early twentieth century discussions of homosexuality in Spain: it is already very apparent in the circles around Carmen de Burgos and Cansinos Assens. The problem with homosexuals, such opinions go, is that they will try to convert everybody else and we must keep firm, a paranoid idea that comes up repeatedly in early twentieth century discussions on homosexual visibility.

It is thus never easy, for anybody who thinks there are important textual consequences of homosexuality, to engage with such positions, as one has to constantly appear to be either defending oneself or pushing an envelope. Pointing out that homosexuality deserves careful attention is a minority opinion that must be justified, whereas the opposite seems evident. And then there is the question of authority: whoever is expressing a gay "perspective" will always occupy an unauthorized position, easy to ignore or reject. Shortly after my book *Para entendernos* came out, authoritative Lorca specialist Miguel García Posada published a column in *El País* in which he posed as an outraged, honest critic who had just been unaccountably "attacked" by one of such envelope pushers (i.e. myself), yet again. Apparently, he had taken offense with the way he had been portrayed in my discussion of the *Sonetos del amor oscuro* affair (actually taken from Daniel Eisenberg's account, which he seemed to be unaware of), especially as he attempted to marginalize or disavow intimations of homo-affectivity and homo-eroticism in the poems. In a blatant case of "protesting [far] too much," he then proceeded to bring out a story on Cernuda, if only to prove that he could discuss homosexuality with the best of them. Then, he ended up suggesting that Cernuda himself would have certainly sided with him: he distorted an assertion by the poet to suggest that he was clearly against the obsession with sex in literature and had, after all, always been discreet with his private affairs (discreet, that is, in front of hetereosexual establishment, as one could not help to be at the time, given that the consequences of any indiscretion were insults or jail). Unlike, that is, other envelope pushers who just wanted to distort and misinterpret (he called gay critics "fraudulent interpreters" and suggested we didn't care about literature, but merely about "affairs of the crotch") the works of the masters.

The strategy, of which this is a typical instance is, then, two-pronged. First, the authoritative critics say that they are as liberal, open minded and accepting as anybody else; the problem is not in themselves, but in others: in a clearly paranoid move the critics portrays themselves as victims of "accusations" and "attacks" carried out by a posse of homosexual critics. If such posse exists in Spain, I would very much like to meet them, as there is some work to be done in terms of counterbalancing the weight of decades of anti-homosexual authoritative voices. Actually, academic scholarship in Spain so far was characterized precisely by its meekness and its acceptance of the status quo, refusing to make waves on this topic. Who is García Posada so afraid of? There are no "gay critics" in Spain that have anything close to the power and authority of the leading "ungay critics" (a label that applies to critics who would position themselves as heterosexuals and closeted gay critics). Actually, part of the problem is precisely that a number of homosexual critics who "don't have a problem" with homosexuality are well placed in key newspaper literary sections and academic departments and have seen it a point of honour to repeat the mantra once and again: there is nothing to say about it.

In a second move, the critic will declare that, after all, nobody thinks homosexuality is relevant in the first place. Authors don't write with their crotches, they write with their brains. And we are all liberal enough to acknowledge that in terms of brains we are all the same.

Fair point, but is homosexuality only a sexual thing? Sex may be the one defining aspect of homosexuality from a normalized perspective, but it is only a minor aspect of homosexual experience for most individuals. The feeling of rejection, fear of the law, doubts, the lack of an authorized language to wrap emotions into words, the awareness of disgust around the individual, the need to accept marginality to find sexual or emotional satisfaction, the feeling of difference, the importance of a close circle of friends, as Sahuquillo discusses in his essay, are far more important aspects of homosexual experience than the actual sex act, and have a stronger influence on any artist's work. His move consists in starting on the need for resistance against the attempts to homogenize homosexual experience on the side of doctors and legislators. And such resistance necessarily involves language, which is the basis of literary work. How could Lorca reach a compromise between dissident experience and social pressure? He had to produce sets of metaphors that would be expressive of such experience but manage to pass mostly unnoticed in their deeper significance right under the noses of the extremely intolerant circles he sometimes frequented and needed in order to pursue a career as a poet.

This is the simple fact that institutional Spanish critics have never brought themselves to face, in spite of grand claims of sympathy for the pariah: they always see homosexuality as a category of otherness, not a category of "experience." It is a simple move, yet so seemingly unachievable for those in hegemonic positions: to think of Lorca, Prados, Cernuda or Gil-Albert not just as individuals with an impenetrable private life and discreet desires, but as people who had to deal with an all too public homophobia and with very unprivate notions of what homosexuality was. The authorized notions of homosexuality never came from homosexuals themselves: they came from doctors, lawyers and those intellectuals that forcefully followed the guidelines of homophobic discourse. In fact, for an individual, identifying publicly with homosexual discourse would immediately marginalize his opinions.

It is living under homophobic structures that actually makes homosexuality not only relevant, but a key aspect in people's lives. True, in terms of the quality of feelings, sexuality does not really matter. What *does* matter, though, is the way people are made to feel *because* they feel in a certain way. Therefore, anybody who is aware of dissidence from majority discourse will be shaped by the need to make compromises, to conceal feelings, desires and attitudes. Still, homosexuality cannot be lumped together with any other kind of dissidence: being a Jew in Germany during the early thirties, or a Republican or an agnostic in Spain during the forties could be said to be facing a similar situation to that of the homosexual until very recently, but homophobia is, we should not forget, also a specific kind of marginalizing discourse. First, because the sense of community in the sense of homosexual is weak and precarious. There is evidence of homosexual communities in Spain at least from the late nineteenth century, but the difficulties in identifying them witness how fragile they were. Homosexuals got together and exchanged knowledge, but found it hard to build a discourse of resistance around what they shared. A Republican, an agnostic, a Jew, wherever they are, have recourse to authoritative, perfectly recognized historical discourses that contribute to tell them that, in spite of oppression, they are somehow "right." Second, because it does not refer to someone's beliefs, but to something yet again, intangible, such as desire. Also, because since the late nineteenth century Western homophobia became all-pervading. There were situations in which Jews, agnostics or Republicans could be made to feel "right," places where they belonged. Nobody dared to speak *for* the homosexual, in case he was rendered suspicious. Homosexual intellectuals had *some* inkling of a mythical past, Ancient Greece, where they could fit. But they were disconnected from the period; there wasn't a feeling of historical continuity. It might even not be real: indeed, there was an effort to turn Greek pederasty into chaste friendship.

Sahuquillo reviews these simple points and proceeds to identify the modes in which homosexual experience could be expressed. On the one hand, he is sensitive to the situation of homosexuals in Spain: the pressure for silence, the need for friends who felt the same. One device to counterbalance the demands for silence and self-expression is especially analyzed: the homosexual writers considered all place themselves within a tradition that had been recognized as explicitly homosexual. The sexualized theme of the ram, Hellenic imagery and other elements are traced back to their origins as materials for the expression of homosexual experience. Of course, nobody writes in a vacuum, and by force such materials also proceded from the homophobic tradition. The clash between "homosexuality as otherness" and "homosexuality as experience" is keenly felt in his description of Lorca's "Oda a Walt Whitman," in which there is the language of homophobia ambiguously mixed with a knowledge that could only proceed from experience.

Out of such textual work, Sahuquillo proposes the legitimacy of describing Lorca, Cernuda, Gil-Albert, Prados and others in terms of "homosexual culture." The existence of homosexual culture is vehemently denied by the intellectual establishment (or marginalized and minimized as "subculture," and therefore irrelevant in discussions of canonic literature). Of course this is not *just* homosexual culture. It is also culture of the Spanish Second Republic, male culture, Andalucian culture, etc. A label such as "homosexual culture" is never exclusive and is simultaneous with a miriad of other labels. Even, one must point out, "heterosexual culture." But if by culture we understand a specific system of signs, rituals, devices, a specific activation of certain signifiers in order to deal with concrete experience, then obviously we will miss what their work is about unless we postulate a situation in which "homosexual culture" is central.

In dealing with homosexuality, it is homophobia that has to be the starting point. It is a point that Sahuquillo has to deal with in his essay, and this means dealing with critical responses to the work of homosexual writers, singling out the way in which the relevance of sexual orientation was muted, censored or distorted. He devotes important sections of his argument to showing how critics have dealt with poems which, he contends, are attempts to express homosexual experience.

It is a necessary step, but a dangerous one. It runs the risk (a risk I run myself in these pages) of demonizing the critic by labelling homophobia, also, as a category of otherness. One of the reasons discourse around homosexuality in Spain is still so distorted and silence has become acceptable, is that "homophobia" is a strong word for anybody to be willing to accept, even in others. From the moment homophobia is described as an almost pathological frame of mind, it is obvious only the extreme attitudes will be thus labeled. Maybe the solution lies in working towards a normalization of homophobia as an expression of the *status quo*. Homophobia can be regarded, rather, as the usual attitude of Western culture to all things homosexual in the past century. Of course homophobes are normal people like you and me, and in the context of our society marginalization of homosexuality is perceived as a guarantee of the rightfulness of certain attitudes. When one says, for instance, that García Posada's attitudes are homophobic, one is not portraying him as evil or wrong: he is just reproducing the hegemonic attitudes in the system he inhabits, which may help to preserve his authority.

The issue at stake here is how legitimate it is to try to counter such attitudes. It has taken decades to be able to identify homophobia as a distinct feature of Western culture, as a particularly insidious resistance to accepting homosexuality as normal, and to recognize that there is discrimination against homosexuals in most walks of life. In the end, it is a matter of deciding whether we think such attitudes, now clearly revealed as something identifiable, should persist or, on the contrary, we should do something to counterbalance them. This is exactly the task Ángel Sahuquillo's book sets itself to perform: by presenting a counterdiscourse it is inviting discussion, it is inviting change, no matter how slow or belated, in predominant structures and attitudes. In this sense, the lack of response was even more frustrating. What could have been used as a tool for an evolution in attitudes was simply discarded. Now the opportunity to engage in such discussion becomes open for English-speaking readers. Although, over the fifteen years after its first publication, other work on Lorca has touched on some of the topics discussed by Sahuquillo, his detailed and systematic focus on formal aspects of literary expressions of homosexuality is still as relevant as it was when it was first published. It remains fresh in considering formal traditions of homosexual expression, and detailing the long history of words and concepts, suggesting that, sometimes, culture does have a sexual identity. It is a new opportunity for dialogue.

Dr. Alberto Mira is a Reader at Oxford Brookes University (UK). He has published extensively on homosexual culture in Spain. His most recent essay, De Sodoma a Chueca (2004), *is a cultural history of homosexuals in Spain during the twentieth century.*

Preface to the English-Language Edition

As I write these lines I realize that it has been more than thirty years since I began the systematic study of Lorca's oeuvre. I presented and defended my thesis in Stockholm in 1986; it dealt with homosexuality in the life and works of García Lorca and the connection between Lorca's writings and those of other homosexuals. I published a revamped and expanded version of my thesis in Spain in 1991; this current book is the third and is a thoroughly revised and updated version of the original. All extraneous material has been eliminated while new information appears throughout the text. The road I have traveled has been long and problematic. I will give some examples so that my American readers can have an idea of the incidents and attitudes that frequently have influenced the research on my chosen topic.

It was during the mid–'70s when I decided to study the theme of homosexuality. I was beginning my doctorate at the University of Stockholm at a time in which Sweden appeared before the eyes of the world as one of the countries that had moved furthest in regard to sexual freedom. This freedom was even greater among university students, intellectuals and other more or less educated and sophisticated people. Therefore, I recall my surprise in the face of certain attitudes I encountered in communicating what was going to be the object of my research. I asked myself, if this happened in Sweden, what would the situation be in other less "liberated" countries?

The first reaction was that of a classmate who inquired in a somewhat rhetorical fashion: "What kind of job do you think you will get with homosexuality as the major theme of your thesis?" Someone who was teaching at the university blurted out soon afterwards, "Everything has already been said about Lorca." Another person asked me if I couldn't work on something "more pleasant." Later on, during a seminar in which I presented an article about the importance of homosexuality in Lorca's work, a classmate tried to divert attention away from the topic by using the *ad hominem* argument. He focused the attention of the participants towards what was, according to him, *my obsession* with homosexuality. When I finally presented the definitive title of my thesis, "Federico García Lorca and the Culture of Male Homosexuality," one of the heads of the department at the university told me that that title could not be used because homosexual culture did not exist or, at the most, was a "subculture." I then asked myself, a subculture of what?

Over the course of thirty years, many changes have transpired in the world and in the mentality of readers. When I began my research, for example, no one or almost no one would speak about "heterosexism" or "hate crimes." One was vaguely aware that these phenomena existed, but they had yet to be named, and in not being named, it was as if, at times, they did not exist. Most readers will surely know that heterosexism is the attitude of disdain, hate or discrimination that some heterosexuals exhibit in discussing homosexuals or in the insolent way heterosexuals address or ignore them. The term can be applied equally when homosexuals manifest this same inclination (see *The Sexual Imagination: From Acker to Zola*, edited by Harriet Gilbert, 1993). Unfortunately, heterosexism and the crimes inspired by hate towards what is different continue to be very much alive, even into the 21st century. Now, at least, we are aware that such phenomena exist, and they are named accordingly.

Many people have helped in different ways during all these years of research, and I would need several pages to name them all. For that reason, I will mention only two, who are very worthy examples of all those who have lent me support: Professor Regina af Geijerstam, who directed almost all my studies during my doctorate, and my energetic North American translator, Professor Erica Frouman-Smith, without whose commitment, passion and determination this book would never have appeared in the United States.

—Ángel Sahuquillo

Introduction

Homosexuality and Lorquian Scholarship. "The Unspeakable."[1]

I've heard there is a secret chord
That David played, and it pleased the Lord
 Leonard Cohen, *"Hallelujah"*

Aunque el tema sea el mismo,
Cada amor tiene su aire,
...
De qué lado estás ya sabes:
Canta tus aires fielmente.
 Cernuda, *"Amor en música," Con las horas contadas* in *Poesía completa,* 437
["Although the theme may be the same, / Each love has its tune, / ... / You already know which side you're on: / Sing your tunes faithfully."—*"Love in Music," With Counted Hours,* trans. Frouman-Smith]

En mi lira tengo yo el secreto de las pasiones—dice David—...Vuestro gran pecado ha sido desligar la carne del espíritu ... Porque, en verdad os digo que vosotros sois los que necesitáis de la misericordia de la carne...
 Lorca, *Visión de la juventud. Mística que trata del freno puesto por sociedad a la naturaleza de nuestros cuerpos y nuestras almas.* quoted in Gibson, *Federico García Lorca,* 1:212, 213
["On my lyre I possess the secret of passion—says David—...Your great sin has been to separate the flesh from the spirit ... Because, the truth is you are the ones who need the mercy of the flesh..."—Lorca, *Vision of Youth: Mystic Treating the Curbs Society Places on the Nature of Our Bodies and Souls,* trans. Frouman-Smith]

En otra ocasión lo has dicho: nada puedes percibir, querer ni entender si no entra en ti primero por el sexo, de ahí al corazón y luego a la mente. Por eso tu experiencia, tu acorde místico, comienza como una prefiguración sexual.
 Cernuda, *"El acorde," Ocnos,* 89
["You have said it on another occasion: you cannot perceive, want or understand anything if it does not begin in you through sex, from there to the heart and then to the mind. For that reason, your mystical tunes begin as a sexual foreshadowing."—Cernuda, *"The Tunes," Ocnos,* trans. Frouman-Smith]

Federico García Lorca's homosexuality is no longer questioned among those professionally involved in literary criticism or biographies. Nevertheless, there are few serious, in-depth studies on this topic with regard to Lorca and his works. In 1977, the year I began a systematic investigation, the scholarship prompted by Lorca's life and works already occupied a total of 54 pages in Aguilar's *Complete Works* (Obras completas), consisting of approximately 1,200 articles and books. If one can judge by what is said and not said in the overwhelming majority of works mentioned there and by the space dedicated to them, that which relates to homoeroticism or to homosexual love seems to have little or no importance for the majority of authors. Not counting a few creditable exceptions, the theme of homosexuality has been considered irrelevant to the study of the life and the analysis of the work of a homosexual poet — in this case, Lorca. A writer friend of the poet has affirmed, indignantly, that Lorca "never muddied his song with unspeakable cries of the flesh" (Vázquez Ocaña 349).

The reality of homosexuality has almost always been something unspeakable, and for many, perhaps, continues so. It is something that ought to be silenced at all cost or, at most, only alluded to. In the prologue to the book *Posible imagen de José Lezama Lima*, José Agustín Goytisolo mentions that at a lunch with Roberto Fernández Retama and José Lezama Lima, one of the themes that dominated the conversation was that of "the lifestyle and sexual practices of the members of the Generation of '27 based on information that could be inferred from their texts, and also through revelations transmitted via oral tradition" (13). No more is said. This can be seen as an example of the allusions or vague terms that are often utilized when oral tradition is transformed into the written word.

Even in 1983, the qualifier *unspeakable* continued to mark the psychological and social reality of homosexuals. In an article entitled exactly that —"Lo inconfesable"— the philosopher Fernando Savater indicated, "The serious thing is that there are still *unspeakable* customs and loves that dare not speak their name" (11). As one can see in the first chapter, this climate does not favor research, although during the latter part of the twentieth century, some articles and books have courageously approached this topic (see chapter 1, "Lorquian Criticism").

Homosexuality and Literary Criticism. The Poetry and Sexuality of Emilio Prados. Prados and Lorca.

Some literary critics have insinuated that only sexually "normal" people can study the work of an author objectively and "impartially" verify whether or not the analyzed texts contain homosexual allusions or symbols. In the preface to his book *Shakespeare's Bawdy*, Eric Partridge quotes Hesketh Pearson, who believes that pedants and pederasts have been a curse to Shakespeare's work. The author thinks that because he himself is neither one, perhaps he can illuminate some neglected, but very important, aspects of the character and art of Shakespeare (vii).

In *Proust and the Art of Love*, J.E. Rivers reminds us that, until recently, homosexuality was viewed as a taboo topic, too difficult to deal with. One took for granted that any intelligent person knew that Proust was a homosexual, and, therefore, that it was impolite and unnecessary to be explicit in this matter (2).

In the scholarship pertaining to Emilio Prados, Luis Cernuda, Juan Gil-Albert and Salvador Dalí, a phenomenon similar to that which concerns Lorquian scholarship can be observed: studies relating to homosexuality are conspicuous by their absence, although some make guarded or hazy allusions. Larrea, for example, affirms: "perhaps one could say" that Prados gradually manifests "that 'otherness'" that made Rimbaud famous (*Poesía de Prados* 18).

The Poetry of Emilio Prados, a book based on a thesis from 1976, appears in 1981 with an ambiguous subtitle "A Progression towards Fertility." The author, P.J. Ellis, seems to allude to a vaguely abnormal sexuality through terms like "sexual inadequacy" (67) but only speaks clearly about homosexuality in a couple of notes (115, 146).

It seems rather ironic that it is a critic of modern music, José-Miguel Ullán, who does speak clearly about Prados' homosexuality in an anecdotal way, with silenced or secret sources, following the oral tradition alluded to by Goytisolo: "It's been said that in the middle of the Civil War, during a bombing, the great poet Emilio Prados felt the necessity of confessing to León Felipe that he thought he was homosexual. And old León, patriarchal by then, instead of repudiating the confessor or delighting in the confidence, went and told him: 'Nonsense! What you are is an angel'" (Ullán 5–9).

In the prologue to the complete poetry of Prados, Blanco Aguinaga and Carreira affirm that for the poet,

> the great figure of the Residencia [de Estudiantes] was Federico García Lorca.... It's even possible that during this period in the Residencia, Prados may have written his first poems under the influence of García Lorca.... In Mexico, among the portraits that Emilio Prados kept on the walls and in the closet of his room — Whitman, Nerval, San Juan, Keats, Rimbaud —, the portrait of Federico always had a special place [xxiv–xxv].

With the consolidation of democracy, homosexual culture has become increasingly visible in Spain. In relation to other homosexual authors of Lorca's group, it is important to indicate that the sexuality of the most discrete or the most oppressed of them, Emilio Prados, finally has been narrated in a work that is a mixture of fiction and biography, *En voz continua* (1997). The author, Carlos Blanco Aguinaga, edited and wrote the prologue for the complete poetry of Prados, together with Antonio Carreira in 1975 (volume 1) and 1976, but without saying anything then about the poet's homosexuality, in spite of including in the book an extensive text that treated Prados' life and writings. In the 1997 work, based in part on the poet's diary and on letters, the homosexuality of the poet is revealed with great clarity.

Cernuda. Exile, Marginalization and the Critical Reception.

Prados, Cernuda and Gil-Albert were exiled poets, physically and psychically. If José Agustín Goytisolo referred to the sexuality of the members of the Generation of '27 in an obscure manner, Juan Goytisolo is a little more explicit in mentioning the motives for Cernuda's marginalization. According to him, Cernuda's poetry was ignored in Spain and abroad, even among "numerous Spanish expatriate communities" ("Homenaje" 161), for two principal reasons: Cernuda's frank expression of his amorous instinct and his attacks on the basic pillars of society. "Cernuda's name disappeared for more than a decade, enclosed in a dense 'wall of silence'" (173). Although the author does not write the word "homosexuality," it is understood what Cernuda's "love instinct" was.

In "I Do Not Like to Talk About Luis Cernuda" (No me gusta hablar de Luis Cernuda), Elena Garro mentions the "invisible curtain" that surrounded the poet (116). Octavio Paz did what he could to help the poet, who "did not appear anywhere, did not attend any parties, meetings or lectures" and who lived "isolated and poor...." "Everything was very difficult in regard to Cernuda" (Garro 115).

Paz himself says, commenting on the tributes made to Cernuda after his death: "Now that the poet is buried, we can discuss his work without risk and make it say what we think it should have said ... And if 'interpretation' seems impossible, we will erase the prohibited words — rage, pleasure, disgust, boy, nightmare, solitude..." (*Signos* 125). Pages later Paz maintains, "in omitting or attenuating his homosexuality, one runs the risk of not understanding the meaning of his work" (142).

Philip Silver does not overlook the homosexual theme but only gives it minimal space. He affirms that the poet's love for boys and adolescents ought to be seen as a nostalgic effort to recover the innocence of youth (*Poetry of LC* 64). Although he mentions the conflict between homosexual love and the established order, Silver does not delve deeply into the significance this conflict might have had for the poet (96).

Derek Harris indicates that the critics, in spite of the eroticism evident in many poems, rarely mention Cernuda's homosexuality. According to Harris, it is tempting to think that the deliberate avoidance of the theme is a sign of the discomfort within literary criticism that puts the emphasis on the neurotic elements of personality. Harris affirms that this behavior could be the result of suppressed moral judgments (*LC: A Study of the Poetry* 13). He is probably referring to "unspeakable" moral judgments.

Christopher Soufas, in a note to his article, "Cernuda and Daimonic Power," believes that, even during the '80s, the theme of Cernuda's homosexuality continued to be something that scholars avoided (175).

Silver summarizes the treatment accorded Cernuda and, also, the indifference official Spanish institutions have shown and continue to show toward his work: "no opportunities in life, not one prize, and until now [1988] in Spain only two 'official' symposiums on his work, the last one this [past] May in Seville. Nevertheless, today in Spain, among poets and critics, Cernuda is considered not only one of the most outstanding poets of the Generation of '27, but of the entire twentieth century in Spain" (*From Cernuda's Hand* [De la mano de Cernuda] 16).

Juan Gil-Albert. The Marginalization of His Work. Belated and Controversial Recognition. The Generation of '27 Members.

Juan Gil-Albert is the only poet studied here who lived to witness the current democracy in Spain. He was also an eminent prose writer who insisted on the importance of homosexuality in his life and work. Francisco Brines calls Gil-Albert's *Heraclés* "perhaps the most lucid treatise of homosexuality ever written in Spanish" ("La voluntaria jubilación" 35).

Perhaps there is reason to wonder why Gil-Albert's name is missing from most of the literary anthologies, histories and monographs on the Generation of '27. In a book by Luis Antonio de Villena that includes a long interview with the writer, Gil-Albert defends his place among the authors of his generation: "I have always said that I belong to this generation based on my age and work. What has happened is that afterwards, life or history has kept me away" (*The Inexhaustable Reasoning* [El razonamiento inagotable] 31–32). Villena believes Gil-Albert has been marginalized threefold: "Marginalized morally, sexually, literarily, Juan Gil-Albert has given us an excellent example of *liberty*, of glory and of sacrifice that occasionally can be equated with being *free*" (9–10).

After Franco's death, the official silence surrounding Gil-Albert's work has become more and more scandalous. In *Insula*'s January 1976 edition appeared an article/interview by Fernando G. Delgado, "Juan Gil-Albert, After the Silence" [JGA, después del silencio]. A year later (in *Cuadernos Hispanoamericanos*) Leopoldo Azancot asked: "To what, then, do we owe this lack of recognition, this silence, that today paradoxically increases his prestige in the eyes of the young?" (524).

In 1982, Francisco Brines notes that although young people appreciate Gil-Albert's work, "The most respectable institutions, the juries of the most important prizes are deaf and blind to it and ignore the swelling rumor from the street from reaching them" ("La justicia").

On January 7, 1984, it seemed that the definitive recognition of Gil-Albert occurred, and *El País* published an article with the important news item: "The Institute of Juan Gil-Albert Studies is being established." The journalist Pere Miquel Campos stated, nevertheless, "In the session of the provincial corporation that approved the statutes and the title of the Institute, the Grupo Popular abandoned the Assembly Room" (*El País*). Juan Gil-Albert, said the Grupo Popular's spokesperson, is "the representative of a generation and of particular attitudes we wish to forget."

It has been noted that Juan Gil-Albert has never been considered a "representative" of the Generation of '27, although certainly of the tastes, inclinations or attitudes of this generation that have been repressed and silenced. The official representatives of the Generation of '27 who have obtained recognition, prizes and rewards have been others: Dámaso Alonso, Cervantes Prize (Premio Cervantes) of 1978, member of the Real Academia de la Lengua from January 1948 until his retirement at the end of 1982; Jorge Guillén, who obtained the Premio Cervantes in 1976 and the Ollín Ylitzli in 1982; Rafael Alberti, National Literature Prize (Premio Nacional de Literatura) in 1924, Premio Nacional in theatre, 1982; also obtained the Soviet order of the Friendship of Peoples (Amistad de los Pueblos) in 1983; Gerardo Diego, Premio Cervantes in 1979; Luis Rosales, Premio Cervantes in 1982, etc. Recognition for Gil-Albert, Cernuda, Prados and García Lorca was much later in coming. After his death, while the Civil War raged in Spain, his works were viewed with disapproval by the "defenders of civilization," the term used pejoratively by Guillermo de Torre in a letter to Eduardo Blanco-Amor. This letter is found in the archive of the library of the Provincial Committee of Orense. It bears the letterhead of the Editorial Losada and the date, May 31, 1938:

> Dear friend and colleague: Excuse my insistence, but Federico's *Book of Poems* [Libro de poemas] and the *Six Galician Poems* [Seis poemas galegos] are of urgent interest because there has to be some immediate action on them. The

mere heading of this paper will forestall any explanations. The "defenders of civilization" categorically refused to publish the works of our poor friend. In order to correct this outrage and many others, that is, in order to publish books, since the ultimate ideal of these people — even being editors — is not to publish them, Losada, very courageously, is creating a new publishing house where I have very direct involvement. For today I'll tell you no more. Begging you for the greatest caution about all of the above, I'll share more explanations verbally when I have the pleasure of seeing you.

The So-Called "Friendship" of Dalí and Lorca

According to declarations made by Dalí to Alain Bosquet, Lorca was very much in love with him. The painter is quite explicit about what happened: "one day I gave in to his desires. We tried it.... It hurt me and we had to stop" (Olano 126; Gibson, *FGL* 1:440; Sánchez Vidal, *Buñuel* 126). Dalí's words could be seen as being inspired by a sensationalistic zeal, but it is doubtful that this is the case. Speaking publicly 30 or 40 years ago about homosexual relationships would have caused a great scandal. Dalí said nothing at the time.

In 1981 Antonina Rodrigo published *Lorca-Dalí: A Betrayed Friendship* (Lorca-Dalí: Una amistad traicionada). With respect to the history of this "friendship," the book is little more than a fraud. The cover seems a shameless attempt to sell something that later disappears from sight. A photo of Lorca and Dalí, alone, in bathing suits, takes up almost the whole cover space. Lorca is seated next to the standing Dalí with his hand on Dalí's knee. Everything suggests that the book deals with the intimate relationship implied by the title and photograph. Carlos Rojas has indicated, nevertheless, that although the author has published important documents, in mentioning Dalí's and Lorca's "friendship," Antonina Rodrigo walks gingerly through her own declarations about their *amitié amoureuse* (*Lorca-Dalí* 7).

According to the poet Louis Aragon, Lorca and Dalí were going to bed for two years, "everyone knows it!" (Fernández and Kobuz 83). (About Aragon's visit to the Residencia in 1925, see Gibson, *FGL* 1:414–15.)

In 1984 Rafael Santos Torroella published *Honey Is Sweeter than Blood* (La miel es más dulce que la sangre), a book based on his doctoral thesis. Homosexuality is mentioned, but not without first giving the reader a long, careful and roundabout preparation. The author names the "intimate conflict" that "tortured" Lorca and Dalí without giving any specific details. Through half the book, the conflict is alluded to without the reader's knowing its nature. Finally, on page 99, the "erotic, sentimental" character of the conflict is revealed.

Such excessive caution in talking about what there was between Lorca and Dalí is an indication of the extremely diseased sensibility of the culture surrounding the criticism, a culture that does not want to face openly and courageously the fact that there was a homosexual relationship between Lorca and Dalí. Dalí himself is very explicit in regard to this: "That was not a friendship; it was a very strong erotic passion. That is the truth" (statements by Dalí to Gibson, "With Lorca and Dalí" [Con Lorca y Dalí 11]).

In spite of the obstacles he encountered, Ian Gibson continued his research on García Lorca and Dalí and published an extensive and detailed biography, *The Shameful Life of Salvador Dalí* (La vida desaforada de SD) (959 pp.). Anagrama published the Spanish version in 1998, and W.W. Norton later published the English version. Some of the pages related to Lorca were also published in *El País*, January 31, 1999, under the title of "The Love of Lorca and Dalí" (El amor de Lorca y Dalí). In 2000 Ian Gibson published a book on the same subject: *Lorca and Dalí: The Love That Could Not Be* (Lorca-Dalí. El amor que no pudo ser) (Barcelona: Plaza y Janés).

Relationships among Lorca, Cernuda, Prados and Gil-Albert

Lorca maintained more or less intimate personal relationships with Dalí, Cernuda, Prados and Gil-Albert. The knowledge that these relationships existed perhaps can help to clarify some of the poetic images utilized by this group of friends. Considering the clandestine nature of homosexual love, the use of a codified language with the power to express the forbidden does not seem improbable. In *Estudios sobre poesía española contemporánea*, Cernuda maintains that his acquaintance with Lorca makes clear to him the symbolic value of certain key Lorquian words and expressions. The author affirms that his friendship with Lorca permits him to decipher passages from his poetry that would otherwise have been impenetrable (218). Also indicated in this book is that Lorca was predisposed to an awareness of injustice based on "intimate personal reasons" (216). In the '50s it was difficult to speak openly without paying dearly for the words, as will be seen in chapter 1 ("Lorquian Criticism").

García Lorca and Emilio Prados knew each other from earliest childhood; they later separated and were reunited in the Residencia de Estudiantes in Madrid when Prados was 20 and Lorca 21. José Sanchis-Banús, who maintained an extensive correspondence with Prados, published 45 of the poet's letters in his doctoral thesis from 1972. Prados wrote to him that Federico was an intimate friend who encouraged him enormously in his debut. He felt connected to Lorca because both had "similar veins" (283). (See chapter 2, "Lorca and Sailors" for more on the symbolism of "veins.") Prados speaks about his relationship with Lorca in his *Diario íntimo*: "I have opened my heart to him and he has known how to understand it.... Once I reached his heart, I understood his childish kindness and affection" (Sanchis Banús 285).

In 1926, Prados spent some time with Lorca. On December 2nd of that year, Pepín Bello wrote to Lorca and asked him about Prados' stay in Granada. He also mentioned the "most pederastic 'Sur' [printshop]" where Emilio Prados was working as a director, along with Manuel Altolaguirre. Accompanying this letter was another one from Benjamín Palencia, illustrated with erotic and phallic drawings, directed to "Emilio and Federico." The sexual organs that were drawn were covered with little red papers that could be lifted. One of the drawings warned: "Anyone other than Emilio or Federico is prohibited from looking" (Gibson, *FGL* 1:459–61).

According to Gil-Albert, he and Lorca saw each other a great deal. In an interview/conversation Gil-Albert says: "I remember him at home, telling me intimate things" (Villena, *Reasoning* 29, 30).

Lorca's Life and Letters: Silences and Secrets

On many occasions Federico García Lorca would express in some letter or other the pain or bitterness he felt at not being able to show his feelings openly nor even speak about them. Already in 1918 at the age of 20, in a letter to Adriano del Valle, Lorca confessed that in the presence of others he feigned a sexual leaning "which is not my heart's truth" (*Selected Letters* 2; *OC* 1095). It seems evident that the reason for Lorca's pretense is a social control that inhibits his true sexuality and awakens in the poet feelings laden with claustrophobic overtones: "I see before me many problems, many entrapping eyes" (2; 1095–96).

Lorca does not clearly say which inhibiting personal experiences he had, but in a letter to Melchor Fernández Almagro, Lorca indicates that he was the object of a direct or indirect compulsion that obliged him to hide what he felt: "There are certain sentiments that shouldn't be displayed ... and I have the papers to prove it (I really do)!" (*Letters* 39; 1095–96).

In contrast to the feelings one has but does not reveal, there are some desires that one supposes Lorca should feel, but which he does not: "It's curious that I don't envy or desire the things of man" (39; 1197). Some lines before, the poet has expressed the emotion he feels in the presence of the sea and has suggested why: "Before the sea I forget my sex...." Lorca forgets that he is a man and, implicitly, he forgets what a man ought to do and feel, according to the dictates of the dominant morality. In this letter, the poet indicates the technique that he utilizes in the play he is writing where "no more is said than the bare minimum and everything else is insinuated" (39; 1127).

In 1927 the outlines of the internal crisis that will culminate in 1929 in Lorca's trip to the United States is evident:

> In my poetry everything seems deplorable regarding what needs *I haven't expressed* and cannot *express*. I find shadowy qualities where there ought to be a fixed light and I find in everything a painful absence of my *own true* person. That's how I'm feeling. I need to go far away [1161].

Lorca does not clarify why he is unable to express himself, but it seems that this is a situation in which a person's innate desire for expression is opposed by something that prevents him from manifesting it: an external pressure or oppression that is internalized by the poet. In terms of his personal experience, this oppression appears in such a palpable way that Lorca realizes that he needs to abandon his familiar surroundings and go "very far" away.

Lorca has lived trying to adapt himself to the dominant values of society. He loves his family and his people and accepts the repression of a part of his being that is not acceptable in the surroundings in which he lives: "I laugh at my passions," he wrote in 1921 to Melchor Fernández Almagro (*Letters* 14; 1112). In the long run, no one can laugh with impunity at what he feels in the depths of his being.

With the internal crisis looming that will make him depart for America, Lorca alerts Jorge Zalamea to the constant tension with which he lives: "trying constantly to see to it that your state of mind does not filter into your poetry, because it will play you a bad trick by exposing the purest in you to the eyes of those who should *never* see it" (*Letters* 143; 1314).

The best part of the poet, "the most pure," is without doubt extremely dirty or undesirable in the eyes of society since Lorca has to be on guard "constantly" in order not to betray himself. In some implicit way, it is revealed that the dirty-pure thing that is silenced has a strong tendency to "filter" into Lorca's poems.

The above letter was written in 1928. That same year, Lorca complains in another letter to the same person: "A famous man knows the bitterness of having a cold breast transfixed by floodlights turned on him by *others*" (145; 1315). The problematics were similar, if not identical, when Lorca was not yet famous and spoke about "eyes that imprison me." There were 11 years of feeling persecuted by continuous and malevolent public control. Not surprisingly, a crisis was brewing.

Far from his family and his country, Lorca writes his most openly homosexual work, *The Public* (El público), a play that, with the exception of two scenes, would not become known until 1978, in a still incomplete version.

Upon returning to Spain from New York, Lorca continued to show the same attitude towards what Marcelle Auclair calls his essential problem. According to Auclair, Lorca kept silent about it, and was totally reserved in his attitude. People confirm that the poet was the personification of discretion with those who did not share his tastes. Auclair declares that she herself and numerous friends had frequent contact with Lorca without suspecting that he was homosexual, but that the poet was less discreet in the last years of his life.

Although he may have been less cautious before his death, Lorca was conscious, until the end, of the prohibitions that weighed on him that made clear and sincere expression of what he felt impossible. In "Literary Conversations," an interview from 1936, the same year he was assassinated, Lorca answers the question, "what is poetry?" by alluding to the strictures that inhibited his inspiration: "One cannot speak about whether a man is a more suggestible object than a woman. With that, I answer your question. No, one can't speak about it" (1076–77).

◆ ◆ ◆

Lorca's significant silences and half words concerning his homosexuality are evident with regard to his letters and his life. To live surrounded by the enemies of "the purest thing" has to be a traumatic experience. Lorca's open secret must have left profound traces in his poetic work, but where do they appear, how do they manifest themselves, what do they reveal, what are the shapes that they take? "Shapes are a lie," affirms Lorca's poetic persona from "Moon and Panorama of the Insects" (Luna y panorama de los insectos) (*Poet in New York* 123 [Poeta en Nueva York 512]). What is there behind the lie of "shape"?

The purpose here is not to read an aesthetic work as a biography. But if there are solid or tenuous connections between Lorca's life and work, they must be disclosed. At the same time, it would be a fallacy to equate the poet's life with his work or pretend that a work of art has no connection whatsoever with its creator, or the context of that creator.

It is easy to observe that, just as in Lorca's letters, in his poetry the acts of pretending and of hiding or silencing something are mentioned or alluded to frequently. In "Elegía" for example, a woman is presented who is a "mirror" of an Andalusia "that suffers gigantic passions in silence, / passions rocked by fans / and by mantillas over throats" (*FGL: Collected Poems* 27; 40). Here the metaphor of the mirror is the axis of two sociological and psychological phenomena: literature as a mirror of society, and the individual as a mirror of the inhibitions and prohibitions of this same society. The silenced passions of the poem are like the covered throats.

The motif is repeated in "Elegía del silencio" and in "The Billy Goat" (El macho cabrío), the latter poem analyzed in chapter 4. (This particular animal has passions attributed to him that are never made explicit. The billy goat is, or seems, "silent.") In "Invocación al laurel" it is affirmed that the title tree produces "fruits of silence" (136). The poetic "I" from "Nido" (Nest) asks what "silent rain" has left him trembling, etc. (145). All these examples are taken from *Book of Poems*.

In *Poem of the Deep Song* (Poema del cante jondo), Lorca continues using the same motif, for example in the poems "El silencio" (160) and "¡Ay!": "All has broken in the world / Nothing remains but silence" (*CP* 111; 171).

First Songs (Primeras canciones) contains a section that Lorca entitled "Palimpsestos." With this word, the author wants to indicate that the original text has been erased and replaced by the ones being read. By calling our attention to this point, Lorca indirectly tells us that those who are interested in the traces left in it can reconstruct the underlying text. Traces are often left in palimpsest manuscripts due to involuntary carelessness. In the palimpsest poems there is a deliberate aesthetic intention.

In several poems from *Songs* (Canciones), there is a poetic "I" that informs the reader of something that the poet has to say that, for some hidden reason, he does not say: "Verlaine" deals with "The song / I'll never speak" (*CP* 453; 321), and in "Narciso" we are told that there is something that can be understood, at the same time that all direct information on this is supressed: "When he vanished into the water, / I understood. But I shan't explain" (*CP* 459; 326). Following the poem "The Voiceless Child" (El niño mudo) (487; 361) comes "The Crazy Boy" (El niño loco) (487; 362). In this way what is suggested is that the impossibility of speaking leads to insanity. Also part of *Songs*, "Two Sailors Ashore" (Dos marineros en la orilla) introduces a man who "washed his words and stopped speaking" (511; 387).

In 1923 Lorca wrote "Wake Up/Ring Out" (¡Amanecer y repique!) and sent it to Melchor Fernández Almagro telling him, among other things, that it is "*getting into problems* that I should have confronted long ago" (*Letters* 63; 1142). Silence appears in this poem accompanied by a double interjection that expresses the strong reaction of someone to the revelation of the androgynous or bisexual nature of the poetic "I": "My soul, boy & girl, / be silent, *silent*! (*CP* 397; 1142). Here it is Lorca himself who associates, in an indirect way, his personal problems with his aesthetic work.

Only in "Ode to Walt Whitman" (Oda a Walt Whitman) from *Poet in New York* will the theme of silenced homosexuality clearly appear in his speaking of "...men with that green look in their eyes / who love other men and burn their lips in silence" (161; 531).

♦ ♦ ♦

Lorca seldom mentioned the word "homosexual" in his public life or in his work. His poetic texts and letters speak only of silences, secrets and pretense, "only," but with great frequency. Often named secrets can be somewhat ambiguous, an example of which is "Song of the Seven-Hearted Boy" (Canción del muchacho de siete corazones) sent by Lorca to Melchor Fernández Almagro. In the accompanying letter, Lorca told him that "There are certain sentiments that should not be displayed" and that he is writing a work in which "no more is said than the bare minimum and everything else is insinuated" (39; 1127). In the poem the poetic "I" says: "And the secrets I wore at my throat, / unbeknownst to me, had come open" (*CP* 391; 1128).

The ambiguity of the poem resides in the fact that there is a poetic "I" that, without wanting to, reveals some secrets; behind the poem is an author who, wanting to, makes his poetic "I" assume the role of an unconscious revealer of secrets. Lorca seems to be playing hide-and-seek with his secrets or those of his poetic "I." He hides them in the text at the same time that he, indirectly, reveals that they are not so hidden. And he hints that the secrets are found very close to the voice of his poetic "I" ("at my throat").

After having observed in Lorca's letters the fear and desire to express something hidden and, also, the recurring appearance of motifs and themes relative to silence and to secrets in his poetic work, the following hypothesis emerges: that the above-mentioned phenomena are signs and signals of a discourse related to the expression of homosexual love. Additionally, this discourse has been and is pushed toward anonymity by family, social, legal and religious oppression going back a thousand years, practiced as much on an individual-personal level, as in Lorca's case, as on a collective level. Although Lorca may have written the texts that will be analyzed, many of the feelings and situations that appear in them, as well as certain symbols, go beyond the personal. They can be found within what we will call a *culture* of homosexuality or *homosexual culture* (explained and defined below under "Clarifications on Homosexual Culture and Homosexuality"), and they are a product and reflection of the conditions under which homosexuals have found themselves obliged to live. The study of social reality is an obvious foundation for this type of literary research — poetic works contain social and political dimensions as Ernesto Sábato suggests in his article, "Reflexiones sobre la obra de arte":

> Let us begin by saying that all art is social, just so, without quotation marks. Humans in an absolute solitary state no longer exist, and all consciousness is consciousness of the world. And even more than ordinary human beings, given

the subtlety and the exaggeration of their sensibility, artists express in their work that interaction of their "I" with external reality [18].

In this work there is a basic isotopy or central unifying thread[2]: homosexuality in Lorca's work, framed within, or contrasted with the culture of homosexuality, all seen in the social context which corresponds to it. In that culture, the works of Cernuda, Prados, Gil-Albert and Dalí are of particular relevance, as has already been demonstrated above.

Clarifications of Homosexual Culture and Homosexuality. The Erotic Dimension of Language.

Homosexual culture is to be understood here as *the linguistic and aesthetic cultivation of all that refers to the expression of homosexual love and its problematics.*

What is or what is not "Culture" or "culture" is something about which there is no consensus, nor has there ever been. Perhaps one could say that a culture or cultivation consists of three principal parts, according to how the term is utilized here: 1) the society or terrain whence the culture originates; 2) the individual and the group or groups in whose interior the culture grows and is transformed; and 3) the fruits that the culture produces, a poetic work, for example.

Homosexual culture has distinctive traits, but it is also, in part, an indirect product of heterosexual culture. This occurs, for example, when homosexuals react by expressing their feelings in the face of repression or persecutions of which they are the object.

As will be seen throughout this work, homosexual culture shows its idiosyncrasy through its themes, symbols, archetypes, position or point of view, by the semantic and semiotic turn it gives to certain words or expressions, etc. Although in the last fifty years a certain evolution has been observed, historically, homosexual idiosyncrasy has been obliged to hide itself or its surface in an extremely subtle, disguised or secret way. This is also one of its principal characteristics. For example, the first two stanzas of one of the most famous poems from *Sonnets of Dark Love* (Sonetos del amor oscuro), by García Lorca, were not known, for the most part, until 1984 (for more details on the history of these sonnets, see Eisenberg, "Reactions to the Publication of the *Sonetos del amor oscuro*," in *BHS* 1988, 261–71):

> O secret voice of dark love!
> O bleating without fleece! O wound!
> O needle of gall, sunken camelia!
> O current without sea, city without walls!

> O immense night of sure profile,
> celestial mountain tall with anguish!
> O dog in the heart, beleaguered voice,
> borderless silence, ripened lily! [*CP* 721; *Sonetos* 54].

At first glance it does not seem that there is anything in these lines that alludes to homosexuality. One of the principal traits of homosexual culture is that it is not obvious. In order to recognize it, it is necessary to study it carefully or belong to it in some way, besides having also studied the personal language of the author under consideration. Nevertheless, today the expression "dark love" as a symbol of "homosexual love" is beginning to be so well known that it almost goes without saying. A writer known to be unsympathetic to homosexuals, Fernando Díaz Plaja, wrote in the weekend section of *El País*, from April 3, 1983, in an article entitled "Los 'gay'": "They wrapped themselves up in mysterious words as if under a blanket ('dark love,' for example)."

The symbol of dark love in Lorca's sonnet acquires greater strength and clarity through its relationship in the poem with three of the most frequent motifs in the history of homosexual culture: persecution, the secret and silence. The voice of dark love is defined as a "secret voice," a persecuted voice and "a boundless silence."

Another characteristic of this persecuted or silent voice is that it indicates the distance or the abyss that separates it from the culture that displays power. In reality, this culture artificially creates, through distancing and discriminatory acts, the limits that help define part of the idiosyncrasy of homosexual culture. The following is an example taken from Cernuda's work.

In "What a Pity It Was My Land" (Es lástima que fuera mi tierra) from "Díptico español," belonging to *The Chimera's Wasteland* (Desolación de la quimera), Luis Cernuda clearly shows that, although he may be Spanish (he is "without enthusiasm"), his work does not belong primarily to Spanish culture, but to a culture of "silent mouths":

> Poetry speaks in us
> With the same language as before,
> long before our birth,
> The people in whom our existence found root;
> Not only the poet speaks there,
> So do the silent mouths of those
> To whom he gives voice and freedom [*PC* 478].

Cernuda did not write for all Spaniards. The poet speaks to those who are disposed to understand and say what he could not or refused to reveal with greater clarity:

> I do not speak for those whom a joke of destiny
> made my compatriots. I speak alone

(those who speak alone hope to speak to God one day),
Or for the few who may listen to me
eager to understand.
Those who, like me, respect
Human free will,
using the life that, today, is ours,
revealing the thought that nourishes our life [478–79].

Homosexuality is the term used here for a sexual or loving attraction towards someone of the same sex, whether or not any sexual act takes place. This definition is quite similar to the one given by the psychiatrist Manuel Gómez Beneyto:

> I understand homosexuality as the capacity to love one's own sex. This simple definition constitutes taking a position before the fact of homosexuality.... The term "capacity" has been substituted for "tendency" in order to underscore the positive and enriching aspect that it contains, fleeing from the apparent neutrality of the word "tendency." In the way I have deliberately avoided introducing into the definition concepts of temporality such as "episodic" or "permanent" [142–43].

Gómez Benyeto's open attitude is very unusual. Homosexuality itself, as well as the fact that it is discussed, seems to have had and perhaps continues to have the property of rousing spirits and rarefying the atmosphere of research. Even doctors and researchers as famous as Masters and Johnson stumble upon difficulties and obstacles that can be disheartening. In *Homosexuality in Perspective* they affirm that the oppressive weight of generalized ignorance, combined with the intellectually debilitating influence of public opinion, has immobilized in an effective way the legitimate search for exact data on homosexuality. Fantasies and prejudices are taken as facts. The above named researchers ask themselves how they could separate certain things from others under the current circumstances. How can scientific objectivity be cultivated when public hatred continues unchanged? So little is known about the physiological and psychosexual aspects of homosexuality that even the extent of our ignorance is unknown (3).

In a similar manner, Alberto García Valdés states in his doctoral thesis: "Sexuality and even more so, homosexuality, are still big unknowns. Few references to them are found in the usual treatises on medicine and neither are they the focus for studies in Spanish doctoral or masters programs where they are not studied in any organized way and are only occasionally mentioned in psychiatry, endocrinology or physiology" (9–10).

Perhaps it is needless to say that this situation was much worse during the times of the Generation of '27 in regard to generalized public ignorance as well as the consequences of that for homosexuals. According to the writer José Mora

Guarnido, Lorca's friend, public opinion reserved and reserves for the homosexual (whom the author calls "poor soul") "all its hatred, ridicule, disdain, its incomprehension, and, if it could, even the scaffold and bonfires. The police chronicles of our civilized world are full of tales of brutal and horrible crimes against those wretched beings, crimes which often are even declared legal" (230).

"I am myself and my circumstances," Ortega y Gasset would say, thus expressing the basis of his whole philosophy, according to Herrero (6). Circumstances, or rather, ignorance and prejudices about homosexuality, obviously influenced what Lorca lived and wrote, and probably has influenced also what is known or believed to be known about Lorca and his work.

Researchers and critics belong in different ways to a historical moment and to a society, and live within determined groups that shape their knowledge. At times it is difficult to separate the importance that something has (in itself or for oneself) from the importance given to it.

In general, as far as Lorca's homosexuality is concerned, there has been a preference to exclude the circumstances surrounding it. It has ended up being accepted in appearance, at least, in order to pass immediately to the analysis of Lorca's work which, divorced from its sexual context, would be the only important thing. A work is born, nevertheless, from the perceptions of its creator. In *Fenomenología de la percepción* Merlau-Ponty maintains that "[b]etween sexuality and existence appears an osmosis ... all the 'functions' of man, from sexuality to motor function to intelligence are, in precise fashion, interconnected" (186, 187).

Octavio Paz in *Conjunctions and Disjunctions* reclaims the sexual or erotic dimension of language in general and of poetry in particular:

> If language is the most perfect form of communication, the perfection of language cannot help but be erotic.... Both the joke and the poem are expressions of the pleasure principle.... I do not deny that art, like everything we do, is sublimation, culture, a homage to death. But it is a sublimation that seeks to incarnate: to return to the body [14–15, 23–24].

In *Love's Body*, Norman O. Brown defends the same ideas: "Knowledge is carnal knowledge. A subterranean passage between mind and body underlies all analogy; no word is metaphysical without its first being physical; and the body that is the measure of all things is sexual" (249).

It will be useful to dedicate the first chapter of this work to the study of the culture or cultures from which Lorca's text and that of Lorquian criticism originate — the culture or cultures that influence Lorca's world and the "knowledge" about that world with respect to homosexuality or homosexual love. In discussing feelings, attractions and homosexual relations, the term "homosexuality" will alternate with "homosexual love." It is often uncertain where sexuality ends and love begins, or vice versa.

Is it appropriate to call a relationship or a feeling "homosexual" in the instances in which there may not be any sex? Let those who are directly involved decide, represented here by Juan Gil-Albert, who answers a question from Luis Antonio de Villena without hesitation: "Do you think that there can be an amorous relationship between two men without sex? And would you also call such a relationship homosexual?" Gil-Albert reponds that:

> Yes, yes, of course, yes. I know such situations in which one of the friends was brought to tears because he couldn't give himself to that total relationship. One didn't want to go to bed with the other one, but he refused to abandon him. Life is very varied, very complex [*Reasoning* 66].

It does not seem relevant and can even be discriminatory to indicate whether the homosexuality under consideration is total or partial. As a general rule, it is not necessary to mention the degree of heterosexual inclination or tendency in heterosexual love. Omitted here are details about the sexual techniques and variations of homosexual love. Nevertheless, there are instances in which the texts that are analyzed seem to allude to concrete sexual acts. In such cases, it seems obvious that these acts should be mentioned.

Overview of the Contents and Methods of This Study

Early on in each chapter there will quotations from Lorca, Cernuda, Prados, Gil-Albert and/or Dalí. Occasionally, others will be quoted based on their pertinence to the discussion. These quotations should be seen as indications of what is to be elucidated, and each chapter will contain a brief commentary to show or underscore their relevance.

Throughout the study, the approach will be based on phenomenology and hermeneutics.[3] Ontological testimony is combined with analytic precision, similar to that proposed by Paul Ricoeur in "On Interpretation":

> I venture to say that to see something as ... is to make manifest the *being as* of that thing.... On the other hand, the testimony to *being as* ... cannot, in my opinion, be separated from a detailed study of the referential modes of discourse and requires a properly analytical treatment of indirect reference [196].

Or, in the words of Jorge Lozano:

> Granted that every action and communication is the result of strategies, games, astuteness, etc.... The attention given to another, the establishment of a fiduciary contract, the reciprocity of perspectives, the principles of cooperation, the definition of a frame of reference, require a constant interchange of roles [147].

In the analysis of vocabulary, symbols and poems under discussion, special attention will be paid to the study of the psychological aspects of the genesis of the work of art and human communication, in their relation to libido.

The first chapter is metacultural and metacritical. Its goal is to create a consciousness of the conditions of existence of homosexuality as a literary theme and of its criticism and interpretation. It will be achieved by reviewing what has been said about Lorca and homosexuality.

The second chapter will examine certain semantic differences in the usage and experience of words that implicitly carry a human polarization: at one extreme, society or the dominant culture, and at the other, the poets who directly or indirectly write about homosexual love, particularly Lorca. Behind the semantic differences and incompatibilities are sketched what one could call class conflicts.

Marxist thinking, which gives the third chapter its direction, has its origin in the concept itself that is studied: *oppressed norms*. If in the second chapter, the point of departure is the meaning of different words, in the third, the focus will be the aesthetic unity of a poem: ("I Know That My Profile Will Be Serene" [Yo sé que mi perfil será tranquilo]). Thus the approach to the theme changes, just like the work's discipline, with the goal of proving the richness of the hypothesis and the solidity of the thesis that were formulated in the above section, "Lorca's Life and Letters."

The fourth chapter comes from the world of semiotics. The Lorquian "billy goat" is seen as a sign, a product of Christian ideology that legalized the persecution and assassination of homosexuals. Lorca himself provided the orientation for his sources: "Ancient Greece / will understand you" (trans. Maurer).

Chapter 5 deals with two poems whose principal common motive is dreams. Since the oneiric dominates in both, it seems obvious that psychoanalysis should make a token appearance in the methodological reasoning of this chapter. In it the relationships of different characters (the billy goat, Verlaine and Bacchus) with the desired and feared world that appears in dreams are examined.

The sixth and final chapter is a detailed study of the poem "Suicide" and its aesthetic and extraesthetic contexts. The Lorquian text is considered readerly and writerly, that is, intertextually related to pertinent texts of homosexual culture and equally related to unwritten texts to which we try to give life with our writing.[4] The poet and his work are seen as creator and artistic creation, respectively, but also as carriers of currents and tensions that need to be exposed (written). The pertinence of this point of view will be based on biographical and aesthetic material.

The changes in the methodological approaches of each chapter are justified by the complexity of what is being researched (homosexual experience and its expression, and the plurality of its aspects). According to Xavier Rubert de Ventós, the only methodological relevancy or legitimacy of that which is fitting to speak about is "that which is relative to its appropriateness to the aspects which are sought" (14).

1

Culture, Homosexuality and Lorquian Criticism

Legal Opposition to Homosexuality

Tu sais que l'on gurit de la lèpra.... Repens-toi. Et tout rentrera dans l'ordre et le vrai bonheur — car même extérieurement una telle réputation n'est vraiment assise que lorsqu'elle devient un souvenir de Cour d'assies.
    F. Jammes, en lettre à Gide, *Correspondence*, 228
["You know that leprosy can be cured ... Repent. Everything will then revert to normal. True happiness will be yours — for a reputation of that sort is only really fixed in the public mind when it has been established in a court of law." — F. Jammes, in a letter to Gide, *The Correspondence*, 213, trans. John Russell]

That you, Oscar Wilde, have been the centre of a circle of extensive corruption of the most hideous kind among young men, it is ... impossible to doubt.
    On the sentencing of Oscar Wilde, in Rivers, *Proust and the Art of Love*, 114

— Que lui reproche-t-on? (à Federico García Lorca)
— Ses œuvres
    Auclair, *Enfances et mort de García Lorca*, 395
["What do they reproach him for?" (regarding Lorca).
"His work" — Auclair, *Chronicle of the Arrest and Subsequent Murder of Lorca,* trans. Frouman-Smith]

At last the dead man walked no more
Amongst the Trial Men
    Oscar Wilde, *"The Ballad of Reading Gaol"* Complete Works, 847

La indiferencia ... es la que habla en las calles con un grotesco vestido de suficiencia y cultura.
    Lorca 1064
["Indifference ... is what is spoken in the streets with a grotesque suit of smugness and culture." — Lorca, trans. Frouman-Smith]

Lo más alejado de posibilidades amorosas se enlaza en un entrecruzamiento de perfecto amor... una serie de conocimientos exactos, cognoscitivos en absoluto por nuestro

instinto y totalmente al margen de los estados de cultura, viene a formar nuestro vocabulario.
Dalí, *"Realidad y sobrerealidad,"* 7
["The most remote love possibilities connect in an intertwining of perfect love ... a series of exact knowledge, absolutely cognitive because of our instinct and completely outside the state of culture, shapes our vocabulary."—Dalí, *"Reality and Superrealism,"* trans. Frouman-Smith]

For Jammes and for those who condemned Oscar Wilde, homosexuality is not a culture; it is an offense to the culture and to the justice that the accusers represent directly or indirectly. The author does not mention the word "homosexuality," and neither does the judge who condemns Wilde. In his letter, he nevertheless mentions a rumor that grows around the name and the work of André Gide, and insinuates that that reputation could bring him to the courts. Consciously or unconsciously, Jammes uses different tricks to get Gide to censor his works. In addition to threatening him indirectly with jail, he coerces him emotionally by asking him if he has forgotten his mother's face (227). He also emits condemnatory judgments about Gide's work and seems to want to suggest to him that he lives and writes under the influence of a terrible and contagious illness:

> your books, since the *Nourritures*, have been a sickly, rending shudder.... What do you want me to say? Either you may hope in hypocrisy to disguise the truth from me, or you must admit that your conduct as a writer makes one doubt your sanity. Unless, alas! you own a truth which I dread.... You know that leprosy can be cured [Claudel, *Correspondence* 212, 213].

This letter, written on March 24, 1914, is not from Gide's enemy, but rather from someone who addresses him as "cher ami," someone who supposedly cares about him.

Rumors about Lorca also circulated, although, according to Vázquez Ocaña, "one shouldn't lose sight of the anecdotal insolence of foulmouthed envy, that for lack of better nourishment on which to feed itself, is accustomed to attribute Wildean inclinations to exceptional men" (349–50).

Lorca not only had "Wildean" inclinations, but he also read Wilde, to which many people, i.e., Carlos Morla, testified (Auclair 107). Wilde's imprisonment and the reasons for his condemnation were in the public domain. Lorca got the news of these incidents during his adolescence, or soon after. José Mora Guarnido recalls that in the meetings of the "Rinconcillo," Pérez Roda would speak to them about "Oscar Wilde's grief, and that his recovery was in full splendor in English literary circles" (57).[1] This grief could only refer to Wilde's condemnation and incarceration.

The quotation from Wilde indicates that the dead man can finally be free of his judges. Given the circumstances, it is difficult to believe that the author was not thinking about the judges who were enemies of his homosexuality. According to the testimony of his brother Francisco, Lorca read the cited book from the 1920s: "The novel and the Russian short story ... and, somewhat later, Proust ... and Wilde's ballad from Reading Gaol were also then in fashion among us" (*Federico* 143).

Ballad expresses the fear of those who could end up like the condemned author. These people prefer not to speak or make any sign:

> We watched him day by day,
> And wondered if each one of us
> Would end the self-same way,...
> Like two doomed ships that pass in storm
> We had crossed each other's way;
> But we made no sign, we said no word,
> We had no word to say;
> For we did not meet in the holy night,
> But in the shameful day [847].

Although in "Reply," by Hart Crane, no name is mentioned, Oscar Wilde and homosexuality are, nevertheless, present in each line of the poem through the situation that is evoked: the lack of communication of the alluded-to people, their "shame," their "guilt," etc. Hart Crane, whose contact with Lorca will be studied in chapter 2, indirectly shows the relevance of a reading based on empathy. A person who reads without identifying with the desire and pain of the one who writes does not know how to read anything:

> Thou canst read nothing except through appetite
> And here we join eyes in that sanctity
> Where brother passes brother without sight,
> But finally knows conviviality...
>
> Go then, unto thy turning and thy blame.
> Seek bliss then, brother, in my moment's shame.
> All this that balks delivery through words
> Shall come to you through wounds prescribed by
>   swords... [Complete Poems of Hart Crane, 177*].

If the highest representatives of culture and justice despise homosexuals, Lorca and Dalí despise "culture" or that which is presented as such. Lorca associates it with the "grotesque" and with "arrogance," and Dalí maintains that his vocabulary, that is, "our vocabulary," is formed by "knowledge" "completely at the margin of the state of culture." Dalí's article bears the date 1928, and,

---

*"Thou Canst Read Nothing..." from *Complete Poems of Hart Crane* by Hart Crane, edited by Marc Simon. Copyright 1933, 1958, 1966 by Liveright Publishing Corporation. Copyright© 1986 by Marc Simon. Used by permission of Liveright Publishing Corporation.

therefore, belongs to the period of Dalí's and Lorca's amorous relationship. The expression, "our vocabulary" marks the linguistic limits of an alienated or marginalized culture. The sexual connotations are evident in the context. Lorca, for his part, in his ode to Dalí, asks his friend to dress and undress his "brush" in the air, and sing "a common thought / that joins us" (*CP* 593; 778–79).

Auclair indicates that according to Ramón Ruiz Alonso, who detained and imprisoned Lorca, the poet's books had caused more harm than revolvers (395). One concludes that Lorca's work was seen as a danger to the values of the culture of power that Ruiz Alonso represented. We are, then, before two conflicting cultures. The results of this confrontation were fatal for Lorca, who left jail only to go to his death.

Homosexuality and Lorquian Criticism

Marcelle Auclair relates that shortly after Lorca's execution, the Huelva newspaper published the news of his death alluding to the "questionable" sexuality of the poet (417). Andrés Sorel has collected a testimony of Lorca's hours in prison. Benet, a barber and Falangist, recalls: "Yes, they tortured him, especially in the ass; they called him queer, and they hit him there. He could barely walk" (203).

About the execution Marcelle Auclair says that "J.T. brags about having finished him off with a bullet in the anus" (409). This fact is corroborated by Dr. Luis de la Torre, who found it out directly from his father, who had studied law with Trescastro: "Trescastro showed my father the pistol with which— I repeat however unpleasant the words—he said he gave Lorca a shot in the ass for being a queer" (Sorel 222).

Ian Gibson presents an almost identical version of the incident:

> Angel Saldaña ... was sitting in the Bar Pasaje, familiarly known as "La Pajarera" when Trescastro swaggered in and exclaimed for everyone to hear: "We have just killed Federico García Lorca. We left him in a ditch and I fired two bullets into his arse for being a queer." ... It seems that Juan Luis Trescastro's implication in Lorca's death is beyond doubt [*The Death of Lorca* 136].

When José Bergamín died, *El País* presented a previously unpublished interview based on a document taped in the poet's house, transmitted in part by radio. Bergamín, the founder of *Cruz y raya*, said the following about Lorca: "The playboys of Granada killed Federico García Lorca for two reasons, because he was famous and because he was homosexual, although he was discreet. The young studs of Granada could not accept it at all" (8).

Lorca may not have been killed solely because of his homosexuality. What does seem evident is that the poet's homosexuality was not missing from the motives that led to his torture and killing.

It also seems important to focus on the values and atmosphere of a society in which it is possible to brag publicly and with impunity about having killed someone "for being a queer." The identity of the speaker of these words was in the public domain. Trescastro would not have mentioned Lorca's homosexuality as a motive or justification for what he said he did if he were not sure that it was an argument of merit at the moment of deciding if someone has or does not have the right to live.

• • •

In 1940 the influence of Lorca's homosexuality on his work begins to be mentioned in public. On the occasion of the appearance of *Poet in New York*, Juan Larrea reports from Mexico:

> Federico García Lorca was a victim, when he wrote this book, of a torturous internal crisis. Everything leads to the conclusion that the crisis was determined in great part by his sexual anomaly. He has not adapted. He cannot live content within a society that repels as one would a poisonous snake his abnormality that is congenital, not perverse or vile ["Murdered" (Asesinado 118)].

Larrea's open attitude is an exception in public life during those years. More common is the tendency to hide or destroy facts and documents that were incompatible with the image of Lorca that the established culture desired. One wanted to recall a charming Lorca, always happy and smiling. The secret melancholy that sometimes appeared in him was Spain's romantic secret. His hidden suffering was the suffering of the Andalusian people.

The great majority of critics and friends opt for a total silence regarding the cause of the poet's crisis. In 1944 Arturo Barea published *Lorca: The Poet and His People*. According to Daniel Eisenberg, who bases himself on an unpublished letter about Lorca, Barea "eliminated from the book any reference to the poet's intimate crisis" (*"PNY": Historia y problemas* 209).

Nevertheless, the importance of homosexuality surges forth when Barea talks about the pagan vein in Spanish eroticism: "there runs a pagan streak through Spanish eroticism ... It breaks forth in the man's delight in the body of a woman or another man" (47).

In his extensive introduction to the North American edition of *PNY*, Angel del Río says that the origins of Lorca's crisis were obscure, but he adds: "at least for those who knew him superficially" (xiv). The author knows enough to affirm that the origins of the crisis are related to the delicate fibers of Lorca's personality, and that it is indispensable to bear them in mind in order to understand the complete meaning of *PNY*. But, how can readers bear in mind Lorca's personal problems when they do not know what these problems consist of? Years later Angel del Río is reproached for his silence on this matter: "It is still surprising today to read the essay about *PNY* by such an illustrious scholar of Spanish literature as Angel del Río — who, in addition, was a personal friend of Lorca's — and not see anything mentioned about the homosexual theme" (Alfaya 52).

In 1955, J.M. Flys published almost simultaneously an article and a book about Lorca. The article criticizes those who deform the poet's personality with purposes "far removed from any attempt at an objective judgment of his literary heritage" (247). The book, presented as a thesis, seems to place less importance on objectivity. Flys states that he bases his study on "intuitive analysis" (9). According to Flys' article, "The poet takes an anti-civic position" that "totally contradicts the logic of our existence" (251). The author, while not explaining what this logic consists of, seems to think it is linked to the established order, but does not elaborate. Unfortunately, when Flys refers to *PNY*, he is unable to recognize the poetic and human logic in it.

Reactions to Homosexuality

In 1948 Kinsey's monumental study on the sexuality of 4,000 Americans revealed that 4% of white American males were exclusively homosexual during their whole lives. More than one third of those interviewed admitted having had homosexual experiences.

D.J. West recalls the indignation that Kinsey's study awakened. It was considered pornographic and morally subversive. In Doncaster the order was given to confiscate the second book, which was declared obscene (35). According to West, the point of view of most of the critics was expressed succinctly by a doctor, whose commentary was that the world would have been cleaner if Kinsey had been content to study his rats (33).

One of the first people to speak with clarity about Lorca's homosexuality was Cipriano Rivas Cherif, Lorca's friend and collaborator for many years. The poet already mentions him in 1923, in a letter to Melchor Fernández Almagro: "Read the cast of characters [of *The Shoemaker's Prodigious Wife* (La zapatera prodigiosa)] to Cipriano [Rivas Cherif], the *charming* and *cultured* playwright and ask him if he wishes to collaborate with me on another thing I'm preparing, which I'll tell him about" (*Selected Letters* 40; 1128). Lorca underlines "charming and cultured" and continues speaking about Rivas Cherif in future letters, so that Rivas appears as someone integrated into the life and daily tasks of Lorca: "Cipriano says that your coming suits me enormously," Lorca writes to Melchor Fernández himself in 1926 (1152).

The feeling of friendship and sympathy seems to be reciprocal. Antonina Rodrigo has publicized a letter from Cipriano Rivas Cherif to García Lorca from February 13, 1927, that can be found in the archives of the poet's family. This letter mentions his romance "of the *asses*:

Come soon. I'm going to give a recital of moderrrn [*sic*] poetry in the Women's Residence and I'm planning to add to the repertoire two of your pieces which have already experienced public success: the romance of the *Camborios* and the one about the *Asses*. In all honesty I must tell you that I cannot compete with you in *your works*, but in any case, I will recite them and they will applaud me. Greetings, and see you soon — Yours. Cipri [*García Lorca en Cataluña* 85].

Rivas Cherif probably refers to the poem "San Miguel," from *Gypsy Ballads* (Romancero gitano), where "some large and hidden asses" are mentioned (411). (San Miguel and other ambiguous archangels of Lorca and Gil-Albert will be studied in chapter 6.)

From exile Rivas Cherif wrote three articles in which he mentioned Lorca's homosexuality in various contexts. He did not have to wait for a reaction. In the same year, Fernando Vázquez Ocaña published a book saying that Rivas Cherif created a "deplorable scandal" with his articles, provoking "angry replies" (349).

Rivas Cherif has spoken of what Federico confided in him after one of his depressions. According to what Vázquez Ocaña himself tells, Lorca was on a spree with a very special friend, "the one from 'La Barraca.'" The friend had gone away "with an ordinary gypsy woman" without saying goodbye (348–49). The next day Lorca did not go to rehearsals, and no one knew where he was. He had disappeared as if the earth had swallowed him up. Rivas Cherif, who was the director of the piece, looked for Lorca everywhere: "at the end of several anxious hours he managed to meet with him in a small, remote café where, with his head in his hands, he was lost in one of his strange sorrows" (349).

Since Lorca and Rivas Cherif were very good friends, it is not surprising that Lorca confided in him about his grief over the circumstances described. Nevertheless, Vázquez Ocaña says that Lorca's confidences are "doubtful and improbable." His principal argument is that Lorca has not confided in others, or that others have not spoken about these confidences:

> Suspicious sorrow? Sorrow from an aberrant sexuality? No man's grief is exactly vile when it springs from his mysterious biological plasma. Rivas Cherif, despite recognizing the discretion, the cleanliness, the delicate and honest designs of that spirit that never muddled his song with the shameful cries of his flesh, has boasted about that sad day that Federico honored him with some confidences which are as doubtful and improbable as they are exclusive. None of Lorca's friends who lived with him so closely, like brothers, and wrote about their life and passions, ever said that the poet had opened up his heart to show them a damaged libido [349].

Note that no one denies that Lorca's troubles were "suspicious" and were related to "an aberrant sexuality." The author recognizes that Lorca possessed "an abnormal sensibility," although he hastens to add: "like that of all great poets," but in order to suggest later that this "abnormality" was not perhaps so "normal": "his modesty and quite noble nature sealed his lips" (349).

It is obvious that the writer does not dare to say that Lorca was not homosexual. It is also obvious that it bothers him that the theme of Lorca's "damaged libido" is spoken about: "Rivas Cherif, pretending to defend the poet's memory and above all to open the way to the miserable version that Lorca's death was due to the revenge of vicious people, believed himself obliged to speak at length on the theme with such delight that it would have gotten the attention of a psychoanalyst" (349).

Vázquez Ocaña uses the *ad hominem* argument. The term "delight" here has the function of inducing the reader to think that Rivas Cherif felt an excessive or sick fondness for the theme of homosexuality.

It is not surprising that Lorca's other friends may have preferred to keep silent, nor that Lorquian criticism avoids showing the interest that is indispensable for any serious research that would deal with Lorca and homosexuality. According to D.J. West, not even psychiatrists seem interested in searching for the means to do research on homosexuality. West believes that the unpleasantness that the theme inspired, and the fear of compromising one's reputation by showing "too much" interest, has a lot to do with this negligence (124).

Although there is a big difference between Kinsey's studies and Lorquian research, the reactions they provoke in regard to homosexuality are very similar.

◆ ◆ ◆

The book *Federico García Lorca: The Man, the Work* (L'homme, l'oeuvre) appeared in 1956 and would reappear ten years later with a new title, *In Search of Lorca* (A la recherche de Lorca), despite having few changes. The author, Jean-Louis Schonberg, gives a homosexual interpretation of Lorca's work, and also includes a great many facts regarding the poet's life. The reaction to the book soon followed. Hardly a year had past when Charles Marcilly wrote an article about Schonberg and his book, saying that without a doubt, it is easier to besmirch the dead than the living. Part of Marcilly's criticism is based on some erroneous translations and interpretive liberties of Schonberg that would unite "so much impudence to so much treachery" (27).

José Mora Guarnido expressed himself in similar terms about one year later. The title of the chapter from his book, *Federico García Lorca and His World* (Federico García Lorca y su mundo), that deals with Schonberg, "The Dogs in the Cemetery" (Los perros en el cementerio), gives an approximate idea of the tone of his criticism. Mora Guarnido indirectly says that Schonberg is a dog, and directly that he is an intruder "searching for a scandalous pretext to make himself known in the literary world" (216 and 236). The author does not deny that Lorca was homosexual. He concedes that the facts "accuse Lorca of misfortune — nothing else but misfortune — of a vital and irresistible tendency to sexual inversion" (229). Mora had even refrained from alluding directly to Lorca's homosexuality, "intentionally, not even out of ignorance, [but because] no Spanish writer of good conscience ... had ever referred concretely and publicly to that aspect to which I allude, despite butting into private conversations regarding the topic" (216).

A few years later, José Luis Cano published an extensive illustrated biography of Lorca. The part pertaining to the poet's love life stands out due to its absence. Cano calls Schonberg's book "lamentable biography," but does not present other arguments against it, save for an erroneous date (7).

Even in 1965, Lorca's homosexuality was denied: "We have not wanted to feed, even minimally, malicious suspicions. The persistent rumors circulating here about Lorca's possible homosexuality seem totally unfounded. Equally arbitrary and unfounded is J.L. Schonberg's book, *Federico García Lorca: The Man, the Work*, Paris 1956, which pretends to demonstrate the writer's homosexuality with absurd arguments" (Alberich 35).

Marcelle Auclair also uses the *ad hominem* argument in mentioning "l'obsession sexuel" of Schonberg (429).

José Caballero attacks Freudian interpretations in general and Schonberg in particular. The Freudian interpretation of the Lorca poem "Blacks Dancing to Cuban Rhythms" (Son de negros en Cuba) is "absurd," according to Caballero, and "even laughable," reaching "an extreme of the greatest critical irresponsibility." Caballero thinks the analysis of the above-mentioned poem, done by Schonberg, is an example of "the grotesque tendency to see in everything of Lorca's a homosexual implication" (46, 48 and 49).

Like Marcilly, Luis Sáenz de la Calzada mentions some drivel that falls on Lorca. He talks about it more than Marcilly, but with less precision. In regard to the urinals and the sewers, one can guess that this drivel perhaps has something to do with Lorca's homosexuality and those who mention it:

> At times drivel falls, Federico, without anyone being capable of avoiding it... men's drivel can fall everywhere in the world, but it is despicable that it falls on the dead.... Perhaps degradation has to exist, not only on the dark walls of urinals, not only in the grey crevices of drains or in the dirty murmur of sewers.... There is thick drivel, mucilaginous drivel that covers, tries to cover, even the memory of blood; there is black, inconsistent drivel [181].

Miguel García-Posada is a renowned Lorquian critic. The appearance of his *Lorca. Interpretación de "PNY"* was greeted by Mauro Armiño with the rubric "Una interpretación modélica" in *El País*, May 30, 1982, p. 8. Motivated by the publication of *Sonnets of Dark Love*, preceeded and provoked by a pirate edition in *ABC*, of May 17, 1984, the attacks against Schonberg are once again renewed, this time with the approval of García-Posada who, with his "monsieur," underscores Schonberg's Francophone origins that, oddly enough, must be borne in mind:

> The rallying cry of the lamentable monsieur Schonberg, a third rank critic, has been well attended, and a number of irresponsible outsiders have flung themselves onto Lorca's work and memory. They have done damage, above all, because they have falsified data, manipulated facts and, what is worse, have induced erroneous readings and interpretations of the Lorquian work ["Un monumento al amor" 34].

Who can these "irresponsible outsiders" who obey Schonberg's orders be, and what exactly is the rallying cry? García-Posada seems to think that it is necessary to create some type of monopoly or control over Lorca's texts and their interpretation. A "concept" like "dark love" "cannot be left in the hands of fraudulent exegetes," he maintains (34).

If professional critics express themselves this way, what can be expected from the average person? Some indications can be found in the interviews collected by Eulalia-Dolores de la Higuera in a book entitled *Women in the Life of García Lorca* (Las mujeres en la vida de GL). The following is an interview with Cristina Gómez Contreras:

> A lot has been written about Federico. And much more has been invented and lied about also. During his life we never heard anything that could stain his character. And much less that he was homosexual. Such a thing was never spoken about. Being homosexual was one of the greatest insults for a man and a family. And neither my husband nor brother-in-law... ever noticed anything abnormal. Nor did they ever comment on his life. And if there were something strange, they would have realized it immediately and would not have allowed Federico to enter their homes and have friendships with their wives, children and relatives. These things are pure lies; a small and evil fantasy that wretched, envious and low people invent [52].

These words are interesting from a sociological point of view as they describe a society with an ideology in which the doors are closed to homosexuals, in spite of their fame and their degree of friendship. (See also Gibson's testimony in chapter 1, below.) The psychic pressures that Lorca suffered can only be imagined, but faced with the threat of those doors that would slam shut, how not to recall the anguish that is expressed in "Childhood and Death": "Alone, here, I see they have closed the door on me. / The door has been closed on me..." (*CP* 643; 794).

It is interesting to observe the qualifiers applied to those who dare to speak of this subject: "wretched, envious and low beings." Higuera chooses her words a little better, but she implies that no work on Lorca's homosexuality will be well received because, according to her, "it is not difficult to distort facts and words, and even find some negative and dark point through which to zigzag and support an obscure thesis" (207). Her book also includes the opinion of M. Vicent, who recognizes that Lorca had a sexual problem, but who maintains that apart from the aesthetes, "most people, not being morbid or overly technical, would not be interested in this drama" (17–18).

Women in the Life of GL presents the testimony or opinion of many women about the poet. The central thesis of the book could be summarized in the words of María del Carmen Prados: "As I said in the beginning, and I confirm it a thousand times, he was a complete man in my female eyes ... A complete and normal man ... there were no signs of any abnormality on his part" (181).

♦ ♦ ♦

In her doctoral thesis from 1967, the eminent Marie Laffranque described the situation in which researchers of less orthodox aspects of Lorca found themselves. As examples of material and moral obstacles, negligence, fear, egotism of those who stopped the publication of Lorca's unpublished works, the impossibility of gaining access to some sources, and also the reticence of the researchers themselves were all mentioned.

For her part, Marcelle Auclair refuses to note the facts relating to Lorca's homosexual loves, in spite of having received information about his "adventures" and the names of those implicated in them (104).

According to what Emilia de Zuleta said in 1971 in speaking about Lorca in *Five Spanish Poets* (Cinco poetas españoles), in spite of the immense mass of Lorquian scholarship, the first essays of Angel del Río and Guillermo de Torre "continue to maintain the primacy of interpretive focuses as a whole" (168–69). Del Río has already been mentioned in this chapter; regarding Torre one can equally say that in his interpretive focus, he does not mention homosexuality. In referring to André Gide, Guillermo de Torre is less cautious; he clearly shows his ideology in qualifying homosexuality as an "aberration" that "some" disguise as Hellenism ("Three Portraits of Rubén Darío" [Tres retratos de Rubén Darío 140]). (See also, chapter 3, "Symbols.") It is difficult to know if in the word "some" there is or is not an allusion to Lorca, but it is less probable that Torre has overlooked the presence of Greece in Lorca's work.

Those who have hidden and destroyed numerous documents complicate research. Dulce María Loynaz tore up and threw out one of the manuscripts from *The Public* because the work had seemed absurd and scandalous to her, according to Auclair (445), although Loynaz denied afterwards having said it or done it. Philip Cummings got rid of a manuscript of 53 pages because, according to him, "as much for Federico as for all those who loved him, it was preferable that everything be destroyed." According to Cummings, Lorca's manuscript was a bitter denouncement of people who were intending to destroy him, destroy his poetry and prevent him from becoming famous. He attacked in a more or less confused way people in whom he had placed his confidence and who did not merit it. I have the impression that he felt physically and emotionally betrayed [Letter from Cummings to Eisenberg; both cited in Eisenberg, *PNY* 181].

Whether it disappeared or was destroyed, the manuscript of *The Black Ball* (La bola negra) presented without evasion the problem of social repression that pursues homosexuals in all aspects of life (Laffranque, *Les idées esthetiques de Federico García Lorca* 308). Having disappeared or been destroyed, the manuscript of *La destrucción de Sodoma* also dealt with the theme of homosexuality (Sáenz de la Calzada 156–57; see also chapter 4, "Lorca's Billy Goat").

In *"PNY. " Historia y problemas de un texto de Lorca*, Daniel Eisenberg names different manuscripts, letters and documents which were destroyed or hidden. The author states that "Rafael Martínez Nadal has a large quantity of letters from Lorca which will not be published while he is alive" (184). Other letters concerning Lorca are published in censored form (see Gibson, *Federico García Lorca* 1:570 and 605, and also Rojas, *El mundo mítico y mágico de Salvador Dalí* 234).

❖ ❖ ❖

In 1966 a doctoral thesis appeared in Minnesota in which Lorca's homosexuality is openly discussed: *Erotic Frustration and Its Causes in the Drama of Federico García Lorca*. According to the author, D.G. Shamblin, Lorca could not satisfy his sexual urges with women, and it was not possible with men without the rejection of society. Shamblin thinks that Lorca transferred his maladjustment to his works, giving similar frustrations to the female protagonists of his dramas (11, 46). The author asks himself what factors could contribute to Lorca's becoming homosexual and he presents various theories (10–11).

In her article "El teatro surrealista español," Barbara Sheklin speaks about the homosexuals who appear in *The Public*, and about the "lascivious woman" who sounds the alarm when she discovers that two men are playing the roles of Romeo and Juliet:

> It is this love scene and the discovery of its homosexual nature that causes a scandal and a revolution in the theatre. The public demands the death of the Director of the scene and of the actors — but only after repeating the scene. This commentary on the public's repugnant curiosity, that delights in exactly what it condemns, is intensified when it is revealed that the public has also killed the actress who was going to play the role of Juliet, 'out of curiosity, to see what she had inside'" [318].

Until then only two scenes from *The Public* had come to light. In 1970 Rafael Martínez Nadal finally decided to make known the manuscript that

Lorca had entrusted to him. Nevertheless, before publishing it he wrote a study on the work and its themes: *The Public: Love, Theatre and Horses in Lorca's Work* (El público. Amor, teatro y caballos en la obra de Lorca). The book was published in England but not in Spain. The first edition of the purged version of *The Public* did not appear until 1978 in Spain. Nadal analyzes the work with a somewhat ambiguous attitude: he recognizes the force of the theme of homosexuality in Lorca but tries to lessen it by saying at the same time that "Lorca looks for love in all forms" (176).

In his critique of the Martínez Nadal book, Francisco Umbral maintains:

> The theme of homosexuality is essential to understanding almost all of the Lorquian work in prose and verse. Let us agree with Martínez Nadal that scholars and biographers, until now, in shamefully avoiding this Lorquian key, have hindered any possibility of complete understanding of one of the most singular creations of Spanish literature ["Análisis y síntesis" 221].

The author also mentions Martínez Nadal's ambiguous attitude:

> after admitting to the homosexual theme in Lorca, he seems to repent of this boldness in regard to his friend, and in the second part of his book he tries to prove to us, for example, that Lorca never utilized "Albertines." That is to say, he never disguised men as women in his theatre or in his poems.... Rafael Martínez Nadal is writing from some morally static positions, from an ethically immobile or at least regressive conventionalism. In any case, he is applying moral judgments to the marvelously amoral work of Federico García Lorca [225, 226].

In *The Death of Lorca*, Ian Gibson states that long before his death, Lorca was viewed as homosexual in Granada. In a city that stood out for its aversion to unconventional forms of sexuality, this was a disaster for the poet. The doors were closing for Lorca and many people distanced themselves from him. Miguel Cerón, who used to receive visits from Lorca, shut his door when he realized that people were beginning to talk (25–26).

During the decade of the '70s, books and articles appear that discuss this issue but do it in a very marginal way. *Eros y Lorca*, according to its author, Carlos Feal Deibe, "is the first attempt at a systematic application of Freudian psychoanalysis to the understanding of Lorca's work" (11).[2]

Rupert Allen believes that too much attention has been paid to Lorca's personal and ambiguous attitude towards sexuality (*Symbolic World* 92). The author does not deal with details about how, what, when and where the excesses are committed. In another work that appeared two years later, Allen observes the androgyny of the Lorquian moon in *Blood Wedding* (Bodas de sangre), and notes the fragmentation of the primordial androgyne mentioned by Plato (199–203).

Suzanne Byrd has pointed out the young man's subtle renunciation of heterosexuality in *Once Five Years Pass* (Así que pasen cinco años). About *La destrucción de Sodoma*, Byrd says that Sáenz de la Calzada still recalls many details of the vanished work, for example, that it was constantly creating the impression that angels were homosexual: "Lorca himself later said to Martínez Nadal, 'What a magnificent thesis! Jehovah destroys the city for the sin of Sodom and the result is incest. What a lesson against the injustice of judgment, and with the two sins, what a manifestation of the power of sex'" ("Paneroticism" 56).

Moraima de Semprún Donahue has dealt with Lorca's homosexuality in several articles. She maintains that in "Sleepwalking Ballad" (Romance sonámbulo) there is an attempt to carry out a homosexual act, or a visual act of a similar nature (259). In her analysis of the poem "The Birth of Christ" (Nacimiento de Cristo), the author interprets the child's cry as an announcement of "what he will suffer because of any possible sexual deviation." In her book, a study of Lorca's short narrations, Semprún defends the thesis that it is difficult to interpret Lorca's work without taking into account "dark love," that is, the theme of homosexuality (*Las narraciones* 10).

❖ ❖ ❖

The ambiguity of Rodrigo's book on Lorca and Dalí was mentioned in the introduction. There is another detail that should be considered. In *García Lorca en Cataluña* Rodrigo published a letter in 1975 to Lorca whose text would appear in *Lorca-Dalí* (1981) with a small change. The 1975 version reads "the little hairs of the horseman's ears" while the 1981 text has "the little hairs of the horseman's *balls*" (232). An underlined word in the original is often of special interest. Was the 1975 letter censored? Rodrigo does not give any commentary that would clarify how the change came about. The "error" can be viewed in different ways, but it leads one to question whether or not there were additional "errors" in works by Rodrigo or others.

In 1975 a work by Franciso Umbral appears with the suggestive title *Lorca, poeta maldito*. In the chapter "Los homosexuales" the author does a brief analysis of "Ode to Walt Whitman," which is accompanied by some commentary. Part of the work had appeared as an article in 1968. Also in 1975, Daniel Eisenberg published a book on *PNY*, which, as was previously seen in this chapter, has to do with homosexuality. There were many difficulties in getting some facts: "because some people strongly resisted, certain information had to be pulled out of them" (9). On homosexuality in *PNY*, Eisenberg states:

> so rarely analyzed, the theme of love in *PNY* is, in a more concrete way, the theme of homosexual love.... In *PNY* there are very few women, only "girls," and the only one who appears in a substantial way is the repugnant "fat

woman" from "Landscape of a Vomiting Multitude" [Paisaje de la multitud que vomita].... On the other hand, there are many men, many phallic images [218].

In 1977 Raúl Andrade used García Lorca's name to do a 77 page "allegory of a reclining Spain." Lorca is placed on the moon, "Because the moon is the gypsy paradise," while homosexuals are placed next to Francisco Franco, in "The hell of the bad gypsy ... who awaits the Caudillo with his entourage of harpy, ducal equestrians; little counts, pimps, homosexuals and invalids; and generals, drinkers of pus..." (26). Andrade's words perhaps would merit silence if they did not come from a person who could possibly influence the entire Latin world. Andrade writes the column "Claraboya" for the newspaper *El Comercio*, edits *ALA* (New York) and collaborates on some thirty daily papers, as is indicated in his book.

Secrecy and half words still seem to be necessary in 1977 among many people who knew the poet. Mildred Adams indicates Lorca's unhappiness and the memories that pursued and tormented the poet because of reasons that should be guessed at rather than made explicit (104).

M.L. Welles points to the incomprehension and even hostility that Lorca encountered when reading *The Public* in public. *The Public* and *Five Years* are linked in their treatment of homosexual love. In both there are similar obstacles confronting psychic realization: "the sexual taboos and prevailing social mores of 'el público' which coerce the conscious mind into deviating from its instinctive reality" (137, 143–44).

The affinities between Lorca and Whitman have been pointed out in several works. Roger Bordier prefers not to speak about certain "tastes" which, according to him, have been "lent" to Whitman and Lorca (188). Laubenthal, to the contrary, mentions both poets' homosexuality, and does not condemn Schonberg's studies, although the latter perhaps was excessively frank in dealing with the theme of homosexuality in Lorca's poetry. In his thesis, Laubenthal presents *PNY* and *Leaves of Grass* as psychological journeys by their respective authors. He states that by examining the libidinous nature of artistic power, one can see the homosexual elements in Lorca's and Whitman's poetry in perspective (11 and 113).

In "The Butterflies in Walt Whitman's Beard: Lorca's Naming of Whitman," Gari Laguardia deals with, above all, the homosexual symbolism of butterflies: "the phonetic relationship between *mariposa* and *marica*. This phonetic association in Spanish also carries over into the conceptual sphere, that is, a person categorized as a *mariposa* frequently connotes a *marica*" (546).

Derek Harris connects the image of the "wounded boys" from "Blind Panorama of New York" (Panorama ciego de Nueva York) to Lorca's homosexuality (*PNY* 22). José Ortega insists that the repression that appears in *PNY* is social, sexual and mental (*"PNY"* 54).

Carlos Ramos states, in regard to Lorca, that "a certain exacerbated preoccupation, maladjustment or dissatisfaction of the erotic-genetic instinct must have conditioned the thematic preferences and extreme recurring attitudes and situations in his work." Nevertheless, the critic considers all these aspects irrelevant: "What is important here is the goal achieved ... That the poet may have made a trophy of his pain and critical literature of his secret is irrelevant. All that belongs to his hidden laboratory" ("Hacia una revisión" 150).

Javier Alfaya has a radically different opinion: "The wall of Spanish prudishness raised around one aspect of Lorca's life which is simply central and without which a big part of his work cannot be explained, will continue to be an inextricable web for the scholar who does not take into account this information" (Lorca's homosexuality). Alfaya includes in his article a long quotation from Blanco Amor, "because few men of his generation had so much access to the intimate secrets of Lorca as Eduardo Blanco Amor." The latter comments on an article that he wrote for *El País*: "with the stupid self-censorship that one imposes in dealing with certain aspects; there, nevertheless, I gave a glimpse of my fundamental conviction that one does not understand anything about Federico's work ... without delving into the problem of homosexuality.... Federico was only himself in his complete relationship" (Alfaya 53).

That article appeared in *El País*, October 1, 1978, with the title "Federico, Again; the Same Time" (Federico, otra vez; la misma vez). Blanco-Amor seems to allude to the content of Guillermo de Torre's letter, cited in the introductory chapter, in mentioning "the *patriotic* dementia of the *saviors* of Western culture" (vi), although he refers to Lorca's death and not to the attempts to detain the publication of his works.

In 1976, the year that Lorca's brother, Francisco García Lorca, died, his widow Laura de los Ríos decided to edit a book about her brother-in-law, a book that had almost been completed by her husband. She did it with the help of Mario Hernández. In the book, which appeared in 1980, Francisco maintains his customary silence about the importance of homosexuality in Federico's life and work. He comments on all the known works of his brother, with the exception of *The Public*. Hernández tries to justify its absence by saying that it was due to the work's late publication. The argument would be valid if two important scenes had not been public for a long time. In addition, it is established that the rest had not been published before precisely because of the insistence of the Lorca family. Martínez Nadal had not been able to count on the proper authorization (Eisenberg, *Historia y problemas* 187). According to Gibson, the theme of Lorca's homosexuality was, for Francisco García Lorca, "strictly taboo," and it was the reason for "a certain distancing between the brothers" (*Federico García Lorca* 1:153 and 632).

In "La poesía erótica del primer Lorca," J. Velasco mentions homosexuality in Lorca's work solely to try and diminish its importance. He underscores "the poet's interest in women ... And not in men," and advises that Lorquian homosexuality be put aside because, according to him, "there is no alternative but to accept the evidence: the beings in whom the poet places the most powerful erotic attractions are women" (446).

Gregorio Salvador appears scandalized because J.M. Aguirre spoke of homosexuality in interpreting "Sleepwalking Ballad," and affirmed that critics had renounced truly submerging themselves in the emotional world expressed in Lorca's work:

> That similar assertions can be made, that there can exist such an absolutely gratuitous reading of a text which in itself does not offer even the most minimal pretext for such an absurd interpretation, is only explicable due to a paradoxical fact, generally ignored, which it seems necessary to address: the existence in the vast world of an endless number of literature professors for whom literature is of absolutely no interest, who do not like it, who do not understand it, who are completely uninterested in it [28].

It seems clear that even in the '80s, some critics decided to continue ignoring the theme of homosexuality and to continue attacking whomever deals with it.

Carlos Rojas feels pessimistic about the possibilities for researching this topic successfully: "the day on which in this crude place one can treat a painter's or a writer's homosexuality with the respect and the critical profundity of Freud in regard to Leonardo, or George Painter towards Marcel Proust is, indeed, far away" ("A Salvador Dalí" 7).

Despite no lack of motives for this pessimism, some authors have already begun to assimilate what may be called a change in the paradigm. José Ortega maintains:

> Lorca, like any Spaniard from the Catholic King and Queen to the present day, lives the internalized repression of the superego or social morals that has stigmatized and defamed anything homosexual.... This social pathology alters the manifestation of any sexual activity, especially that of a homosexual nature, and partially explains the erotic explosion in Lorca's work as an aspiration to love free from any obstacle ["Surrealismo y eroticismo" 87].

In 1984, Antonina Rodrigo published a new book, *Memoria de Granada: Manuel Angeles Ortiz, Federico García Lorca*. Granada at the beginning of the century is described with a luxury of details, and Manuel Angeles' (heterosexual) relationships are referred to with obvious sympathy. Lorca's relationships do not appear (200–01).

After finishing the first three volumes of his biography of Lorca, Gibson was interviewed in *El País*. According to Juan Cruz, the interviewer, Gibson's biography "begins by giving normalcy to Lorca's homosexuality." Gibson states that: "For a long time, Spanish Lorquistas have refused to speak about this aspect of the poet, fleeing from it (in public, of course) as if one were dealing with something terrible, or criminal" (*Federico García Lorca* 1:2).

At the end of his introduction to the biography, Gibson cites some words of Eduardo Blanco-Amor ("Lorca's friend and a homosexual, like him"), words that the biographer has had in mind during the long editing process of his book:

> Some day, García Lorca will be rescued from the darkness that obscures his genius and allows the root and flowering of his life-work to remain inexplicable. We who have known him, and therefore, have loved him, cannot permit ourselves to die and take with us the rot of this complicity — a silence that will be judged as cowardice by those who come in times of greater naturalness and freer intelligence to understand and judge their fellow creatures, fellow creatures in more than one sense [22].

Emerging Changes in Lorquian Criticism and Gay Culture

Lorca: the Gay Imagination appeared in 1985, a book dedicated almost exclusively to the study of the theme of homosexuality. The Spanish translation appeared two years later. Paul Binding, its author, maintains that the development of Lorca's homosexual consciousness is present throughout his work, and that he has read Lorca's writings largely from that perspective (9).

Binding's book has received more varied criticism than Schonberg's. Ian Gibson believes that it represents a valiant attempt to read Lorca's poems from within, from the perspective of a marginalized homosexual ("Concerning Lorca Today" [En torno a Lorca hoy] 88). Nevertheless, for Daniel Eisenberg, Binding's book has little to offer a Lorquista. Eisenberg states that Binding's readings are simplistic and literal, and, in some cases, contain errors. Eisenberg presents the example of the term "maricón" as more dignified than "marica" ("Reviews of Lorca" [Reseñas de Lorca] 414; Binding 139). Certainly these terms can create a problematic reading. Binding probably had difficulty explaining where to find the "more dignified" *maricón* at the end of scene 2 of act 1 in *Ocaña, the Infinite Fire* (Ocaña, el fuego infinito):

> NEIGHBOR 3. Oh! We already have this fucking queer in Cantillana, and for the parties.
>
> NEIGHBOR 4. (*Stressing fury and anger.*) This fag is probably a fairy! [49].

During the years 1986–89 there was a veritable explosion of works on Lorca, due to the 50th anniversary of the poet's death. Many of the following deal with Lorca's homosexuality.

All of the issues of *Cuadernos Hispanoamericanos*, 433–364 (two double volumes), are homages to Lorca. In his article "Annotations for a Portrait of Lorca" (Anotaciones para un retrato de Lorca), Francisco J. Satué maintains, "No one talks about Lorca's homosexuality. But it is like an open secret. They have made it that way, and so, it is a secret stained with shame" (48).

In the very same issue of this journal, Eduardo Tijeras criticizes the fact that Andrés Sorel picks up "with insistence" Trescastro's sentence, "We came to kill García Lorca. I shot him in the ass for being a faggot." The author does not present examples of this "insistence," nor does he indicate the pages from Sorel's book on which it appears. According to Tijeras:

> it is more elegant, given the impracticality of it, to do without sexual anomaly. "It is evident," as Manuel Vicent carefully states, "that Lorca had a sexual problem." But no one, other than an expert or a sick person, is more interested in this personal drama than in any other drama like *Yerma* or *Blood Wedding* or *The House of Bernarda Alba* [La casa de Bernarda Alba] [95].

In his article in these same issues of *Cuadernos*, "García Lorca como poeta petrarquista," Andrew A. Anderson points out and documents important details that many critics who write about the death motif in Lorca's work often forget. For example, "the figurative representation of orgasm as death ... has a long history in ancient times before becoming a commonplace in Elizabethan poetry, and that in Lorca's work the words 'to die' and 'death' principally take on a metaphorical and sexual meaning" (505, 506). Anderson's observations are in accord with what is stated here in chapter 2, in the sections dealing with death and decapitation.

Equally important is Anthony L. Geist's article, "Butterflies in the Beard: A Reading of *PNY*" (Las mariposas en la barba: una lectura de *PNY*). The author states, among many other things, that "In Lorquian poetry the change in gender (masculine-feminine) is as much a rhetorical strategy (an integral part of the multivalence of its symbols) as a survival tactic. Buñuel's *My Last Sigh* [Mi último suspiro] gives eloquent testimony to the intense and violent homophobia present in Spain in the 20s and 30s, even in a very good friend of Lorca's" (555).

Lorca's juvenilia, some of which finally became available, together with Eutimio Martín's observations, in *Federico García Lorca, heterodoxo y mártir*, confirm several significant points. The author studies "El estigma de la homosexualidad" in a section in chapter 4. He presents an innovative focus: the "Christlike dimension of Lorquian homosexuality." This sexual orientation is, according to Martín, "the cross from which the poet cannot remove himself" (219).[3]

Nevertheless, the poet is seen as totally removed from his sexual passion in the film, *Lorca, the Death of a Poet* (Lorca, la muerte de un poeta), that Juan A. Bardem screened in October 1987, to "public acclaim" (*El País*, October 29, 1987, p. 42). It can be said that it deals with a television series produced by "our culture," that is, the heterosexual culture,[4] for a public not far from the one that Lorca presents in *The Public*. This is a public that certainly would not find it pretty to "see Romeo urinate" (scene 1), and that, perhaps, would complain bitterly if the small screen were to show Lorca kissing some of the men he loved, or if scenes were suggestive of the sexual intimacy that was the poet's norm. In the culture of the norm "of breast and hip" ("Two Norms," *CP* 765; "Dos normas" 784) a piece of merchandise or *thing* (in the Marxist sense of the word), like this series on Lorca's life, is sold more successfully by purging it or stripping it of feeling and of the vital force of that "obscene practice" (homosexuality), that inspired a big part of the poet's life and work. The result is visible: six chapters of a 6½ hour film which contrasts enormously with other movies and series that one is accustomed to seeing in the "liberated" times that now exist. In theory, the series deals with the life and death of one of the most passionate homosexual poets of this century. But in reality, Bardem's Lorca is practically an asexual being. Out of the many ways to castrate a homosexual poet, this is one of the most refined and ingenious (for *castration*, see chapter 4, "Heavenly Lucifer").

In 1987, the second part of Gibson's biography of Lorca was published. There are many valuable and informative details in this work in relation to the theme of homosexuality. One example that might suffice has to do with the attacks aimed at La Barraca, in general, and against Lorca and his homosexuality in particular:

> The ultra-right magazine *Gracia y Justicia* did not delay in resuming its attacks. On July 23 (1932) it published an article whose title contained a direct allusion to Lorca's homosexuality: "FEDERICO GARCIA LOCA OR ANYONE CAN BE MISTAKEN" [FEDERICO GARCIA LOCA O CUALQUIERA SE EQUIVOCA]. The use of "*LOCA*," [a feminine adjective meaning both "crazy," and "effeminate"] instead of "Lorca" was no printing error [197].

Gibson publishes the complete article and comments on the "information" given there about the fact that Lorca traveled with women: "That is to say that Lorca — because he was 'loca,' as the title of the unfortunate little article indicates — did not travel with the 'men' from La Barraca, but with the girls.... The 'license' taken by the magazine to stain the poet's name is the same liberty his murderers will take four years later" (198).

In Spain's Ministry of Culture important changes in attitude took place during the 1980s. In 1981, the then Minister of Culture, Iñigo Cavero, attracted public attention by labeling as immoral a program on homosexuality, played on National Radio in the segment *From Coast to Coast* (De costa a costa).[5] In contrast, in 1987, two publications that deal with homosexuality were supported by this same Ministry of Culture. The first, *Cuadernos El*

Público (issue 20), contains a selection of texts on this very theme, accompanied by a review by Juanjo Guerenabarrena and articles by various authors. Ian Gibson's "El insatisfactorio estado de la cuestión" is the one that most closely approaches the theme. The second one, issues 27–28 of the journal *Poesía*, is published with the title "Salvador Dalí Writes to Federico García Lorca" (Salvador Dalí escribe a Federico García Lorca). Those readers who thought that they knew the letter where Dalí makes his famous comments on *Gypsy Ballad* will be surprised by reading this letter in *Poesía*. They will discover that the final part of the letter had been suppressed in previous publications.[6] The following is a small sample of what had been censored: "Little Federico, in your book, which I have taken with me to read by the mineral sites nearby, I've seen in you the little beast that you are, an erotic little beast, with your sex ... your thumb that almost exactly matches your penis and the moisture of the slimy lakes of certain species of hairy planets that exist.... I love you for what the book reveals about you" (92, 93).

A Federico García Lorca, also from 1987, is a volume of critical essays, poems and drawings by various authors published by the Ateneo Obrero de Gijón. Of the many works it contains, the one by Inés Marful, "Passion and Death in Lorquian Drama" (Pasión y muerte en el drama lorquiano) is of special importance. The author states that "Lorca projects onto his characters the definitive fulfillment of that prophecy by Coleridge that a great mind is androgynous" (34). Marful alludes afterwards to the price Lorca had to pay: "There is no doubt that, in addition to 'heavenly fury,' another kind of more earthly fury hovered over homophile passion; if any kind of erotic state has had to remain true to Epictetus' recommendation, 'abstain and hide your life,' it certainly is homosexuality" (35).

In this same volume, in the article "The Other Side of the Moon" (La otra cara de la luna), Carlos González Espina reveals the opinions of several people who were open in their antipathy or hostility towards Lorca. For example, the author cites César González Ruano: "Federico García Lorca never came across to me as appealing.... He dressed gaudily and boasted about being charming, spiritual and the queen of the South" (66).

In 1988, the French journal *Magazine Littéraire* published a Lorca dossier. In the very first pages there is a long interview with Ian Gibson, who destroys the myth that it is currently much easier to research the theme of Lorca's homosexuality. Gibson tells about the difficulties he has had and the insults that he has experienced due to his addressing this issue. He has been treated like a sick person and a specialist in looking into other people's bedrooms, and he feels obliged to repeat once again that one cannot write the biography of a man without taking into account his friendships, love affairs and sexuality. The researcher maintains that he is tired of having to defend the work he does. In Spain, according to Gibson, among left-leaning people it is considered a betrayal to speak about Lorca's homosexuality (Gibson, "Les vies múltiples" 16).

Other articles of interest in the same journal are, for example, "Mémoires d'un enfant du siècle," by Francisco Umbral, who mentions the attitude of "the illustrious Francisco Ayala" (to ignore or hide the homosexual love object in *Sonnets of Dark Love*), although he does not document where and how it is shown (26–27), and "Un demi-siècle de silence," by Armando Llamas (51–52).

In *Buñuel, Lorca, Dalí: The Unending Enigma* (Buñuel, Lorca, Dalí. El enigma sin fin), Agustín Sánchez Vidal presents various letters and other documents and testimony of some interest. The friends that Lorca had in the Residencia knew that the poet was homosexual and left him out "when they would go whoring." The adversity that the poet experienced is mentioned, but without going into any details. The poet "would disappear" (53). Sánchez Vidal is not the first to speak about Lorca's disappearances. In general, they are presented as a fact that needs no further commentary. At times, one has the impression that what Lorca was looking for during the occasions on which he disappeared was tacitly known.

During some of his "disappearances," around the years 1928–30, it is more than likely that Lorca would go off to Vicente Aleixandre's house, where there were very special gatherings. In "Cernuda Recalled by Aleixandre" (Cernuda recordado por Aleixandre), from *To One Truth* (A una verdad), Luis Antonio de Villena speaks about those gatherings (and other things) "because the protagonists have already died.... (I respect the silence which one of them was concerned about while he lived)." Villena's article primarily deals with the friendship between Cernuda and Aleixandre, but:

> [this friendship] is shared by Federico, and on occasion, by the musicologist Adolfo Salazar. The center is Aleixandre's house where the latter — delicate in health — organizes afternoon parties with young boys and with his literary friends. Federico sometimes plays the piano, and they have cocktails. And some days (Vicente would talk about it as small excess) they even dance. Obviously, one is dealing with a homosexual circle, facilitating — in its seclusion — the greatest intimacy [83–84].

With *Federico García Lorca* (essays in Spanish and Italian) the fiftieth anniversary of the poet's death was also recalled in Italy. The article of greatest interest is "The 'Dark' in *Sonnets of Dark Love*" (Lo "oscuro" de los *Sonetos del amor oscuro*), by Víctor Infantes. The author does a detailed study of these sonnets and what has been written about them. At the end, he states that "In (almost) everything I have read about the *Sonnets of Dark Love*, what is carefully and cautiously avoided is to mention, suggest, point out García Lorca's homosexuality" (86).

Along the same lines as Víctor Infantes' article, and complementing it on some points, is Daniel Eisenberg's "Reaction to the Publication of the *Sonetos del amor oscuro*." Like Infantes, Eisenberg defends the title of the work and suggests that those who insist on calling these poems *Sonnets of Love* or *Sonnets*, alone (members of the Lorca family, García-Posada and Mario Hernández), not only fight against the original title itself, but also against any tone or nuance of homosexuality that the title might have (263). To vindicate the title Eisenberg supports his position based on the words of different people. He cites, for example, Neruda's statements about his last meeting with Lorca: "The last time I saw him, he took me to a corner and, as if in secret, recited six or seven sonnets by heart that continue still in my memory as exemplary sonnets, of an incredible beauty. It was an entire book that no one yet knew. He called it *Sonnets of Dark* Love"[7] (264, 265).

One important addition to the study and comprehension of Lorca's homosexuality is, without a doubt, John K. Walsh's article "'Las cintas del vals': Three Dance-Poems from Lorca's *PNY*." Among the many accurate observations presented is that of the thematic parallelism of homosexuality between the "waltz of the wounded rose," from the poem "Childhood and Death," and "Little Viennese Waltz," just like the similarity of image (and of the situation to which it alludes) in "Ode to Walt Whitman" and in "Little Viennese Waltz." In "Ode," the faggots tremble "between the legs of chauffeurs." In "Little Viennese Waltz," the speaker asserts that he will leave or forget his mouth between the legs of someone (two variations exist) (513–14).

♦ ♦ ♦

The interest that García Lorca awakens does not seem to have diminished, to judge by the large quantity of books and articles that continue appearing year after year on his life and work. Nevertheless, to what degree the majority of those books and articles offer something truly new to Lorquian studies is very debatable.

To do a detailed review of everything published on Lorca during the 1990s would require a great deal of time and space. In reality, one would need to write a new book. Therefore, I will limit my comments to a lecture and a few articles and books which, to my understanding, are fairly representative of all that is being published on what concerns, recognizes or ignores the importance of the theme of homosexuality in Lorca's life and work.

♦ ♦ ♦

In 1990 the writer and then Cultural Minister of Spain, Jorge Semprún, gave a lecture at an international seminar in Madrid celebrating the 50th anniversary of the publication of *Poet in New York*. There Semprún stated that "It is time for homosexuality to assume its place in a democratic society," and "it is impossible" not to speak about homosexuality when one speaks about

García Lorca. The journalist José Méndez did a review of Semprún's lecture published in two articles in *El País*, on April 3, 1990. In the one entitled "Homosexuality" he quotes, among others, Semprún's words which seem to confirm the hypothesis that Lorca's shooting was related to the poet's homosexuality: "I recall that in one of our frequent conversations, Dionisio Ridruejo told me that during an official dinner, a still politically active general of the Falangist Movement shouted to another from his table: 'So-and-so! What was the name of that faggot we shot in Granada?,' Semprún explained."

Also in 1990, the results of Agustín Penón's research appeared in an edition edited by Ian Gibson. As in the article about Semprún's lecture, Penón's book came out shortly before the publication of my thesis, so there was only time to mention it, but not to study it in detail. The book is very important in many respects. In it, the author collects, among other testimonies, the statements of Angelina Cordobilla González, who saw how some guards mistreated Lorca in the San Vicente Orchard, shortly before they arrested him and killed him. According to this woman, who was then working as a maid, they struck Lorca with the butt of a rifle and insulted him, calling him a "faggot." When they left him, "his whole body ached" (89). If this occurred in front of Angelina, before Lorca was officially arrested, it is frightful to consider how they would treat the poet in jail, when no one could see or hear what they did to him. When Gibson visited Angelina ten years after she spoke to Penón, she repeated, almost word for word, what the latter had left written (84, 88–89). Miguel García-Posada believes that *Agustín Penón: Diary of a Lorquian Search* (Diario de una búsqueda Lorquiana) is a persuasive and sad testimony of what Spain and Granada were like during those years (31). Others, like Nicolás López Calera, author of *The Granadan Being* (El ser granadino), are convinced that "if Lorca was again born in Granada, they would kill him again" (Arias).

◆ ◆ ◆

"Journeys from Frustration to Empowerment: *Cat on a Hot Tin Roof* and Its Debt to García Lorca's *Yerma*," from 1992, is a comparative study of two important works by two great homosexual playwrights, García Lorca and Tenessee Williams. Christopher Brian Weimer presents several very interesting ideas, but does not go into great detail on those that most concern us.

The article begins with an exposition of the evil nature of silence and of its explosive potential through the words of Yerma and Maggie, the heroines of both plays. In regard to the masculine protagonist of Williams' work, Weimar indicates, "Brick's moral deterioration and alcoholism both stem from his inability to accept the possibility of a homoerotic element in his friendship with his teammate Skipper" (522). As far as the masculine protagonist's "sexual apathy" and the lack of interest in having children in *Yerma*, the author does not offer any theory. Juan's paleness also remains unexplained: "the question of Brick's suggested homosexuality remains just as unresolved as that of Juan's sexual apathy.... Juan's malady may be nothing more than the result of his relentless labor — although if this is the case, his long hours in the Andalusian sun should be darkening his skin, not the reverse" (527).

On two occasions Weimer quotes from Paul Binding's book on Lorca, *The Gay Imagination* (discussed in chap. 1, "Lorquian Criticism") but without suggesting that the theme of silence or the problems of the masculine protagonist of *Yerma* can have any connection to Lorca's homosexuality. Nowadays, however, we know that the different characters in a work, although they are never identical to the author, often incorporate the different feelings, problems or conflicts that live in the mind of the one who has created them.

Another article, "Un-masking the Masculine: Transvestism and Tragedy in García Lorca's *El público*," by Antonio Monegal, moves closer to the theme of homosexuality, although without transforming it into the central point. The author indicates that the male figures who change appearance by going behind the changing screen and becoming feminine or ambiguous figures, in reality, are not disguising themselves: "The change is not perceived as a disguise but as an uncovering of the true identity that was hidden under the masculine clothes" (207). It seems relevant to recall here that Lorca also did not identify himself with the masculine persona. As was observed in "Lorca's Life and Letters" from the introductory chapter, Lorca found it curious to observe that he did not desire "the things of man."

Basing himself on critics such as Michelle Gellrich and David Lenson, Monegal suggests that we read *The Public* as a tragic work. He is most likely not lacking in evidence to do so: "If we define tragedy from the point of view of the inescapable conflict, in which all the options are terrible or destructive, and where the unavoidable outcome is disastrous, *El público* becomes one of the most innovative propositions for a contemporary reformulation of tragedy" (213).

◆ ◆ ◆

In 1991 Cátedra published María Clementa Millán's edition of *The Public* that contains an introduction that is longer than the play (9–115), apart from the 52 endnotes. It is a very carefully done edition, and there is little to object to with regard to its formal elements. What is surprising to observe are the author's many efforts to avoid discussing the theme of homosexuality.

Lorca's "psychological necessity for change" when he wrote *The Public* and *Poet in NY* is mentioned and recognized in "Preliminary Comments." There María Clementa Millán states that in *The Public*, "the introspective and complex Lorca ... shows himself with greater thoroughness than in any other of his theatrical productions" and also that this work "is an act of personal and artistic self-affirmation" that cannot be excluded in analyzing the poet's work. An informed reader perhaps understands that Lorca's "psychological necessity for change," his introspection and his "personal self-affirmation" are all linked to the poet's homosexuality. But, can a less-informed reader understand some of this?

One part of Millán's introduction is dedicated to the "Superrealist Contagion" and to the figure of Jean Cocteau. Cocteau was also homosexual, but Millán does not study the importance this detail may have had in his influence over Lorca.

On several occasions, the author mentions her other previous studies on Lorca, among them, an article from 1986, "Líneas de una biografía," that also avoids the theme of homosexuality. When Lorca, invited by Dalí, goes to Cadaqués, the poet's stay at the home of his friend and lover is described as if one were dealing only with a trip relating to studies or something strictly professional: "On this trip, Lorca settles into his knowledge of the new art, at the same time that he changes his regard for his plastic creation" (60).

Millán mentions the importance of Jesus Christ in the Lorquian oeuvre. She speaks of it in "Líneas" as well as in her long introduction to *The Public*, but in neither one does she speak of anything close to the homosexual connotations that the cross and the Passion of Christ have in Lorca's work. The author fails to inform her readers that there are critics who have elucidated this and other similar themes, although several of these names appear in the bibliography she includes at the end of her introduction (Ian Gibson, Eutimio Martín, and Ángel Sahuquillo, for example).

◆ ◆ ◆

At the beginning of the book interestingly entitled *Lorca and Popular Moroccan Culture* (Lorca y la cultura popular marroquí), the author, Ahmed el Gamoun, states that the approach to Lorca's work "is found channeled beforehand by a series of prejudices and clichés that have been transmitted to us by Western criticism, and that we either adopt consciously or unconsciously" (27). The truth of these words stimulates the reader's interest in this work, which is presented as an alternative to Western criticism. Some sections have titles as suggestive as "An Exotic Bird within Western Culture" (28) and "The Hidden Part of the Iceberg or Lorca's 'Mythic Conscience'" (62). Already in the first of these sections, the author states that the hidden part of the Lorquian oeuvre "is the most important" and, in making a reference to the Lorquian poem "Ghazal of the Bitter Root," maintains that "Lorca's esoteric world" needs "a preliminary initiation to discover the secret of that *bitter root*" (28–29). Nevertheless, it remains unclear as to what that initiation consists of.

According to the author, Lorca's world "demands a kind of trance, which frees us from false cultural convictions" (29). Roger Garaudy and Nietzsche are mentioned as sources of inspiration: "For Garaudy and Nietzsche, the salvation of our current civilization consists of a return to Dionysian enthusiasm, to play, to delirium and to intoxication." Nevertheless, in spite of his insistence on the importance of states of trance and intoxication, Ahmed el Gamoun takes no notice of Lorca's drunken sailors nor of the contexts in which Lorca himself used alcohol (see chap. 2, "Lorca and the Sailors"). The kind of intoxication the author proposes as an alternative to Western logos in order to reach Lorca's hidden side, turns out to be very selective and aseptic.

Símbolo y simbología en la obra de Federico García Lorca, by Professor Manuel Antonio Arango, is a book that, for its length, 480 pages, as well as for its long and detailed index, seems very ambitious. The connection between the author's formal ambitions and his analysis of Lorca's work, nevertheless, does not seem clear.

In the first 55 pages, as well as in the second chapter and in the majority of the rest of the work, Arango shows what symbols, allegories, myths and archetypes are and what they mean according to different dictionaries and authors: J.E. Cirlot, Jung, Northrop Frye, Mircea Eliade, Lévi-Strauss, Martin Buber, etc. But by not presenting a theory that shows the relevance of all these names to the study of Lorca, Arango gives the reader the impression that he could be referring to the poetry or to the dramatic work of many other authors using the same symbols.

In chapter 4 of the second part, the author announces that he is going to do a study of Lorca's erotic symbols, but in reality, what he does is a not very profound study of heterosexual eroticism. The study of homosexual eroticism is glaringly absent here, as well as in the rest of the book. An extensive bibliography is included at the end.

Without commenting on them in great detail, I would like to conclude this section by mentioning some new books and a few articles related to Lorca, his friends and homosexuality. The first is an anthology of Lorca's amorous and erotic poetry that a new publisher, Altera, published in 1995: *Sonnets of Dark Love, Poems of Love and Eroticism: Unpublished Poems of Maturity* (Sonetos del amor oscuro, poemas de amor y eroticismo. Inéditos de madurez). There are 10 previously unpublished poems that appear in this volume. The most clearly erotic is perhaps the one which begins: "Oh hotel bed / Oh sweet bed!"

No well-known name appears in the title of the second book. Many of the pages from *Writings on Spanish Poetry* (Escritos sobre poesía española), by Francisco Brines, nevertheless deal with García Lorca, Luis Cernuda and Juan

Gil-Albert. Although the theme of homosexuality is not central to the book, it is treated in a clear and direct way in relation to the analysis of works by Cernuda and Gil-Albert, the ones the author studies in great detail (73–125 and 127–243).

Many journals of gay studies have also included articles about García Lorca. One of the most serious ones that is published in Spain, *Orientaciones*, includes several interesting articles in issue number 6: Alberto Mira, "Between Sodom and Helade: Homosexual Traditions in the Poetry of the Beginning of the Century (Entre Sodoma y la Hélade. Tradiciones homosexuales en la poesía de principios de siglo); Eladio Mateos Miera: "Mask and Truth: Homoerotic Identities of the Generation of '27" (Máscara y verdad. Identidades homoeróticas del '27) and Werner Altmann: "Sadomasochistic Games: The Modern Work of Federico García Lorca" (Juegos sadomasoquistas. La obra moderna de Federico García Lorca).

The Heritage of the "Queer with the Bowtie"

Homosexual culture has become more consolidated in the terrain of criticism, literature, film and painting, and gay studies are offered in some Spanish universities. The book *ConCiencia de un singular deseo*, for example, resulted from a summer course given at the University of Vigo (Galicia) in July of 1995 and contains diverse essays on homosexuality and lesbianism in history, literature and art. The book was published in 1997 and was edited by Xosé M. Buxán Bran, who also organized the course. Another important book of essays is the extensive study by the sociologist Ricardo Llamas, *Queer Theory: Prejudices and Discussions on "Homosexuality"* (Teoría torcida. Prejuicios y discursos en torno a la "homosexualidad") (1998).

Almost all the novels of Eduardo Mendicutti have a predominately homosexual theme: *The Lame Dove* (El palomo cojo), *Anyone Can Have a Bad Night* (Una mala noche la tiene cualquiera), *The Bulgarian Lovers* (Los novios búlgaros), and *March Fire* (Fuego de marzo). Something similar has occurred with the abundant works of Luis Antonio de Villena, in which many different genres are found (novels, biographies, poetry, articles, essays, translations, etc.) and, also, in the majority of Terenci Moix's writings: articles, novels and, principally, the three extensive volumes of his memoirs, *The Weight of the Straw* (El peso de la paja), entitled *Film on Saturdays* (El cine de los sábados), *Peter Pan's Kiss* (El beso de PP) and *Stranger in Paradise* (Extraño en el paraíso).

One of the greatest writers of the Spanish postwar period, Juan Goytisolo has aroused a great deal of irritation by abandoning his life as a heterosexual and crossing over to the homosexual "camp." Additionally, he is no longer committed to social realism and leftist politics and is now involved in a literature of mystic and "postmodern orientation." For some "intellectuals," Goytisolo's decision is even more alarming since he has chosen to live in Morocco on a more or less permanent basis. As a result, it seems as if Arabs are the ones who awaken the writer's amorous attraction and sexual desire. Goytisolo's evolution is also related, in part, to his rejection of Western culture in general and Spanish culture in particular. Almost every book that he has written since *Marks of Identity* (Señas de identidad) touches on, in one way or another, the theme of homosexuality: *Count Julian* (Reivindicación del Conde don Julián), *Juan the Landless* (Juan sin tierra), *Landscapes after the Battle* (Paisajes después de la batalla), *The Virtues of the Solitary Bird* (Las virtudes del pájaro solitario), *State of Siege* (El sitio de los sitios), *The Garden of Secrets* (Las semanas del jardín) and, of course, *A Cockeyed Comedy* (Carajicomedia). The latter, like many other novels of Goytisolo, contains both allusions to García Lorca and explicit mentions of the poet, as well as a lot of homosexual symbols, like the bird. His autobiographical works, *Forbidden Territory* (Coto vedado) and *Realms of Strife* (En los reinos de taifa), are actually where the author expresses himself with greater clarity. Goytisolo's oeuvre has sparked great interest in England and in the United States and has given rise to the publication of numerous articles and books. In *Significant Violence: Oppression and Resistance in the Narratives of Juan Goytisolo*, Bradley S. Epps, for example, deals in great detail with the theme of AIDS and the homosexual and mystical meaning of birds in *The Virtues of the Solitary Bird* (see chapter 5).

In film, the art of Pedro Almodóvar has marked the presence of a new aesthetic and moral paradigm for many reasons: the humorous and carefree style with which Almodóvar approaches traditionally serious or tragic subjects such as pornography, prostitution, incest, rape, sex change, drugs, etc. In addition, the filmmaker has placed homosexual love or passion as a central cinematographic theme in two of his movies, "The Law of Desire" (La ley del deseo) and "Bad Education" (La mala educación), and has made homosexual desire visible in others. The latter occurs even in movies and in scenes that deal with something else or that treat many things at the same time. Almodóvar evokes homosexual desire, for example, in causing his camera to take pleasure in the physique and in the nudity of some of his masculine protagonists in scenes in which most directors show only women in the nude. In "Live Flesh" (Carne trémula), 1997, the only scene with highly visible full frontal nudity is portrayed by the actor Liberto Rabal. Other directors, like Imanol Uribe, previously had shown the political dimensions of the oppression of homosexuals in fairly daring contexts as occured in the film "The Death of Mikel" (La muerte de Mikel), from 1984. The death to which the title of the movies refers is that of a married man, a leftist militant from the Basque region, who falls in love with a transvestite. The censorship and rejection of that love by the family and by colleagues involved in the political battle is not long in coming. Mikel dies under confusing circumstances, and the same people who distanced themselves from him when they realized that he was gay use his death for political ends. Mikel's death, although it belongs to the world of cinematic fiction, causes one to think about Lorca's death. The history and the landscape are different, but the socio-political, sexist manipulation of the dead homosexual figure is fairly similar in both cases.

Almodóvar and other Spanish film directors have inspired important works in the English-speaking world, for example, those of Paul Julian Smith, who has also written about Juan Goytisolo and Terenci Moix (among others): *Laws of Desire: Questions of Homosexuality in Spanish Writing and Film (1960–1990)* (Oxford: Clarendon Press, 1989), *Representing the Other: "Race," Text, and Gender in Spanish and Spanish-Anerican Narrative* (Oxford: Clarendon, 1992) and *The Body Hispanic* (Oxford: Clarendon Paperbacks, 1992) are perhaps his most well known works.

In the Spanish American world of literature and analysis, a lot more work remains to be done. In the preface to the pioneering work by David William Foster, *Gay and Lesbian Themes in Latin American Writing* (1991), the author mentions some of the difficulties he had to confront:

> Of all the acts of critical inquiry I have indulged myself in, this has been the most exhausting. To attempt to pursue doggedly a topic that has no ontological status in most realms of literary criticism, and especially much less so in the case of Latin American culture ... is to be set up for a heavy dose of frustration....
>
> Moreover, to talk about homosexuality in Western culture at the present moment is to venture into a minefield of issues, ideologies and opinions....
>
> As a consequence of the foregoing, I often had the sense, while composing this monograph, of engaging in something "dirty." ... Nevertheless, criticism should be a dirty word, if it is ever to deal with the real issues of human history and the social dynamics that disable the individual's quest for decency and dignity [vii–viii].

◆ ◆ ◆

For the many readers who surely will want to know the places where Lorca lived, in 1989 Ian Gibson published an excellent work-guide, accompanied by beautiful pictures. *Guía a la Granada de Federíco Garcia Lorca* is much more than a guidebook for tourists. It is a book rooted in Lorca's life and work, and in the history of a city and its surroundings, a book that shows the beauty as well as the shame of Granada. The beauties are there to see. The shame is this: "The rebels were decided on killing all the followers of the Popular Front, and for them the author of *Yerma*, the anti–Catholic Lorca, the 'queer with the bowtie,' as the city's comfortable bourgeoisie knew him (as one of Captain Nestares' sons assured me) was one more 'undesirable'" (195).

The reference to the heritage of the "queer with the bowtie" has nothing to do with the economic inheritance of Lorca's legal heirs. The concern here is for the richness of another kind of inheritance that for some might be less desirable, but yet is quite a vital inheritance.

Ocaña, the Infinite Fire is a drama by Andrés Ruiz López that received the Calderón de la Barca prize in 1987 and that was published by the Centro de Documentación Teatral in 1989. It is a work that reconciles, in part, homosexual culture with "our culture," a drama that, as Antonio José Domínguez indicates in his presentation, manages "to connect with the Lorquian dramatic world and, at the same, with Valle-Inclán's absurdist assumptions" (12). Many people do not know, or do not want to know, the world of subtle Lorquian allusions and homosexual symbols. But their traces are so visible in *Ocaña* that it is hardly necessary to demonstrate anything. It will be sufficient to put both Lorca's and Ruiz López' texts side by side so that even the most hard of hearing will find themselves obliged to hear that silenced voice, the *ancient* voice of homosexual love:

Lorca	**Ruiz López**
Ay, my love's ancient voice, *ay*, voice of my truth. ... "Double Poem of Lake Eden" *PNY* (81; 489)	I want to discover what is ancient in man. To fight against mockery and lies. Scene 10 (116)
Throw that ring in the water. "Marriage Vow" *Songs* (*CP* 489; 363)	I'll marry when I find the little ring I threw in the water! Scene 6 (63)
Green sound intact. The fig tree's arms open to me. ... Like a panther "Bacchus" *Songs* (*CP* 453; 321–22)	And, little green panther, what happened to you that God and his Saintly Mother left you this way? Scene 6 (65)
Nude (crowned with ... thorns) Everything has been consummated. *The Public* Scene 5, (33, 38; 511, 521)	*the space of the door-symbol opening upon a young, crucified man.* Scene 7 (67)

What rivers on their feet
her fantasy has glimpsed!
   "The Gypsy Nun"
     The Gypsy Ballads (*CP* 533; 405)

... trying constantly to see
to it that your state of mind
does not filter into your
poetry, because it would play
you a bad trick by exposing
the purest in you to the
eyes of those who should never
see it.
   "To Jorge Zalamea,"
   Autumn, 1928
   (*Selected Letters* 143)

What aching pain! All through
the house I race, insane.
I drag my braids across the
floor...
   "Ballad of Black Pain"
     Gypsy Ballads (*CP* 539; 409)

How did Romeo urinate, Mr.
Director? Isn't it nice
seeing Romeo urinate?
...
You could've seen an angel
carrying off Romeo's sex ...
   The Public scene 1 (5; 467)

O love of my heart, living death,
In vain I await your written word,
...
Fill, then, with words my madness ...
   "The Poet Asks His Love to
    Write Him"
     Sonnets of Dark Love (*CP* 715)

DIRECTOR
And my lipstick?
BELL FIGURE
... you'd be nothing more
than a little powder box ...
   The Public, scene 1 (7; 471),
   Scene 2 (13; 479)

Like an ocean on its feet.
   Scene 8 (70)

I will have to resign
myself, like the faggot
who doesn't want others to
know, and direct my eyes
towards the heavens and tear
out my purest feelings by the
roots!
   Scene 9 (75)

Do you know, sweetheart,
when you were speaking to me
I was a quiet silence
surrounded by shouts? Look at
my braids on the floor.
   Scene 9 (75)

why do the angels possess
enormous wings and not one
little piece of a branch?
My God, how do they urinate?
   Scene 11 (126)

Crazy love that I carry inside
my eyes!...You refused to write me,
to answer my letters...
   Scene 13 (128)

A badly wounded queer.
Two young men seated on the
floor distribute what was
stolen.
Look, he was carrying
lipstick, a compact and a fan.
   Scene 14 (133)

Summary and Conclusions

As result of being manipulated and oriented in only one direction, the culture of everyone, "our culture," in most public spaces is in reality the culture of heterosexuals. This situation is presented as natural, but in fact is a construction with an ideological basis, "the social construction of reality," as Berger and Luckman would say. By obliging homosexuals to hide, "our culture" shapes the style and themes of their culture: worlds of silences, secret languages, veiled allusions, etc. Afterwards, the "science" of "our culture" questions the existence and the relevance of that which has been condemned to live in the shadows. Their logic is irreproachable: darkness cannot be seen clearly. Nevertheless, as Cernuda points out in "Apologia pro vita sua" from the "dark cave": "These latterly shadows painfully surge: / Shadows of those of my blood, / Clamoring for a recognition..." (*Selected Poems* 143).

Lorquian criticism is part of the established culture, and assumes, many times, its values and points of view. The most generalized pattern has been to abstain from openly declaring the ideological bent of a study. The work gives the impression of being objective. In the name of this pseudo-objectivity, some "scientists" have attacked and do attack critics who see "ghosts," or realities that, according to those "scientists" *are not* in the analyzed texts. Lately, however, a change in attitude has been observed. Some renowned Lorquian critics already recognize the importance of the homosexual factor in the interpretation of his work. One part of "our culture" has also begun to realize that homosexual culture, that "ancient voice," as Lorca called it, is an integral part of the culture of humanity, or, to say it in Cernuda's words:

> What man's spirit
> Won for man's spirit
> Through the centuries,
> Is our patrimony and heritage
> for future men.
> In allowing them to deny it to us
> And seize it, man then descends
> And how much?, that hard ladder,
> That from the animal reaches up to man.
> ["Spanish Diptych" (*The Chimera's Wasteland*) 476].

2
"The Other Half": Homosexual Purity in the Sewers

Rage of the Marginalized Towards the Establishment

Each one of us when separated, having one side only, like a flat fish, is but the indenture of a man, and he is always looking for his other half. Men who are a section of that double nature which was once androgynous are lovers of women.... But they who are a section of the male follow the male."
 Plato, *Five Great Dialogues* 180–81

Yo denuncio a toda la gente
que ignora la otra mitad,
la mitad irredimible
...
Os escupo en la cara.
 Lorca, "Nueva York" *Poeta en Nueva York* 518

I denounce everyone
who ignores the other half,
the half that can't be redeemed,
...
I spit in all your faces.
 Lorca, "New York," *PNY* 133, trans. Simon, White

Ahora vivo y me arrastro sobre el llanto que escupo,
como el amor que digo, la sangre que no escuchan.
 Prados, "El llanto subterráneo" in Ellis, 320

I live and crawl now over the lament that I spit,
like the love that I speak, like the blood they don't hear.
 Prados, "Underground Weeping," trans. Frouman-Smith

Se hace imposible ya no morir con un asco de rabia,
con un furioso vendaval que se desata,
golpeando con la feroz saliva del instinto
las caras rasuradas de estos monstruos.
    Gil-Albert, "Cultura estallante" *Obra poética completa* 1:55

It's becoming impossible to die without an angry disgust,
without a furious gale unleashed,
hitting the shaved faces of these monsters
with the fierce spit of instinct.
    Gil-Albert, "Shattered Culture," trans. Frouman-Smith

Contra vuestra moral contra vuestras leyes
Contra vuestra sociedad contra vuestro dios.
    Cernuda, "Vientres sentados" *Poesía completa* 550

Against your morality against your laws
Against your society against your god.
    Cernuda, "Seated Bellys," trans. Frouman-Smith

    In 1930, Fernando de los Ríos was taken to see those arrested for being homosexuals.[1] Some of the "fags" were dressed as women. Don Fernando was so shocked that he could hardly believe his eyes. Marcelle Auclair relates the incident to clarify that it is understood why Lorca had a nervous breakdown when he learned that Soriano Lapresa, who was well known in Granada, had publicly accused him of being a homosexual (101).
    According to the myth told by Plato, men are divided into two different "halves": one half looks for his complement in a woman, and the other half needs to be completed with the love of another man. Lorca not only knew Plato's *Dialogues*, but "was also enthusiastic" about them, according to his brother's (Francisco García Lorca's) testimony (*Federico y su mundo* 99). It is not necessary to search a great deal to discover the sources that inspired the poet's use of "the other half."
    If Soriano Lapresa accused Lorca, in the second epigraph Lorca's poetic voice stands as an accuser and denounces and spits in the faces of all those who ignore or marginalize "the other half." An important detail in Lorca's poem is that "the other half" is described as "unredeemable," a point discussed below. After saying, "I spit in your face," the poetic voice confirms: "The other half is listening to me." This sentence indicates that the poetic voice is keenly aware of selecting those to whom he directs his poetic message. These addressees pay attention to what the powerful ignore or do not want to know. The other half is also characterized by its "purity." The speaker as well as the

addressee of the message seems to belong to a separate culture. The message is probably then codified according to the norms or semantic and linguistic customs of that culture.

If Lorca's poetic "I" spits its disdain at people who contemptuously ignore the group with which Lorca identifies, Prados spits-cries-weeps to whoever does not pay attention, and Gil-Albert spits out an instinctual rage against the outwardly impeccable "monsters" with "shaven faces." The title of Gil-Albert's poem alludes to the nature of the conflict: it deals with a cultural war. Further on, the poem affirms that "this society" is "crazed."

Cernuda underscores the condition of dispossession of his poetic persona by insistently using the possessive form "your" in connection with morality, laws, society and God.

Lorquian Criticism and "The Other Half"

Lorca, in using the expression "the other half," was referring to homosexuals like himself who were marginalized from society (although they are not the only ones being referred to). "New York (Office and Denunciation)" (Nueva York. [Oficina y denuncia]) is a poem that has been studied by many Lorca experts who fail to note the significance of "the other half." Gustavo Correa, for example, has dealt with the poem on two occasions, but not in regard to this particular issue (*La poesía mítica* 35; *"PNY"* 226–27). Richard Predmore has also analyzed the poem in an article and in a book. Both works say approximately the same thing: that the poet denounces the indifference and cruelty of the monstrous metropolis ("Nueva York" 37; *Lorca's New York Poetry* 60–61). Predmore, however, does not ignore the importance of homosexuality in Lorca's work (see chapter 3, "Oppressed Norms").

In his thesis, Halliburton maintains that the poem "New York" deals with the condemnation of people who are blind in the face of their sins of omission, and ignore their neighbors. According to the author, the protagonist's mission in the poem is not very clear (*"Lorca's Rejection"* 178–80).

Betty Jean Craige asserts that "the other half" with which Lorca identifies is the most primitive world of Spain, its streets and fruit stands (74). According to María Clementa Millán, the poet "steps forth to offer himself as the propitiatory victim to save the type of humanity that he reclaims" ("Voces poéticas" 104). The author does not explain the details which are characteristic of that "class of humanity." For Derrick Harris, the rich are the ignorant half and the exploited poor are the other half (56). García-Posada supports the thesis of those who believe that "the other half" is made up of the victims of capitalism: "Oppressors and oppressed, two 'halves' ... This world of owners and slaves has a neuralgic center, a conducting wire and supports the whole capitalist system: it is Wall Street" (*Interpretación* 75–76).

None of these authors explains why the half exploited by the capitalists would have to be "unredeemable." The idea of being or not being redeemed has Christian roots. Redemption is associated with sin and guilt. Those who are exploited do not sin because they are the victims of capitalism, but homosexuals indeed sin by fulfilling their amorous potential, according to the Catholic Church. Homosexuals are "unredeemable" since they cannot stop being what they are. According to Gibson, Lorca's *Místicas*, which have still not been published, "show that already by the fall of 1917, Lorca's rebellion against the Christian God is quite developed" (*Federico García Lorca* 1:200). A few pages later he adds, "The adolescent Federico who appears in his *juvenilia* is of an intense, unrestrainable eroticism.... It seems clear that if the adolescent poet rebels against the Catholic God it is mainly because this God does not tolerate eroticism" (206, 207). It is evident that in Lorca's work, the tension between the values of the church and those of prohibited eroticism is as old as the appearance of the poet's "secret" conflict. In one of the texts from the *juvenilia* published by Gibson, the pride of an implicit "other half" who does not want to be redeemed from his "sins" is already outlined:

> Do not grieve for my soul. You are the wretches of faith, of greatness, of Love, of Good and of Passion.... Away, deicides of the God of the heart! Do not rise up against the one who like me hates you.... Observe that there is someone who runs joyfully after sins.... But you only think about the matter of the soul and you have formed a ridiculous scheme of piety and salvation [*Federico García Lorca* 1:202–03].

Orality. Flight. Purity and the Pure.

"The other half listens to me / devouring, singing, flying in its purity" (518).

The other half is "devouring" and "singing." Bernard Sesé has analyzed the eroticism and aggression of orality in Lorquian works: "from eroticism to aggression, the boundary is unclear" (*Les valeurs* 35). The author gives an example from *Blood Wedding*, act 1, which in reality is from act 2, scene 2. The mother is speaking: "...caress her in a way that will hurt her a little: a strong hug, a bite and then a soft kiss" (76, 633).

The mixture of eroticism and aggression mentioned by Sesé and its association with orality takes on an openly homosexual character in scene 3 of *The Public*, a work that belongs to the same period as "New York." The fight between two men who love each other is described as a bloody "party." Both would be demigods "if they did not have an anus" (485). In the *Enciclopedia Ilustrada de Sexología y Erotismo* it says that hunger and sexual instinct "often appear intertwined" (803).

Flight evokes birds, a concept whose homosexual connotations will be studied in chapter 6. A personal, ontogenetic antecedent for the poetic flight can be seen in a letter from Lorca to Sebastian Gasch, dated September 8, 1928, one or two years before Lorca made reference to the flight of "the other half": "Yesterday Dalí wrote me a very long letter about my book.... My poetry now tends towards another even keener flight. It seems like a personal flight" (*Selected Letters* 136; 1299).

Lorca is probably referring to the letter where Dalí criticizes *The Gypsy Ballads*, asking himself or Lorca if in reality there is an organic connection between the rider, the reins and the horse, that seem to symbolize the Freudian ego, the superego and the id (see Rodrigo, *Lorca-Dalí* 212). Lorca's personal poetic flight precedes the flight of "the other half," and seems to be equally circumscript. It is not an escape-flight, but a flight within the terrain itself.

In *Signs of Being* (Signos del ser, *PC II*), Emilio Prados mentions an inverted flight that takes place in the life of the poetic "I." *Inverse* and *inverted* are analogous terms that have homosexual connotations: *inverse* alludes to what is opposite or contrary to the "natural order," and *inverted* is generally used as a synonym for homosexual (*Pequeño Larousse* 591). In Lorca's *juvenilia*, the protest against God and against the "natural order" is juxtaposed with the verb *to invert* and is accompanied by an implicit desire for flight in the souls-sails swollen by the wind: "We have to implore, to fight with God ... so that he stops playing with our hearts ... that he abandon us to ourselves so that the sails of our souls swell towards pity and tranquility. We have to protest inverting the natural order of things" (Gibson, *Federico García Lorca* 1:200).

The church tries to impede the above-mentioned flight, according to what is affirmed in a text that, in Gibson's opinion, is the most furious antiecclesiastical protest in all of Lorca's works: "You are miserable politicians of evil, exterminating angels of light. You preach war in the name of God of the battles and to those who do not share your ideas you teach them to hate in a refined way ... the world that has been educated by you is an idiotic world with clipped wings" (*Federico García Lorca* 1:202, 203).

Returning to an earlier poem by Prados, the character, identity and inspiration of the flight had been hidden:

> "Aren't you flying?"
> "Yes; but my flight hides
> its nature and towards what it's taking me,
> which propels me to flight" [*PC* 1:775].

While the poem where the "inverse" of the I that flies comes from a book whose title suggests a certain degree of clarity, *Signs of Being*, this other one is from a book with a more mysterious title: *Semi-Darkness I* (Penumbras I), poem XVI.

For Lorca, purity is even more personal than flight. A letter was mentioned in the introduction in which Lorca confessed that he tried to avoid having his intimate feelings appear clearly in his poetry; what was "the purest" ought to be hidden. One concludes that Lorca's purity is very much connected to that of "the other half"—both are persecuted and in danger.

The association of purity with oppression and censorship appears clearly in the poem, "Your Childhood in Menton" (Tu infancia en Mentón). A "pure mask" is mentioned that is "from another sign." The poetic persona wants to speak about the love object, but there are those who try to prevent it: "Yes, I do love! Love! Leave me alone, all of you. / And don't try to cover my mouth..." (*PNY* 15; 518).

It would be logical to interpret Lorquian purity, starting from the connotations that the concept has in the marginalized culture rather than in the oppressor, after having seen this division and incompatibility between what is pure for Lorca and his poetic "I" and what is pure for those who surround and pursue him.

Purity and Lorquian Criticism. Lorca and Walt Whitman.

In "Ode to Walt Whitman" (Oda a Walt Whitman) the Lorquian poetic "I" says to the fags: "Let the confused, the pure, / the classical, the celebrated, the supplicants / close the doors of the bacchanal to you" (*PNY* 163).

According to Betty Jean Craige, "Whitman's homosexuality is not that of the 'maricas' ('perverts') but that of the purer love of universal brotherhood" (79). Can Craige mean that "universal brotherhood" practices a homosexuality of greater value? It seems unlikely. Surely she means that pure love is that which abstains from sex. How does one then explain that the Lorquian "pure ones" are participating in a bacchanal? When one closes the door on someone, one person is inside and the other one is outside. If the pure close "the doors of the bacchanal" to the "queers," this means that "the pure" have the keys and are in the bacchanal.

García-Posada tries to deny the importance of the Lorquian bacchanal. In his edition of *Ode and Mockery of Sesostris and Sardanapalus* (Oda y burla de Sesostris y Sardanápalo), the critic includes a note about the bacchanal from "Ode to Walt Whitman" where he passes judgment: "It is clear that the bacchanalian is seen here from a poetic perspective, not a philological one, and it would be nonsensical to apply an irrelevant focus to it. Doubly nonsensical because, as is well known, the question is invested with special complexity" (39).

García-Posada seems to think that poetry, or words and poetic expressions, are born with their own focus which has absolutely nothing to do with the point of view of the critic that focuses on them. The author does not clarify what he means by "poetic perspectives." Can he believe that Lorca uses the word *bacchanal* only because it seems pretty? A similar "poetic" perspective would not jive with the personal experiences that Lorca himself had in relation to poetry. In his lecture on Góngora, Lorca maintains that the poet "must ... discharge all his arrows at living metaphors, avoiding all that is florid and false ... and keep wary lookout for the quivering flesh of reality that accords with the shadowy map of the poem that he carries" (Belitt, *PNY* 175, 176; 1044).

The poetic perspective that Lorca presents in his talk "Children's Cradle Songs" additionally suggests the thought that criticism should proceed carefully before rejecting totally the philological perspective: "I am on a poetic plane where the yes and the no of things are equally true. If you ask me 'Is a moonlit night a hundred years ago identical to a moonlit night ten days ago?' I could show ... that they were identical and they were different." (1044).

The association of purity with "the bacchanal" is evident in Lorca's work as well as in his life. In a letter to Jorge Zalamea from the fall of 1928 the poet states: "All day I turn out poems like a factory. And then I go in for the manly, in the style of a pure Andalusian, to a bacchanal of flesh and laughter" (*Letters* 139; 1312).

Also 1928, Lorca was "deeply in love" with the sculptor Emilio Aladrén Perojo, who exploited him shamelessly, according to García Carrillo (Gibson, *Federico García Lorca* 1:545). The painter Maruja Mallo asserts that Aladrén was her suitor, and that Federico took him away from her (*Federico García Lorca* 1:544). One could say that Lorca was pure when he gave into his homosexual feelings in body and soul, as a complete man. The "impure" were probably the "queers" and perhaps those who practiced homosexuality because they were attracted primarily to money, pleasure, fame or other factors.

López Castellón also speaks about "Ode to Walt Whitman," as well as "the pure" and "the impure," but not about the bacchanals. According to him, "None of those who knew him affirm that Federico was an effeminate man and, much less, carried on openly homosexual relationships. (With the exception, perhaps, of some cynical declarations from his intimate friend, Salvador Dalí...)" (*Federico García Lorca* 53). The detail about "effeminate" may be correct, but the other information is not, as already demonstrated in chapter 1 (unless one reads "openly" as "exhibitionist").

Some critics suggest or maintain that there is no proof that either Lorca or Whitman ever engaged in homosexuality (Laubenthal 111). Laubenthal believes that if one speaks from the point of view of psychological criticism, the nature of *PNY* and *Leaves of Grass* is a result of the sublimated homosexual attitudes of both poets. Nevertheless, he recognizes that their best poems are filled with sexual images (111).

Walt Whitman seems very conscious of the "indecency" of what he expresses, for example, in section 24 from "Song of Myself": "Through me forbidden voices, / Voices of sexes and lusts, voices veil'd and I remove the veil, / Voices indecent..." (68).

What most characterizes Lorca's and Whitman's poetry is not the song to sexual abstinence. The purity that Whitman represents does not hide the impassioned kisses exchanged between two men: "Why do you think that I take up the pen and begin to write?," he asks readers in the clearest and most direct style. It is not to speak about a battleship, nor about the splendor of day or night, nor the glory of the great city. It is only to speak about two simple men who say goodbye by embracing and kissing passionately: "The one to remain hung on the other's neck and passionately kiss'd him, / While the one to depart tightly prest the one to remain in his arms" (125–26).

Whitman is not pure because he might be chaste but because in him the division between body and soul, between homosexual practice and spiritual love has been avoided, at least in his poetry: "I have said that the soul is not more than the body, / And I have said that the body is not more than the soul" (section 48, "Song of Myself" 94).

Bacchanalian Purification. Homosexual Purity.

Bacchanals are associated with unchecked sexuality and with Dionysian rituals which are no less uncontrolled. They connote the presence of a very different culture from the Judeo-Christian heterosexual one. Bacchanalian purification does not mean that one must abstain from practicing sex. On the contrary, it implicitly means the annihilation of what separates the soul from the body. It fuses the spiritual or religious experience with the sexual one.

Men who would not approach women have also been called pure. In the *Enciclopedia Ilustrada de Sexología y Erotismo* it states that in ancient societies, when women had their first menstruation, generally "they were placed away from human groups and were prohibited from having sexual relations" (739–40). According to Charles Segal, "Dionysus, in his first birth from Zeus's 'immortal fire' and 'male womb,' acts out a fantasy of the male's independence from female cycles of menstruation and birth with their attendant uncleanness, and achieves that independence from [the] female which recurs wishfully through early Greek literature" (181).

The "impurity" of women or of the heterosexual relationship is mentioned at times in the texts of homosexual culture, perhaps as a reaction against the condemnation of the "purity" of love between men. "Bíblica" by Gil-Albert states that women themselves "barely do anything that does not / stain the original" (*OPC* 2:163). According to Forberg, it seems that among the Celts, the "impure" were those who did not practice homosexuality. These men could not aspire to receive honors (90).

The Ambiguity of Victorian Purity. Whiteness.

During the Victorian period an ambiguously pure love flourished between men. Women were divided into two basic groups: good women or "saints" (mothers, sisters and wives) who must not becomed stained, and the other women, the more or less evil ones, who stained men. In *The Victorians and Ancient Greece*, Richard Jenkyns summarizes the situation of heterosexuality during the Victorian period by saying that a man had to choose between violating a saint or going off with a prostitute. Heterosexual activity under those conditions becomes exciting, but degrading, according to the author (284). A homosexual did not have to dedicate himself to these "repugnant" acts. His emotions seemed nobler and purer. It is only a step away to the thinking that the kiss of a young man is purer than that of a woman, adds Jenkyns (284).

It is undeniable that many relationships between men were platonic, but one does not always know if those relationships had concrete boundaries, nor if those boundaries could be broken at certain moments. Jenkyns presents several examples of a Victorian homosexual purity that was not always chaste. He also notes the existence of other terms semantically analogous to "pure" like "white" that connote the same ambiguous homosexual purity. The author analyzes the essays of Walter Pater, in whose prose the word "white" emerges with "troubling overtones" whenever the critic speaks about sculpture. A sweet insinuating voice seems to murmur a message that it dares not say out loud (Jenkyns 149). The author analyzes how Pater uses different metaphors centered around the idea of whiteness. In erasing the distinction between different forms of purity, Pater implies that the emotions condemned by his contemporaries could seem innocent in a Greek context. According to Jenkyns, the reader is "coaxed" into believing that the Greek cult of beautiful young men is acceptable, since it is enveloped in a halo of apparently religious associations (150).

The Accursed "Breed" or "Race."[2] Animal Blood. "Sailor's Blood." Those of a "Different Blood."

In his drawing "The Drunken Sailor" (no. 187 from the exposition catalogue, 1986), Lorca shows how the term *Roma* becomes *Amor* when reversed. Both words revolve around the head of the drunken sailor, and seem to come out of a bottle that carries the label *Rom*. As the reader probably understands, it is more than a matter of simple words. What revolves around the head and, implicitly, *inside* the drunken sailor's head, is the impossible equation of *The Church of Rome* and (homosexual) *love*. The conflict is presented with hardly any disguise in *The Public* and in "Cry to Rome" (Grito hacia Roma). In the scene called "Roman Ruin" from *The Public*, the Roman Centurion says to the two masculine figures who love each other: "May all of your kind be damned!" (14; 482). In "Cry to Rome," Lorca returns the stone, an object with phallic meaning, making it very clear what he thinks and feels about this center of civilization that cursed homosexuals, and about its representative, "the man dressed in white": "loves covered with worms / will fall on you" (149; 525). (This "cry" is no longer the same as that of the weeping character who compares himself to a worm in "Rhythm of Autumn" [Ritmo de otoño] [*Book of Poems*]. The cry that Lorca hurls towards Rome in *PNY* is a shout of rage that, at the same time, demands justice: "Because we demand that Earth's will be done, / that its fruits be offered to everyone" (153; 527).

The Roman Centurion's utilization of the concept of the accursed "breed" raises the question of homosexuals' being seen as a breed. *Breed* is a synonym for *lineage* and also evokes animal blood (animals are crossbred to improve the breed). The poem "New York" speaks about animal blood and "sailor blood." The poetic "I" mentions the blood of real animals, but it should be noted that Lorca easily identified with animals and projected his feelings onto them. This will be seen in the figure of the billy goat in chapter 4.

Homosexual feeling is often expressed through what could be called an "animal" symbolism. Two of the animals mentioned are lambs and dogs. In the sonnet whose first line begins "O secret voice of dark love," the poetic voice is presented as a "bleating without fleece" and a "dog in the heart" (*CP* 721; *Sonetos* 54). Chapter 3 discusses how Dr. Gregorio Marañón denounced the animal-like roundups that the police organized for the "hunting" of homosexuals. In "New York" the poet mentions the "delirious hunts" of dogs. Lorca himself is an "erotic little beast," according to what Dalí says to him affectionately in one of his letters (*SD escribe* 92). In "The Poet Prays to the Virgin for Help" the poet seems even to prefer animal light or instinct to the light of understanding[3]:

> I pray to the Divine Mother of God
> Heavenly Queen of all things,
> that she grant me the pure light of the little animals
> that have a single letter in their vocabulary.
> Animals without souls, simple shapes [*PNY* 193; 810].

A comparable symbolism with clearly homosexual connotations can be seen in the work of Walt Whitman, the poet for whom Lorca felt affection and admiration. Whitman spoke about the "animal purity" of wounded soldiers "with whom he had exchanged long kisses, as he continuously repeated" (Bedient 218). Whitman also shows his preference for what could be called "the pure light" of animals in section 32 of "Song of Myself":

> I think I could turn and live with animals, they are so
>   placid and self-contain'd,
> ...
> Picking out here one that I love, and now go with him on
>   brotherly terms.
> A gigantic beauty of a stallion, fresh and responsive to my
>   caresses, [73].

In studying "sailor blood" it is obvious that in Lorca's poem there is a unifying link between animal blood, "sailor blood" and "the other half." In *Androgyny*, June Singer reminds us that the process of division or fragmentation of the platonic androgyne occurred in two stages. Men and women came forth from the first division, heterosexuals and homosexuals from the second. In this way, the homosexual "race" was created (112). In Lorca's poem, "sailor blood" appears "Under the divisions." The homosexual "race" afterwards became an "accursed race" or "outcast (damned) part of humanity" according to Proust's expression (Hahn 97, Viers 11). There is no difference between "caste" and "race" in regard to the present topic.

Lorca quotes Proust in his lecture on Góngora: "Only the metaphor can give a kind of eternity to style" (1036). In *Sodome et Gomorrhe*, Proust alludes several times to the homosexual "race." Charlus belonged to it. It is a race that lives under a curse, a race that must live in the middle of lies (18, 19). For Proust, there is a clear parallel between the persecution of homosexuals and Jews: "Joined with those like them by the ostracism that wounds them, the disgrace into which they have fallen, having finished by taking on the physical and moral characteristics of a race, because of a persecution similar to that of Israel" (20).

The idea that homosexuals are of "another blood" or belong to a different race continues making a token presence in literature: "It was as if he were born of different blood" (Hobson 17).

In using the expression "sailor blood" without the article, Lorca confers on this blood the distinction of a race. Since one is dealing only with one drop of blood, only one "drop of sailor blood," some might question the importance of that drop. The answer is given by the Director in *The Public* in the last scene of the work: "that law is a wall that dissolves into the tiniest drop of blood" (45, 532).

In *The Homosexual Matrix* C.A. Tripp mentions a traditional connection between sailors and homosexuality, the origin of which is from different sources. We feel that this link should be taken into account. Ocean trips lasted a long time. When arriving at a port, the crew's freedom would be restricted. The idea gained popularity that, under these conditions, men were more or less "forced" in the direction of homosexual practices. Tripp shows that there are data indicating that men who chose to live at sea were not concerned about living apart from women. Additionally, lost in the censored pages of history, there is a long tradition of homosexual practices at sea. In the Spanish galleons, for example, there was a detailed code which specified the sexual freedom or loyalty of the men who "belonged" to each other during a trip. Its objective was to control jealousy in order to avoid fights and maintain order on board (209–10). The author also speaks of direct prohibitions against research during our century and the sequestration of statistical data: "To this day, the U.S. Army keeps under lock and key the second largest statistical study of human sexual behaviour ever conducted — refusing to share any part of it with the numerous professionals who have requested it.... This huge study examines the effect of military service and confinement upon the sexual behaviour of males" (215).

Sailors as Archetypal Figures in the Homosexual World

In Sarotte's thesis four essential archetypes of the homosexual couple are presented: adolescents, the professor and the student, the military man and his subordinate, and the black and the white man. For his part, Kleinberg, in his book *The Other Persuasion*, speaks about themes or archetypal motifs. He mentions as an example the scene or issue of the confession that one is homosexual (xi). His use of "other" in the title refers to "other" as "other half." Apart from the introduction, Kleinberg's book is an anthology of texts on homosexual themes. J.T. Farrel and William Faulkner are represented for having described two of the most characteristic scenes in the homosexual world: "rough trade and men at sea" (xiv). Also included is a short novel by Hemingway, "The Sea Change." The connection between sailors and homosexuality is obvious.

Jean Cocteau was very fond of drawing sailors. Some of his drawings have been published in a very limited edition of *The White Book* (Le livre blanc). The most erotic ones have been published only in books not easily accessible and in homosexual magazines. For example, see "Jean Genet's Sailors through the Eyes of Jean Cocteau" (*In Touch,* May–June 1976, 58–61) or "Jean Cocteau Censored" (*Gay magasin,* Jan. 1984, 44–45). According to Milorad, the theme of the sailor found a source of enrichment thanks to the seamen from the French and American wars whom Cocteau met along the Mediterranean coast, especially in Villefranche and Toulon (15). *Querelle de Brest* would be the meeting point for three different kinds of artists who have dealt with the motif of sailors and homosexuality: Genet wrote the book, Cocteau drew the sailors and Fassbinder made living cinematographic images out of the theme.

Lorca and Sailors

David Loughran undoubtedly thinks that sailors are important figures in the work of Lorca. The second chapter of his book *Federico García Lorca: The Poetry of Limits* is entitled "Lorca's Sailors." Nevertheless, either the author ignores the importance of homosexuality in this context or chooses to ignore it. Loughran recognizes that sailors appear to be associated with love, but he suppresses the importance of this fact in affirming several times that the word *love* appears frequently in Lorca's work without any erotic connotations (18). It is unclear what pertains and what does not pertain to the atmosphere of the erotic, nor what methods Loughran has followed to be sure of the absence of erotic connotations.

Already in 1976 García-Posada showed that the motif of the sailor is a "decisive symbol in the New York poems," although he did not explain what it symbolized. The author does not ignore the presence of the homosexual theme in *PNY*. In a longer study he states: "A new morality rises up over the ruins of Judeo-Christian morality, to which [Lorca] delivers a crucial blow in justifying the legitimacy of homosexual love, situated at the same level as heterosexual love" ("Nota previa," "Estudio" 107).

García-Posada speaks about Lorca's sailors as much in the second as in the third part of his detailed and extensive study *Lorca: Interpretación de PNY*, but not in connection with the theme of homosexuality. He maintains that "the sailor ends up transformed into a paradigm of what is human" and that "the sailor is the symbolic representation of some concrete navigators, the

Christians" (145). He says nothing about the link between "sailor blood" and the "other half." Could Christians be irredeemable?

The critic refers to the biographical aspect of Lorca's poems and its relationship to the poet's drawings: the sailor appears "as a victim of love and in this guise is identified with the poet himself, thus joining with Lorca's fine arts production" (145). If the sailor is identified with the poet in his capacity as "victim of love" as stated so well by García-Posada, would it not then be relevant to study this link? Lorca has indicated the place and the year in which he wrote *PNY*. These details are included at the beginning of the book and are also relevant for the interpretation of its symbols. Did Lorca meet a sailor or a few sailors during his stay in the United States? And, if so, what were the circumstances and the events involved in the meeting? The answers to these questions come primarily through Mildred Adams' *García Lorca: Playwright and Poet* (122). Nine years later, B. Bussell Thomson and J.K. Walsh would complete and correct in part the information given by Adams in their article "A Meeting Between Lorca and Hart Crane in New York" (Un encuentro de Lorca y HC en NY 1, 12). Lorca was taken to Crane's home. According to Adams, the friend who introduced them described the encounter with hesitation. Crane's homosexuality could hardly be called secret. When Lorca arrived, Crane was surrounded by young sailors, all of whom were drunk. According to Adams, the meeting was not very fruitful. Bussell Thomson and Walsh maintain that Adams received the information "very second hand and pretty distorted by the informers in order not to offend the poet's family, particularly Lorca's brother." The critics name the friend who took Lorca to see Crane: it was Angel Flores, a young scholar from Puerto Rico, who states, "he suddenly realized that Lorca and Crane had a lot in common, that Lorca 'also was interested in sailors.' ... Crane invited Lorca to remain with the sailors; Flores left and Lorca remained with the group. Flores' last recollection was a glance at Crane joking with a group of sailors, and Lorca surrounded by another group" (12).

Lorca liked to drink; the poet was not an inveterate drunk but drank when the occasion called for it, or when his feelings demanded it. Alcohol's stimulating effects and its ability to loosen sexual inhibitions are well known. But, what was the poet's relationship with drinking during his stay in New York? In a letter written to Angel del Río, dated August 1929, that is, the same year that Lorca met Hart Crane and the sailors who were in his home, the poet begs his friend: "Angel: tell me by return mail how to meet you. When I think that I can *drink* in the house where you live it makes me very happy.... Urgently need cognac for my poor heart. Write me and I'll go to meet you" (*Selected Letters* 150; 1329).

In spite of the prohibitions in the United States in regard to drinking as well as to homosexuality, Crane's house had both alcohol and sailors. What Lorca did or did not do there on that day or on other days may never be known with certainty. Nevertheless, Lorca has left his poetry, and what, in fact, can be confirmed is that some of the central motifs of several poems from *PNY* are alcohol, sailors and a poetic voice that barely recognizes himself in comparison to what he was before. In the poem "Landscape of a Vomiting Multitude" (Paisaje de una multitude que vomita), it is suggested that the poet has had a lot to drink and that the alcohol awakens something in him or makes him see something in himself that creates fear. His look is no longer his own, no longer the one from before, the one he knew and controlled. It is now a look free from masks and from the clothes or the disguises which had been imposed on him. A naked look, whose nakedness probably has existential and erotic dimensions. A look that comes from "waves where no dawn would go," that is to say, from the hidden and proscribed sides of the poet. The following lines from the poem refer to what has been described:

> The look on the face was mine, but now isn't me,
> the naked look on my face, trembling for alcohol
> and launching incredible ships
> through the anemones of the piers.
> I protect myself with this look
> that flows from waves where no dawn would go,
> I, poet without arms, lost
> in the vomiting multitude, [55; 474].

The poet's look that the alcohol has unmasked is in reality the friend or ally of the poet since, according to the poem, that look allows the poet to defend himself. It is suggested here then that the enemy is the social "I" of daily life or the clothed look.

What happens often to Crane is the same thing that happens to Lorca. Some critics prefer not to mention certain things, despite all the relevance they may have. Virginia Higginbotham, for example, compares the work of both poets in her article "García Lorca and Hart Crane: Two Views from the Bridge," without entering into the homosexual issue, in spite of the fact that the author observes Walt Whitman's presence as an important link in the work of the two poets. Extra-literary material is considered to be of interest since Higginbotham mentions Crane's letters. But the author is content to observe that Lorca and Crane are indignant over oppression and social or human exploitation (219–21).

A.L. Rowse is much more explicit than other critics and mentions the "orgies" and Crane's drunken binges. According to Rowse, there were always "available" soldiers and sailors (314).

In *Howl and Other Poems,* Allen Ginsberg refers to Crane and mentions the sailors. The name itself does not appear in the poem but Ginsberg makes the reference to Crane explicit: "who blew and were blown by those human seraphim, the sailors" (12). There are two translations, one from Argentina and the other from Spain. The first uses the verb "soplar," "to blow," while the other employs "mamar," "to suck." The second one seems more exact in its use of the Spanish verb "mamar" (to suck) as the equivalent of the English "to blow" since Ginsberg himself says he is describing the "acceptance of the basic realities of homosexual pleasure." In Criado de Val's dictionary (*Dictionary of Ambiguous Spanish* [Diccionario del español equívoco]), "mamar" is "an ambiguous designation for the sexual act" (107).

The following is from "Sleepless City" (Cuidad sin sueño), a poem that Lorca wrote after his meeting with Crane and the drunken sailors (Adams 122): "raw flesh. Kisses tie mouths / in a tangle of new veins" (*PNY* 67; 480). The tied mouths can be prisoners in a double sense: tied — busy with the sex act — and tied — silenced by the nature of the act or by the above-mentioned love which cannot be made public. The first meaning is already found in Marcial, whose writings were familiar to Lorca, who names him in the poet's lecture on the *duende*. In epigram 96 from book III, the speaker assures another that since he is fucking him his tongue will stop moving. Before mentioning kisses, Lorca's poem refers to a "flesh" which is raw. The contiguity places the kisses in connection with the referred to flesh, and the mouths with "veins." According to Cela's *Diccionario secreto,* vein is a synonym for "cock" (475). In "First Lamentation of the Flesh," Miguel Hernández uses the word *flesh* in such a way that there can be no misunderstanding: "Oh flesh of urination, active and evil" (*OPC* 148).

One can observe the similarity of poetic expressions in Lorca and Hernández: "raw flesh" and "active flesh." That there was communication between the two poets so that words and expressions were used rather freely is seen very clearly in a letter published by Juan Cano Ballesta in his article "Vicissitudes of a Friendship: Lorca and Miguel Hernández" (Peripecias de una amistad: Lorca y MH): "Federico, I would love to have a member for urinating for each one of these women who fade away" (217).

Among Lorca's unpublished texts made public in 1986, "Mística" surfaces to show clearly what type of love and what kind of flesh attract the poet: "I dream of a love that is my own flesh" (28).

Gil-Albert refers to the masculine organ through *veins* in *Presencia misteriosa,* first calling it "Porción prohibida": "How abundant, how fleeting life is in the veins, / How the cockhead imprints on the chest / The thread of your fluid erect being" ("Sonnet XII," *OPC* 1:26).

In the poem "Flesh" (Carne), Lorca also mentions "veins" that grow longer: "Look what tender sighs, what mobile sounds / press on the waist of the frenzied youth! / Come, come! The tips of the veins will grow longer" (795). The erotic evocation in the "tender sighs," the movement and the waist seems evident. Further down (so there is no mistake about the kind of love being evoked) appears the line "the green blood of Sodom shines."

Veins and *waist* are again mentioned in "The Poet Asks His Love to Write Him" (El poeta pide a su amor que le escriba), also known as "Sonnet of the Letter" (Soneto de la carta). Here the poet suggests that his blood (that is to say, his semen) spilled onto his love's waist while the two exchanged lovebites: "But I suffered you, tore open my veins, / tiger and dove on your waist / Caught in a duel of bites and lilies" (*CP* 715; 795).

Vein is also used in daily life to refer to very pronounced features of homosexuality or to belonging to a homosexual group, in expressions like "to have a very pronounced vein" or "to be of the same vein." In "Uncertain Solitude" (Soledad insegura), Lorca writes about a night of "hidden vein" where there is a "mute fish" who bathes "lasciviously" (*CP* 763; 782).

In regard to the interpretation of words like "veins," "flesh," and "kisses," it is to be noted that the sexual variant referred to in speaking about kisses and flesh was utilized by Lorca as well as by Philip Cummings. According to Daniel Eisenberg, in a letter to Ángel Sahuquillo dated July 19, 1989: "Cummings was Lorca's lover. He told me how they blew each other — at least he did it to Lorca — there in the Vermont woods, ... I would have to get out my notes, these memories are from fifteen years ago. He speaks of it in front of his wife without the slightest reservation."

Perhaps for understandable reasons given the nature of what has been narrated, Cummings does not speak about these things with everyone: "(he denies having mentioned homosexuality to researchers)," clarifies Eisenberg in a parenthesis from his letter. Nevertheless, the author believes what Cummings told him is "true." In a postcard marked Tallahassee, September 22, 1989, Eisenberg gives us permission to quote him and adds: "They often were in the woods."

The meaning of *fellatio* that *kiss* can have would explain, among other things, the dénouement of *Yerma*, as J.A. Parr also suggests in his article "La escena final de *Yerma*" (26–27). The violent reaction of the protagonist of the work when her husband asks her to kiss him "...like this" is not easily explainable if one does not think that the kiss that Juan desires is something different from what one usually understands as such. "That I'll never do," shouts Yerma, and she repeats "Never" and chokes her husband until he dies (*Three Tragedies* 153; 744).

"Sleepless City," the poem in which veins and kisses are mentioned, is of an implacable clarity. Indirectly, the addressee is asked to be conscious of what the poem tries to communicate and also causes others to be so. The poetic voice provokes those who do not want to see to open their eyes, even though it may be by force:

> No one sleeps.
> But if someone closes his eyes,
> whip him, my children, whip him!
> Let there be a panorama of open eyes
> and bitter inflamed wounds [*PNY* 69; 481].

To sum up: the "fresh veins" from Lorca's poem can be a symbol for newly "kissed" penises. They can also refer to the distinctive features of a homosexuality recently assumed by those who perhaps have tried to escape their destiny by closing their eyes in the face of their own feelings or in the face of reality and the weight of social marginalization.

◆ ◆ ◆

In *The Drawings of García Lorca* (Dibujos de García Lorca), Gregorio Prieto recalls Lorca's words and also the setting and the atmosphere in which he said them: "a beautiful summer afternoon in Madrid, seated in the cool shadows of the poplar garden of the Student Residence, the poet told me: 'Gregorio, the poetry of your painting and the painting of my poetry are born from the innermost recess of the same source'" (28).

Much more suggestive is the book that Prieto published in 1972: *Lorca y su mundo angélico*. In a few pages, Prieto expresses himself with great clarity: "Earthly man; earthly woman; celestial and eternal Archangel. Man and woman at the same time, transfigured into divinity, perpetuated in perfect equilibrium of creative superabundance. Created by God for the perpetuation of the artistic and valuable species that never dies" (195).

Three figures illustrate the text: one masculine, one feminine and a third one with the physical and sexual attributes of the first two. Only one name, Prieto's signature, appears on the page, yet the book deals with Lorca and his world. On page 54, a large open eye covers half the sex of the masculine figure. Lorca wrote, "May there be a panorama of open eyes." Some drawn wings make the semi-nude masculine figure seem like a pagan archangel. The sailor motif takes up many pages in Prieto's book. Of particular interest is the one on page 110. In capital letters it reads: "ONLY MYSTERY LETS US LIVE, ONLY MYSTERY." Although there may be no signature, these are the words that Lorca used to illustrate a drawing entitled "Sailor" [Marinero]. Three photographs accompany the text: one of a sailor alone, another of three sailors and the third of a sailor and a woman. In the first two, the sailors have an almost identical posture. The sailor alone, who seems to be urinating, as well as the other three who seem to be praying, have their hands on their sex organs. Under each photograph the word "Mystery" appears.

Prieto knew Lorca well and lived with Cernuda for some time, a fact that is important to bear in mind. "Everything you say about my love is certain, and I already knew it," writes Cernuda to Prieto, who is the only one who can excuse and understand his secrets ("Letter to Gregorio Prieto" [Carta a GP]). In his book Prieto suggests that the mystery that helps Lorca live has a direct relationship to "race" or the archetype of the sailors. This concurs with what Lorca himself says in maintaining that the *duende*[4] through which true art is manifested and created is not a *duende* primarily engaged in artistic form, but rather a *duende* who is a descendent of another one who, "glutted with circles and lines, went out on the canals to hear the drunken sailors singing" (Belitt 155; 1099). Drunken sailors like the ones Lorca encountered in Hart Crane's homosexual circle.

Miguel García-Posada has observed the repeated association of sailors with alcohol in Lorca's work, but does not arrive at any conclusions about it ("Comentarios," *Interpretación*).

Sailors appear often in Lorca's drawings; two different drawings even have the same title: "Sailor." In the second one are the words "BIERE" and "VINOS" on the building walls where a sailor seems to be leaving. On a bottle label appear the letters "AMO." The sailor, drink and love are thus related. One part of the sailor's body is drawn with small dots that resemble earth. A root grows or comes out of the left armpit. In the poem "Ghazal of the Bitter Root" (Gacela de la raíz amarga) love appears as the enemy of the ego or conscious "I," that is to say, of one's social being, a love that is of "bitter root." If the roots of a love are bitter their fruit will probably also be bitter and perhaps, also, their shells. The bitter shell is a well known homosexual symbol that appears in Spanish books and dictionaries (León 80, Coll 28).

The Symbolism of Death, the "Bitter One," Knives, and the Act of Mounting

Many critics have noted that death is one of the biggest Lorquian motifs (see Lima: *The Theatre of GL*). In "Life and Death in the Drama of Federico García Lorca" (Muerte y vida en el drama de Federico García Lorca), Betty Rita Gómez, in the space of two pages, alternates her discourse on death with an exalted song to procreation and maternity: "Juan, the sterile man, is the negation of life and has to be destroyed.... Yerma's yearning for maternity is the echo of the earth's eternal pregnancy" (376–77).

In "Lorca and the Poetry of Death," Pedro Salinas states that the "culture of death" is very Spanish and gives some examples in popular culture, but does not mention the homosexual act as a symbol of death (104–06).

Martínez Nadal somewhat approaches the issue in the chapter added to the English version of his study of *The Public*, "Death in the Work of García Lorca." The author mentions the world of apparently negative values in *PNY*, its Goyaesque dreams, a nightmare in which disintegration appears to triumph. A detailed study of those years and the poet's personal problems would help to clarify some elements and the logic of many of the so-called "disconnected metaphors" and truncated images, according to Martínez Nadal (*Federico García Lorca and The Public* 168–69).

In "Deaths of the Bitter One: The 'Ballad of the Summoned One,'" (Muertes del Amargo: El "Romance del emplazado") F. González Cruz has observed that the character dies two times, although in different ways. The author adds that death is an obsessive central theme in all of Lorca's work, but the death of the Bitter One is "disturbing in its vagueness" (27, 32–33). The vagueness of this death is an interesting sign. According to Loughran, a tone of predetermined death extends throughout the "Diálogo del Amargo" which is interpreted as a conversation with death. L.F. Vivanco sees the dialogue similarly and believes that darkness, the knife and the horse indicate the presence of death (56, 57). Alvarez de Miranda feels it is insufficient to say that the characters die in order that everything may be explained: "the important thing is to see why they die and how they die." The death of Amargo, the Bitter One, states Alvarez, is "hidden and magical" (31). Carl Cobb is one of the few critics who has spoken directly of the phallic dagger offered to the Bitter One and of the deliberate ambiguity of the images of death and homosexuality (*Federico García Lorca* 50–51).

In the "Dialogue of Amargo, the Bitter One," it is night and Amargo, the Bitter One, goes with other young men along a road. He willingly remains further behind and encounters a man on a horse. The latter insists that he mount and gives him a knife as a present. Finally Amargo mounts and the rider gives him the knife. The majority of critics state that he is Death. The two men exchange enigmatic words in connection with the knife: "AMARGO: A knife doesn't have to be any more than a knife. RIDER: There you're mistaken. AMARGO: Thanks" (159).

Generally, when someone says one is mistaken, a dispute follows or an explanation is requested. That Amargo immediately thanks the rider because he tells him that he is mistaken indicates that he knows that he is and that he did not want to be right, although something obliges him to deny, indirectly, that a knife can be a symbol of something else. According to Freud, the phallus is symbolized by objects which have the property of penetrating the body and harming it, for example, weapons with a point: knives, daggers, lances, sabers, etc. (*Psychoanalysis* 137–38). In *Surrealismo y sexualidad*, X. Gauthier has indicated that this symbolism was adopted by many surrealists and is "particularly visible in the paintings of Picasso and Masson, where the penis almost always has the shape of a dagger" (61).[5] Lorca also mentions the knife ambiguously in a postcard from April 1927. In the middle of the Sierra Nevada, the poet feels as if he were in the *heart of the soul* of Africa. He says that there one understands "the taste for the piercing knife" (1303). If in his postcard Lorca associates "taste" with "the piercing knife," in the poem "Earth and Moon" (Tierra y luna) he associates love with a "long death that I relish" (*CP* 645; 809). *Love and Knife* (Amor y cuchillo) then seems to have very similar values in the mind and in the heart of the poet. Or perhaps one can say that the "knife" can be an instrument of love, and that it can "kill" in a pleasurable way.

The image from "Earth and Moon" which relates love with death and pleasure supports the hypothesis that *death* often is a symbol of *orgasm* or of the homosexual act in Lorca's work. The knife that pierces in "killing" is the phallus, as Andrew Anderson also suggests in his analysis of *Blood Wedding*: "The knife fight at the end of act 3 scene 1, is thus a confrontation of rival penises ... and the knifing is like an act of sexual love.... During the moment of death of the two men, 'suddenly two long, ear-splitting shrieks are heard.' This 'shriek' is a moan of grief in death, but it can also be, in an ambivalent way, from the agony and ecstasy of orgasm" (60).

In "Dagger" (Puñal), which is also from *Poem of the Deep Song*, the dagger is compared to the most luminous of things, the sun:

> Like a ray of sun,
> the dagger sets
> the terrible bottomlands
> aglow [*CP* 109; 169].

The "dagger" then is not cold, nor does it cause cold, but it "sets aglow," that is to say, it *inflames*. It enters the heart, "...a plowshare entering, / breaking fallow ground" (109; 169).

Dalí states in *El mito trágico del "Angelus" de Millet*: "It is already known that peasants ... tend to eroticize ... all the work instruments which fall into their hands." As a complement to these words, a folkloric illustration from the nineteenth century is included. In it a peasant is used as if he were a plow: the man "plows" the earth with the erect phallus stuck in it (11, 12). Freud also indicates that the masculine sexual organ is symbolized by diverse work instruments, among which the plow stands out (*Psychoanalysis* 146). For García Calvo this paradox regarding the penis seems curious: "on the one hand, it is the organ apparently designated for love, designated for pleasure, but at the same time it is the one which because of its own constitution converts that pleasure into a plow at work, according to the traditional metaphor" (50).

Yermo is a synonym for *desert* or *barren land*, and *Yerma* is the title of Lorca's famous play that deals with a woman's infertility. Lorca associates the act of driving a dagger with that of putting the "plow" into earth, which does not bear fruit, an unusual and very significant association. Since time immemorial, the plow and the sowing have evoked the sexual act and its fruit. Lorca quotes from the Bible in *Impressions and Landscapes* (Impresiones y paisajes), when he had not yet turned twenty: "...Because he who sows for his flesh..." (853). The quotation is located before the chapter "The Carthusian Monastery" (La cartuja), which contains various sexual references, some of which are very clear.[6] The dagger-plow that "inflames" evokes the fall of semen or seed that will not germinate since the place where "the plow" is put is infertile.

Miller has explained "dagger" in these terms: the dagger is A, the plowshare is B, the heart A1 and the fallow ground B1. Two diagrams are used. The purpose is to do a "close analysis" of *Poem of the Deep Song*, a book that, according to Miller, has been passed over or treated too superficially by the majority of contemporary critics (9 and 127). The profundity of Miller's analysis nevertheless seems somewhat uncertain. The critic concentrates almost exclusively on the study of superficial structures and relationships of the type mentioned and forgets to dig deeply into the soul or instinct that gives life to the structures.

Having studied the symbolism of the dagger, it is essential to look at the plot of "Dialogue of Amargo, the Bitter One" to see if there are more indications that support the relevance of a homosexual reading.

Although the majority of critics believe that the Rider symbolizes death, Panebianco maintains that it deals with a persecutor (in a Freudian sense) who embodies the ghost of homosexual rape. Amargo does not have the slightest intention of fleeing from the supposed persecution, but rather, the opposite. The knives that the Rider speaks about seem "beautiful" (*CP* 161; 238). The Rider is interested in having Amargo mount, and insists on wanting to give him a knife as a gift:

> Why don't you mount up behind? [159; 235].... Come on, climb on up [161; 238].... Now you'll get up here with me, right? [163; 240]. Come on! Get up! Let's get going [163; 240].... Want a knife? [159; 237].... Hey, I'm giving it to you [159; 237].... You won't have another chance [159; 237].... Hey, how about this one? [161; 237].... Take this knife. It's yours for the taking! [163; 240].

The sexual connotation in general and the homosexual one in particular of the verb "to mount" already existed in ancient Greece: "Heraclitus was very beautiful, when he was young. Now that the bloom of youth has left him, his skin is a shield to those who want to mount him" (Meleagro. In Villena, *The Boys' Muse* [La musa de los muchachos 38].)

The Rider therefore, wishes to mount Amargo. Both characters begin by addressing each other formally and are informal at the end. It is suggested that the two men become intimate rather quickly.

It has been seen that the idea that "a knife doesn't have to be any more than a knife" is contradicted by the Rider. Amargo thankfully accepts that he has been refuted. The Rider speaks disdainfully of an unusual category of knives: the "soft" ones (159; 237). Although it is not said explicitly, one supposes that there are hard knives, or that they can become hard, and that the knife given to Amargo at the end is a hard knife. This knife is made "of gold." Amargo seems to anticipate, and before the Rider gives him the knife, his hand feels "as though he were gripping a chunk of gold" (161; 237). The horseman pulls out a knife with a shining point "like the flame" (161; 237). Prior to this, it is seen that the dagger "sets aglow," or inflames. Thus, Lorca suggests that the hard knife with the shining point that the Rider gives to Amargo is a phallic symbol. The "gift" is followed by an "Ay yayayay!" from Amargo that indicates that the Rider is driving in the "knife." This "Ay yayayay!" is similar to what comes out from the door to a bedroom in Lorca's drawing, "Bedroom" (1310). Lorca thus associates it with something done in bed. After Amargo's "Ay yayayay!" the two men take the road to Granada. Amargo, in reality, has not encountered death, as some critics maintain. The sierra is covered with hemlock and nettles, the former a homosexual symbol. The fags from "Ode to Walt Whitman" are in "rigid hemlock landscapes" (*PNY* 163; 531). A sonnet from *Sonnets of Dark Love*, "Wounds of Love" (Llagas de amor) ends by showing the connotative relationship between the hemlock and bitterness with loving passion: "And though I seek the summit of discretion, / your heart gives me a valley spread below / with hemlock and passion of bitter wisdom" (*CP* 715; *Sonetos* 47).

Heads and Necks. Biting and Beheading. Oscar Wilde's Salomé *and "Beheading the Baptist."*

"Head," according to Cela in his *Diccionario secreto*, is an antonomasia for the head of the prick, cock, etc. "Point" is used in an analogous way. This same sense is found in Shakespeare, for example, in act 4, scene 2 of *Measure for Measure*. The scene begins with the question, can one cut off a man's head? One can, if it is the head of a single man. According to Partridge in *Shakespeare's Bawdy*, the head here symbolizes the foreskin (126): "*Prov.* Come hither sirrah. Can you cut off a man's head? *Clo.* If the man be a bachelor, sir. I can: but if he be a married man, he is his wife's head."

In his analysis of the motif of the masturbator's head in Dalí's work, Rafael Santos Torroella sees a head-phallus erection in the *Portrait of Paul Eluard* (Retrato de Paul Eluard): "Let us notice the now icto-phallic head of the masturbator, which, as if forming an imaginary diagonal, would cross through the lower part of Eluard's face, and be found below, at one end of it" (169).

In *The Butterfly's Evil Spell* (El maleficio de la mariposa) by Lorca, Alacranito wants to "swallow" the Butterfly's head (see Laguardia's commentary on the butterfly in the penultimate section of chapter 1): "if I weren't so senile / I'd just gulp down / your tasty skull!" (*Five Plays*, act 2, scene 4, 227; 47). Alacranito wants a taste, although it may only be "the tip": "Just a little sample / from where the wound is. / Just the tip of an antenna" (227, 47).

In scene 2 of *The Public* a "head of love" is mentioned (15, 483). In addition to being associated with the mouth and love, the Lorquian head can be "full of excrement," which obviously lends itself to diverse interpretations.[7]

In "In the Frame of Don Cristóbal: A Farce" (Retablillo de DC) a sick person appears whom Cristóbal pretends to cure "with a de-necking." Previously we have been warned that speaking clearly is prohibited. The Director says: "As a poet you have no business prying into the secrets in which we all live" (*Four Puppet Plays* 20; 544).

The neck that Cristóbal is going to "cure" has the unusual property of stretching a great deal, and the invalid is pulling out more and more of his neck. Initially he could not, but Cristóbal heats it up and hits it so that the invalid "pulls out" and "places" his long neck resulting in his immediate killing by don Cristóbal. During the whole time, the patient has had "twenty bucks" placed "in my ass's little eye" (22; 546). Soon after the killing, Rosita's mother appears, praising, among other things, her daughter's "little ass round" (23; 548).

In Shakespeare, "beheading" is used as an unequivocal symbol of "deflowering." For example, act 1, scene 1 of *Romeo and Juliet*, where Sampson says he will cut off the maidens' heads or their heads' maidenhead. The expression's double meaning is made explicit, and Gregory is given the freedom to take it whichever way he may want: "the heads of the maids or their maidenheads; take it in what sense thou wilt." The reader, nevertheless, is left with little freedom to choose the preferred meaning. It seems that the object of "beheading" will be a "pretty piece of flesh."

In the Lorquian poetic world there seems to be a preference for beheading men in general and sailors in particular. Lorca's short narratives contain numerous beheadings. In "Beheading the Baptist" (Degollación del Bautista), the "knife" of the beheader enters through "a deep hole" which is open in the place where the "neck" ends ("where the neck swoons"). The final piece of the narration does not appear in Aguilar's *Obras completas*. Juan Marinello published it in 1965 with the following commentary: "It has always surprised me that in the final version of the incredible *Beheading*, Federico suppressed one of the paragraphs that appears in the original he gave me and that was included in the *Revista de Avance*" (22).

The ending is as follows: "First he made a deep buttonhole in the place where the neck swoons searchingly into the shoulder. He made his entry there, cutting away the entire moon, and turning livid the upper part of the forehead. This was a stroke of genius much applauded by the experts; the rest was mere technique, without the least bit of inspiration" (*CP* 839; 22). The incident is described in positive terms; the beheading, or part of it, is "a stroke of genius" and the "experts" applaud.

Several times Dalí had painted Lorca's decapitated head and also his own (Santos Torroella 95, 103, 107 and 203). "The Great Masturbator" (El gran masturbador) is the title of a painting and a poem by Dalí; almost the whole painting is filled with an enormous head and the poem mentions a "swollen neck" (Santos Torroella 249).

In *Salomé*, Oscar Wilde had clearly shown that "the head" is only a substitute for "Sodom's daughter." In the prologue to the edition of *Salomé* from 1979 in Spain, Terenci Moix says that Wilde's text has "a completely homosexual content," and recalls that there was a way of embodying *Salomé* with "handsome, naked and ambiguous young men." The author mentions

> the furious moralists who tried to prohibit, on the one hand, the representation of Wilde's work, and, on the other, Strauss' opera based on that text.... In the New York productions (1917), the Metropolitan met one of the most unusual scandals in its history when the soprano Olive Fremstad kissed the lips of the severed head of the Baptist... [Moix quotes G.R. Marek].

> During the period 1949–50 it was shown (in London's Covent Gardens) decorated by Salvador Dalí. His staging ... was so scandalous that the issue led to the fall of Peter Brook, who resigned as artistic director of Covent Garden [8–9].

In "Beheading the Baptist" Lorca mentions the police, perhaps a reference to the prohibitions Wilde's *Salomé* fell victim to due to prudish public morality: "At Police Headquarters they are certain of a thousand percent rise in blushes" (*CP* 627; 986).

The "beheading" of the Baptist is ambiguous, as is purity in Wilde's *Salomé*. The Baptist is pure in the sense that the establishment tends to give to this word, but for Wilde's Salomé everything related to purity is a loving-sexual stimulus when she hears and sees this man. One could say that whiteness becomes an aphrodisiac: "I am amorous of thy body! Thy body is white like the lilies of a field that the mower has never mowed. Thy body is white like the snows that lie on the mountains.... The roses in the garden of the Queen of Arabia are not as white as thy body.... There is nothing in the world as white as thy body. Let me touch thy body" (*Complete Works* 558–59).

Moix thinks that what is most appropriate is to give a homosexual meaning to Salomé's monologue: "Of course one must not forget that it is not the Salomé character who is speaking but the disguised homosexual which Salomé is. The whole series of metaphors provoked by Jokanaan's body would not be comprehensible disconnected from a homosexual vision of the world" (16).

Semprún analyzes Lorca's narratives that contain beheadings: "In reality what is being described is a mass castration" (35). Lorca's poetic voice speaks about Salomé's dentures and Semprún interprets that as a reference to the famous Freudian vagina with teeth. Baseless or not, the fear that some men feel towards women can cause the vagina to be perceived as a mouth with teeth that can eat up the phallus, or castrate it in one bite. According to the critic, that "vagina dentata" is attributed to Salomé. It may be noted nevertheless that Lorca's poetic voice says that Salomé's dentures are "false." What is false is used to simulate or to cross-dress. If the interpretation that Salomé's dentures are a symbol for the vagina is accepted, this vagina would not be a true vagina, but a simulacrum or substitution for one. Lorca's Salomé, like Wilde's, is perhaps a transvestite.[8] A representation of *Romeo and Juliet* takes place in *The Public* in which the protagonists turn out to be two men. In the second scene, the association or analogy between the amorous kiss and the beheading is shown: "If you kiss me, I will open my mouth so you can drive your sword into my neck afterwards" (15; 483).

Upon receiving the Emperor's kiss, "one" probably opens his mouth to allow the other's tongue in. Afterwards the Emperor's "sword" itself will be driven in. Any further comment is unnecessary.

When Wilde's Salomé kissed the mouth of the head of the Baptist, the public at the Metropolitan Museum was scandalized, resulting in the work's being prohibited. In Lorca's *Public*, when it is discovered that "Romeo was a man thirty years old and Juliet a boy of fifteen" (38; 521), the public asks for the "death of the director" (33; 511) and "that the poet be dragged off" (35; 515). Afterwards, they murder the two men playing the roles of Romeo and Juliet (38; 522). Student 3 comments on it by saying: "doctrine, when it lets its hair down, can trample without fear even the most innocent of truths" (39; 522).

In Lorca's *The Beheading of the Innocents* (Degollación de los inocentes), "innocence" and "purity" are frequently used as synonyms or as terms that connote each other. The innocents can be pure, and the pure can be homosexuals. The beheading of innocents is also very ambiguous. The innocents are the victims of the dominant power, but victimization, that is to say, the beheading, goes together with the reference to the practice of homosexuality: "the bee's stinger made it possible to wield the sword" (*CP* 625; 88). Despite the widely known symbolism of bees and flowers, it is noteworthy that here it is not an issue of fecundation but the possibility of handling "the sword." According to Viers, Proust constructs the whole first part of *Sodome et Gomorrhe* as a parallelism between the bumblebee's visit to the orchid and that of Charlus to Jupien: "What happens between the two men is commented upon and explained by very learned botanical notions. The visit of the bumblebee to the orchid should serve as a backdrop to the scene of homosexual love" (103).

In a letter published by Gibson, Emilio Aladrén tells Lorca that he is reading Proust (*Du Côté de Chez Swann*), and copies a paragraph from the book for him into the letter (*Federico García Lorca* 1:548).

In the matter of the "beheading" of sailors or the accursed "race," Lorca's "Christmas on the Hudson" presents us with "my throat just cut open," and also a "sailor whose throat was just cut." It is not specified who slashes them and it is not unthinkable that they slash each other. What does appear to be clear is that the slashing is not a tragedy in and of itself, since the poetic voice continues speaking and the sailor sings. Manuel Valls has amply documented the traditional connection between sexuality and singing in his book from 1982 *Music in the Embrace of Eros* (La música en el abrazo de Eros), and numerous examples can be found in Lorca's work. In "Serenade" (Serenata), "The Night Sings Naked" (La noche canta desnuda); in "Song of the Fairy" (Canción del mariquita), the fairies, who provoke a scandal... "sing on roof terraces"; in "Ode to Walt Whitman," "boys were singing, exposing their waists," etc.

The hypothesis of an erotic singing is supported by the clearly amorous character of the perhaps mutual throat slashing of the sailor and the poetic "I": "That keen blade, my love, that keen blade / ... / Oh, the keen blade of my love, oh, the cutting blade!" (*PNY* 63, 65; 478–79).

At the end of "Beheading the Baptist" there is a repetition of the words "light" and "blade" alternating in a crescendo. If Lorca suppressed the ending presented by Marinello it was, perhaps, because he thought that this was the way to reach a poetic climax, and it would suggest the arrival of another climax.

The phallic neck and the "hole" through which "the knife" enters in "Beheading the Baptist" symbolize a double or ambiguous sexual potential. It is referring, perhaps, to the platonic myth of the primordial androgyne. The difference is that in Lorca, the two enamored figures which in *The Public* are said to be "one" are two complete men, and their ideal is manliness:

"FIGURE IN VINE LEAVES ... because I'm a man, because I'm nothing more than that, a man ... more of a man than Adam, and I wish *you'd* be more of a man than I" (scene 2, 11; 476). The Centurion addresses these two men, speaking to them as if they belonged to an inferior race: "May all of your kind be damned!" (recall the "damned" homosexual race mentioned by Proust). The "race" is contrasted with the incredible fertility of the centurion's wife, who, according to the work, "gives birth out of four or five places at a time" (14; 482).

The Lorquian androgyne is not an ambiguous being of two different sexes, but a man, "more of a man than Adam," with the possibility of playing the sexual role of both sexes. The mutual "beheading" actualizes this potential. The two men in *The Public* sustain a bloody fight in which the anus plays an important role. The symbolism of death appears again: "MAN 3. Both should have died. I have never witnessed such a bloody feast.... MAN 1. But the anus is man's curse. The anus is man's failure, it's his shame and his death" (17; 485–86).

It is not very clear if the two men already practiced homosexuality before their "bloody feast," but the mutual loving dependence of both is clear. As there are no reasons to suspect that they were cannibals, "feast" is understood as an "orgy." This "bloody feast" is therefore very similar to the "bacchanal" of "the pure" from "Ode to Walt Whitman" in which what is animal has not been alienated from what is human; nor has the feminine part of man been alienated from his manliness: the purity of an entire half, the purity of "the other half."

Otherness, Homosexuality and Childhood. Rimbaud. Cernuda. Gide. Green. Ruiz López. Lorca's "Childhood and Death." Rats and Sewers.

The term *the other* will be used here to refer to the marginated part of a being, of people, of groups, of societies or of the world. The term is current in psychiatry, and its use extends to other spheres. Tzvetan Todorov employs it in *La conquête de L'Amerique: La question de l'autre*. According to Esther Ferrer, "Todorov presents a typology of relationships with the other, in which what predominates is not the recognition of the other as different, with its implication of inferiority, but its negation or rejection of difference, which invariably leads to the destruction of its identity" (1).

As this is the case for homosexuals and homosexual identity, it seems appropriate to speak of the homosexual being as an Other. A capital letter will be used to differentiate this word from its common usage and to avoid misunderstandings.

The homosexual is alienated, and does not recognize himself in the image of his being that an openly or covertly inimical society presents to him. "The I is the other," says Cernuda in 1931, quoting Rimbaud (*Crítica* 63). André Gide recalls that one day, at the age of eleven, he was crying, probably because he sensed his condemnation: "I am not like others! I am not like others!" (*Si le grain ne meurt* 135).

In *Ocaña, the Infinite Fire*, Ruiz López puts the same words into Ocaña's mouth: "I am not like the others, mama ... I am not like the others! (*With bitter premonitory irony:*) A feather in flames on top of shit" (scene 4, 52).

In his thesis Sarotte shows the technique used to dehumanize homosexuals through literary means. In *The Turn of the Screw*, by Henry James, the homosexual characters do not have names in order to distance them better from readers and deny them any human privilege. None is described physically in order to make them abstract types, beings without consistency, but with evil principles which have to be suffocated, if not in reality, at least through a vocabulary and syntax which make them more like things and keep them at a distance (4).

Among homosexuals, the personal experience of being or possessing an otherness generally begins at a very early age, when they still have not had time to develop their defense mechanisms and they live dependent on adult truths. Consciously or not, with words and with silences, parents and educators direct the homosexual child towards the splitting of his psyche into two halves, converting the homosexual side into the enemy of his social and spiritual being.

When he was still a child, Julien Green learned to separate the drawings he did for his family from those that he did for himself and for the Other ("l'autre"). In school, he would flee from what he found to be more attractive: the company of "certain boys," but he felt a sexual drunkenness invade him when he saw the statues from the Louvre in their "criminal nudity" (53, 89 and 167). Conditioned by his education, Green associates what attracts him with what ought to suffer the punishment of God and men.

Lorca felt the awakening of his amorous feelings at the age of ten; "I was ten and I fell in love..." (1096). The context and the ellipsis make the sentence somewhat ambiguous. Lorca can refer to the fact that he fell in love with Poetry, that he began to be interested in Poetry because he fell in love, or both things at once. The autobiographical poem "Childhood and Death" is of special importance in Lorca's life and work. Martínez Nadal, keeper of the manuscript, observes that, "because it was badly erased one can still read 'Federico defeated in school'" ("Prólogo, transcripciones y notas" xxxv).

The wish to discover that the poem deals with one's own life is resisted later, probably due to Lorca's reflections on the consequences that such revelations would cause. He attempts to erase the name itself, but it seems that it is done unwillingly because the name is not clearly erased. In Lorca's *Obras completas* it is absent. Martínez Nadal was the protagonist of a significant incident: "Several years later, when Lorca was arranging the poems he planned to include in the future book, I warned him that the one he had sent me from New York was missing. He did not remember. When I showed him the rough draft he became visibly disturbed and without finishing the reading he threw it on my desk: 'Keep this and don't ever show it to me'" ("Prólogo" xxxv).

In the poem, Lorca sees his childhood as an otherness. Towards the end of the poem, the boy's body "eaten by the rats" becomes himself as a rat: "...my childhood was a rat that scurried through a dark, dark garden, / a satisfied rat, soaked in simple water ... / carrying a golden streamer between its teeth" (*CP* 643; 798). What is repugnant ends up being associated with satisfaction, and the poetic persona shows a positive attitude towards the rat in affirming that it is soaked in "simple water" and in seeing something "golden" between those same teeth that perhaps have eaten the child.

"Fish" and "rats" appear together in Martínez Nadal's manuscript, although "fish" has been erased. Fish are often a phallic symbol. According to Cela, fish is a formal metaphor: "The penis resembles a fish" (401). In *The Love of Don Perlimplín and Belisa in the Garden* (El amor de don Perlimplín con Belisa en su jardín) the masculine sex is evoked through the sun-fish:

> Voice of Belisa, *within, singing.*
> Ah love, ah love.
> Tight in my thighs imprisoned
> There swims like a fish the sun [*Five Plays* 108; 325].

Cirlot's *Dictionary of Symbols* (which also mentions the phallic symbolism of fish) says the following about rats: "The rat occurs in association with infirmity and death. It was an evil-doing deity of the plague in Egypt and China. The mouse, in mediaeval symbolism, is assimilated into the devil. A phallic implication has been superimposed on it, but only in so far as it is dangerous or repugnant" (259–60).

In his book on Lorca, Vásquez Ocaña quotes Wildgans: "well next to well, / in food and repugnant coitus / the rats live!" (248). In *The Public*, at the end of scene 2, the Centurion shouts to one of the masculine figures who loves another one: "Shut up, you old rat, you son of a mop!" (15, 484).

Like rats, homosexuals are associated with a dangerous and repugnant sexuality, and also with the plague. In 1900 they were regarded as infected with the plague, as stated by Paul Morand: "In 1900 homosexuals were plague-stricken" (quoted in Viers 103).

In *Our Perverse Ancestors* (Nos ancêtres les pervers) certain physical and psychic illnesses and deformities are mentioned that the "science" of the previous century attributed to the practice of homosexuality in general and to pederasty or sodomy in particular (Hahn 33, 193–201).

It has been seen that Federico's childhood "was a rat that scurried." In "Ode to Walt Whitman," which is from the same period as "Childhood and Death," faggots are presented as rats, "emerging in bunches from the sewers" (*CP* 157; 529). The lover in "Ghazal of Desperate Love" is associated with love as much as with the abode of rats: "But you will come / through the murky sewers of darkness" (*CP* 657; 575). What awaits the children in "Cry to Rome" is not the marvelous light which schoolteachers show them: "but what arrives is a junction of sewers" (*PNY* 151; 526).

Federico's sailor's suit appears in "Childhood and Death." For Martínez Nadal perhaps it is "that first sailor's suit in which he was photographed at the school in Fuente Vaqueros, a photograph which today recalls certain defenseless characters from Velázquez" ("Prólogo" xxxv). To say that the sailor suit from the poem can be the one from the photograph is an anecdotal fact. That Lorca puts the suit in the poem is a poetic fact. And that the author recalls that suit precisely and puts it next to the rats that eat up his body in a poem that he later prefers to forget, is, in addition to being a poetic fact, a semiotic one as well. It is a signifier that Lorca, through the untransferable phenomenon of inspiration, first *felt* that the sailor suit from the past had a direct or relevant relationship with his situation and his feelings in the present.[9] He later *decided* to use the image of the sailor suit as poetic material. Ultimately, he *felt* and *decided* that what evoked "Childhood and Death," the degradation of the awakening of his homosexuality, was something too strong, too painful to see published. Something that he should, perhaps, try to forget, in order to be able to continue living in the midst of that society whose moral order places in its system the humiliation and degradation of the dawning of some children's sexual instinct.

In the first half of the twentieth century, it was very common to dress children as sailors. But poetic art is something more than an objective description of facts, customs or objects. Although they may be relevant, anecdotes about images from a poem run the risk of becoming trivialities if one does not explain the nature of their relationship to the feelings evoked in the poem being studied. As Lorca himself has said in his lecture on Góngora: "a poetic image is always a transference of meaning" (Belitt, *PNY* 167; 1032).

In "Childhood and Death," the sailor suit is associated with this child, Federico, "defeated" and "amazed by the dark dawning of the thighs' soft hair" (643, 795). One is dealing with a pubescent boy whose sexuality is referred to through the mention of the soft hair that unexpectedly appears on his thighs. The little "sailor" has not been prepared for what he discovers, since he is "amazed." In connection with the awakening of sexuality, the sailor's suit uniform indirectly evokes the "blood of sailors" from "the other half." The two images belong to the same period; "Childhood and Death" is dated October 7, 1929.

The image of childhood transformed into "a satisfied rat," that the critics generally ignore or avoid explaining,[10] becomes very understandable if we think that Dalí would approach Lorca, calling him "little erotic beast," and placing "death" in the back part of the poet's body: "You, beast with your little nails, you whom death at times grabs half of your body, or raises you by your little nails up to your shoulder in a very sterile effort! I have drunk death in your back..." (*Dalí escribe a Federico García Lorca* 92, 93).

Federico the boy, therefore, wears a sailor suit, and is "eaten by rats," but in the rot to which those who close the door on him implicitly have condemned him, hope and eroticism live. In "the rat" ghetto, among tin cans and shirts full of blood, a song is heard: "the sewers sing" (*CP* 643; 797), as well as the pursued "other half" which listens to the poetic "I" of Lorca, "devouring, singing, flying in its purity" (518). The boy of the "dark" soft hair informs us about his childhood, transformed into a rat, distances itself "through a dark, dark, garden." The "rat" knows what it is and accepts it. It is "a satisfied rat" (643, 798).

"Everyone" and the Other

In "The Crazy Boy" (El niño loco), Lorca's poetic "I" warns that the language he uses—that is to say, the lexical meaning of the language he employs—does not correspond to his reality: "I said: 'Afternoon.' / But it wasn't so. / The afternoon was something else" (*CP* 487; 362).

It is evident that for Lorca death is not always what one understands as such; but why does the poet speak so much about death?: "Everyone understands the pain that accompanies death," he says in "Blind Panorama of New York." The poet is cognizant of the readers who do not want to know about the pain of the Other whom they themselves marginalize. The problems of homosexuals are not of interest, unless, of course, they are presented in such a way that what is specifically homosexual disappears, and only a human pain remains which all can identify with and feel in harmony with, for example, the pain that accompanies death. What "the rats" feel is not important. The doors of society and the theatre should be closed on "the rats." The boy-rat of "Childhood and Death" says: "Alone, here, I see they have closed the door on me. / The door has been closed on me..." (643, 797).

In the final scene of *The Public*, the Prestidigitator warns of the dangers of opening the theatre door: "If you were to open that door, this place would be filled with mastiffs, with madmen, with rain, with monstrous leaves, with sewer rats" (45; 531).

The poetic "I" speaks, then, of death so "everyone" understands, but it also communicates with a smaller group by saying that "genuine pain was on other plazas" ("Blind Panorama," *PNY* 75; 483). An adverbial otherness corresponds to the substantive otherness. Whoever wants to know about this other pain, "the genuine one" will have to abandon the platitudes of the establishment and search for the pain of the poetic voice "on other plazas." The unscathed remains of a culture of antiquity are still on these plazas. Its art and its sexuality, its sky and its gods were marginalized or erased from the cultural patrimony of humanity when representatives from the Judeo-Christian religion took power.

Lorca's Doves. The Incompatibility of the Christian Dove and the Lorquian Dove. The Doves of the Sewers.

In Christian countries the dove usually symbolizes the Holy Spirit. Nevertheless, the Lorquian dove is despised and persecuted, as can be seen in several poems, and the highest representatives of religion are those who lead in the abuse. In "Cry to Rome," "a man pisses on a dazzling dove." "The man who scorns the dove" is "dressed in white" and has "rings and diamond telephones." He also seems to be "acclaimed by millions of the dying" (*PNY* 149, 151; 525–26).

Many critics prefer not to comment on the scatological image here; others make brief comments, without going into detail. Carl Cobb states that the spirit of man has been despised (93). Formulating the sentence in the passive avoids having to say who the agent of disdain is. Betty Jean Craige acts similarly by indicating what the dove symbolizes and saying only that "a man" urinates on it (23). Derrick Harris identifies the man as Pope Pius XI, although the poem does not clearly say it (322). García-Posada is fairly explicit on the subject when he mentions the emblematic meaning of the dove which, according to him, is the one emphasized by Lorca:

> Another positive meaning is the *emblematic* one — innocence, purity —, that Lorca promotes: thus, the "dazzling dove" on which the Pope "urinates" ("Cry to Rome"). This "dove" is related, without a doubt, to the traditional representation of the Holy Spirit: but in the Christological context of the poem, one must shade this meaning and think of a displacement of the image towards Christ, a Christ-child; the Pope "urinates" on him [*PNY* 168].

It does not seem that García-Posada's explanation clarifies why the Pope urinates on Christ, or on the symbol of a culture to which he himself belongs. We do agree that "dove" can have an emblematic meaning of "purity," but this does not say it all. An interpretation based on the emblematic values of Christianity does not seem relevant in this context.

Perhaps it is helpful to read what Lorca himself says about the dove in his lecture on Góngora. Lorca indicates that Góngora calls the dove a "lascivious bird," and he is in total agreement, because he says that Góngora "rightly" eliminates the adjective "guileless" (1049). Lorca, therefore, associates the dove with sexuality, and not only in his lecture. In act 1 of *Yerma*, María relates that the child she is awaiting is like "a dove" that entered her on her wedding night (*Three Tragedies* 108; 675–76). It is obvious that this is a reference to the Holy Spirit as well as to the sexual act.

The sexual gender of *paloma* is ambiguous. Ayala indicates that "although the masculine *palomo* is also used, *la paloma*, like *la perdiz* (patridge), belongs grammatically to the epicene gender." In the slang of marginalized Spaniards, the "palomar" (pigeon house) is the "Place in prison designated for homosexuals" (León 118).

It is not only the Pope who despises and persecutes the Lorquian doves; in "Little Stanton" (El niño Stanton) people, in general, do the same: "Because it's true, there are people / who want to dump doves in the sewers" (*PNY* 93; 496). People want to throw the doves into the same place with homosexuals and rats. In "Ode to Walt Whitman," homosexuals are presented "emerging in bunches from the sewers" (157; 529). For many there is no difference between pure homosexuals and fags; they are all like rats.

Daniel Eisenberg has discovered two earlier texts of *PNY*. In "Little Stanton" there is an important variation: "Because it is true that people want to dump mouse traps into the sewers" ("Dos textos primitivos" 172). "Mouse traps" and "dove" are modifications of the same thing and represent a "dangerous and repugnant" sexuality like that of rats, which is, at the same time, "pure" and "lascivious" like a dove. Its enemies abound: people want to confine it to the sewers, Rome urinates on it, and the law declares that it does not belong to the culture nor to the social surroundings. One is dealing with the sexuality of the Other; it is not "our" sexuality, but the sexuality of "the other half."

Lorca suggests, nevertheless, that there is a limit for everything, and that "the other half" is not going to continue forever accepting the thankless role that they have been assigned. In the prose poem "Beheading the Baptist," the narrative voice asks: "Is it possible the doves that had remained silent are pounding on the door so furiously with the "immortelles?" (*CP* 627; 986). The Lorquian doves are already more than appalled with keeping silent, and the anger with which they knock on the door proves it.

Homosexual Purity in the Sewers and the Messianism of the Other

The Swedish photographer and artist Elisabeth Ohlson developed one of Lorca's big themes, the parallelism between the Passion of Jesus Christ and homosexual passion, in EuroPride, in the exposition "Ecce Homo." "Homo" in the context of the exhibition refers to Jesus Christ sacrificed as a human being on the cross, but also, at the same time, refers to the passions of homosexuals and to homosexuals sacrificed by hate crimes. Later, the exposition was moved to the cathedral of Uppsala and other churches thanks to the positive attitude of the Swedish archbishop, Karl Gustav Hammar, and to other people. This awoke the indignation of some groups of traditional Christians, and during the second half of 1998 and the beginning of 1999, there was a long and heated debate on homosexuals and the figure of Jesus Christ. Newspapers and magazines published more than 100 articles for or against Elisabeth Ohlson and her exposition, and for or against the presence of homosexuals in the church. Echoes of the debate extended even to Rome, and the Pope, as a "punishment" against Sweden or as an expression of his disgust, cancelled a meeting he had planned with the archbishop, Karl Gustav Hammar. The archbishop had been invited to go to Rome, but afterwards, he was the first to permit the exposition "Ecce Homo" to be shown in a church. Some journalists, for example Olle Svenning in *Aftonbladet*, interpreted the Pope's attitude as an "ideological fight" against Hammar, the prolongation of another, very ancient fight, or moral war, of Rome against homosexuals. Svenning's article titled, "The Pope's Secret Armies" (Pavens hemliga arméer), was published in *Aftonbladet*, November 2, 1998, p. 2. Other critics applauded Rome's censorship. The meeting with the Pope finally took place at the beginning of May 1999, but Hammar has maintained, at every step, his support of "Ecce Homo" and of homosexuals.

In the face of the first reaction by Christianity's highest authority, it is easy to recall Lorca's words in his "Cry to Rome." That cry was directed at a previous Pope, but it is a cry that has not lost currency since the current Pope has proven to be just as insensitive in regard to the "leprosy" of homosexuality and the "flesh shredded by thirst" of those affected by "leprosy" (on "leprosy" as a metaphor of homosexuality, see the first epigraph from chapter 1 and the commentary that follows it).

◆ ◆ ◆

> The man who scorns the dove should have spoken,
> screamed naked between the columns,
> and injected himself with leprosy
> and shed tears terrible enough

> to dissolve his rings and diamond telephones.
> But the man dressed in white
> ignores the mystery of the wheat ear,
> ignores the moans of a woman giving birth,
> ignores the fact that Christ can still give water,
> ignores the money that burns the prodigy's kiss
> and gives the blood of the lamb to the pheasant's idiot
> beak.
> ...
> Love is in the flesh shredded by thirst,
> [*PNY* 149, 151; 525–26].

This poem, like most of Lorca's poems, can be read in several ways. Obviously, it is a protest against the luxury and insensitivity of the Pope and the Church of Rome. The protest and the indignation of the poetic voice, nevertheless, have more personal roots that can be surmised by the line that mentions thirsty "flesh." Water often has sexual connotations.

The Lorquian theme of parallelism between the Passion of Christ and the love and suffering of homosexuals appears in a more obscure form in the poem "Crucifixión" and with more clarity in *The Public*. As we saw in chapter 1, "Lorquian Criticism," Eutimio Martín has pointed out this connection as did María Clementa Millán (although in a much more vague way) in her edition of *PNY*, in tracing the fundamental lines from various sections of the book and by dwelling on "Crucifixión": "The poet establishes in his lines a relationship between the death of Christ and the amorous situation of the poetic protagonist ... in 'Crucifixión,' this parallelism takes place in a mode similar to that of *The Public*" (270).

Millán frequently avoids being specific and does not speak clearly about the amorous situation to which she refers as homosexual love. Lorca's homosexuality or that of his poetic protagonists is only mentioned on two or three occasions, for example, in a note about the fabulous and "terrible" animal that appears in several of Lorca's drawings (81) and in a commentary on "Oda a Walt Whitman" (86).

The tree of the homosexual cross is referred to in the first poem of *PNY* "After a Walk" (Vuelta de paseo), where the first verse implicitly carries an accusation: "Cut down by the sky."[11] This poem has inspired the artist Eduardo Naranjo in a painting of the same title as the poem's first verse, in which one sees a man lying down lifeless on the outskirts of a city with the silhouette of buildings on the horizon.[12] Elisabeth Ohlson shows a very similar image in "Ecce Homo," presenting a homosexual lying over some rocks, beaten up, or perhaps, "cut down," with the city in the distance and the shadow of a cross projected above his body. In "After a Walk," Lorca evokes the cross through the image of the "amputated tree that doesn't sing," but the poet also evokes the scene of paradise lost through the presence of the serpent. The "cutting down," inspired or instigated by the "sky," appears in the poem in relation to another violent death: that of the butterfly "drowned in the inkwell," the butterfly being an obvious reference to a homosexual. This use of butterfly is found in many dictionaries of slang and vulgarisms, for example, in the *Dictionary of Spanish Slang* (Diccionario de argot español) by Víctor León, and in the *Glossary of Obscenities* (Glosario de la mala palabra), by Francisco Hernández Castanedo. Of course the butterfly can also be the symbol of the psyche or the soul, but here it is the case of a homosexual soul. Lorca himself suggests the relationship between "butterfly" and "fag" in his "Oda a Walt Whitman." Lorca shows us the beard of the American poet "full of butterflies" to indicate soon after that the "faggots" land on that same beard (*PNY* 157; 529). In other words, the faggots were there, or rather, they were themselves the butterflies that filled the beard (see also Laguardia, "The Butterflies," and Sahuquillo, "El asesinato de 'Vuelta de paseo' de Federico García Lorca"). In reality, the symbolism of the butterfly and the problems related to the love of "butterflies" were already suggested by Lorca in his first play, *The Butterfly's Evil Spell* (El maleficio de la mariposa). There the poetic voice falls in love with a butterfly and senses that that love will end with his life:

> Who gave me these eyes I hate?
> And these hands that try
> to clutch a love I cannot understand
> and that will end with my life? [*Five Plays* 235; 57].

The theme of passion or of homosexual cruxification is also suggested in the above mentioned "Oda," when the great American poet appears with his sex pierced and the poetic voice of Lorca addresses him by saying: "you moaned like a bird / with its sex pierced by a needle." The bird is often a homosexual symbol and appears in the works of many authors, as I try to show in my article "Juan Goytisolo, Severo Sarduy and San Juan de la Cruz: Birds, Passion, Homosexuality, AIDS, and Sainthood." This theme took on a sad topicality in the United States in October of 1998, when the young Matthew Shephard was abused, burned and murdered in Wyoming, and his body was discovered tied up, like Jesus Christ on the cross.

In his 1990 article "The Messianic (Christlike-Quixotesque) Utopia of Federico García Lorca: *The Love of Don Perlimplin and Belisa in the Garden*," (L'utopie messianique [christo-quichottesque] de Federico García Lorca: Amor de don Perlimplín con Belisa en su jardín), Eutimio Martín presents new proof about the Lorquian association of the figure of Jesus Christ with homosexual passion. In connection with the theme of utopia, the author reminds us first that for Lorca, his most authentic works were a *Teatro imposible* (272–73). Afterwards, the author goes on to examine the traces that the Jesus Christ figure has left in Lorca's work and to state that in *The Public*, the identification of the poet with Christ is quite obvious. For Martín, this work loses all meaning if we deprive it of its messianic foundation (274). Martín analyzes *Don Perlimplín* and points out that the spilled blood, due to the self-sacrifice of Don Perlimplín, is described by Marcolfa as "the most glorious blood" of her master and is associated with the redemptive blood of Christ (279). The author also discovers that Lorca read Unamuno's *The Life of Don Quixote and Sancho* (Vida de don Quijote y Sancho) (1914 edition) and underlined different passages from it, among which is the following:

> There are loves that cannot break the glass which contain them and they spill out within, and there are unspeakable ones which formidable destiny oppresses and constrains in the nest in which they arise; ... And there, prisoners, ashamed and hiding themselves, insisting on being dumbfounded, struggling to die, since they cannot flower in daylight and in view of everyone, and less fruitful, they become a passion of glory and of immortality and of heroism [284].

Martín suggests that the stigma of homosexuality led Lorca to identify with Christ and, after reading Unamuno's book about Don Quixote, the poet associated Jesus Christ as well as Don Quixote with his own passion, in which "the vine of Bacchus becomes the blood of Christ" (286, 287). (For Bacchus, see the first epigraph of chap. 4.)

At the end of his article, Martín confirms his hypothesis that Lorca's literary activity is inscribed with a messianic perspective that is doubly utopic because of its Christlike-Quixotesque character. He states that it was conceived as a necessary complement to Christ's redemptive work: "what the author has wanted to write is, without doubt, a fifth Gospel," concludes Martín (287).

It also seems relevant to mention here an article by Christopher Maurer in which he comments on and analyzes an unpublished work by Lorca on Charles Chaplin (Charlot) and his mother. It appears pertinent because Maurer mentions that when the poet wrote it, "Lorca was undergoing two crises which cannot be easily separated: one, of an amorous nature, and the other, aesthetic." Maurer points out that "Chaplin had no voice" and Lorca compares him to Jesus Christ. That they put "Caiaphas' pants" and "a hat of thorns" on Chaplin can be read in the Lorquian text that accompanies Maurer's analysis. The feminine dimension of this Christ now transformed into Chaplin is present here: "Chaplin has fainted. This has been the most compromising characteristic of his work, so ineffable, so expected that it is incredible. Suddenly one has discovered the heart of a young woman that he kept inside himself.... Affected. Beautiful. Feminine..." (14, 15).

Summary and Conclusions

After having examined the conceptual field of some items in connection with "the other half," it has been seen that they share a common denominator: homosexual love. To the disgust of "the normal ones" who persecute them, homosexuals respond with their own disgust and cultivate an artistic sensibility that distinguishes their "purity" from what is generally understood as such. The "accursed race," artificially created by the "racists" of sex, has learned to purge the vein of their inspiration. Behind the Lorquian concept of the "blood of sailors" appears the figure of a homosexual archetype. Against the denominating accusation that they are "from the bitter shell," Lorca transforms the bitterness of their feelings into poetry. Obligated to be the Other, he defends his otherness with pride.

The spirituality of homosexual love has been the object of outrage and depredation on the part of the highest representatives of Christian culture. Lorca protests by launching his "Cry to Rome," and at the same time seizing the symbol of the Christian spirit. Lorca transforms the dove, a symbol of the Holy Spirit, into a homosexual symbol that connects to the purity of the love of "the other half."

All the symbols analyzed here are a mirror and a product of the conditions under which homosexuals are forced to live. They are, therefore, a true reflection of the efforts of this author to conserve his human dignity and affirm his existence in the midst of the surrounding opprobrium, a test of his valor or *courage to be*.[13]

The man from Rome will be able to urinate on the Lorquian dove. People perhaps will continue throwing doves into sewers. Homosexual poetry will then come out of the drains, as Lorca suggests in "Childhood and Death": the sewers "sing" (*CP* 643; 797).

Rivas Cherif relates that, in a conversation with Lorca, he was surprised that the poet assured him that he had never known a woman (in the Biblical sense of the word). Rivas Cherif asked Lorca how he was going to convince him that someone with so much curiosity for life and for all that the world has to offer was going to deprive himself of half of the human genders. Lorca then answered him quickly: "Haven't you deprived yourself of the other half?" ("La muerte y la pasión de Federico García Lorca," 2nd article).[14]

3
"Oppressed Norms": Homosexuality and Class Struggle

libre signo de normas oprimidas / seré...
    Lorca, "Yo sé que mi perfil será tranquilo" 699

I'll be a free sign of oppressed norms...
    Lorca, "I Know That My Profile Will Be Serene"
Collected Poems 733

Federico García Lorca era víctima, cuando escribió este libro (*Poeta en Nueva York*), de una torturadora crisis interior. Todo induce a creer que esa crisis se hallaba en gran parte determinada por su anomalía sexual.
    Juan Larrea, "Asesinado por el cielo" 113

When he wrote this book (*Poet in New York*), Federico García Lorca was a victim of a torturous internal crisis. Everything leads us to believe that this crisis was found to be determined principally by his sexual anomaly.
    Juan Larrea, "Murdered by the Sky," trans. Frouman-Smith

the "yo" has been regarded ... as "abnormal."
    Ellis, *The Poetry of Emilio Prados* 233

Oye sus marmóreos preceptos
sobre lo útil, lo normal y lo hermoso.
    Cernuda, "La gloria del poeta"

Poesía completa 185
Hear their marbled precepts
About the useful, the normal, and the beautiful
    Cernuda, "The Poet's Glory" *Young Sailor* 68

—¿Para ti la homosexualidad es normal?
—Sí, por supuesto. Es vieja como el tiempo.
    Gil-Albert, en respuesta a Luis Antonio de Villena en Villena,
    El razonamiento inagotable de Juan Gil-Albert 65

"Is homosexuality normal for you?"
"Yes, of course. It's as old as time."
   Gil-Albert's reply to Luis Antonio de Villena in Villena's
   The Inexhaustable Reasoning of Juan Gil-Albert, trans. Frouman-Smith

The Economic and Determining Factors

The focus of this chapter is Lorca's sonnet "I Know That My Profile Will Be Serene" (Yo sé que mi perfil será tranquilo) from a Marxist point of view, with psychoanalytic influences. First, it is necessary to clarify the debate over some concepts and what they imply or what they ought to imply.

According to Paul Ricoeur, "Marxism should take its research in the same direction as psychoanalysis." The author sees psychoanalysis as "an interpretation of texts" that finds "*in the work itself* the process of distortion analogous to those of dreams and neurosis," and is related to the "psychoanalysis of culture" ("Psicoanálisis y cultura" 210, 212, 221).

The previous chapters have shown that linguistic, semantic, literary and semiotic factors exist that give a distinctive profile to homosexual culture. The very important factor of resistance also exists, along with the active fight against oppression. Thus homosexuals perhaps can or ought to be considered an oppressed class. Their fight should then be seen within the framework of a class struggle, since it is the struggle of a "race" considered inferior or damned to stop "our Culture" from exploiting it culturally and economically.

Janssen-Jurreit affirms that sexuality as well as fertility has an economic dimension in human socialization (339). Additionally, Engels himself clarifies a frequent misunderstanding in his famous letter to Block, written in 1890: according to a materialist conception of history, the determining factor is, ultimately, the production and reproduction of real life. Neither he nor Marx affirmed anything else. Consequently, if someone distorts this proposition in order to make it say, for example, that the economic element is the only determinant, it is transformed into an empty, abstract and ridiculous phrase (Vovelles 3).

Often the concept of class is automatically associated with the working class. Ernesto Laclau refers to this in mentioning the *reductionism of class* typical of classical Marxism and ends by saying that "The working class does not possess any ontological privilege" (qtd. by Paramaio in "Ernesto Laclau"). To the question of whether he believes that it is fitting to speak of a class consciousness in connection to homosexuals, Foucault answers: "of course, homosexual consciousness exceeds the individual experience and includes the perception that one belongs to a socially determined group. This is an indisputable fact" ("Opción sexual" 18).

In *A Dialogue on Power* (Un diálogo sobre el poder) Michel Foucault points out the connection between the homosexual and revolutionary movements:

> Women, prisoners, inducted soldiers, patients in hospitals, homosexuals have at this moment begun a specific fight against the particular form of power, of coercion, of control which is exercized over them... And these movements are connected to the revolutionary movement of the proletariat itself in that it has to fight against all the controls and coercions which accompany power everywhere [18].

❖ ❖ ❖

What is stated in "I Know That My Profile" implies that some oppressors and governing norms exist in whose name the "oppressed norms" are pursued. No names are mentioned, but an analysis of the poem perhaps can help to identify the "oppressed norms" and, indirectly, the oppressive norms.

In the second quotation Larrea speaks of Lorca's "sexual anomaly"; he sympathized with Lorca and, in his way, tried to defend him. Nevertheless, in centering the discourse on the poet's internal crisis, Larrea diverts attention from the external factors that provoked it. Crises do not have an a priori existence. The problems of homosexuals are materially constructed with propaganda and concrete political acts such as the promulgation of laws, incarceration, insults, threats and precepts. Cernuda's poetic "I" denounces precisely some "marbled precepts" which, in the poem, are related to heterosexual norms or behaviors:

> Look at them, how they straighten their invisible crown
> While they are erased in shadow with their women on their arm,
> ...
> ...in the dense conjugal darkness
> Of their dens... ["La gloria del poeta," *Young Sailor* 67; *PC* 184].

In *"Et in Arcadia Ego": A Study of the Poetry of Luis Cernuda*, Philip Silver states that already the Cernudian title of "The Forbidden Pleasures" openly proclaims that the love the poet advocates is a threat for society, almost an act of political violence (99). Harris maintains that the attack against the sacred convention of the family obviously is motivated by Cernuda's homosexuality (*Luis Cernuda* 72).

A Study of "I Know That My Profile Will Be Serene"

> I know that my profile will be serene
> in the moss of an unreflecting north.
> Mercury of vigil, chaste mirror
> to break the pulse of my style.
>
> For if ivy and the cool of linen
> were the norm of the body I leave behind,
> my profile in the sand will be the old
> unblushing silence of a crocodile.
>
> And though my tongue of frozen doves
> will never taste of flame,
> only of empty broom,
>
> I'll be a free sign of oppressed norms
> on the neck of the stiff branch
> and in an ache of dahlias without end [*CP* 731–33].

The poem demonstrates a lucid consciousness oriented towards the future. Only five verbs are used: *to know, to be, to break, to leave behind,* and *to taste. To be* is the most important one. Used in the future, at the beginning and at the end of the poem, it connotes a desire to be. Implicit in the fourth line, it indicates the place where being serene will be realized (in the style) and the act that will accompany this realization (the breaking of the pulse of the style).

The poetic voice traces its own profile and situates it in the sterile sand. It mentions its ambiguous silence; in other words, it indicates that something is not said with clarity. What it keeps silent/reveals, it says/keeps silent without false shame. Its tongue, numbed by the cold or by fear, gives everything it can under the circumstances in which it finds itself. The profile of "blanks," "gaps" or silences has to be broken by another so that the "I," at the end, is and achieves the desired serenity. When this occurs, the "I" will be transformed into a sign or symbol of oppressed norms that are not made explicit.

The content or plot of the poem could be seen as a poetic testament. The "I" leaves its whole being in the hands of whoever accepts the task of breaking-interpreting the sign that is attested to, so that it may be placed in the service of "oppressed norms."

Different Versions of the Poem

There are three very similar versions of the poem, dated 1929, 1930 and 1932. The first manuscript was published by Marinello (1965, appendix) and the second by Mario Hernández (*Introducción* 124). The third version is mentioned and transcribed in the critical edition of *PNY* and *Earth and Moon* (Eutimio Martín 298–99). As Hernández indicates, the differences are the following: in the version from 1930, the second line is "in the north of an unreflecting sky"; in the second to last stanza there is a comma after "I'll be," and in the last line, the word for without end, "sinfín" is written as "sin fin." Lorca prefers the title of "Sonnet" because the poem was published with it. This is understandable. What is less understandable is to find the change in Mercury (Mercurio), written with a small letter, instead of a capital letter. According to Hernández, it is a matter of "regularization" (182).

The first version, dated 1929, was written in New York. The concepts of the ignored "other half" and "oppressed norms" appeared in the same place and, approximately, at the same time.

Because of the use of the adjective "old," attention is focused on the antiquity of silence. It is possible that the poetic voice may have had to keep silent all his life, but perhaps it is a reference to a more vast silence: that which falls on the part or forbidden profile of poets and their themes, a silence of centuries. Homosexuality is "as old as time," indicates Gil-Albert.

The poetic "I" does not live in the present, that is to say, it lives in it in an unsatisfactory way since the whole poem is directed toward the future, toward the day on which the speaker can become a defense or sign of oppressed norms. Lorca bequeathed to his readers signs of a being that could not fully realize itself among his contemporaries.

Technical Elements. Hernández and the Reading of the "Autoepitaph."

According to Hernández, the poem can be viewed "as a kind of autoepitaph in that García Lorca poeticizes, as he already did in *Book of Poems*, his reincorporation, after death, into the uninterrupted flow of nature" (127). Yet, this positive view does not fit under closer examination. The poem does not mention the flow of nature but what is biologically sterile. "North" (or "sky" in the variation) does not have a reflection, that is, it cannot be reproduced. The profile is in "the sand," the tongue tastes "empty" and the free sign will appear on a "stiff" branch, that is, one that does not bear fruit through its "neck." Such an accumulation of words suggestive of biological sterility cannot be fortuitous. Neither can the connection between what does not bear fruit and suffered oppression.

The Author's Presence

It has been seen that the demarcation line between the poet and the poetic "I" is at times very diffuse. The separation between both is even more problematic during the personal crisis that Lorca had, since the author placed himself as the "central protagonist" of several poems he wrote in the United States. One of them was discussed in the section in chapter 2, "Otherness, Homosexuality and Childhood." Marinello has even published a version of "Double Poem of Lake Eden" that includes the entire name of the poet. Nevertheless, the use of the terms "poetic 'I'" and "poet" continues here because in spite of the undeniable links that join them, the two are not identical.

Symbols and Homosexual Intertextuality

A profile is associated with silhouette, that is, with something external, but can refer to something internal as well. *El Pequeño Larousse*, nevertheless, gives examples of fairly common usages which refer to the internal: *the profile of a building* is its vertical section or section on a plane. In geology, the profile or section of a terrain "allows one to see the arrangement and nature of the layers" (789). It may not be irrelevant to consider this in examining the Lorquian profile.

Lorca's poem is an artistic profile that the author has traced, but it also contains a human profile. There are two profiles: the form of the poem and that of the person who is in it. Lorca has written-drawn-created the layout of the sonnet-terrain and that of the feelings of the protagonist so that both profiles are seen *from within*. The implicit desire is not that the style triumph but that "the pulse" of the style is broken in order that what gives life to the poem may come forth. Whoever has read "The Duende: Theory and Divertissement" will have been able to confirm that, for the poet, style is not what is most important. On the contrary, the *duende* that Lorca admires is a power "that breaks styles" (1100). Lorca relates that the "flamenco singer" (cantaora) Pastora Pavón was not successful in communicating with her public before seeing her voice "broken" and "torn." The *duende* did not want to appear. It was necessary "to kill the whole scaffold of the song" in order to insure "that everyone listening tore at his clothing almost in the same rhythm with which the West Indian negroes in their rites rend away their clothes" (Belitt 158). Indirectly, Lorca maintains that artistic communication does not take place if the external is not broken, and that a certain amount of violence or possession and passion may be necessary.

◆ ◆ ◆

The two variations of the second line of Lorca's sonnet are: "in the moss of an unreflecting north" and "in the north of an unreflecting sky." Moss is a cryptogamous plant. The adjective "cryptogamous" comes from two Greek words: *kryptos* (hidden) and *gamos* (union). Moss has masculine and feminine organs, although the feminine ones can be less visible. Several thousands of species of moss exist. The Swedish doctor Nils-Erik Landell indicates in an article that the masculine organs can grow in great abundance and be like cocoons or bananas. When a drop of water falls near the masculine parts of moss, some organisms with the color and characteristics of man's semen can immediately color it white and carry it towards the feminine parts, according to Landell (114). Therefore, Lorca situates his poetic profile in an androgynous plant of hidden sexuality, in an "unreflecting north." The absence of reflection evokes the lack of physical reproduction as well as the hidden sexuality that is not reflected or does not appear openly in the poem.

One might wonder if Lorca was knowledgeable about the properties and characteristics of moss and other plants that appear in his works. That Lorca was very interested in natural history is clear in reading the chronicle by Alfredo Mario Ferreiro. According to Ferreiro, the poet stated he was a big reader of works of natural history (156). In act 2 of *Doña Rosita the Spinster* (Doña Rosita la soltera), Lorca calls the reader's attention to the fact that botany "is a science" (772). It is more likely that the poet mentions moss with a clear consciousness of what this plant and his choice of it can suggest to the reader.

In his book on Dalí, discussed in the introduction, Santos Torroella includes a poem by the painter that mentions a "god of snow" who is "melting from desire" "among the quiet moss," while "the heterosexual group ... conscientiously hefts the libidinous cataclysm" that approaches (259–60).

The *sky* symbol is introduced in the variation of "Sonnet." Years before, in "Mediterranean" (Mediterráneo), Lorca already had written about the sky's possessing a very specific organ: "The sky's fat penis" (*CP* 305; *Suites* 133). The sky in the famous "Ode to Walt Whitman" "has shores where life is avoided" (*PNY* 159; 530).

The affinity of the rhyme in lines 2 and 3 (in the Spanish) runs parallel to the analogy of the evoked concepts, semantically and semiotically: "chaste mirror" in an "unreflecting" north-sky. The chaste man does not lie with a woman. The pure homosexual does not reproduce, nor does he openly show himself. He is an unreflecting mirror (see below).

◆ ◆ ◆

"Mercury" is written with a small letter in the 1929 manuscript. Obviously, the poet changed his mind and with strong strokes put an *M* on top, as is seen in the manuscript published by Marinello. The *M* was used from the beginning in the 1930 and 1932 manuscripts. Lorca probably thought of the metal, but preferred the symbolism of the messenger god.

Lorca's interest in Greek mythology is very well known. But the myths that most interested him were, for obvious reasons, the ones that had some connection with homosexuality. Lorca knew much more about these myths than what is generally known. In "Bacchus and Cyssus" (Baco y Ciso), Martínez Nadal states that the story that Lorca told him was not recognized by any of the university colleagues who were consulted years later (230). (See the abbreviated story in the first epigraph from chapter 4). Gibson has shown that already in the juvenilia, Lorca praises the religion of "warm Greece" (*Francisco García Lorca* 1:214).

Mercury or Hermes is a god of many facets: the *Dictionary of World Mythology* (Diccionario de la mitología mundial) states that "he was represented with a rooster (a symbol of watchfulness)" (160). Perhaps, therefore, Lorca's poetic persona sees himself as Mercury "on watch." The most common image of the god was, nevertheless, according to *The Meridian Handbook of Classical Mythology*, a herm.

In "Possible Sources of Some of Whitman's Ideas and Symbols in *Hermes Mercurius Trismegistus* and Other Works," Esther Shephard reminds us that Hermes or Mercury was especially the god of boys, and was celebrated in their orgies (80). Whitman's poetic "I" participates in the boys' orgies in "Native Moments": "Give me now libidinous joys only, / ... / I am for those who believe in loose delight, I share the / midnight orgies of young men" (*Leaves of Grass* 110). This poem belongs to the group called "Sons of Adam." Lorca seems to know these poems since he calls Whitman "Adam of blood, Macho" (*PNY* 157; 529). He also calls him "Apolo virginal."

According to J. Duché, the *Himno homérico a Hermes* was the first picaresque novel. Hermes-Mercury was also the god of thieves, a "joyously immoral" libertine, as Duché says (77). In the orgies in "Native Moments" the indecent as well as those outside the law participate. The calls perhaps allude to the messenger aspect of the god: "The echoes ring with our indecent calls, I pick out some low person, for my dearest friend, / He shall be lawless, rude, illiterate, he shall be one condemned by others for deeds done" (111).

Points of contact exist between the god and the metal. Cirlot states that

> Probably, it was the alchemists, with their lofty speculations, who penetrated farthest into the archetypal structure of Mercury. In many cases, they identified their transmutation-substance with the "lively planet," that is, with the god whose metal is white and decidedly lunar. However, since Mercury is nearest to the sun (related to gold), the resultant archetype has a double nature (of a chthonic god and a celestial god — a hermaphrodite). Mercury (the metal)

symbolizes the unconscious because of its fluid and dynamic character; it is essentially *duplex* [198].

Hermes was evoked by means of a stack of phallic stones that also served as tombs (Duché 91), and he is the god who best symbolizes the synthesis of sex and death. Mercury had a very important role in religious homosexual rites from the earliest centuries,[1] and his name continues to be associated with homosexuality.[2]

♦ ♦ ♦

In several poems, Lorca associates what is chaste with an internal fire or another erotic symbol. The thematics that will be developed in "New York (Office and Denunciation)" are profiled in "Invocación al laurel." The people who ignore "the other half" here are "all" those who overwhelm the I-Other and have nothing to do with his "chaste fire":

> All of you overwhelm me with your songs;
> Uncertain I only ask you for mine;
> No one wants to suffocate the yearnings
> of this chaste fire that burns up my chest [136].

It is well known that the laurel invoked in the poem is the tree of Apollo. It has already been seen that Lorca calls Whitman "Apolo virginal," that is, chaste or pure. The same expression is used in "Moon and Panorama of the Insects," subtitled "Love Poem": "This chaste, burning desire of mine" (*PNY* 125; 513).

"Little Stanton" presents "cancer" "with an apple's chaste longing" (*PNY* 91; 495). The usual sexual connotation of the symbol of the apple is reinforced through the allusion to the bed: cancer "wants to go to bed with you" (93; 496). It is clear that here eroticism is seen as if it were a devouring illness.

The billy goats were born "in the chaste foam of the sea" (trans. Mauer) according to *Book of Poems*. In mythology, this "chaste foam" is the sperm of Uranus, the god-planet of homosexuals (see chapter 4, "Celestial Lucifer") (Duchén 39; Fernández-Galiano, "The Gods of Lorca" [Los dioses de Lorca] 85). For Lorca, Mercury and the chaste function as a prefiguration of Bacchus and his purity—what they evoke is realized in the integrating experience of the bacchanals, in a love that exceeds both the spirit and sex and which is found beyond life and death.

♦ ♦ ♦

Pulse is made up of the intermitent beats of a body, but it can also refer to the certainty or force by which a job is carried out. In the present consideration, they are two facets of the same thing. The poem beats, has life, because the poet has put in it his blood and his trade that, together, constitute the style. Nevertheless, one hopes that the style's "pulse breaks." The poetic "I" or the poet knows very well that if the poem is not dissected, if the form is not broken, the blood that inspires it will not appear. It will not be a "free sign of oppressed norms" because these norms will continue to be ignored by people. As was seen at the beginning of this chapter, when the *duende* "breaks the styles," what makes art and people live is also freed, which is also what "kills." True life is inseparable from a continuous death. With the form broken, the person "destroyed," the voice is finally transformed into "a gush of blood" (1101).

♦ ♦ ♦

The body of the poetic "I" is characterized through the information that its norm was ivy and had the cool of a thread.[3] Ivy belongs to the family of plants whose seeds have two cotyledons. It was utilized in bacchanals because it was thought to have stimulating properties (Frazer 125). Therefore, it is associated with Bacchanalian purity that does not separate spiritual and orgiastic experience, and is also associated with a norm of being or of behaving.

In his lecture on Góngora, Lorca states that Bacchus changed into a vine "Out of love for his dancer Cyssus, who dies and is transformed into ivy" (1049). In "Sketch for an Ode" (Apunte para una oda), the poet refers to homosexual love through the metaphor of ivy: "Like ivy of light and green frost, my soul creeps up the / wall of day, searching for you. / ... / Cyssus cries in the ruins, Bacchus in the grapes" (*CP* 753; 773–74).

Lorca has mercury appear in connection with the north ("northwest") and the symbol of ivy in "Lovers Slain by a Partridge" (Amantes asesinados por una perdiz): "They loved one another despite all the museums.... The sole of the foot with the left cheek. That left cheek! Northwester of dories and quicksilver ants! ... They all went to bed..." (Belitt 152; 995–96). "...They often had to separate the dogs who moaned around the bed's very white ivy. But they loved each other" (trans. Frouman-Smith).

The narration is surrealistic in style with apparently illogical images that are not the subject of the current discussion. It is important to point out the conjunction of the three symbols in the quoted love scene. When "they" love each other in the bed of "ivy," cheeks have the function of "north" (left is "northwest"), the direction in which the "dories" and the "quicksilver ants" approach. "Cheeks" can refer to those in front as well as to those behind, the buttocks or gluteus, "those roundfaced, jovial parts," which emulate "the rosy chubby cheeks of Aeolus" (Goytisolo, *Juan the Landless* 7 [Juan sin tierra 17]), and which Octavio Paz has addressed in his gloss on Quevedo's book, *Graces and Disgraces of the Eye of the Ass*, "a long comparison between an ass and a face," according to Paz (*Conjunctions and Disjunctions* 3).

Similar to ivy, thread is associated with love and with activities done in bed, as can be seen in "Nocturne of the Void": "When I look in the bed for the murmurs of thread / you have come, my love, to cover my roof" (505). *Cover* has a sexual meaning. In act 3, scene 1 of *Yerma*, the protagonist complains about her husband: "When he covers me, he's doing his duty, but I feel a waist cold as a corpse's..." (*Three Tragedies* 140; 723).

The profile of the poetic "I" in the Lorquian sonnet "I Know That My Profile" is situated in a sandy landscape. Martínez Nadal refers to this expression in scene 6 of *The Public*: "for the Prestidigitator — this is death, championed *per se* by the reproduction of the species — the word love from the lips of the director, defender of the legitimacy of homosexual love, awakens the idea of 'a sandy landscape' reflected in a cloudy mirror ... a lost seed, sand in the desert, says the biblical sentence" (*Four Lessons* [Cuatro lecciones 73–74]). Richard Predmore maintains that in "Living Sky" (Cielo vivo) the Lorquian sands are utilized to suggest sterile love, that is, love between men (*Lorca's New York Poetry* 31).

◆ ◆ ◆

A blush, like tears, is the expression of a feeling; false tears are called "crocodile tears." The crocodile's blush is then a false or hypocritical blush that the poet will not feel. The "unblushing silence of a crocodile" is in the last line of the second quatrain; "the pulse of ... style" appears in the last verse of the first quatrain. In the original Spanish version of "I Know That My Profile," there is a correspondence between "pulse" and "blush," and "style" and "crocodile," as much for the rhyme as well as the place that they occupy, and also for what they evoke. Pulse and blush elicit blood while style and crocodile conjure up the external, the shell, deceit.

When the feeling that corresponds to the expression is shown, when the form and the context are illuminated (the profile of silence in the sand), the poetic "I" will not blush, since he is not ashamed about what he feels. On the contrary, he wants to defend his norms without any shame. Mentioning the absence of a blush implicitly means that the oppressed norms are pointed to or condemned like something shameful. The poetic "I" will not blush either for having kept silent, since he has spoken as clearly as possible.

On Pentecost, the Holy Spirit descended on the apostles. He alighted on their heads like a tongue of fire, and the apostles began to speak in languages they did not know. The flame as well as the tongue of fire and the dove are symbols of the Holy Spirit.

The tongue of doves of Lorca's poetic voice "will never taste of flame;" it is frozen from the cold or from fear. The Lorquian dove does not give shape to the Holy Spirit, but to the spirit of homosexual love. Power is in the hands of Christian culture. "Two Sailors Ashore" (Dos marinos en la orilla) mentions "the tongue" that represses words and, also, "the Pope's balconies": "He had a tongue of soap. / He washed his words and stopped speaking. / ... / He has seen the Pope's balconies" (*CP* 511; 387).

The "dirty" homosexual tongue can be punished as was seen in "Ghazal of Desperate Love" (regarding the reference to Sodome's shower of salt, see the section in chapter 4, "The Billy Goat"). "But you will come, / with your tongue burnt by the shower of salt" (*CP* 657; 575).

Christian culture has always refused to recognize the worth of homosexuality. The dazzling Lorquian dove is used as a sewer by the man from Rome, "surrounded by thousands of small bells."

◆ ◆ ◆

"Broom. *Bitter like broom.* Said about anything that gives off a bitter flavor as is the case of this plant" (Sbarbi 252).

In act 1 of *Yerma* reference is made to the bitterness of the broom: "Hillside of bitter weeds. / What child is killing you? / The thorn the broom-tree bore!" (*Three Tragedies* 117; 690). In "The King of Harlem" (El rey de Harlem) there is hidden and raging blood under the broom. These brooms are associated with "cancer" as well as with what is chaste (see above). As in "I Know That My Profile," Lorca mentions the absence of blushing. In *Yerma* the "the spine of the dagger" is evoked. Here, the "spine of the broom" (for dagger, see chapter 2, "Death, the Bitter One..."): "No blush in your face. Blood rages beneath the skin, / alive in the dagger's spine and the landscape's breast, / under the pincers and Scotch broom of Cancer's heavenly moon" (*PNY* 33; 461).

Although there can be other readings of these and other lines, it can be confirmed that Lorquian sensuality is associated with death and with the bitter "taste" of the broom. In "I Know That My Profile," this taste also evokes the presence of infertility by mentioning "desert." It is clear that the desert taste is related to the "profile in the sand." In *Juan the Landless*, Goytisolo refers to the type of love that is usually associated with the desert: "MAIS DIEU CREA LES ARABES ... and the love that you will find in their company will be burning and sterile like the desert plains" (71, 86).

In "Speaking of Flowers" (A propósito de las flores), Cernuda shows that purity and bitterness are paired in life and in the work of some poets. If one takes into account everything analyzed up until now, the following could be asserted: the ending of the poem suggests that what is entailed by the concepts of "purity" and "bitterness" is a product of the conditions in which homosexuals live, dignified or embellished at times by the poet's art:

> Bitterness? Purity? Or, why not both at once?
> The iris rots just like the bad herb,
> And the poet is not only pure or only bitter:
> He gives back to the world just what the world has given him,
> Although his genius, pure and bitter, may give something more [*PC* 500].

Cernuda clarifies the following about García Lorca: "He was not tormented, but I believe that he couldn't enjoy something unless he felt at the same time the rubbing of a thorn. This is one of the most profound roots of his poetry: *the bite of the bitter root*" (*Crítica* 172).

♦ ♦ ♦

Although oppressed norms may not appear explicit in "I Know That My Profile," the study of the symbols and their contexts seems to give a sufficient basis for supposing that Lorca was thinking about homosexual norms. As Roman Jakobson states: "In poetry, not only the phonological sequence, but also, in the same way, any sequence of semantic units, tends to construct an equation. The superimposition of similarity and closeness confer on poetry its symbolic, complex, polysemous essence" ("Lingüística y poética" 40).

Little by little, the symbols, signs and metaphors from "I Know That My Profile" have been strengthening the metonymic nuances of the homosexuality of "oppressed norms." The concept evokes the presence of a homosexual rhetoric[4]; it implies an *experience-view from within* and is a linguistic marker of a subjugated class, as discussed below.

♦ ♦ ♦

The philosophy of language has begun to demonstrate interest in the implications of the existence of social and linguistic norms which are despised, ignored or classified as "abnormalities." In "Sistema y norma," from *Principios de filosofía del lenguaje*, Hierro indicates that "the concept of norm represents a level of linguistic analysis in which it is easy to raise a whole series of problems of a strictly social nature about which it is not possible to reach clarity with the mere distinction between language and speech" (55). Hierro mentions Coseriu's list of norms and states:

> it invites adding new categories, such as the *language of class*. If it is appropriate to distinguish between a familiar language, a vulgar language and a literary language, with even more reason one could distinguish a language of class, that is, a linguistic norm connected to the nature of the class of a social group and whose manifestation in speech expresses the membership of the individual in that class. Taking the term "class" in its Marxist sense, the linguistic norm of class fundamentally would be of two kinds, depending on how it characterizes the dominant classes or the dominated classes [55].

From the *view from within* of the subjugated class which Lorca belonged to as a homosexual, homosexuality as a norm of life or norm of love is somewhat obvious.[5] "What I gave you ... was the standard of love," says the Lorquian "I" in "Your Childhood in Menton" (Tu infancia en Menton) and, anticipating the reactions, exclaims: "Leave me alone, all of you. / And don't try to cover my mouth..." (*PNY* 13, 15; 452, 453).

Norms and Criticism

Homosexuality is not generally seen or accepted as a "norm," but as an "abnormality," with the entire negative "implications" that this term "connotes." In a strict sense, homosexuality is only abnormal if one accepts the ethnocentrism and the voluntary ethnological and historical blindness of "civilized" countries, with their implicit disdain for the "primitive ones." Charlotte Wolff reminds us that homosexuality was practiced openly during the Hellenic period "as an ideal way of life." According to her, "*bisexuality is the origin of human sexuality and the matrix of all biopsychic reactions*" (*Bisexualidad* 9–10, 18). The results of research carried out by Ford and Beach show that in 49 (64%) of the 76 societies different from "ours" from which it is possible to obtain information, homosexual activities of one type or another are considered normal and socially acceptable for certain members of the community. In some societies, for example, that of the Siwanes of Africa, all men and boys practice anal intercourse and male as well as female sexual relations are openly discussed (170–72).

◆ ◆ ◆

Chapter 1, in the section "Lorquian Criticism," makes reference to a work that Lorca began to write but about which only one scene is known: it was published by Laffranque in 1987. In her "Estudio y notas" to the *Teatro inconcluso* of Lorca, the author indicates that *La bola negra* (The black ball) is a compromising title: "The alluded-to custom (when members of a court put a black ball to confirm the prisoner's guilt) as well as the colloquial, critical use of the formula imply, in this title, the calling into question of a social condemnation" (82).

Laffranque quotes the summary of the work facilitated by Rivas Cherif in the third of his articles from 1957 on Lorca's death and passion:

> A provincial capital. A man behind an office desk. He rings the bell and a servant enters:
> FATHER: Let the young man come in. (His son enters.)
> FATHER: What does this mean? (And the father shows his son a letter.) What is this — you applied for membership in the Casino and they've thrown you a black ball? Why?
> SON: Because I'm a homosexual [84].

For Marie Laffranque the focus of a "social drama" seems incompatible with the purpose of creating a biblical tragedy. The title and part of the plot of "The Black Ball" are found in Proust's *Sodome et Gomorrhe*; "the black balls" appear toward the end of the first part of this book (36). With these so-called black balls, a sodomite can be denied membership to a club or casino. But other homosexuals who condemn sodomy throw the majority of them because they have inherited the lie thanks to which their ancestors could abandon the accursed city. By throwing the black ball, that is to say, by lying and accusing others, the sodomites who are ashamed free themselves from being condemned. This plot ties in perfectly with that of Lorca's other incomplete work, *La destrucción de Sodoma*. At one level of meaning it does not seem incompatible with the plot of the tragedy of Cain and Abel, which also occupied Lorca's thoughts. There are homosexuals who betray their brothers, the same as a large part of the heterosexual half of the world pursues, and even murders, "the other half" or homosexual half of creation. People "ignore the other half" just as Cain ignores where his brother is: "Am I my brother's keeper?" (*Genesis* 4:9). Proust mentions *Genesis* on the same page where the black balls appear. (For *La destrucción de Sodom* see chapter 4, "The Billy Goat.")

According to *Sodome et Gomorrhe*, when homosexuality was the norm there were no abnormal people (20). In an analysis that one supposes is purely literary, H. Peyre, after mentioning Proust's "obsession" with "abnormal" love and his "excessive " preocuppation with "abnormal sexuality," exclaims: "even the broadest-minded among Proust's readers may protest, on aesthetic grounds, against a vision of the world that sets up abnormality as the norm" (28, 30). In not accepting Proust's perspective, the author indirectly supports oppression. Nevertheless, he pretends that the basis of his criticism is aesthetic.

The reactions against the eroticism described or evoked by Whitman in *Leaves of Grass* have appeared previously (chapter 1, "Lorquian Criticism"). The first poem of the "Calamus" section is entitled "In Paths Untrodden." In it norms or "clear" patterns are mentioned, but not published. Just like Lorca, Whitman indicates the absence of blushing and, more openly, declares that he sings of masculine adhesion or attachment and celebrates the necessity of comrades:

> Clear to me now standards not yet publish'd...
> ...
> No longer abash'd, (for in this secluded spot I can respond
> as I would not dare elsewhere,)
> Strong upon me the life that does not exhibit itself, yet
> contains all the rest,
> Resolv'd to sing no songs to-day but those of manly
> attachment,
> ...
> To celebrate the need of comrades [112].[6]

"I Know That My Profile," Lorca's poetic testament, is similar in theme to the second poem from "Calamus." Whitman states that he writes to be read or studied after his death. Whitman and Lorca express the desire that the leaves of the body, dead and alive at the same time, from what they are and write, serve to reveal their hidden meaning:

> Tomb-leaves, body-leaves growing up above me above death,
> ...
> Grow up taller sweet leaves that I may see! grow up out of my breast!
> Spring away from the conceal'd heart there!
> ...
> I will sound myself and comrades only... [113].

Toward the end of the poem, Whitman's poetic "I" declares the hope that perhaps some day, death will dissipate "this entire show of appearance" (114).

What follows is a discussion of what the critics believe about the norms referred to in "I Know That My Profile."

♦ ♦ ♦

Guillermo de Torre refers to homosexuals who inspire Lorca and his colleagues, using the following terms from a book of literary criticism: "beings like André Gide, resolutely univocal in their deviousness, more clearly in their abnormality" ("André Gide" 156). Guillermo de Torre graduated in Granada, together with García Lorca ("Presencia de Francisco García Lorca" 9). By reading only what he writes about Lorca, one gets the impression that they were friends: "with Federico there couldn't be any 'differences,' because what overwhelmingly came to the foreground were the affinities and 'congenialities'" ("Francisco García Lorca" 270).

In order to realize the importance certain "differences" had for Torre, one must observe what he states in referring to others. In "Reverse and Obverse of André Gide" (Reverso y anverso de AG), the author maintains that homosexuality or its defense is a "deviousness," an "abnormality," an "anomaly," "a clinical case," a "notorious immorality," a "cynical delirium," and a "defect" whose variants "within the same species" seem to contain "abysses" and "grotesqueness" (156–59). Like Peyre, Torre utilizes his position as a critic to support implicitly the oppression of homosexual writers and homosexual literature. His technique is well known. Before the oppressor demands freedom from oppression in its nakedness, says Simone de Beauvoir, he preferentially presents himself as the defender of certain values: "It is not in his name that he fights: it is in the name of civilization, institutions, monuments, virtues that objectively realize the situation that he intends to maintain" (131).

Torre's criticism can be seen as an example of what Girard calls "stéréotypes de la persécution." The persecutors seem to be incapable of seeing any other norm but their own: "It is not the other *nomos* that one sees in the other but anomaly; it is not the other norm, but the abnormality" (35).

Marguerite Yourcenar also mentions this incapacity of "our Culture," in her book on Mishima, that "almost paranoid necessity of 'normalization,' the obsession with social shame that, as well stated by Ruth Benedict, has replaced sin in our civilizations, without any true benefit for human liberty" (23–24).

In "The Natural Norm in the Plays of Francisco García Lorca," C.M. Wells believes that natural existence in Lorca's works is a way of rejecting dualisms like sacred-profane, spiritual-earthly, ugly-beautiful, etc., a rejection called "norm of nature" (299). Two pages later, one wonders if Wells might not be confusing the "norm of Nature" with societal norms. In the prologue to *The Butterfly's Evil Spell*, Lorca maintains that "love is born with the same exaltation in all planes of life.... In nature, all things are equal" (194). But according to Wells, "The principal violation of this equality is desiring beyond one's station — desire engendered by dissatisfaction with one's own position" (301).

The prologue of the cited play promotes nonconformity, the rejection of schemes, and it is a veiled accusation against the phobias of society. This accusation is not directed against the character Boybeetle (Curianito), as Wells believes, but against men:

> Why do the clean, bright insects, moving so charmingly through the grass, cause a feeling of repugnance in you? And why is it that you men, full of sins and incurable vices, are filled with loathing for the good grubs who creep quietly a-long in the meadows, taking the sun of a warm morning? What right do you have to scorn the meanest of God's creatures? [194].

Wells shows disdain for the "absurd" Boybeetle, but tries to convince the reader that it is Lorca who despises or satirizes the insect:

> Lorca describes him as "painted charmingly in yellow" and with "a bereaved and upset face." Another device used to satirize Curianito's romantic excesses and consequent violation of the natural norm of instinctual sensuality is dramatic contrast. Frequently, Lorca juxtaposes the absurd Curianito with spokesmen ... for the natural order [302].

The "norm" is "natural," and so is the "order." Evidently, Wells associates the prescriptive and the established with the natural. The author seems to ignore the fact that in Spain, an attractive face is far from being a ridiculous or absurd face. If someone is painted with grace, he or she is not, necessarily, being satirized.

One of the crimes or "violations" of the "natural norm" that Wells attributes to Boybeetle is that he is insensitive to the charms of Sylvia, the "beetle." Worse, "the principal violation," nevertheless is, according to Wells, Boybeetle's desire for a butterfly: "In *El maleficio*, Curianito's rejection of Silvia (whose attractiveness Lorca goes to considerable lengths to demonstrate) is mocked with equal zeal. Curianito loves 'algo que nunca tendrá' [something he will never have]" (301).

In chapter 1, "Lorquian Criticism," it was shown that the butterfly is the symbol for a homosexual (Laguardia 546). Boybeetle's love seems to allude to the sexual ambiguities of adolescent love. At the end of the prologue to the play, Lorca has made insects speak "like men or like youngsters." It is unclear what Wells' opinion is based on when the critic states that Lorca goes to a considerable distance to "demonstrate" Sylvia's attractiveness.

In being a prisoner of his emotions, Boybeetle does not violate the norm of *his instincts*, but rather the established norm that Wells confuses with the "natural norm." The type of criticism that Wells practices contains normative elements. It is, therefore, relevant to recall the words of Goldman: "it is very important for the sociologist to show the normativeness of even that which one refuses to recognize" (54).

Dennis A. Klein interprets Boybeetle's attraction for the butterfly in a very different way. In his article from 1974, published in the *García Lorca Review*, "El maleficio de la mariposa: The Cornerstone of García Lorca's Theatre," Klein maintains that the butterfly encompasses everything that Boybeetle would desire for himself: someone who is united or at peace with nature (n.p.).

Predmore has recognized the Lorquian concept of "yesterday's norm" as corresponding to the homosexual norm (*Lorca's New York Poetry* 76). On the issue of "oppressed norms" the critic asks himself: "What are the oppressed norms? Probably those of homosexual and heterosexual love, often in conflict with each other or with the norms of society" (73).

It could be assumed that the author thinks that homosexual and heterosexual norms find themselves in the same position in society and are, more or less, equally oppressed. He does not specify in what way the norms of heterosexual love are in conflict with the norms of society, nor how the supposed conflict coincides with the well-established nature of some institutions and basic pillars of society, such as marriage and family.

García-Posada does not speak clearly about the psychological and social conflict implicit in the linguistic usages "normal-abnormal" versus "two norms." Nevertheless, it is evident that he is referring to heterosexuals in mentioning "the guardians of 'normal' love" or, at least, the most fervent heterosexuals. The author interprets the poem "Your Childhood in Menton" and states that "the norms of the dominant orthodoxy" are "tied to Judeo-Christian culture which demands fecundity as a condition of love" (*PNY* 130–31).

In *Francisco García Lorca o poética de la libertad*, A. Estévez Molinero refers to the *Sonnets of Dark Love* in affirming that knowing that one is a *prisoner in the jail of dark love* produces "the movement of rebellion and denunciation against the norms which strangle the freedom of love" (15). Two pages later the author adds: "Dark love, yes, because the moral norms of society have established it in that way," and on another page, the critic approaches a significant point: "what is prohibited from being expressed through habitual language, is then communicated through poetic translations."

❖ ❖ ❖

In *My Last Sigh* (Mi último suspiro), Buñuel relates how he offered himself as bait to hunt homosexuals, with the intention of beating them up: "In our youth, we did not appreciate pederasts.... I came to play the role of a provocative agent in a Madrid urinal. My friends waited outside, I entered the small building and played the part of bait. One afternoon, a man bent down towards me. When the wretch left the urinal, we beat him up, something that today seems absurd to me" (144).

The situation of homosexuals in Spain in the 1920s appears with clarity in several of the writings of one of the great authorities of the period, Dr. Gregorio Marañon. In a book from 1929 the same year that Lorca wrote about the "oppressed norms," Marañon says:

> Unfortunately in Spain (it might possibly occur elsewhere), police customs often do not honor the elevated intentions of our legislation. The police are accustomed to inflicting, if not grave penalties, then at least depressing and above all, counterproductive humiliations, on homosexuals caught in the "raids" which from time to time are organized to hunt them. Not too long ago, a recently nominated governor was arriving in his district and wanted to make a show of his energy. He ordered the arrest and subjection to a scandalous demonstration of all homosexuals who, justifiably or not, appeared on police lists. Among them were many scoundrels, prostitutes, blackmailers, cynics, etc., but also people affected by this sad deviation of instinct. The newspapers applauded this "manly governor who had not stopped in the face of any prejudice" [*Los estados intersexuales en la especie humana*, qtd. in García Valdés 116].

The raids, which were organized to hunt homosexuals, bring to mind the situation of the animals and "the other half" in the poem "New York (Office and Denunciation)." It is clear that homosexuals were also treated like animals.

It is worth noting the press's presentation of the described incidents. Abstaining from hunting homosexuals is having a "prejudice." Marañón was right: the situation was not, nor did it approach being, benevolent. By virtue of the "Law for the Prevention of Morbid Inheritance," many homosexuals were castrated and eliminated in Hitlerian camps, without their consent and with the help of doctors (García Valdés 112). Another aspect indicated by García Valdés is the oppression of homosexuals in the bosom of their own families:

Before the last great war, and now still, hypocritical Puritanism gave rise to true tragedies. When parents became horrified at discovering the homosexual condition of one of their children, from then on they would ignore or evict them from their home because they could not tolerate coexistence with such degenerates. For these types of parents, their child's homosexuality was worse than cancer or any other type of incurable illness" [119].

In "Little Stanton," Lorca's poetic "I" states:

> In the house where there is cancer,
> the white walls shatter in the delirium of astronomy
> ...
> you looked for my agony in the grass,
> the terrible flowers of my agony,
> while the speechless, acid cancer that wants to go to bed with you
> pulverized red landscapes on the bedsheets of bitterness
> [*PNY* 91, 93; 495–96].

In addition to associating cancer with bitterness, Lorca also refers to its purity: "cancer springing to life ... / with an apple's chaste longing" (91; 495).

◆ ◆ ◆

In Spanish, the *neck of the stiff branch* rhymes in a contrast of opposition or dissimilarity with *taste of flame*. *Neck* corresponds to *taste* and *stiff branch* to *broom*.

The word *stiff* in Spanish, *yerto*, comes from *erctus* (Corominas 239), and is indirectly associated with *erection*. Lorca also uses this adjective in a poem of special interest: "Flesh." Its relevance is evident since "Flesh" was written in the same place, in the same year, in the same month as "I Know That My Profile." In addition, Lorca works on it with the same symbols and semiotic signs as in "Profile":

> Look what tender whimpers, what mobile sounds
> press on the waist of the frenzied youth!
> Come, come! the tips of veins grow longer
> to bite the crest of the moonstruck cayman,
> while the green blood of Sodom glows
> in the room of a rigid aluminum heart.
> It's necessary for weeping to spill into the armpit,
> and for the hand to remember soft nocturnal rubber.
> And for the necessary rhythms of systole and diastole
> to tarnish the sky's inhuman blush.
> ...
> It is your body, oh gallant, your mouth, your waist,
> the taste of your blood through frozen teeth.
> It is your flesh — defeated, broken, and trampled on —
> which conquers and shines on our flesh [795].

It is obvious that "sound" and "rhythm" are related. The movements of the young man's waist correspond to the entering and leaving of "blood" of the "rigid heart." The "blood" enters the mouth "("the taste of your blood"). The sky blushes, but the poetic "I" maintains that it is necessary. Probably, "the sky's inhuman blush" is no more than the "unblushing silence of a crocodile" ("Profile"). The blood of Sodom "shines." The "conquered" flesh "conquers and shines." The affinity of sounds is completed by the affinity of concepts.

The stiff or erect neck of the branch on which the "I" will be a "free sign" can correspond to the erection that the images of Hermes-Mercury often have, evidently, in a symbolic or referential way (regarding these phallic figures see the *Enciclopedia Ilustrada de Sexología y Erotismo* 560). Mercury and the sign on the stiff branch would then have a triple semantic-semiotic relationship in their common connotations of *death*, *sex*, and *messenger-message*.

The masculine body is compared to a tree in several Lorca poems. In "Adam," the boy who was just born is described as a "tree of blood" (*CP* 731; 264). The body-tree grows in different places, but the poet indicates a particular place to us in "Dance of Death" (Danza de la muerte): the crossing of thighs (471). In addition, Lorca shows that he is following a precise line in his poetics of the stiff-erect associated with the "branch." *Stiff* and *cold* are related concepts. Consequently, "the cold men" are "those who grow in the crossing of thighs."

Lorca's influence on Ruiz López' *Ocaña* was studied in chapter 1. In that work there also appears a reference to what the branch or "little branch" symbolizes: "why do the angels possess enormous wings and not one little piece of a branch? My God, how do they urinate?" (scene 11, 126). In the scene with the Masks of Male and Female in the final act of *Yerma*, the Male says "ah, how the sad wife sways," (*Three Plays* 148; 736) and the Second Man urgently states: "Strike her now with the branch!" (149; 736).

❖ ❖ ❖

Flowers symbolize the transitory as well as what is permanently renewed. According to Cirlot, "the flower is an image of the 'Centre,' and hence an archetypal image of the soul" (105). In "I Know That My Profile," "dalia doloridas" (ache of dahlias) rhymes with "normas oprimidas" (oppressed norms). Lorca evokes the grief of living oppressed by heterosexual norms. The "endless" number of these dahlias probably refers to the large quantity of descendants of the men of Sodom that Proust mentions at the end of the first part of *Sodome et Gomorrhe*: "So numerous that one can apply to them the other verse from Genesis: 'If someone can count the dust of the earth, he will also be able to count these descendants'" (35–36).

Dahlias symbolize a negation or a rejection that can be paid for dearly.

In act 2 of *Doña Rosita the Spinster*, Lorca has his protagonist say the following: "the dahlia speaks of shy disdain" (*Five Plays* 168; 801). Doña Rosita is indirectly disdained or evaded by her boyfriend. What is evaded in *Yerma* is more concrete: "to beg a son to suffer, and for the wind / to offer dahlias of a sleeping moon!" (*Three Tragedies* 131; 710). The dahlias appear in this scene as something that is in place of, or an impediment to, having a child. The seeds of the Lorquian dahlias are things that do not seem to be worth much since people trample them, as is seen in the beginning of *Doña Rosita*: "Uncle. I say that because of everybody. Yesterday I found the dahlia tubers trampled underfoot.... You must have more respect for my plants" (133; 748). Intertextually, Lorca perhaps relates these "trampled" dahlia tubers to the "trampled" flesh of the poem that contains "the green blood of Sodom" (see above). The color green symbolizes the erotic as well as the vegetable.

Doña Rosita's housekeeper does not like flowers but, rather, prefers what bears fruits. For her flowers evoke the accursed fruit of men and are associated with something hidden or suspicious: "To me flowers smell like a child's funeral" (133; 748). In contrast, fruit trees are linked to heterosexuality, something that is clearly alluded to. The housekeeper would eat them: "That's what I have a mouth for ... as they used to say in my village: The mouth is useful when we eat, / The legs are useful when we dance, / And women have a thing quite neat... (*She stops, goes to the Aunt, and whispers*)" (134; 749).

The dahlia seeds are trampled in *Doña Rosita*. In "I Know That My Profile," the dahlias have human reactions, they "ache," perhaps because they have been trampled or the symbol of sexuality that is referred to has been trampled. The "ache of dahlias" corresponds to the "frozen doves" and to the "oppressed norms" because of their location in the sonnet, because of their rhyme (in Spanish) and because of their meaning. Form and substance are aptly interpenetrated through the conscious and purposeful elaboration of Lorca's homosexual feeling.

◆ ◆ ◆

Summary and Conclusions

"I Know That My Profile" alludes to two bodies of analogous norms that probably are the standard for "oppressed norms": the body of the poet and the body-text of the poem, Mercury and the messenger, the poet-god messenger and the message that represents him, the text as fluid metal that rises up or grows in contact with the reader, the same way moss is revived with water.

The pulse of style broken, the homosexual cloth comes forth from the profile of silence with which Lorca has sewn the thematic unity of the poem. Together with loving and Bacchanalian ivy, this cool linen was the norm of the poet's "body," and it is the norm of the body of the poem that the poet bequeathed to us. The symbols of the sonnet's text are somewhat ambiguous, but their ambiguity is considerably reduced by the accumulation of words that refer to a sexuality that does not reproduce. The oppressed norms are first and foremost homosexual norms.

The physical and psychic violence exercised against homosexuals has the characteristics of a class struggle. Lorca lived during the years of the proletariat revolution; his sensitive chords replaced the atmosphere of economic oppression with that of the sexual and ethical oppression that his love suffered. The revolutionary tones of the "International" song of "flesh" are clearly audible in the rough draft of "Cry to Rome" presented by Laffranque: "Colleagues of the entire world, / men of flesh, with a violin and with dreams, / the hour of breaking down doors has arrived"[7] ("Puertas abiertas" 78).

The doors did not break open. Lorca's love was not recognized or accepted, not even among those who said they loved the poet. On one occasion, Marcelle Auclair commented that Córdoba did not seem to appreciate Góngora very much. Lorca answered sharply: "Well, do you think they indeed love me in Granada?" (Auclair 206). Without the support of his family or his friends, Lorca did not have the strength to defend openly his "oppressed norms." He willed his "sign" to those who, in a distant future, perhaps could break the pulse of his style so as to, as Walt Whitman would say, put an end to "this entire show of appearance" (*Leaves* 114).

"I Know That My Profile," therefore, is Lorca's homosexual testament, an inheritance that grants his readers a right that can be seen as being close to a duty; to bring to light what Lorca could not openly show so that the murdered poet can finally rest in peace, his profile serene in the sand, being what he hoped to be: a free sign of oppressed norms.

4
The Metamorphoses of the Billy Goat: Hell, Gag and the Rebellion of Homosexual Love

Baco ... es primero macho cabrío de retorcidos cuernos. Por amor a su bailarín Ciso, que muere y se convierte en hiedra, Baco ... se convierte en vid. Por último, muere para convertirse en higuera.
    Lorca 1049

Bacchus ... is, first of all, a billy goat of twisted horns. Out of love for his dancer Cyssus, who dies and is transformed into ivy, Bacchus changes into a vine. Finally, he dies in order to become a fig tree.
    Federico García Lorca, trans. Frouman-Smith

...su boca como el higo maduro
...
¿cómo hablar de su voz que apenas dice nada
pero cuya densidad hace desprenderse las hojas
para mejor oirle pegadas a la tierra
y a cuyo son se llenan de un rumor oscuro los racismos de la vid?
    Gil-Albert, *Fuentes de la constancia* 164

...his mouth like the ripe fig
...
how to speak of his voice that barely says anything
but whose denseness causes leaves to fall off
and stick to the earth to hear him better
and to whose sound bunches of grapes from the vine fill with a dark murmur?
    Gil-Albert, *Origins of Evidence*, trans. Frouman-Smith

Yo pertenezco
...
a esos largos racimos que duelen contra el cáñamo
que abandonan sus nombres...
    Prados, "Si yo pudiera...," Ellis 317

I belong
...
to those long bunches of grapes that ache against the hemp
that abandon their names...
    Prados, "If I Could...," trans. Frouman-Smith

Ese es el hombre que ama al Emperador en silencio y lo busca en las tabernas de los puertos. Enrique, mira bien sus ojos, mira qué pequeños racimos de uvas bajan por sus hombros.
    Lorca, *El público* 79

He's the man who loves the Emperor in solitude and seeks him out in the taverns of the ports. Enrique, look deeply into his eyes. Look how little bunches of grapes go down his shoulders.
    Lorca, *The Public* 18, trans. C. Bauer

Soy un racimo maduro
...
Andando estoy por el mundo.
Cuál es mi nombre no sé
y cuando lo sé lo oculto
    Prados, *Poesía completa* 2:467–68

I am a mature bunch of grapes
...
I am walking through the world.
What my name is I do not know
and when I know it I hide it
    Prados, *Complete Poetry* 2, trans. Frouman-Smith

Dream
May 1919

I was riding upon a
a billygoat.
Grandfather spoke to me
and said:
"That is your path."
"It's that one!," shouted my shadow,
disguised as a beggar.
"It's *that* one of gold," said
my clothes.
A big swan winked at me.
"Come with me," it said.
And a serpent was nibbling
on my rough pilgrim's robe.

Looking at the sky I thought:
"I have no path.
The roses at the end will be
like the ones at the beginning.
In the fog, the flesh
turns into dew."
My fantastic horse carries me
over the reddish fields.
"Let me alone,"
my pensive heart
cried out, sobbing.
I left it on the ground,
full of sadness.
    Then came
the night, full of wrinkles
and shadows.
    Lighting the way,
the luminous, bluish eyes
of my billygoat.
    trans. Christopher Maurer

The Billy Goat
1919

The group of billy goats has gone by,
near the water of the river.
On an afternoon of rose and sapphire,
full of Romantic peace,
I stare
at the huge billy goat.

Hail, mute devil!
You are the most
intense of animal,
Eternal mystic
in the hell
of all flesh.

What charm there is
in your beard
and wide brow,
you rough don Juan,
and the [sharp] accent of your look,
passionate as that of
Mephistopheles.

You go through the fields
with your flock,
turned into a eunuch
when you are a sultan
Your thirst for sex
is never slaked
How well you learned
from father Pan!

The she-goat follows
slowly after you,
humbly in love,
but your passions are insatiable.
Ancient Greece
will understand you.

Oh creature of deep, holy legends,
of frail ascetes and Satan
with rough, black stones,
tame beasts, and deep caves
where they saw you, in the dark,
blow upon the flame
of sex!

Oh, horned machos
with your unkempt beards!
Black epitome of the Middle Ages!
You were born next to Filomnedes
in the chaste foam of the sea,
and your mouths
caressed her
as a world of stars stared in astonishment.

You are from forests full of roses,
where the light is a hurricane.
You are from the pastures of Anacreon,
full of the blood of immortality.
Ah, billy goats,
you are the metamorphoses
of old, lost satyrs!
You spill virgin lust
greater than that of any animal.

Mystics of the South!
Pull up short and listen:
from the depths of the fields
the rooster tells you
hello, as you go by.

    trans. Christopher Maurer

Introduction: "Book of Poems" and the Critics

According to Guillermo Díaz Plaja, *Book of Poems* is "a work of extraordinary importance, and is in no way classifiable as 'promising,' but rather as an already mature achievement of a series of skills of the best lyricism" (74). García-Posada agrees: "because of all its concepts, it is a very important work ... and in no way can be judged as a novice work" (*García Lorca* 97). Nevertheless, the majority of critics have not shown much interest in the book. In Colecchia's bibliography only four names appear which have dealt with the work. What is missing is Gibson's detailed study of "Sad Ballad" (Balada triste). One can now also add Newton's article "Nostalgia del paraíso infantil en *Libro de Poemas*: el poeta sobre su Pegaso."

In Schonberg's opinion, of the 82 poems from the book, some 30 deal with sterility. Whether or not this theme is so ample, it is a significant fact that one should consider, together with the words of the poet's brother: "*Libro de poemas* is essentially an act of impetuous personal affirmation" (*Federico* 194). In this context it is not redundant to recall Gil-Albert's exclamation from "Once Autumn," where the referential meaning of the referent "sterile" is obvious: "Unfortunate are those who call such a union sterile" (*OPC* 3:178).

The lack of precision in the words of Federico's brother is remedied in part by one of the poet's friends, Fernando Vázquez Ocaña, through a combination of decisive assertions and rhetorical questions: "This book is not in any way consistent with normal influences from youth. For Federico, living is an enigma that produces more grief than delight. Why? By virtue of what violence, either suffered or felt, of what anxieties or childish terrors, of what warnings of his being...?" (118–19).

The billy goat personifies the violence to which Vázquez Ocaña refers. This is one of the principal motives which has guided our choice since our hypothesis deals with a violence similar to the one exercised against the "other half" and the "oppressed norms" that were previously analyzed.

◆ ◆ ◆

With regard to the first epigraph, Lorca relates that Góngora refers to Bacchus' transformation in a *Solitude* (Soledad) in such a way as to be "comprehensible only to those who are in on the story's secret" (1049). The understanding of the text is presented as an initiation, an entrance into a distinct and secret world.

Four symbols relating to Bacchus and his lover are named: for Bacchus — the billy goat, the vine and the fig tree — and ivy that symbolizes Cyssus. Two of the symbols that refer to Bacchus, the vine and the billy goat, already appear in one of Lorca's first texts, *Fray Antonio* (*Poema raro*). Almost unknown, this work has been commented on and summarized by Eutimio Martín, who believes that it is "of an autobiographical nature," and that the "huge billy goat" in the text represents "the overwhelming presence of the flesh" (Martín, *Federico García Lorca* 161, 168). In contrast to an obviously unattractive "potbellied Christ," "an ancient fountain, embraced by a shady vine" appears in this "strange poem" (167).

A man goes looking for homosexual love "in the taverns," as seen in Lorca's second epigraph. The reference to drink as well as to "bunches of grapes" makes one think of Bacchus. The taverns are in a precise place: "The ports." The presence of the archetypal and concrete love of sailors is evoked indirectly (see chapter 2; see further on in this chapter for the "sea" and homosexuality).

The bunches of grapes in Prados' first poem above are personified since they have names (that are not pronounced). The poem's title, "If I Could..." is almost identical to that of a poem by Cernuda from *The Forbidden Pleasures*: "If Only a Man Could Say." Cernuda completes the sentence within the poem: "...what he loves." He denies saying what the loving instinct itself discovers or identifies, but the reason is obvious. Prados also says, "I am a mature bunch of grapes ... I hide it." Now the poetic "I" is a grape cluster that does not know his name. It is possible that he does not know if *this* term or *these* names are related to what he really is. At times, nevertheless, he does in fact know what his identity is and prefers not to discover it.

The person who does not know that Bacchus, out of love for Cyssus, changed into a vine, and later into a fig tree, will not understand why Gil-Albert compares the lover's mouth to a ripe fig, nor why "bunches of grapes from the vine fill with a dark murmur." Whoever does not know about the fear that homosexuals have of being discovered cannot sense why the "bunches of grapes" from Prados "abandon their names," nor why the "voice" in Gil-Albert's poem "barely says anything," because it is more significant that its sound causes a reaction in the bunches of grapes.

The reader who does not know or feel the ambivalence and the conflict of having to live in dichotomic cultures will not intuit why Lorca presents fags as "bunches of grapes" emerging from the sewers and asks that the doors of the "bacchanal" be closed in his "Ode to Walt Whitman" (529 and 532). Perhaps the reader will think that it is illogical and contradictory: Are grape clusters associated with pure homosexual love or with degradation? The contradiction is illusory. In Bacchus as well as in homosexuals two dimensions of being converge that are sometimes in harmony and other times in disagreement: the pure and the impure, the masculine and the feminine. The religious experience of the bacchanal can be transformed into an unbridled search for physical pleasure. Homosexuals can change into "faggots." Segal indicates that in the rituals involved in *The Bacchants* there are no boundaries established; rather the limits become confused. Pentheus sees the maenads or bacchants as "bitches" in the hunt for sex (Segal 36–37). According to the Lorca of "Ode to Walt Whitman," the "ambushed" "faggots" are "bitches" (*PNY* 163; 531). The idea of changing himself into a bitch of love is not, nevertheless, absent from the brain nor the heart of the poet, as one can observe in "Sonnet of the Sweet Complaint" (Soneto de la dulce queja) (for "dogs," see chapter 5, "Bacchus"):

> If you are my hidden treasure,
> if you are my cross, my dampened pain,
> if I am a dog, and you alone my master,
> never let me lose what I have gained,
> and adorn the branches of your river
> with leaves of my estranged Autumn [*CP* 713; *Diván* 141].

The idea of the hunt also appears implicit in the Surrealist-Freudian text by Dalí "Fish Pursued by a Bunch of Grapes" (Pez perseguido por un racimo de uvas) (Gibson *Federico García Lorca* 1:564) (for erotic and phallic symbolism of the *fish* in Dalí's work, see Santos Torroella 93–94, 170). The homosexual also finds scapegoats to pursue; the faggots "in bunches," the degraded version of oneself. Prados associates bunches of grapes with pain: "Long bunches of grapes that ache."

"A branch of wounds and an absolute disorientation" is the only thing that the people can conclude when they kill the homosexuals in *The Public* (522). The scapegoats have been needlessly sacrificed. Their victimization does not clean away anyone's sins.

The Sociopsychological Function of the Scapegoats

Cirlot asserts that the billy goat is the symbol of the projection of one's own guilt on another with a repression of one's conscience. From this comes the meaning of "emissary" traditionally given to this animal associated with the devil (178). It also has the secondary meaning of "bearer of evil" that connects with buffoons and anomalous beings. As one can see, evil is associated with abnormality in a more or less gratuitous way. In projecting the "diabolical" evil on the person who is different, persecution is disguised as justice. What can also occur is that even the ones who are identified as evil begin to act as expected, or are afraid that they have to do so. This has been demonstrated by Sartre in his famous study on Genet (*Saint Genet*). The mechanism is explained by Laing in *Self and Others*. It is born from the desire of each man to be confirmed as what he is and even as what he can become, according to Buber, whom Laing quotes before he himself expands on the theme (98).

Girard maintains that, due to the weaknesses of those considered to be abnormal, the persecutors always end up convinced that a small number, even just one, can cause enormous harm to all of society.

In "March Nocturne," an unpublished poem publicized by Eutimio Martín, the poetic voice speaks to the Devil, telling him:

> All the Christians
> slander you.
> They, they themselves are
> your Evil Enemy [*Federico García Lorca* 259].

Popular Fantasies about the Billy Goat. The Religious Connection.

The most well known stereotypes on this animal appear in the *Dictionnaire des sciences occultes* by F. Boutet that speaks of the diabolical animal par excellence, a principal figure in the witches' Sabbat and a favorite mount of the latter (103). These fantasies which provoked cruel realities seem to have greatly influenced the Lorquian creative mind.

Like a witch that heads toward an unknown Sabbat, the Lorquian poetic "I" from "Dream" appears "riding upon / a billygoat" that is called a "fantastic horse." Boutet names as relevant the "luminous" eyes of the witches' billy goat. In the Lorquian poem the reader's attention is called as well to the importance of "the luminous eyes" of the billy goat that illuminate the road where the poetic "I" is found. In the poem "The Billy Goat" the diabolic image of this animal is realized even more through the names "devil," "hell" and "Satan."

It is probable that the Bible is not completely unfamiliar with the fantasies about this animal. According to the *Encyclopedia of World Mythology,* "The scapegoat ritual tended to connect the goat with evil and, through the link with Azazel, with the fallen angels and the Devil. This association was hammered home by St. Matthew's gospel (chapter 25) in which Jesus likens the righteous to sheep and the wicked to goats" (215).

The connection appears even clearer in Leviticus, chapter 16. Of the two billy goats or goats mentioned, one will be sacrificed as the propitiary victim, and all kinds of iniquities and sins of the children of Israel will fall on the other.

Like goats, homosexuals also have to be sacrificed. In passage 20 from the same book, the killing of a man who goes to bed with another man is mandated.

The Billy Goat and "Perverse" Sexuality

Caro Baroja maintains that the billy goat has always been associated with dirty rituals and those of a sexual nature" (*Las brujas* 120). Corominas states that "witches' Sabbat" means "a secret meeting of witches with the devil."

The word is made up of the words *larre* "meadow" and *aker* "goat." *Akerlarre*, in the Basque language, is "meadow of the billy goat" (58). According to the *Pequeño Larousse*, it is synonymous with "orgy" (85). Plutarch mentions that in the Dionysian rites a billy goat was taken in procession and presiding over it all, "walked the one who carried the phallus," states Koning (152–53). F. King comments that it is certain that many celebrations of the witches' Sabbat culminated in "an indiscriminate sexual orgy," but doubts that it was always so: "many of the grossest descriptions of sexual perversions contained in the treatises on witchcraft from the end of the Middle Ages and the Renaissance owe more to the frenzied imaginations of their authors than to the actual practices of witchcraft" (94).

The inquisitor Pierre le Broussard described the rituals of the "Sabbat" in which a billy goat participated (qtd. by Caro Baroja):

> They make an offering and do homage to the Devil and many adore him, giving him their souls and at least part of their bodies. Then they kiss the Devil, in the form of a billy goat, on the hindquarters.... They would also commit the sins of sodomy and homosexuality and other obscene and enormous crimes, as much against God as against Nature [*Witches* 123–24].

The association of the figure of the billy goat with orgies and "perversions" is an undeniable fact. The cases in which this association is owed to the fervor of some imaginations are no less interesting. The "scapegoats," homosexuals as well as others, are frequently persecuted or sacrificed because of the fantasies that their persecutors project on them. What follows are some of the historical proofs of these sacrifices and persecutions during the periods alluded to in "The Billy Goat."

Christianity and Homosexuals.

In *Homosexuals Before the Law* (Los homosexuales frente a la ley), Victoriano Domingo Loren does an intense review of the laws utilized to kill homosexuals legally in the name of the God of the Christians. The Bible seems to have been the principal source of inspiration in administering "justice" by burning homosexuals at the stake. Loren reminds us that the famous councils of Toledo had the force of law, and he quotes from the acts of the Sixteenth Council of Toledo, celebrated almost at the end of the Visigoth kingdom: "III. On Sodomites ... just as the horrendous and detestable crime in previous times handed over the people of Sodom to be burned by the fire that came from heaven, in the same way the fire of eternal condemnation will consume the men who give themselves over to similar filth" (8–9).

The *Legal Code* deals with homosexuals, "sodomites" or "men who lie with other men" in book III, law V, of King Flavio Egica, and law VI, of King Flavio Rescindo. Both laws mandate that homosexuals be castrated (Loren 9–11). The period of Municipal Codes is "fairly brutal and expedient in its justice. The repression of homosexuality is almost a constant; an example is the *Code of Albarracín*, one of the most ancient, which punishes homosexual acts in this way: '...both together should be burned'" (Loren 11). Alfonso X "the Wise" (el Sabio) established the *Royal Code of Spain*. In book IV, title IX, "sodomites" are to be punished before the whole town, "and afterwards, on the third day, they may be hanged by the legs until they die" (12). In *Las siete partidas* homosexuals are also condemned to death. According to law I, the sin of sodomy causes God to send "hunger, and plagues, and storms and many other evils" (Loren 13).

The Catholic Monarchs looked at sodomy as a crime against God, against nature, and as a personal offense against them. On the 22nd of August of 1497 they arrived at the conclusion that

> the current established sentences are not sufficient to eradicate and completely punish such an abominable crime; wanting thus to account to God our Lord ... we establish and command that any person, of any state, condition, pre-eminence or rank whatever it may be, who commits the heinous crime against nature, being convinced of it by way of proof, that according to Law is sufficient to prove the crime of heresy or high treason, may be burned in the flames of fire [Loren 14–15].

H. Kamen also indicates that in the Middle Ages as well as in the era of Ferdinand and Isabel, homosexuals were burned alive (201).

According to the Lorquian speaker, the billy goat is the "Black epitome of the Middle Ages!" (149). In calling the billy goats "Mystics," the poet indirectly refers to the persecution of those who did not see anything bad in sexuality. In *L'homosexualitat a Mallorca a l'Edat Mitjana*, the author, R. Rosselló, examines homosexuality during the Middle Ages and states that homosexuals were always burned and that the persecutions and punishments have lasted until this century (11). García Valdés indicates that "In Madrid, midway through the seventeenth century, the burning of homosexuals was not uncommon" (59–60). The author documents the burnings that took place in 1622, 1626, 1636, 1637, 1639 and 1640. Many Christians from different countries have been convinced that homosexuality was something diabolical. These fantasies have influenced the psyche of homosexuals and have left traces in literature, as will be seen below. The persecution of homosexuals in the name of God has not yet ended.[1]

◆ ◆ ◆

In *Le Thème de l'Homosexualité masculine dans le Roman et le Théâtre américains, de Herman Melville à James Baldwin*, Sarotte states that before

1940 homosexuals in literature were seen only from an external point of view, which impedes any possibility of identifying with them. Objectified, animalized or presented as the principle of evil, a ghost or hallucination, the homosexual is anything but a being of flesh and blood (ii). Melville, as well as Henry James, speaks secretly of homosexuality, utilizing pejorative epithets and associating it with the forces of evil, as Sarotte demonstrates. The author analyzes the work of Sherwood Anderson, in particular the novella *Hands* from 1919. The protagonist of *Hands* is objectified, since his personality and his life are reduced to the story of his hands. The story of this person-thing is somewhat shameful: his hands are alarming and his owner wants to keep them hidden (Anderson 28). The protagonist seems possessed by his hands when close to a boy. The fire from his eyes underscores the reference to the wickedness of his desire: "Wing Biddlebaum looked long and earnestly at George Willard. His eyes glowed. Again he raised the hands to caress the boy and then a look of horror swept over his face" (30).

In a letter from 1895 reproduced in *Our Perverse Ancestors*, Émile Zola compares a homosexual to someone possessed by the devil (Hahn 234). The devil seems to be incarnated in an adolescent who shows his sex, according to the description of the scene done by J. Green in *Leaving before Daylight* (Partir avant le jour). The young man's "blazing" eyes and the "wickedness" of his joy are mentioned: "His eyes flaming, he unbuttoned himself from top to bottom and showed himself to us.... I turned my head violently and felt myself blushing up to my ears. Still today, I have before my mind's eye that dominating look with which he covered us and the diabolical jubilation which radiated from his whole person" (93).

In *Julien Green o la obsesión del mal*, J. Sémolué has shown that "the evil" that horrifies Green is, at the same time, what most attracts him and inspires all of his works. His experience with sex, and homosexuality in particular, as something diabolical is inseparable from the vision that the institutions of Christianity have propagated for centuries. The author quotes Green on different dates and occasions:

> Green himself recognizes this: "my true diary is found hidden in what I invent" ... "the novelist's talent submerges its roots in sin" ..."A novel is made of sin like a table is made of wood" ... "what is a novel made of but evil?" ...
>
> 'If I had fallen amongst the powerful hands of that holy Spanish Inquisition ... perhaps my body would have been destroyed on its racks or imprisoned in its terrible dungeons, saving myself at the end" ... In such sentences, beyond a frightful masochism, the hope of saving oneself from certain temptations emerges, at the cost of torment. The autobiography and, well before, the novels have specified the nature of these temptations [14, 17 and 83].

In Gide's *The Fruits of the Earth*, the Commandments are accused of having made the protagonist's soul sick: "*Will you teach that there are still more forbidden things? New abundantly promised punishments of all I would have found beautiful on earth? ... God's Commandments, you have made my soul sick*" (115).

Maxence Van der Meersch is one writer who with great refinement has presented homosexuals as possessed by a demonic power. The literary approach used in *The Mask of Flesh* (La máscara de carne) is as if the writer gave homosexuals the right to speak as representatives of of their majority. The characters think and speak continuously in the first person, presenting their homosexuality as an objective evil. It is the perfect objectification for the construction and consumption of expiatory victims. The despised homosexual-thing considers himself despicable and he himself justifies persecution. Author and society wash their hands. At the beginning of the book one of the narrator's "companions of servitude" speaks (a possible reference to the "companion from hell" from Rimbaud's *Une saison en enfer* 93):

> We are frustrated beings. It's preferable that no one speak about us. Our history doesn't have any meaning. We don't have any solution or way out. Our existence contradicts freedom and perfectability. It's unpleasant and disturbing that beings like us exist whose lives lack meaning and are worth nothing other than to corrupt whatever surrounds them [4].

Lorca's "other half" is "unredeemable." The homosexuals from *The Mask of Flesh* say they have no "solution." The narrator knows himself to be "incurably evil," and feels "hopelessly like a malignant beast, surrounded by other equally malignant beasts" (8). The first homosexual experience is presented as on a par with selling one's soul to the devil and crossing the threshold of hell: "because of the diabolic appetite for knowledge, with the same gesture with which Faust signs the end of the parchment that opens a new life for him, softly I knock at the door of the unknown, on the threshold of a new, repugnant and sordid destiny which awaits me behind that closed door." (26). From now on the protagonist will live possessed by "that devil which lives in me and is at times stronger than I" (97). The realistic style of the narration, combined with the confessional style of the many paragraphs in the first person, truly succeeds in giving the impression that homosexuality is the door to hell on earth and that homosexuals are the most disgusting and unfortunate beings that one can imagine.

That same year Mauricio Carlavilla del Barrio published *Sodomitas* in Madrid, wherein the homosexuals are described as "ferocious beasts and perfidious reptiles." The clinical psychologist Manuel Soriano Gil quotes from this book that presents the attempts at contact by homosexuals as assaults that contaminate homosexuality:

The herd of sodomite beasts by the thousands is launched through the undergrowth of the city streets in search of their young prey.... Disguised as a person, the sodomite beast looks for his preferred object, the innocent boy, amongst the traveled thicket of sidewalks, ... "Better off dead!" ... , you all will shout desperately.... Yes, your son is better dead... Better off devoured by any vermin. Better for him, for all of you, and better for God. No greater torment for him nor for you, nor greater abomination towards God [44–46].

Sodomitas appeared 20 years after Lorca's death. One might think that it does not have any direct connection to Lorca. In that case, it would be forgotten that the Spain of the dictatorship was the one that killed Lorca. The author of the book was a policeman in a Spain in which homosexuals had the mandatory role of scapegoats (Soriano 23 and 43).

The homosexual relationship between Verlaine and Rimbaud was presented in their time as something demonic. Upon Rimbaud's death Verlaine himself wrote in 1891: "*Mortal, angel AND demon, you might as well say Rimbaud*" (from the sonnet "A Arthur Rimbaud," qtd. by Mayer 224). In *A Season in Hell* (Une saison en enfer), Rimbaud describes a colleague from hell who presents himself as a "slave of the infernal Husband." The poetic voice says that he does not love women and one must again invent love (93, 94).

According to Houston in "The Symbolic Structure of Rimbaud's Hell," Rimbaud had the vision of the advent of a new religion that would replace Christianity, although it maintained some of its characteristics (71). Barbachano is more categorical: "if Rimbaud fought against something throughout his trajectory it was against Christian culture, against the new morality that Christianity imposed on earth" (166). The new religion mentioned by Houston evidently contains elements that many Christians would call demonic, as being an inversion of the symbols and values of Christianity as well as being directly related to homosexuality. This double inversion appears so clearly in some of Verlaine's poems that publishers prefer not to include them in his so-called complete works.[2] Nevertheless, it is perceptible in many other poems of Verlaine and it finds an echo in Lorca.

In "Luxures," Verlaine speaks about "love and flesh" and about "the bread of the condemned who choose the Sabbat." The flesh is "the only fruit eaten from the gardens from here below" (58, 59). For his part, the Lorquian voice in "Cry to Rome" states: "Love is in the flesh shredded by thirst" (*PNY* 151; 526). Like Verlaine, Lorca also mentions bread and fruits:

> Because we demand our daily bread,
> alder in bloom and perennially harvested tenderness,
> because we demand that Earth's will be done,
> that its fruits be offered to everyone [153; 527].

Verlaine associates bread with the Sabbath. Lorca changes the text of the "Our Father" prayer that precedes "our daily bread." "Thy will be done on earth as in heaven" is changed into "Earth's will be done." God's name has been replaced and "earth" is written with a capital letter to give it the category of a proper noun. The "Earth" has will, as does God.

In his introduction to *Parallèlement* by Verlaine, Jacques Borel states that Verlaine was going to show the idea of a "hell" for his Christian work, a parallelism "between mysticism and eroticism, which seems to have been born from a deliberate will" (Verlaine, *Oeuvres poétiques* 470). A very similar parallelism between mysticism and eroticism can be observed in Lorca's "The Billy Goat": "Hail, mute devil! ... Eternal mystic / in the hell / of all flesh" (148).

Verlaine's homosexual, mystical and carnal hell is not easily accessible. Almost 100 years after having been created, the poems from *Men* (Hombres) continue to be jealously kept in the "Hell" of the Biblioteca Nacional (Hell nos. 1050 and 1150).[3]

The mysticism of Lorca's carnal homosexual hell has recently begun to be discovered, above all thanks to the publication of some parts of his *Mysticism That Treats the Curbs Society Places on the Nature of Our Body and Souls* (Mística que trata del freno puesto por [la] sociedad a la naturaleza de nuestros cuerpos y nuestras almas) (Gibson, *Federico García Lorca* 1:212–13). This text was written in 1917, two years before "The Billy Goat."

Myth and Criticism. The Mythic Reading of "The Billy Goat."

Myth can refer to very different things. Many books have dealt with the classic myth as rooted in the deepest part of the human being's complex psyche. The other acceptance or groupings of acceptances for *myth* is that of something false, twisted or superficial, which is repeated as if it were a profound truth or the great Truth; for example, the myth that Lorca was not homosexual, that homosexuals are wretches or are sick, and the myth of Lorca's gypsy lifestyle.

As is the case with other myths, Lorquian criticism can be divided into two major groups. One is the illuminating criticism that tries to show what is behind the facades or in the most profound part of images; the second is criticism that does what Pedro Córdoba calls a "mythic reading of Lorca" or which converts the poet into "an object of mythic consumption" (140, 141), that is to say, the criticism that does not go beyond what deceitful appearances or superficial details suggest, no matter how beautiful the former nor how exact the latter may be.

For Córdoba one of the dangers of the "mythic reading" is that "Myth imposes itself by imposing silence around its borders, condeming the rest to muteness." These words of Córdoba have a special relevance to our study, not only in regard to criticism, but even regarding the figure being analyzed, since Lorca's billy goat is called a "mute devil" in this very poem. We are then before a mythical, classical figure that today is mute, perhaps because other more trivial or twisted myths have silenced it. A mute figure can only speak through intermediaries. Before ceding the word to Lorquian criticism, some questions may be reflected upon as an important point of departure for the elucidation of the character. For example: what aspects of the billy goat figure activate Lorca's sensibility, giving rise to the creation of the poems "The Billy Goat" and "Dream"? Why does this activation take place? Which facts from objective reality have been able to influence Lorca's psyche, causing him to bring this character to light?

Many Lorquian critics point to the influence of Rubén Darío in the creation of the previously mentioned poems, for example, José Mora Guarnido (120) and Emilia de Zuleta (201). Fernández-Galiano mentions the influence of Rubén and underscores the erotic elements in the symbolism of the billy goat: "encarnation of an old satyr dead, perhaps, from excessive love. The lustful animal is a disciple of his father, Pan, and comes from a forest filled with bursting roses of such lascivious passion as the venereal Gongoresque dove, where furious and thunderous Venus of the great erotic hurricanes rules" ("Federico" 33).

André Belamich asks himself what prescience caused Lorca to define a world conception and religion that would impose themselves on him until the end of his life. All of this is found in "The Billy Goat": mysticism, love of the flesh and the hell that results from their union, from which Lorca will be unable to escape (*Lorca* 97).

In his biography of Lorca, Gibson publishes the photograph of a monument to Ganivet to which, he maintains, "The Billy Goat" is related. In effect one sees in it a billy goat ridden by a naked man (or almost naked, since in the photograph one cannot see whether or not he wears a fig leaf). For Gibson, the billy goat is a symbol of all the Lorquian characters who "passionately give themselves over to the search for dionysian love" (*Federico García Lorca* 1:206).

Marcelle Auclair seems to want to deny the importance of Lorca's Satanism. She does not speak directly about "The Billy Goat" but states that in Lorca's first book of poems there is a naive Satanism that will never again appear in his work (92). Francisco Umbral believes exactly the opposite: "*The Billy Goat*" ... is already a decisive and significant song to the dark powers which will forever carry the poet" (*Lorca, poeta maldito* 42). For his part Gustavo Correa dramatically maintains: "Satanism takes hold of the poet's spirit and the symbol of the 'billy goat' emerges" ("El simbolismo religioso" 42). More well meaning, Eutimio Martín believes that it is relevant, to a certain point, to identify the poet with the billy goat, as does Belamich in calling Lorca "a carnal mystic." Nevertheless, for Martín, "the denomination 'carnal mystic' applies to Lorca to the extent to which sexuality is elevated to a mystical sphere with which an attitude of decisive heterodoxy in regard to the official position of the Catholic Church is adopted (*Federico García Lorca, heterodoxo y mártir* 247).

What follows is a discussion of what is behind Lorca's Satanism and his billy goat.

Lorca's Billy Goat.

In his extensive and detailed study of the concept of character, Philippe Hamon states that its meaning or "value," if speaking with Saussurean terms, is not constituted only by *repetitions, accumulations* and *transformations,* but also by *oppositions* (128). By first examining the accumulations and repetitions, one observes that those who state that the Lorquian billy goat is "satanic" are not completely lacking a basis for their assertions. Lorca presents it as a "demon," a mystic from "hell," with a "Mephistophelian" look, a being from the legends of "Satan." Others that transform the "Satanism" of the character, nevertheless, accompany these words. His hell is "carnal," and in this hell of flesh he is a "mystic." The importance of the loving-sexual dimension of the character is underscored by means of diverse adjectives and nouns. The billy goat is an "intense" animal, a rude "Don Juan," of a "passionate" look, with a "thirst for sex" and with "insatiable" passions, who blows "the flame of sexuality" and spills "virgin lechery," the former word related to *pure* (see the sections in chapter 2 on purity).

After having confirmed that sexuality is one of the principal features that characterize Lorca's billy goat and his hell, an examination of what this trait contrasts with is to follow.

◆ ◆ ◆

The satanic billy goat of Christian culture invariably practices all kinds of sexuality. In contrast, the Lorquian billy goat, in spite of its "thirst for sex," does not show any interest in the type of sexuality within its reach. It is made explicit that Lorca's billy goat has at its disposal a whole flock of goats. One goat in particular humbly follows him. Nevertheless, the contacts of the Lorquian billy goat with the opposite sex are nil or unsuccessful since he has "become a eunuch." To become a eunuch does not mean *to be* a eunuch, but rather to function as such in a particular context. How can one understand the sexual incapacity of an animal that Lorca repeatedly presents as passionate and erotic to an extreme? When I defended my thesis in 1986, the designated opponent, Poul Rasmussen, proposed the idea that Lorca perhaps was inspired by a type of chastity belt which, in some places, was used on these kinds of animals so they do not mount the females excessively. It may be so. Nevertheless, in Lorca's poem it is the female who follows the male, and not the reverse. In addition, Lorca himself points to where we should direct our attention if we are looking for a relevant meaning for his character: "Ancient Greece / will understand you."

• • •

Lorca uses the verb "to understand" in the future tense implying that in the time and place in which the billy goat lives, there is no comprehension of his sexual appetites.

In sexual matters, the most important difference between our culture and that of ancient Greece is an open secret. In Greece, Baudrillard states, "love is homosexual and pedagogical" (23). Many authors use the expression "Greek love" as a synonym for "homosexual love" (Azancot 530, Fonvieille-Alquier 28). The Romans called this type of love "the Greek vice" (Koning 164). Whether it is called a vice or love, homosexuality is associated with Greece and Antiquity, and is alluded to by Lorca through the use of the adjective that accompanies the country: "ancient Greece."

Cernuda uses the same adjective to evoke the same thing in "Lightkeeper's Soliloquy" (Soliloquio del farero) from *Invocaciones*: "the old forbidden pleasures" (*Young Sailor* 63; *PC* 175). In *En Memorabilia* (1934–39), Gil-Albert comments on Cernuda's poem where the poet addresses the Devil, calling him "my brother." Gil-Albert also mentions "old" affinities, whose relationship with "ancient Greece" and with "the old forbidden pleasures" seems undeniable: "In the dedication that I keep in his book, one can read: 'To Juan Gil-Albert, with the already old friendship of Luis Cernuda.' And we had only known each other for two weeks. Given that affinities which do not depend on frequency are as old as the world" (*OC en prosa* 261).

Valle-Inclán, named by Zuleta and Umbral as one of the authors who inspired Lorca, also associates "beautiful sin" with Greece:

> I have sighed more than once lamenting that the centuries have made an unknown sin of the divine, voluptuous feasts. Today, only in sacred mystery do the ghosts of a few chosen wander, causing the ancient time of the Greeks and Romans to be reborn, when the ephebes crowned with roses would sacrifice on the altars of Aphrodite [*Sonata de estío* 135 (Autumn sonata)].

In "Jardines" (Gardens), from *Impressions and Landscapes*, Lorca uses the superlative and the plural to refer to "beautiful sin." Somewhat further down, some "hidden lechery" is mentioned as well: "A garden is a chapel of passions and a grandiose cathedral for very beautiful sins" (923). Valle-Inclán's character does not share the ancients' affection for the "beautiful sin," but sees it as something positive. Other contemporaries of Lorca express a very different attitude toward what "ancient Greece" symbolizes. Guillermo de Torre attacks those who disguise their "aberration" as Hellenism ("Rubén Darío" 140).

* * *

The poetic "I" greets the billy goat with a "Hail, mute devil!" Pointing to the animal's muteness underscores its significance in the poem. The speaker endows the billy goat with feelings, intelligence, pyscho-sexual problems and with the necessity of being understood instead of speaking about his own problems. That is to say, he projects his muteness and his feelings onto the figure of the billy goat.

There is a section in *Impressions and Landscapes* titled "The Tombs of Burgos." In the first part, Lorca observes the "paganism," the "lust," and the "mysticism" of the tombs from the Renaissance (the billy goat in Lorca's poem is called a "mystic"). Lorca mentions, in particular, an urn with "two completely naked men showing their sex to the air" (895). The poet realizes that in the ornamentation of the tombs he admires, "a perverse intention" is hidden. Perhaps the artist is homosexual. Whatever the case may be, the artist *inverts* or transforms the meaning "normally" attributed to death in Christian culture, underscoring the (homo)sexual aspects of funereal art. The sculptors could not express themselves more clearly. Lorca understands very well why: "There is an anxiety about saying things which could not be said for fear of being burned alive or locked forever in a dark prison" (892).

According to Hahn, who also cites Gregorio López and Nicolás Gorranus, homosexuality was called a *pecatum mutum*, an unmentionable vice, a crime that ought not occupy or "dirty" the works of medicine, a crime that is not allowed to be named. Lord Alfred Douglas, the lover of Oscar Wilde, called it "the love that dares not speak its name," and Wilde himself used this expression before his judges (Rivers 114). F. Porché published a book entitled *The Love That Dares Not Speak Its Name* (L'amour qui n'ose pas dire son nom), and today this rhetorical figure is a commonplace for alluding to homosexuality. In *García Lorca: Life, Canticle and Death* (GL. Vida, cántico y muerte), Vázquez Ocaña utilizes the expression "unspeakable cries of the flesh" (349).

Daniel and Baudry state in *The Homosexuals* that, in reality, we find ourselves facing what could be designated as a "conspiracy of silence." The "conspiracy" was probably initiated by Saint Paul in the Epistle to the Ephesians in prohibiting that "such things" be named. The authors do a concentrated review of what has occurred since then:

In the era of Louis XIV, the preacher Bourdaloue, in crying out to the king to pursue homosexuals in his court, would use all kinds of periphrases to designate those "whom the Scriptures prohibited him from quoting." ... Even in 1880, a famous doctor, in writing one of the first scientific works devoted to "aberrations of a genetic kind" (the title is a whole program) concluded: "Let us put a veil over such a sad theme for the honor of humanity" [16].

In the work *Yerma* it is never clearly stated at any moment why Yerma and her husband cannot have children. The closest explanation is the words of Juan, shortly before being strangled by his wife: "for dark things, outside of life — for things in the air." These words are like a revelation for Yerma who repeats: "*with dramatic surprise.*" "Outside of life, you say? In the air, you say?" (*Three Tragedies* 152; 741).

What is in the air can be what the whole world knows or senses, but what no one confesses. Air is also a sexual symbol in general (as can be observed in "Preciosa and the Wind" [Preciosa y el aire], from *The Gypsy Ballads*), and a homosexual symbol in particular (see "Symbols and Homosexual Intertexuality" in chapter 3).

Often fed up, the poetic "I" of Lorca's poems has a voice that suffers and cannot speak. In "Cry to Rome" the voice is "heartrending" (*PNY* 153; 527); in "Cave" (Cueva) "cracking voice" is encountered (*CP* 113; 174); in "Joke about Don Pedro on Horseback" (Burla de don Pedro a caballo) the voice is "secret" (*CP* 579; 438); and in "Idilio" it is made of "still waters" (*CP* 497; 373). The voice can also be characterized by its antiquity, as in "Double Poem of Lake Eden" (*PNY*), where "ancient voice" is repeated twice (81, 489). The ancient voice is the voice of love of the poetic "I"; it is his "truth."

In a Lorquian poem from *Songs*, "The Voiceless Child" (El niño mudo), the voicelessness is due to external things. The boy has a voice, but it has been robbed. The thief is a "king of the crickets" (*CP* 487). Carlos Feal reminds us that the sound or song of the crickets "serves to attract the female" (36). The "captive voice" puts on "cricket's clothes," that is to say, it disguises itself as a heterosexual call.

• • •

Works in which the text of homosexuality has been erased or deformed have occurred in countries other than Spain. C.A. Tripp gives some examples from the prestigious translation that Jowett did of *Symposium and Lysis*. The original states that it is honorable for a man to concede sexual favors to good men, and shameful to grant them to the insatiable ones. In the "translation," this is transformed into the affirmation that the good ought to be accepted and the bad not (217–18).

Gide names other examples of similar "translations" of the classics and of Walt Whitman in *Corydon* (17–20, 141, 183). In the preface of the second edition, Gide relates that some "friends" intended to stop the book: "Friends disuaded me from completing the writing of it. That is so. I try to explain what it is. And since one does not ordinarily admit that that exists, I examine, I try to examine, if it is really as deplorable as they say it is" (*Corydon* 11, 12).

Two things are of interest in Gide's preface. On the one hand, seeing how "friends" utilize their influence to silence homosexual discourse, even before it begins to be uttered, and, on the other hand, also observing that Gide makes long detours in order to avoid using the word "homosexuality." He alludes to homosexuality in underscoring *it exists* ("*est*"), and *that exists* ("*cela est*"). In the book's text, Gide speaks in a much more direct way.

Pierre Démeron denounces the silence in teaching: "I have studied Greek and Latin for ten years without anyone's ever teaching me about the essential role of pederasty in Greek civilization, most notably in education. There is a kind of tacit agreement to maim texts, censor history, and mutilate cultures" (Daniel and Baudry 17).

In *Sodome et Gomorrhe*, Proust shows that what for others is the greatest pleasure of living, the homosexual "race" is forced to view as something unmentionable ("inavouable" 19). Pier Paolo Pasolini, who was murdered, like Lorca, writes in the preface to *Actos impuros* and *Amado mío*: "I suppose there would be some that, if I said the name of the sin ... perhaps they would not read even the first page of the book" (201).

H. Mayer states that "A critic of *Los baños de Lucca*, who before Heine experiences only disdain, insists with regard to the theme of pederasty, he only dares to write it with a P.: 'the customs, the most profound moral sensibility, the basic principles of our people, even more, of the Christian people, demand that such mistakes, if they have to be mentioned, be treated only with sincere horror'" (196).

Mayer believes that Wilde's *The Portrait of Dorian Gray* is "a homosexual narration... The narrator does not ever specify with exactness the scandals which isolate the already along in years Dorian Gray in social life, even to the point at which the archdukes abandon the club when Dorian appears and the doors to previously hospitable houses are closed to him" (238). Mayer relates that in Hamburg, the first translation of *Querelle de Brest* by Genet, gave rise to a trial with the condemnation of the editor" (268).

Fire and Blinding Light

In Lorca's work, the voice, the tongue, the look and other physical organs or senses often appear related to fire. "Some Souls" (Hay almas que tienen)

"...speak of a burnt voice / that comes in / from a distance" (*CP* 53; 84). Walt Whitman's voice is compared to "a column of ash" in the famous ode (529). In "Suicidio" "soft ash" falls from the hands of the lad (365). In "Idilio" a "voice's still waters," a "secret" and the "ashen sky of your glance" are mentioned (*CP* 497; 373). The "phallus of the horses" is burned in "Crucifixión" (545). The "I" of "Invocación al laurel" feels a "fire" burning in the chest (136), and in "Ghazal of Desperate Love" the speaker states that his lover will arrive "with his tongue burnt by the shower of salt" (575). Lorca refers to a particular shower ("the" shower and not "a").

A fire destroyed Sodom because of the homosexuality of its inhabitants. Salt is associated with this city through Lot's wife, transformed into a pillar of salt for looking back. The shower of sulphur and fire is mentioned in Genesis 19. In naming "the shower of salt," Lorca makes a poetic synthesis of several biblical scenes. In Proust's *Sodome et Gomorrhe*, it states that some sodomites managed to escape. They were not changed into pillars of salt although they turned back to look at a youth.

Lorca wrote a play on these themes that, according to Mildred Adams, is rumored to be hidden in a strongbox in Madrid (173). Several friends of Lorca's heard about the work; some heard it read by the author himself. "At the begining of 1935 Lorca announces that he already has *La destrucción de Sodoma* 'almost done'" (Vázquez Ocaña 325).

> an act from *La Destrucción* read to Rapún and to me in my room in the Residencia de Estudiantes.... What Federico does in the work is to counter incest with sodomy.... I don't know what has become of the manuscript.... I haven't heard any more about *Destrucción*, but I'm sure that it took up vast regions of Federico's mind, thinking and time [Sáenz de la Calzada 156, 157].

In her article "La destrucción de Sodoma: A Reconstruction of Federico García Lorca's Lost Drama," Suzanne Byrd gives a summary of the work. Her informant was Luis Sáenz de la Calzada, who, according to the author, vividly recalls many details of the drama. The summary relates that in the work, Lorca creates the impression that the two angels, guests of Lot, are homosexuals (106). Marie Laffranque has released a dialogue from *Destrucción* in Lorca's *Teatro inconcluso*. The author indicates that the manuscript bears a title, subtitle, description of the scenery and an incomplete dialogue, which is what has been published (56 and 215–17).

In Genesis 19 some sodomites became blind, and the sun came out when the city was burned. In "Ghazal of Desperate Love" the poetic "I" assures that he will be reunited with his love "though a sun of scorpions feed on my temples" (*CP* 657; 575). A sun that feeds on a temple is a sun that burns and blinds. One is again before the poetic condensation of several incidents. The blinding light is mentioned in "Oda a Salvador Dalí," where a "statue" is also named which seems to be by all indications "blind." The "rose," object or cause of "the buried struggle" is like a butterfly or "like an eyeless statue." What causes the blindness of the Lorquian "I" as well as of Dalí, to whom the ode is dedicated, becomes explicit: "The light that blinds our eyes is not art. / Rather it is love..." (*CP* 595; 778).

"I'm blind, don't you see? / Give me your hand" begs the slandered Devil from "March Nocturne," an unpublished poem by Lorca released by Eutimio Martín, who sees in it "an autobiographical splitting of the poet" (*Federico García Lorca* 258, 260).

"Lacking a sense of touch and nameless / we walk around like blindmen..." states one of the poetic voices from Prados' *Persecuted Body* (*PC* 1:342), and in Gil-Albert's "Didáctico" from *Life Is a Dream* (La vida es sueño), blindness is also mentioned and a race of hidden blood is alluded to: "that a divine or almost blind lineage / flows through the hidden veins / of our presence" (*OPC 2*: 180).

In "Return to the Shadow," Prados mentions blindness as much as the punishment from hell that threatens those who practice "infertile" sexuality, to which the poetic persona dedicates himself with fear:

> frightened seed alone I deliver,
> infertile and opaque
> — blind pupil —, flesh from hell:
> where, through where does the wind spill?
> ...
> that in being born again I find myself blind [*PC* 2:202, 203].

"You'll wind up blinding me!" complains one masculine figure to another in the second scene from *The Public* (13; 478).

"Old report in the world calls them blind" says the poetic voice in canto XV of the "Inferno" from *The Divine Comedy* (75), and among the Florentines there were many. In the introduction to the canto they are called "violent against Nature" (for "anti–Nature," see the section "Culture" in chapter 1). Soon after mentioning the blindness of the condemned, Dante's speaker exclaims "but far from the goat will be the grass!" (75). In "Cry to Rome," the Lorquian poetic voice laments that there is no one to "make grass grow in the mouths of the dead.... / Only a crowd of laments" (*PNY* 149; 525).

In *La escritura y la experiencia de los límites*, Philippe Sollers believes that *The Divine Comedy* still keeps "its secret" because it has been "commented on and repeated with manic erudition" (14). Sollers presents a new interpretation or vision that has a certain relevance to the theme of homosexuality, although the author does not deal with its interpretation: "To be in hell means to be persecuted by one's own word; it is the obverse, the inversion 'where the sun keeps quiet,' the place for the reaction and confusion of languages, for definitive metamorphoses, for lack of communication" (38).

In the case of homosexuals, to be "persecuted by one's own word" is to be persecuted from within and from without. From within, by self-censorship and self-disdain produced by the alienated vision that the "education," of which they were the object, incited. Blind because they have been blinded. "Dogs" because they are harassed like dogs (see chapter 3, "Oppressed Norms," the beginning of chapter 4; and chapter 5, "Bacchus"). From without, the word itself pursues them in another way: whatever is said or written about homosexual love can turn against them and be used as proof of their "crime," as occurred in the case of Oscar Wilde (see the beginning of chapter 1). This is the hell of the lack of homosexual communication. Hell "is others" as Sartre would say, although some convicted people, like Genet, perhaps can learn to affirm themselves as individuals within that hell.[4]

The title of Lorca's poem "Ghazal of Desperate Love" indicates that the lovers have abandoned or ought to abandon all hope, as prescribed on the doors to Hell: "ABANDON EVERY HOPE, YOU WHO ENTER HERE" (Dante 17). But in spite of all of this, Lorca's poetic "I" will go to encounter his love, "and cede to the toads" his bitten carnation (*CP* 657; 595).

Toads are known to be associated with witches, with the devil and with sexuality. In *Arte y humanismo*, Santiago Sebastian reminds us that

> Throughout the Middle Ages, the frog or toad remains related to the sin of lust, and we see it next to those condemned to hell, be it on the facade of Bourges, or in the archivolts of Paris or Leon, and more concretely in miniatures and in paintings in which we find the lustful couple, united in a tight embrace, naked, and next to them the little symbolic animal.... Also in a painting "Death" [La muerte] from Memling's workshop which presents a man's body, half decomposed and naked, whose sex is replaced by a toad [209].

The different sections above can be summarized by saying that Lorca's "mute devil" is not mute, but rather it has been silenced in the same way that the voice of passion that it symbolizes has been. The Lorquian poetic voice is imprisoned and "burnt" as is the lover's tongue from "Ghazal of Desperate Love." Homosexual love has been controlled and condemned to fire and desperation. The Lorquian motif of desperate or hopeless homosexual love is also adopted by Ruiz López in *Ocaña* (see "Lorquian Criticism" in chapter 1). In scene 3, the protagonist states: "Life has not taught me to hope; to cry, yes, and with a lot of rage, and even to despair, but never to hope" (43). The work is dedicated to some proletarians of sex who confessed ironically: "despair unites us for hope."

❖ ❖ ❖

In addition to Lucifer from hell there exists another Lucifer or another aspect of Lucifer that is relevant to the study of Lorca and his billy goat. The purpose in the following sections is to prove that in Lorca's work there is a great poetic cohesion among such apparently disparate motifs and symbols as the billy goat, the fall of the angels, the sea and the stars, and that the internal agglutinating agent of all of them is the underlying theme of homosexual love and its problematics.

❖ ❖ ❖

The biblical fall has been interpreted as a split from the fundamental man associated with Plato's androgyne (Eliade 128). As June Singer explains in *Androgyny* (108–116), the fall would have given rise to the separation of sexuality into heterosexuality and homosexuality. J. Jiménez studies the "Angels of '27" in *The Fallen Angel* (El angel caído). According to the author, paradise and the angel that Cernuda lost are very different from those of Lorca whom Jiménez sees as an "angel of light" (88). Between this reading and what Pedro Córdoba calls "the mythic reading of Lorca" it does not appear that there is any difference. Jiménez does not mention Lorca's or Cernuda's homosexuality.

Kolakowski indicates that "according to the Book of Enoch," the angels fell because of sex's fire. For his part, Saint Augustine explains in *La ciudad de la luz* that there is a relationship between the devil and knowledge (chap. 20, book IX). Kolakowski thinks that there are no contradictions between the books since *libido sciendi* and *libido sentiendi* match (143–44). It seems that Lorca's lost work *La destrucción de Sodoma* implicitly expresses an analogous idea about the sexuality of angels: he was creating the impression that angels were homosexual (Byrd 56) (see also chapter 1, "Lorquian Criticism").

For a homosexual, the fall consists of, among other things, knowing a homosexual in the biblical sense of the verb. In "falling" he sins, but also is fulfilled and gives birth to his idiosyncrasy. Prados implicitly expresses this idea in "Hour of Birth" (Hora de nacer), from *The Written Stone*. As in the Platonic myth of Venus, man gives birth: "he was taken / slowly to give birth there." He alludes to the ambiguous inversion of the fall and, in separating the adjective "inverted" from the noun "walking," Prados acts against the natural syntax and gives a preferential place to "inverted": "The immanent, transcends walking / inverted, and in falling, is conceived" (*PC* 2:719; *Piedra* 92).

❖ ❖ ❖

In Lorca's work there are two essentially distinct skies: a powerful (omnipotent) sky that cuts down ("Cut down by the sky," presented in "After a Walk" (Vuelta de paseo 447) from *PNY* 7) and a victim-sky, a fallen god-devil or fallen angel. The latter is located in "Ocean" [Mar], a poem of special importance to the interpretation of the figure of the billy goat, since Lorca puts it before "Dream," where for the first time the symbolic animal makes its appearance. "Ocean," dated April 1919, one month before "Dream," begins in the following way:

> The ocean is
> the Lucifer of blue.
> The sky fallen
> for wanting to be light [*CP* 37; 128].

The ocean is the fallen Lucifer and it is also the father-mother of the Devil since the billy goat is born in the ocean's foam (129). In its Venus dimension, it is even a spirit: "Venus ... / ... / the depth of the soul..." (37; 129). One could say then that fallen Lucifer is the father, the son and the "pure" spirit. Lorca inverts the meaning of the religious symbols of his time, paying back in kind the Christians who distorted or inverted the meaning of the myths and the religions of Antiquity. According to Gibson, who bases himself principally on Lorca's unpublished juvenilia, "In the Church's history, Lorca finds few Christian leaders who escape the qualification of 'miserable politians of evil'" (*Federico García Lorca* 1:206).

Uranus was the sky and was also the god of the sky (*Meridian Handbook of Classical Mythology*, 1954, 596). The fallen sky, "pure" father-mother, is associated with the castrated sky:

> Oedipally *avant la lettre*, Cronus cut off the genitals of his father Uranus. The cult of Aphrodite Uranus, in addition to being Phoenician, was based on the former's name and not to fantastic concomitance with heavenly things. They [the genitals] floated in the sea surrounded by white, spermatic foam from which the goddess was born" [Fernández-Galiano, "El mundo clásico" 85].

From Uranus' foam-sperm the billy goats were born, as is suggested in Lorca's poem that also alludes to purity: "You were born next to Filomnedes / in the chaste foam of the sea" (trans. Maurer).

In "Uncertain Solitude" (Soledad insegura), Lorca refers to the "pure" and ambiguous birth resulting from the wound-castration: "The sky exalts a smudgy scar / to see its flesh turned into flesh" (*CP* 761; 783).

Lucifer, the sea and Uranus-sky all refer to the same myth of homosexual "purity." The term *uranism* was in style in the nineteenth century and in part of the twentieth century to designate male homosexuality. As Daniel and Baudry say, it was "elegant and practical" (21). Gide uses this term and its derivations on numerous occasions. In *Le voyage d'Urien* he does it indirectly, since he changes the name a bit, although it is understood that "Urien" is related to "Uranus" and "Urania." On the first page of the book there are already three references to the morning extinction of Venus-Lucifer in three parallel incidents: the lamp turns off by itself, the protagonist's dream is consumed and his soul, which had "burned" during the whole night, is also extinguished at dawn (31). Then the trip or literary fantasy begins. The topic of the anonymity of homosexual contacts and the homosexual fraternity or "union of uranists," as Fonvieille-Alquier would say, takes shape immediately. The narrator-protagonist does not know if he has seen or not seen his traveling companions previously somewhere else. Nevertheless, he recognizes all of them. They seem to be united by certain "virtues" or characteristics which are not made explicit ("our virtues were the same") (10). The trip is made by sea and begins on a "pure night," on a ship called *Orion* (16) (see the various sections on "purity" in chapter 2). At the end, the narrator confesses that, instead of writing about the things that truly concern him, the whole trip has been a lie. These things are so serious and terrible that the narrator does not dare name them: *"I am afraid to cry too loudly / and to overwhelm poetry / if I have spoken the Truth, / the Truth that one must hear; preferring lying still / and waiting, waiting, waiting..."* (165).

Uranism is not only alluded to in *Corydon*, but it is discussed openly. It suggests that doctors who usually treat these issues only find ashamed uranists. The book that the narrator will write will deal with healthy uranism. It is maintained that sadism usually accompanies heterosexuality rather than uranism. Finally, attention is called to the fact that Schopenhauer and Plato understood that they should take uranism into account in their theories (Gide 35, 38, 53, 61).

Sarotte indicates in his thesis that Uranus is named in the first American literary work of the twentieth century in which a homosexual couple appears, *Bertram Cope's Year*, by Henry Fuller, 1919. The word "homosexual" could not appear in a novel of those years, but the nature of the relationship of the two male characters is suggested by Uranus' benevolent look when Cope inserts the Freudian key (Freud, *Psychoanalysis* 141): "The author shows us Arthur and Betram returning home: 'As Cope ... bent to put the key in the lock, Lemoyne impulsively flung an arm around his shoulders. "Everything is going well now," he said in a tone of great satisfaction; and Uranus, from the whole breadth of his starry firmament, cast a benevolent look upon a household made happier'" (Sarotte 21). Sarotte does not state that the author is indicating that Arthur and Bertram are lovers, but suggests it through the help of a technique of reflections, echoes and repetitions.

Uranus, that is to say, the homosexual sky, appears in a more or less open way in the works of Rimbaud and Lorca. Lorca mentions Rimbaud in "The *Duende*: Theory and Divertissement": "Rimbaud's delicate body." In *A Season in Hell* (Une saison en enfer), the "companion from hell" of Rimbaud's poetic "I" is presented as a "crazy virgin" (Rimbaud, *OPC* 93). With the kisses and embraces of the infernal Husband, the poetic "I" enters a dark "sky" (95).

This dark sky in which Rimbaud's "crazy virgin" is placed resembles the sky "without exit" from Lorca's "Nocturne of the Void" (Nocturno del hueco): "Within you, my love, for your flesh, / ... / what a sky without exit, love, what a sky!" (505).

The sexual aspect seems fairly clear in both poets. The "infernal" is more evident in Rimbaud, although Lorca's "sky without exit" also probably refers to the entrance into the flesh as well as the entrance into the Uranus-sky of homosexuality, and the entrance into the Inferno without exit from *The Divine Comedy*, canto III. The so-called sexual inversion is also an inversion of Christian values. In being assumed and dignified, the homosexuality-hell "without return" is transformed into a "sky without exit." The horror of the Christian legacy is transformed into affirmative exaltation. Poetry's alchemy permits the homosexual to make a heaven out of his hell. Heaven is in his feelings and in his voice, not in his objective reality, and it is always a heaven that is hidden.

In the original version of "Nocturne of the Void," the Spanish "cielo sin salida" (sky without exit) rhymes with "silencio de trenes bocaarriba" (505) (silence of trains face up). "Face up" is an adverb usually associated with the human body and not with trains. The trains are in an inverted position. They have left their usual course and have derailed. This may refer to "abnormal" love as well as to the loving feeling that causes the lovers to feel as if they were living outside of time. André Breton also uses the image of the train that derails in the poem "Without Knowledge" (Sans connaissance): "This instant makes the train, round with clocks, derail." Riffaterre explains this by saying that in such a moment, time seems to be suspended (48).

Time is Cronus, also called Saturn, who castrated Uranus. With the same sickle with which he castrated his father, he reaped the lives of men like ears (Hinostroza 122).

In his reader's guide to *The Public*, Martínez Nadal indicates that Lorca gave dramatic form to the idea that "the fruit of love is only nourishment for death" ("Guía" 204). Lorca sees reproduction as something similar to providing death with lives, lives which time-Cronus-Saturn will reap as if they were ears. The poetic parallelism of concepts and events that can be observed in "Your Childhood in Menton" indicates that Lorca tried to evoke four different occurrences or facts that are closely related: l) the castration of Uranus; 2) the muzzling, censorship or castration of uranism or homosexual culture; 3) the connection of this censorship or castration to those who promote reproduction at all costs, that is to say, those who search for lives or ears that time will reap; and 4) the pressures or duress the poet suffered directly or indirectly in order not to speak about homosexual love (the analogy between *muzzling* and *castration* is found in the *Diccionario de Casares* 79):

> Yes, I do love! Love! Leave me alone all of you.
> And don't try to cover my mouth, you who seek
> the wheat of Saturn in snowfields,
> or castrate animals on behalf of a sky,
> anatomy's clinic and jungle.
> Love, love, love. The sea's childhood [*PNY* 15; 453].

✦ ✦ ✦

As previously indicated, Lorca's sea is the sky-fallen Uranus, that is to say, "pure" homosexuality defeated by Christianity. The poet's love is inspired by this sea-love of remote times, the sea of Antiquity, "the sea's childhood." Childhood evokes as well that period of life in a human being in which sexuality or eroticism is unfamiliar with differences, the period of "perverse" sexuality. To understand the Lorquian sea as well as the poet's billy goat, we cast a glance towards Greece: "All the sea / is Greek," says the poetic "I" in Lorca's "Visión" (*Suites* 213).

Rimbaud presents a sea of similar connotations in "The Drunken Boat" (Le bateau ivre). The poetic "I" receives him like a woman ("ainsi qu'une femme"). Rimbaud describes the encounter with a verb of strong sexual connotation (penetrate), having previously mentioned "flesh" and some symbolic "apples": "Sweeter than the flesh of sour apples to children, / the green water penetrated my pine hull" (63).

The homosexual association is even clearer in one of Cocteau's erotic texts. Referring to some young men who are like ancient athletes, the speaker states: "I love their assholes, they smell of the sea!" (139).

"Sea" and "ass" appear equally associated in Lorca, in the third scene of *The Public*: "Oh, sea resting against the twilight, and flower in the ass of the dead man!" (25; 499).

Lorca dedicated "Seawater Ballad" to Emilio Prados (111). It is clear that Prados also felt inspired by the sea. Ellis has indicated that in *Time* the landscape is more maritime than terrestrial and that in *The Daily Heart and Other Songs* (El corazón diario y Otras canciones), out of 22 poems, 20 specifically refer to the sea (6). In "If I could...," Prados' poetic "I" states that he belongs to "firm" waters that wake up "erect" (Ellis 317). Like Cernuda's sailor and Rimbaud's drunken "boat," the speaker in Prados' "Solitudes" (Soledades) (*Río natural*) sensually gives himself to the sea, which also gives itself to him: "My body enters the foam / that undresses in my arms!..." (*PC* 2:411). In "Cross of the Sea" (Cruz del mar) from the same book, the poetic persona identifies with the sea. Its body "is" the sea. The sexual association is ambiguous: the "I" penetrates (enters) the sea, but he also opens his body: "My body is the sea! / ... / The sea calls me and into the sea I enter. / ... / I open up my body!" (469, 470, 471). The poem "Naked Angel" (Angel desnudo) states

"The sea is beautiful," referring to Lucifer, "and my sin is beautiful," that is to say, "satanic," or homosexual (*PC* 2:204, 205).

Cernuda expresses himself with diaphanous clarity in poem VI from *Where Oblivion Dwells*: "The sea is a lover, / Faithful response to desire" (*Young Sailor* 52; *PC* 155). Gil-Albert has analyzed this and other Cernudian poems where the sea is mentioned. It confirms, among other things, that women are barely named in Cernuda's poetry ("Luis Cernuda" 83, 88). In "Before the Sea" (Ante el mar), Gil-Albert's poetic "I" perceives the parallelism between the beating of the sea and that of his heart. They are "hidden" blows that become agitated for "secret" reasons. Purity is mentioned and alluded to: "Pure life / we are both / ... / Oh virgin water." The symbol of bitterness is equally present: "my bitter love" (*OPC* 3:189).

It is clear that the sea is associated with homosexuality in an implicit way in the texts discussed. It is not certain that the connection is always deliberate on the part of the poets, but Gil-Albert shows that this is a detail of minor importance:

> The very explicit allusion that I made then to the significance of the sea in Cernuda's poetry and very particularly in one of his poems, was hidden to me, and I don't know if the same was true for him. Our interpretation of these things is delayed at times in showing itself to us, it moves among mine sweepers and, one day, those walls of smoke will become extinguished and the light will shine through ["Cernuda" 53].

In *Ocaña*, the homosexual painter exclaims: "Oh! How many little oceans, seas and rivers in some men's bodies!" (43). In "To an Andalusian Boy," the first poem in *Invocations*, Cernuda says to the boy in the text: "You were the sea," "You were an unconscious force of your very own beauty" (*Young Sailor* 61; *PC* 173).

♦ ♦ ♦

The connection between Lorca's billy goat as devil and stars is through Lucifer, the devil for Christians. Can Lorca's bearded and demonic fallen star be distinguished from other stars, or do they share the same symbolic baggage? The following is a consideration of some examples.

The first Lorca in "The Silver Poplars" (Los álamos de plata) shows a split "I"; he has stars within his chest, but he believes that it was Satan who put those symbolic stars there:

> One must put to bed the body within the restless soul!
> One must blind the eyes with light from beyond.
> We have to look out at the shadow in our chest,
> and pull out the stars which Satan put in us [118].

The Satanic stars are associated with parts of the poetic "I" that his conscious "I" rejects: the body and the eyes, that is to say, the *libido sentiendi* and the *libido sciendi* mentioned by Kolakowski (see heavenly Lucifer in the section "Lorca's Billy Goat" above, in this chapter). The speaker is afraid of feeling and seeing. He wants to sublimate his impulses and blind himself, fairly common reactions in societies that instill in the young the idea that "the flesh" is one of the enemies of the soul.

The butterfly is often used as a symbol of homosexuality (Laguardia 546, León 104). The title of Lorca's first work, *The Butterfly's Evil Spell*, already evokes the presence of evil. In scene 5 of act 1, the butterfly is called a "fallen star." At the same time the already familiar symbols of bitterness and dawn are mentioned: "What bitter dawn did your eyes look into as you fell?" (216; 35). Boybeetle does not love Sylvia since it would be "the normal thing": "He loves a star now," says Sylvia (216; 35). This love for the butterfly-star is presented as something undesirable which can be Boybeetle's ruin (217–18; 37–38). Boybeetle himself tries uselessly to fight against his feelings, but his eyes and his hands, as was the case with the protagonist's eyes in "Hands" (chapter 4, "Christianity and Homosexuals") seem to have a life of their own:

> Who gave me these eyes I hate?
> And these hands that try
> to clutch a love I cannot understand
> and that will end with my life? [235; 57].

The billy goats are born "in the foam." The butterfly is "like a flower from another world, / or like water's foam" (*Butterfly's* 235; 56).

The poetic "I" of Lorca's "My Shadow's Soul" (La sombra de mi alma) from *Book of Poems* realizes that for him, "the word love" has crumbled. His illusion is entangled in a murky labyrinth of "smoky stars" (*CP* 43; 32), that is, stars which have been or are in contact with the fire (of passion, of hell, of Sodom or of the bonfires). The shadow that the speaker describes in his soul is incompatible with what he had heard said about love. Observe that it is "the word," and not love, which has crumbled. What remains for the poetic "I" is the reason and substance of his "old midday of lips" and his "old midday of gazes" (43; 32). "Old midday" is repeated two times. In "The Billy Goat" "mystics of the South," "old satyrs" that "ancient Greece" will understand are mentioned. Both poems are dated 1919.

In "The Premonition" (El presentimiento), Lorca relates the stars that will be in his protagonist's bed to a secret that will be revealed. As in "The Billy Goat," what is not said is associated with the past, with "the old" which is mute or silenced:

> We cannot
> extract a sigh
> from the old.
> ...

> But the future child
> will tell us some secret
> when he plays in his bed
> of bright stars [54, 55].

This poem is from 1920.

The stars are confused with water in "Spring" from 1919: "there was a torrent of bright stars" (125). The sky and sex are related in a fairly explicit way: "sex without stain," "sky without stain" (124, 125). Lorca presents a protagonist who feels something in the water that makes him shudder and who pretends that his heart "doesn't understand anything." The water-stars activate in some way his feminine part since he is compared to a nymph: "Manly Daphne who flees fearful / of an Apollo of shadow and nostalgia" (126). It is a question, therefore, of an intention to flee from homosexual love. In her analysis of Garcilaso's Apollo and Daphne, M.E. Barnard states that the transformation of Daphne in Ovid has ontological implications because the nymph abandons a body split by opposing forces in order to acquire a form that adapts to an ideal of a body without sexuality (256). One observes this same division in Lorca's masculine Daphne, sad and full of anxieties as he/she flees. "Spring" has been placed in front of "Ocean" and "Ocean," as has already been seen, before "Dream," the first poem in which the billy goat appears.

• • •

One of the poems that is often presented as an example of heterosexuality in Lorca's poetry is "Summer Madrigal" (Madrigal de verano). Auclair, who seems very conscious of the sexual ambiguity of almost all of the *Book of Poems*, states that this time, indeed, one is dealing with a woman ("on ne saurait en douter") (92). For J. Velasco, the poem even acquires an "autobiographical value." The author reads it like a kind of definitive proof of Lorca's heterosexuality that will annul "the accusations that were formulated, some years ago, against the Granadan" (452). Although Velasco does not explain what he is referring to, the "accusations" are surely related to Lorca's homosexuality that this author decides "to leave aside" (446). Schonberg observes that of all the poems in the book, this is the only one where the poetic "I" directly addresses a woman, as long as this woman is not a man (150). The author does not deny or affirm that Estrella's trail may or may not lead towards the most beautiful woman of Granada, Asunción P.

Sáenz de la Calzada recalls that during the tours with the Barraca, Lorca could choose to do a presentation in particular towns which were not on the previous itinerary, and in those for which they had to take long detours along highways in poor condition, only because of the sonority of a name. The poet thought that the name of a town was an indicator of the mentality of its inhabitants (134).

A poet, above all a poet like Lorca, does not choose by chance the name "Estrella" nor any other name. The proper name is also a sign, maintains Barthes, a voluminous and dense sign, loaded with meaning (*Le degré zéro* 125). Derrida as well as Lévi-Strauss are in agreement about the significance of the proper name.[5] Grace Alvarez-Altman, in several articles, has called attention to the significance of the names utilized by Lorca, and the importance that the absence of names can have.[6]

Lorca gives the name "Estrella" to the object of the loves of the poetic "I" in a poem dated 1920 (one year after "The Billy Goat"). We are informed that the "flesh" of this "Star" has the flavor of "dawn," and that her body is "scorched," a reference to the morning star and to fire. "Star" offers "stars to the wind" (a new allusion to Lucifer-star) and is called a "feminine Silvanus" (*CP* 67, 69).

The *Diccionario de la Mitología Mundial* states that Silvanus was a god of the forests or fields: "He was presented as an old man of happy appearance, crowned with pine tree branches, with the posterior part of his body that of a billy goat" (284). The connection between Silvanus and the billy goat and, through him, with the Devil, is revealed in the words of Caro Baroja who says, referring to the latter, that although he may appear in different forms, "in the supreme moment of the cult it adopts that of the billy goat." The form in which he is characterized "seems inspired by that of satyrs, sylvans and fauns of Antiquity although at times he may possess anthropomorphic traits" (*Las brujas* 120, 121). *Mythology and the Renaissance Tradition in English Poetry* contains numerous examples of the connection between the Devil and "Pan or Silvanus or Faunus (Bush 293).

When Lorca mentions other women in the poem, the context is superficially positive but internally negative. Estrella the gypsy is called a "Danaid of pleasure." The Danaids are known, first and foremost, for having killed their husbands.[7] The gypsy *kills* "the pleasure" of the poetic persona. This reference is reinforced some lines further down: The "pegasus" or winged horse of the poet's inspiration will fly freely only when he sees the "dead" eyes of the "Danaid of pleasure."

One could then affirm that although Estrella the gypsy may have existed, the poet associates her with symbols that evoke the presence of a masculine god-devil. As Danaid, that is, in its feminine dimension, the rhetorical figure of Estrella symbolizes, rather, the death of pleasure and the chaining up of inspiration. Therefore, "Summer Madrigal," as proof of the attractions that heterosexuality could have for Lorca, is very questionable.

◆ ◆ ◆

In "The Encounters of an Adventurous Snail" the stars appear related to perversity and death. A "half dead" little ant that has been pursued, beaten and dragged by its group says repeatedly: "I have seen the stars" (11, 12). The society of ants reacts violently: "We'll kill you; you're / lazy and perverse" (13). There are no apparent motives to kill the little ant based on how it seems like a scapegoat of unknown sins. It is not specified why the society of ants calls it perverse. The punishment of killing it seems totally disproportionate to the crime of saying that one has seen the stars. Evidently there is something charged with symbolism and danger in that *seeing*. This was noted previously in a poem that stated: "We must blind the eyes ... and pull out the stars."

In *Once Five Years Pass* a sexually ambiguous cat appears who at times is called "Boy-Cat" and at times "Girl-Cat." This Boy-Girl Cat is stoned to death, and the exactness with which the number of stones that cause the death is stated makes one suspect a possible reference to the Commandments: "Ten stones those children hit me with" (act 1, 39; 381). Henry Kamen relates that a usual punishment inflicted on homosexuals in the Middle Ages was to castrate them or stone them to death (201). The boy in the play evokes the castration that goes along with the death in saying that they eat "our peepees" (45; 383) and makes reference to the death by stoning in mentioning the "slingshots for shooting stones" (45; 384). He also names "a dove lying dead on the sand" (47; 385) (for the symbolism of the dove, see "Symbols and Homosexual Intertextuality" in chapter 3). In the stage directions, Lorca specifies that the boy should enter the scene "dressed in white, as though for his first communion, with a crown of white roses on his head" (35; 384). The boy has been prepared for a rite of passage; he must leave childhood and enter puberty. Knowing or foreseeing that for him growing will mean going deeper into the knowledge of something that will separate him from others, a knowledge that is punished with death, the child exclaims terrified: "I want to be a boy. A boy!" (45; 384).

The child is executed without being told why: "They tied my hands together..." (37; 379). His death is matched by the appearance of the fateful Lorquian stars: "a man with a hammer who drove / paper stars into my coffin in rows" (37; 379).

❖ ❖ ❖

The Lorquian stars present anthropomorphic traits and are victims of violence. In "Martyrdom of St. Eulalia" (Martirio de Santa Olalla) the stars' noses are broken. The "dawn" evokes the presence of the morning star: "A night of scattered torsos / and stars of broken noses / waits for cracks of dawn" (*CP* 571; 433). As in the case of "Estrella," the sources of Lorca's inspiration for Eulalia are probably fairly ambiguous. According to Gregorio Prieto, a friend of Lorca's (see chapter 2, "Lorca and the Sailors"), "the most beautiful statue in Spain is St. Eulalia, which is in Cáceres. And that sculpture is of a Roman soldier on whom a halo and a crucifix have been placed. But underneath he is a soldier" ("Gregorio Prieto" 11). In the fourth line of the poem, Lorca mentions the "soldiers from Rome."

The star from "Song" (Canción) has been beheaded (for the ambiguous symbolism of beheading, see chapter 2, "Heads and Necks"). The poetic "I" wants to remain alone in "the poplar's decapitated star. / In the broken and submerged compass" (780).

In the Lorquian universe, the moon can be transformed into a star:

> Gigantic
> spider
> turns moon
> into star [*CP*, "Portico" 181; 619].

The moon resembles Lucifer. In "Song for the Moon" (Canción para la luna), the moon stares closing an eyelid: "Satan's one-eyed too... / Perhaps / it's a relic" (*CP* 71; 56). Like Lucifer, the moon rebels and protests

> the abuses
> of Jehovah, that despot,
> who sends you packing
> down the same old path [73; 57].

The Lorquian protest intensifies in "Prologue." The poetic "I" sees something in his heart that displeases him. He complains to God who does not seem to listen to him and he reproaches him:

> Are you deaf? Blind?
> Or are you cross-eyed
> in spirit
> seeing double in the human soul? [*CP* 63, 65; 88].

It is notable that in Spanish Lorca uses "invertidos," i.e. seeing the human soul with "inverted" tones. "Invertido" was and may still be a synonym of "homosexual."

The demonic (filthy) spirits attack or perhaps counterattack in "Crucifixión": "they smashed vials of water on the temple walls" (546).

Like a rebellious angel, Lorca's poetic "I" in "Ocean" denies what the biblical preacher states. He interprets it as an attack against the love symbolized by Venus-Lucifer: "Venus ... (Silence, Ecclesiastes!) / [is] the depth of the soul..." (*CP* 37; 129).

Summary and Conclusions

Although there are important differences between Lorca's billy goat and the one that appears in Christian culture, there is also something that both have in common: they are related to Hell, Lucifer-Venus, the fall and homosexuality, although from different points of view.

In the poems studied above one can note the different kinds of falls that are interrelated in the poetic experience. They have archetypal overtones and a common denominator: their association with homosexuality of a more or less direct, more or less clear form. They are falls *of* or *from*, and falls *into*. The following are the principal ones:

1. The fall — split of the androgyne or primordial man.
2. The fall into heterosexuality or into homosexuality.
3. The fall — decadence and censorship of "ancient Greece."
4. The fall — castration of the sky — Uranus or Uranism.
5. The fall of Lucifer — Satan from Christian culture.
6. The fall of the angels.
7. The fall into the "sin" of pride and disobedience.
8. The fall into conscious knowledge and libidinous knowledge.
9. The fall — dawning — birth, beginning of idiosyncracy itself.
10. The fall into enemy society-world.

It has been established that Christian culture has shown in its mirror a deformed and filthy image of homosexual love and has contaminated or poisoned homosexuals with that vision, to the point that some see themselves as devils. Lorca has mirrored in his works the fire of Sodom and the burning of homosexuals, as well as the silencing-castration of homosexual culture. Nevertheless, a singular metamorphosis takes place in reflecting the ambiguously inverted image in Lorca's works: the dirtiness bequeathed by Christianity to homosexual love is purified; the ugly vice is transformed into poetic beauty and the "mute devil" speaks at last.

5
Shadows and Dreams: "Verlaine," "Bacchus," and Criticism of the Dominant Reality

trained, the ego becomes "reasonable," is no longer controlled by the pleasure-principle, but follows the REALITY-PRINCIPLE.
    Freud, *A General Introduction to Psychoanalysis* 312

Mentís, mentís, me habéis mentido siempre
...
ya no podrá importar lo que decíais,
cuando se siegan bandas de muchachos,
cuando cazáis horribles venturosos
por respeto a la ley que os hizo infames.
    Gil-Albert, "Vuestras mentiras" *Obra poética completa* 1:81–82

You lie, you lie, you have always lied to me
...
what you said will no longer matter,
when groups of boys are cut down,
when you hunt horrible fortunate ones
out of respect for the law that made scoundrels of you.
    Gil-Albert, "Your Lies," trans. Frouman-Smith

La realidad y el deseo me ha vencido con su perfección sin mácula, con su amorosa agonía encadenada, con su ira y sus piedras de sombra.... La pluma que ha escrito con sangre una carta de amor sobre la que después se ha escupido ... es la que ha sostenido entre sus dedos Luis Cernuda mientras oía la voz que dictaba su *Realidad y el deseo*.
    Lorca, "En homenaje a Luis Cernuda" 1231, 1232

Reality and Desire has conquered me with its unblemished perfection, with its loving, linked agony, with its wrath and stones of shadow.... The pen that has written a love letter in blood that has been spit upon ... is the one that Luis Cernuda has held between his fingers while he heard the voice that dictated his *Reality and Desire*.
    Lorca, "In Homage to Luis Cernuda," trans. Frouman-Smith

¡La sombra en su capullo nos cobija!
  Prados, *La piedra escrita* 117

The shadow in its cocoon gives us shelter!
  Prados, *The Written Stone*, trans. Frouman-Smith

Surgen dolientes esas sombras postreras:
Las sombras de la gente de mi sangre,
Clamando identidad...
— Cernuda, "Apología pro vita sua" *Poesía completa* 309

These latterly shadows painfully surge:
Shadows of those of my blood,
Clamoring for a recognition...
— Cernuda, "Apología pro vita sua" *Selected Poems* 143

Lorca, Prados, Cernuda and the Rejection of "Reality"

Freud maintains implicitly that pleasure should adapt to reality. Nevertheless, he avoids mentioning that "reality" is a construction of ideologies that prevail in each historical moment. The dominant "reality" has denied now the existence, now the dignity of homosexual love. For Lorca and other homosexuals, the only possible form of adapting to "reality" was to disappear from it. Only by denying themselves as homosexuals was a social reality conceded to them.

Gil-Albert's "Your Lies" does not clarify who are the ones doing the lying, but they are presented as a power that has tried to control the poet's persona from childhood, above all his "burning, morning look." Thus, a new allusion to the burning morning star is seen. Bacchus also seems to draw himself behind the "fertile winegrower who accepts the orb," in contrast to the intransigent and deceitful reality of those who exert a power that institutes despicable laws. Homosexuality was called a "despicable vice," or "disgrace," and homosexuals "despicable" (Hahn 12, 109, 167). Gil-Albert returns the blow: the disgrace is in the laws.

Those who advocate the reality of the establishment probably believe that the oneiric is of lesser importance, or that it is not "reality." In his lecture, "Imaginación, inspiración, evasión," Lorca opposes these ideas. He calls the world of dreams "very real" and states that the "poetic norms" found in him have "true" emotion. The dream "has logic" (1069). The reality and logic to which Lorca refers are those of the Other; they do not count for the established power.

Cernuda gathered his books of poetry and gave them the name *Reality and Desire*. This title can be interpreted as a conflict between both things and as a requirement or demand from one who is not satisfied with only one of the two. The book, states Lorca, contains "stones of shadow." It is not specified against what or against whom these stones and anger of Cernuda's art are directed, but it is not unthinkable that it be against those who spit on the kind of love alluded to in the above letter. Lorca maintains that in Cernuda's book there is a grief, a cry and a "deviation" that are "norms" (they are "expressed in norms"; 1233). The "norm" of *Reality and Desire* does not correspond, therefore, to the norm or norms of reality from which the book emerges. It is a norm diverted from the dominant or imposed reality.

In Prados' quotation, the shadow appears associated with that which provides shelter, as well as being a symbol of obvious phallic connotation, the cocoon. The untitled poem is number IX from the section "Tower of Signs" (Torre de señales) from *The Written Stone*. Prados makes signs for us and, like Cernuda, throws a stone in the form of a book. The poet begins with a quotation from Hölderlin taken from the poem "Sokrates und Alcibiades": "*He who thinks the most profound things, loves the liveliest ones.*" In the critical edition of *The Written Stone*, J. Sanchis-Banús offers the translation of the poem proposed by J.I. Murcia who facilitated the information relating to the quotation:

> "Why, divine Socrates, do you spend time
> courting that young man? Don't you know anything more noble?
> Why do your eyes contemplate him
> with so much love as if he were a god?"
> "*He who thinks the most profound things, loves the liveliest ones*" [87–88].

According to Ellis in *The Three Nights of Man* (Las tres noches del hombre), the symbol of the stone will reveal the direction of the sexual impulses (92). In "Mirror That Does Not End" (Espejo que no acaba), from *Closed Garden*, the poetic "I" receives the stone in his body: "You were a stone in the middle of my flesh" (*PC* 2:253). It is understood that the stone, in addition to being an instrument of attack, is a religious symbol and a symbol of the unity of man (Franz 225–26). It is also a phallic symbol, as was seen in chapter 2, "'Everyone' and the Other." Additionally, it has this connotation in the line of Prados' poetry quoted above and in "Nocturne of the Void," by Lorca, because of the parallelism of the first lines of the two stanzas that follow: "Within you, my love, through your flesh, / ... / The stone in the water and the voice in the breeze / are edges of love that escape from their bleeding trunk" (505).

Implicitly, Cernuda, Lorca and Prados attack established reality by throwing stones of poetry and sex at it, along with their books. Cernuda's "those of my blood" in "Apología pro vita sua" refers to the so-called accursed race, studied in chapter 2, "The Accursed 'Breed' or 'Race.'"

"Reality"

In his article "Beliefs and Cognitive Schemes," A. Fierro indicates that "Important elements of our construction of what is real refer to our social environment, to people and to values." The author reminds us "For Piaget, the 'world,' 'objects,' 'reality' are always constructed" (12).

Berger and Luckmann state that among the multiple existing realities there is one that presents itself as the reality par excellence: it is the reality of daily life. Its privileged position gives it the right to being called the capital or supreme reality. When we are children, this reality reaches us through our parents. When we reach adulthood, institutions and authorities are the ones who construct, to a great extent, our daily reality through laws, information and propaganda. These institutions of which criticism is a part, do not always embrace fantasy and literary realities. Julio Caro Baroja mentions critics and scholars "with cultural pretentions," who initially showed their hostility "to Lope or Tirso as well as to Zamora." They were also hostile to "any theatre which used fables and facts not in keeping with 'reality'" (*Teatro popular* 225).[1]

Rivers has shown that some critics actively oppose the presentation of a literary reality positive towards homosexuality. Justin O'Brien, for example, pretends that true love and good literature are incompatible with homosexuality. With these arguments, he attacks *Remembrance of Things Past*. Rivers replies that "This point of view is perverse since one of the goals of Proust is to show what homosexual experience has in common with the human experience in general" (3).

It is clear that the reality of homosexuals has been principally constructed by the enemies of their sexuality at an international level, as well as at a national and social level, and even within the bosom of the family itself. Under these circumstances it is easy to understand that the idiosyncrasy of their feelings finds itself obliged to seek refuge in diffuse areas like oneiric or literary shadows and dreams.

According to Esther Bartolomé Pons, "Cernuda never knew how to accommodate the real world" (1). This assertion appears to be a half-truth. Before *knowing how* to adapt oneself, one must *want* to adapt. For Cernuda and other homosexuals of his group, "to accommodate" the "real" world meant renouncing their own and abdicating the right to be what they were and to love whom they loved. Cernuda did not know *nor did he try* to adapt to the so-called real world, since his reality was another.

Freud and the Generation of '27.
Art against "Reality."

In *Surrealism and Spain*, C. Brian Morris shows that Pío Baroja anticipated Breton by some twenty years in seeing contemporary art as "pure psychic automatism" (34–35). Morris presents some parts of Baroja's article "Towards the Unconscious" (Hacia lo inconsciente), dated May 18, 1899. Baroja fluently uses terms from psychoanalysis and states that contemporary art is born in the subconscious. Inspiration is not governed by the Ego, states Baroja in the quoted article (35).

Freud's theories were soon known in Spain, thanks to Ortega y Gasset. Rof Carballo indicates that Ortega introduced psychoanalysis in 1911 in two long articles in the journal *La Lectura*. Rof Carballo also speaks of the concept of "VerdrAngung" ("repression" or "expulsion").[2]

According to Dr. Valentín Corcés, Spain was the first country in the world that bought Freud's work, thanks to the interest of Ortega. In "Fifty Years after the Rebellion" (Cincuenta años después de la rebellión), Lola Galán quotes Corcés, who relates that Ortega spoke with the editor Ruiz Castillo. Ortega was enthusiastic and the editor decided to buy every work by Freud, "which would arrive in Spain in 1917 ... to be subsequently translated by Luis López Ballesteros" (Galán 44). In 1922 the first of the seventeen volumes of Freud's works appeared. On May 17, 1923, Freud, who had learned Spanish to read *Don Quixote*, wrote to his translator admiring "the very correct interpretation of his thought" (Muñoz 8).

Parallel to the development and the expansion of Freud's ideas, two artistic movements came forth, which broke with the prevailing moral ideas: Dadaism and surrealism. Carlota Hesse recalls that May of 1916 was the official birthdate of Dada in Zurich (349). Like psychoanalysis and surrealism, the Dadaist movement brought the unconscious to light. The establishment also reacted against sexuality and the inversion of order and morality that Dadaism advocated. Hesse relates the following episode, which has Breton as a protagonist who makes use of a play on words of Duchamp: "In the Palais des Ftes he presented some paintings of Picabia, pulled out a canvas with the words 'up' down and 'down' up, which presented in large red letters the pun *LHOOQ* (*Elle a chaud au cul*), which made the audience shout and, before the eyes of the world, finished the destruction of a 'work of art'" (357).

According to Morris, certain scenes from Lorca's *Trip to the Moon* (Viaje a la luna) are "mockery reminiscent of Duchamp's painting of a moustache on the Mona Lisa in his LHOOQ" (132).

Many of the members of the Generation of '27 have recognized the importance the oneiric has for the analysis of symbols and of literary works. In "Initial Words" (Palabras iniciales) from *Superrealismo poético y simbolización*, Carlos Bousoño states that "Psychoanalysis and Ethnology ... have shown ... the extreme importance of symbolization as a general human tendency; the symbolizing tendencies of the primitive mind and their relationship to tribal customs, myths, etc., have been studied" (17–18).

Kessel Schwartz has indicated that Vicente Aleixandre recognized the influence of Freud in his work in general and in *Pasión de la Tierra* in particular (48). According to Colinas, "Aleixandre knows Freud's work through the first world edition of his complete works, the Spanish edition from Biblioteca Nueva edited in 1921 at the suggestion of Ortega y Gasset" (11).

Freud also influenced the bullfighter Ignacio Sánchez Mejías, immortalized in the famous Lorquian poem that bears his name. According to Morris, the work *Withoutreason* (Sinrazón), written and premiered by Sánchez Mejías, contains dialogues that at times seem to be Freudian lectures or psychiatric manuals (*Surrealism* 37). Morris also speaks of the influence of Freud on different members of the Generation of '27, and recalls that Luis Buñuel believed that Freud was one of the greatest men of the century, together with Lenin and Einstein (36). *Withoutreason* was reissued in 1988 with an extensive prologue by Antonio Gallego Morell, who points out that the work premiered in the Teatro Calderón of Madrid, March 24, 1928, and was published that same year in the collection "El Teatro Moderno" (16–17).

As far as Dalí is concerned, Mildred Adams says that Moreno Villa recalls Dalí from the Student Residence days always immersed in the readings of Freud. Adams believes that Dalí managed to guide Lorca through the subterranean roads of the subconscious. The painter dedicated a lot of time to these studies before beginning to exploit them in his paintings (45, 50). Santos Torroella indicates that Dalí spoke of Freud, according to what Julien Green would say, "like a primitive Christian from the Gospels," and that he started using the expression, "my father Freud." For Gershator, Dalí's influence on Lorca above all appears in *Trip to the Moon*. According to the author, the Lorquian script contains virtually a Freudian manual of symbology (217–18).

Since "reality" has declared war on instinct or "insanity" of people, Dalí declares war on "reality." In 1929 he announces that by means of a process of an active and paranoiac nature, it is going to be possible to systematize the confusion of the world of reality. More and better informed than perhaps he seems due to the unusual nature of his assertions, the painter praises "the admirable thesis of Jacques Lacan: 'Of paranoic psychosis in relation to personality'" ("Nuevas consideraciones" 389, 392). According to Luis Racionero, "Dalí tests out a pioneering attitude in his personal life to overcome the opposition between the pleasure principle and the reality principle by means of a calculated and deliberate fusion of art and life" (103).

Perhaps this attitude is not so pioneering since, as Racionero himself observes further on, "it is what Wilde intended when he said to Gide: 'I only put my talent into my works, I save my genius for life.' It is already known how much the establishment made Wilde pay for his intentions, since there is nothing more subversive than the introduction of art into life. For this very reason, Dalí's lifestyle is irritating" (108).

Arrington observes in his thesis, *A Study of FGL and Surrealism*, that Freud is frequently named in speaking about Lorca's works but that no study has been done which examines the specific Freudian concepts and symbols that Lorca uses (8). Freud's influence on the Generation of '27 is evident but perhaps one should recall that Freud's attitude was not always clear or unequivocal. On the one hand, Freud tried to free the expression of repressed impulses, but, on the other hand, he advocated that instinct should adapt to "reality." Ronald de Sousa states that behind Freud's evolutionist point of view there are implied value judgments: an ideal of objectivity and rationality (203).

In "Civilization and Its Dispossessed: Wilhelm Reich's Correlation of Sexual and Political Repression," Phil Brown indicates that Freud seems to have put himself at the service of social conformity in some of his last works, for example, in *Das Unbehagen in der Kultur* (Discomfort in Culture): "This was his definitive work on the nature of civilization and its requisite social control. For Freud, the pleasure principle, as enticing and pleasurable to the individual, is to be controlled by the reality principle which dictates correct social conformity" (45).

Freud thought that persecutory paranoia is the means of defending oneself against a very strong homosexual impulse (*Psychoanalysis* 368). The criticism of the mechanisms of society that make people ill and oblige them to defend themselves and flee from their own impulses is notable here for its absence. Freud presents paranoia as a sick person's problem. Nevertheless, the persecution of homosexuality does not exist only in the mind of the paranoid; it is an objective fact.

The necessity of evading "reality" is expressed rather explicitly by Lorca in a lecture in 1928, "Imaginación, inspiración, evasión," reconstructed by Marie Laffranque: "The 'evasion' of reality through the path of dreams, through the path of the subconscious ... let us rejoice, he adds, that poetry can flee, evade the cold clutches of reasoning.... This poetic evasion can be done in many ways. Surrealism uses dreams and their logic in order to escape" (1067, 1069).

"Dream"

Lorca's poem is situated between two currents: the influence of modernist art, discussed in chapter 4, "Myths," and the consciousness that contemporary art is born from the subconscious, as Pío Baroja said above. In *Withoutreason*, the relationship of the subconscious to the world of dreams and repressed desire is explicitly indicated. Sánchez Mejías puts the following words in Dr. Ballina's mouth: "According to modern theories, dreams are desires repressed by our consciousness. In the realization of process of this desire, materials in our life related to this very desire are taken incoherently" (*Sinrazón* 72).

In "The Billy Goat" it can be established that the symbolic animal's contemporaries did not understand his "insatiable" passions. In "Dream," the figure of the billy goat searches for refuge in the domain of the subconscious towards which the poet's inspiration consciously steers it. What is not acceptable in the dominant reality is manifested in the oneiric, that is, in "the very real world of dreams," according to Lorca's expression (1069).

In the beginning of "Dream," the poetic "I" finds itself riding on a billy goat. It is a typically "demonic" or witchlike image. As Caro Baroja indicates:

> the images of witches riding more or less fantastic beasts and others related to them, are found in churches and cathedrals as part of the imagery which, rightly, has been considered equivalent to writing, as an ordered imagining of the dogmas of knowledge and of medieval society. Thus in Lyon we find the classical witch mounted on a billy goat [*Las brujas* 94–95].

The poem's protagonist is dressed as a pilgrim. In his *Dictionary of Symbols*, Cirlot reminds us that the figure of the pilgrim is related to the "fall" (243). Man feels strange or foreign in the world surrounding him. He then goes on a pilgrimage searching for his center, trying to find himself.

Several roads open up to the Lorquian speaker. He is at a crossroads, a place where offers are made to Hecate, which consisted of the "residues of purifying sacrifices" (*Las brujas* 45). Later the crossroads became the place for witches' meetings, a place where infernal pacts and demonic parties were carried out (101–02, 117, 287–88). According to Caro Baroja, there is a passage "which is fundamental to the History of Witchcraft." In it the practices of the secret society of the heretics of Stedinger are described. When a novice is received, if there are more men than women, "men satisfy their depraved appetites among themselves" (105).

Several figures try to influence the choice of direction: the grandfather, the shadows, the protagonist's clothes, a swan, and lastly, a serpent who nibbles the pilgrim's robe as if it were an apple.

The first figure who tries to influence the protagonist's decision is a member of his family. The road that the grandfather indicates surely implies the continuation of family traditions (career, marriage, children, etc.) and the renunciation of a personality different from the one prescribed by family morals. In his epistolary, Lorca gives the impression of having felt very frustrated in his own home. At the beginning of the 1920s, he states in a letter to Regino Sainz de la Maza: "*I haven't been born yet. The other day I studied my past attentively (I was seated on my grandfather's easy chair) and none of the dead hours belonged to me because it wasn't I who had lived them*" (*Selected Letters* 5; 1188).

In this letter as well as in "Dream," Lorca mentions a disguise: "I'm living on borrowed time, what I have within is not mine.... I'm sad now and bored by my false interior" (5; 1188–89). It is interesting to observe that Lorca realizes that his life does not belong to him *when he is on his grandfather's easy chair* (emphasis added) and that he considers it relevant to mention this detail in two sentences, just before voicing his frustration. Therefore, there is an association of ideas between the life not lived and this low, comfortable chair that belongs to his grandfather. No matter how you look at it, there had to have been a conflict, which was probably unarticulated, between Lorca's homosexual being and life within the bosom of the family.

The second figure who tries to influence the poetic "I" is the shadow, symbol of great richness and complexity, that will be studied in greater detail in chapter 6. Only in the work *Shadows* do seven distinct shadows appear of which only that of Socrates has a name (Martín, "Sombras" 51) (see below "From 'Dream' to 'Verlaine'" for the symbolism of Socrates). The shadow evokes all that is not seen with clarity and, also, the dark or "cursed" part of people, all that society rejects but from which one cannot flee. The shadow follows us always. In the poem, the shadow is disguised as a beggar; it has an impoverished appearance. Lorca points out, nevertheless, that it is only a matter of a disguise, indicating in this way that there is no such poverty. Perhaps the shadow hides something of value that, for various reasons, cannot show itself.

As the external or superficial part of the "I," clothing is naturally inclined towards what shines, the money and fame that the poet can obtain, the path of gold.

The swan is a symbol that proliferated at the end of the nineteenth century and beginning of the twentieth, above all among the symbolists (Balakian 131). In *The Wilde Swans of Coole*, by Yeats which like "Dream" is from 1919, the swans symbolize a creative relationship with Nature, according to Cowell (52, 54). Lorca's swan winks at the poetic "I." A wink is frequently an indication of amorous incitement or suggestiveness. The bisexual Zeus took the form of a swan to seduce Leda (on Zeus' homosexuality, see "Wings and Birds," in chapter 6). Cavendish states that the swan is a symbol of satisfied desire (131). It seems probable that the person or god symbolized by the swan is intending to seduce the poetic "I," which does not dare to cede to that desire.

The symbol of the serpent is no less complex than that of the shadow. Cirlot dedicates four pages of his dictionary trying to clarify it. As a masculine sexual symbol, it is very well known (Freud, *Psychoanalysis* 139). It can evoke a more earthly and erotic seduction than that of the swan, which is not necessarily in contradiction with the fact that the serpent is also an energy or vital force which determines births and rebirths. This is relevant in Lorca's poem since the pilgrim is perhaps reborn or is reincarnated into a new "I," a serpent who changes skin if, at the end, he finds himself.

Pressured from within and without and feeling divided by everything that wants to push him in different directions, the "I' in crisis tries to evade the anguish and the necessity of having to choose: "I have no path," he claims. The "flesh" is a problem. Not choosing, the speaker hopes or wishes that the problem be dissolved in the fog or distilled, transforming itself "into dew." But not choosing is also a choice, and the flesh does not change into dew, no matter how much fog is around. The poetic "I" eludes its responsibility; the poet assumes it by writing about the subject. Each allows or causes the billy goat to choose the path to follow. The choice turns out to be incompatible with what the heart wants. The heart here does not seem to represent the most intimate thoughts of the speaker. Rather, it represents the interests of the ego, the familiar or social feelings since it is a heart that thinks. The "pensive" heart probably fears the consequences of allowing itself to be swept along by instinct, symbolized by the billy goat, and wants to get off. The "I" now sees itself obligated to make a decision. In light of modern psychology, it is a matter of a fairly relevant choice. Sousa indicates that the "I," just like the rider of a horse, obtains energy from the "id," that is to say, from its libidinous instinct. Conquering or subjugating this source of energy is like killing the horse in order to control it better (218).

The poem "Dream," therefore, tells the evolution of Lorca's poetic "I" until it comes to assume the "demonic" and exiled sexuality symbolized by the billy goat and ancient Greece. At the beginning of the poem the narrator says that he is mounted on "a" billy goat. At the end it is no longer "a" but "my" billy goat and "the luminous eyes" of this symbolic animal are what light the way and guide the protagonist in the darkness of the surrounding reality. The indefinite "a" shows, first of all, the insecurity or alienation of those who do not recognize or fear recognition. The possessive "my" at the end shows the affinity between the billy goat and the poetic "I": the animal is not at all strange, but, to the contrary, is something of one's own. The "id," the interior demon and homosexuality have been recognized and accepted in spite of the danger they entail.

The Symbolism of Mounting and Blood. Blood Wedding.

In "Dream," the billy goat is called a "fantastic mount." Among the studies dedicated to the symbol of horses or mounts in Lorca's work, Martínez Nadal's work stands out. In it he states: "The suspicion that there is a clear relationship between horses and men is inevitable." In *The Public*, the Director's love for horses is "a secret, but impassioned love" (223, 226). Another critic also states, "Generally, the horse in Lorca's work represents a vital force, a libidinous instinct, an uncontrollable demand and the traditional phallic symbol" (Viera 81). Lorca uses the symbol of the mount as an instinctive and demonic alter ego of different poetic "I"s in his poems as well as in his theatrical works. Dalí also uses it in communicating with Lorca.[3]

In act 3 of *Blood Wedding* we see that Leonardo's mount realizes the instinctive wishes of the character, in spite of the conscious I's resistance:

> And when I saw you in the distance
> I threw sand in my eyes.
> But I was riding a horse
> and the horse went straight to your door [87; 648].

Juan Villegas has indicated a use of the indefinite article in *Blood Wedding* that recalls the above: "The Servant's 'did you hear a horse' indicates a first sign. It refers to something real. It makes it remain anonymous and indeterminate.... The reply by her interlocutor alters the previous 'It carried a rider.' The unit horse-rider has returned, but now anonymously" (Villegas 29).

The wedding ends up being formal only for the couple that marries. The bride says they can bury her without any man having seen himself in the whiteness of her breasts (96). Her marriage has not been realized physically with Leonardo either. She remains intact "as a new-born little girl" (97; 659, 660).

It is suggested that the act of mixing bloods equals the sexual act: Third Woodcutter: "They'll find them and they'll kill them" (Leonardo and the Bride). First Woodcutter: "But by then they'll have mingled their bloods" (80; 638).

Blood is often associated with sexuality: according to F. King, it was a popular belief that "one drop of semen is equal to an ounce of blood." In Victorian thought, masturbation was like a loss of blood that explained the pale complexion and haggard appearance of some young men (King 62). Alvarez de Miranda places the example cited from *Blood Wedding* under the epigraph "*Blood-Sexuality*" and recalls that in Leviticus, "blood is the soul of flesh," and that the theme of blood is intertwined with those of fertility, generation, sexuality, etc. (20, 25, 26). In Prados' work, the sensual or sexual nature of blood appears fairly clear, for example, in "Ascensión" from *Pursued Body*:

> Like a river my blood
> goes crossing your body.
> What a perfect possession
> of your entire path! [*PC* 1:329].

The blood that mixes in *Blood Wedding* is not that of Leonardo and the Bride, as the first Woodcutter would suggest, but rather belongs to Leonardo and the Bridegroom. The bride and bridegroom of the wedding alluded to in the title of the work are two men. Lorca seems to have had a deliberate intention in choosing such an ambiguous title. In the "Notes to the Text" it reads that there is a variation on "they're bringing the dead from the arroyo": "they're bringing the bride and groom" (657; 1517). The diminutives that follow in the lines of verse (in Spanish) applied to the physique of the two men color "them" with a sensual and affective hue: "Dark the one / dark the other" (94; 657). The flight of a nightingale "over the golden flower" is mentioned immediately afterwards. Cirlot indicates that in alchemy "this nonexistent flower" is mentioned and that "in the *Epistola ad Hermannum Arch. Coloniensem* (*Theatr. Chem.* 1622) it is given the name of 'the sapphire-blue flower of the Hermaphrodite'" (105).

Antonio Gades and Carlos Saura have observed the importance of "the wedding" of the two men in the ballet and in the movie *Blood Wedding*. A slow motion scene is added to Lorca's text that accentuates the sensuality of the dancers' movements without diminishing the tension of the fight. The details about the movie appear in *García Lorca y el cinema* (Utrera 16–17). Recall in this context that in *The Public*, a work written years before, the fight between the two men who love one another is described as a "bloody" feast" (485) (see "Heads and Neck" in chapter 2). Andrew Anderson also mentions the homosexual aspect of Leonardo's wedding-fight with the Bridegroom in his article, "What Does *Blood Wedding* Deal With?" (De qué trata *Bodas de Sangre*):

> the wedding ought to precede the blood that flows in the deflowering of the Bride — as is expressed ambiguously in the Servant's song — but, ironically, the blood that stains the Bride's hair and dress is that of the two men; both men are, in a certain sense, united in their fight to the death.... At the moment of the death of the two men, "Suddenly, two long, ear-splitting shrieks are heard."

This shriek is a lament of grief in death, but it can also be, in an ambivalent way, [a lament] of agony and ecstasy in orgasm [60].

The Horse's Lullaby. Water. Green. Tail. Branches.

Several critics have directed their attention toward the lullaby from *Blood Wedding*, whose protagonist is the horse. The studies by Allen and Doménech stand out for their profundity and detail. The latter supports Correa by maintaining that "It is a matter of, or said another way, a subtheme parallel to the action or principal theme; a technical recourse which is traditional and particular to the tragedy" (203). Allen, who does not differ on this point adds, for his part, that to put the child to sleep is to submerge him in the waters of the subconscious (171, 172). The aspects of the lullaby related to "Dream" and "The Billy Goat" have not been observed, although Allen indicates that the horse of the lullaby is related to sex, evil and the Apocalypse, among other things. The author states that the horse is Leonardo, the principal sexual force in the work (181).

It is important to note that the horse in the lullaby is called "horse of the dawn" (42; 578). Lorca associates him in this way with Lucifer-Venus or the morning star. The poetic "I" of "The Billy Goat" mentions a "she-goat," "in love" with the animal that does not seem to be interested in her. The horse in the lullaby seems equally uninterested in going where "the mare" is (579). In "Dream" the poetic "I" cries in going deeper along the road that the billy goat takes; in the lullaby the horse cries when starting to drink. In "Dream" the night arrives full of shadows; in the lullaby the horse drinks a black water.

Doménech says that one must observe, "that throughout the composition there is a shying away from openly explaining why the horse refuses to drink." That the water may have "the blackness of blood and of death" does not appear to be a sufficient answer (204). Water is an erotic love symbol that Lorca has used with these connotations in his theatre as well as in his poetry. In "Meditation Under the Rain" (Meditación bajo la lluvia) the speaker is confused "before the murky fountain that springs from me out of love" (123), like the murky water that the horse does not want to drink. In "Morning" (Mañana) the symbolism is repeated: "it is love of love we drink / when we drink water" (*CP* 15; 30). In "Ode to Walt Whitman" some solitary men are named "who drink prostitution's water with revulsion" (*PNY* 161; 531).

These men "who love other men" "have that green look." The water in the lullaby goes through a "green parlor." In his lecture "Children's Lullabies," Lorca states: "I have fled from all my friends, and I leave with that boy who eats up the green fruit" (1073). There are three things to note: 1) Lorca's flight from his friends is, at the same time, a flight from his daily reality in search of lullabies which provoke sleep; 2) in his flight, Lorca chooses to leave with a boy; whether or not it is a real reality or a "reality" from Lorca's fantasy is not relevant in the context; and 3) the boy is characterized by, among other things, eating "green fruit."

The horse does not want water but for some hidden reason feels pushed to drink the black water in "its green parlor." In "The Moon Appears" (La luna asoma) it states that "Fruit must be eaten / green and ice-cold" (*CP* 471; 339). There is, therefore, a resistance and, at the same time, an attraction or necessity of eating and drinking what is unripe (green) or is actually green. In contrast, the boy with whom Lorca flees from his friends eats green fruit in a natural way.

In "Flesh" Lorca associates green with "blood" and with a city whose name possesses unmistakable connotations, "green blood of Sodom" (795). Love escapes towards "the green current," states Cernuda's poetic "I" in "River" (Río) from *Ocnos* (63).

Another characteristic of the water from the horse's lullaby is "its long tail" (41; 571). The water and the horse are similar in that both have a "tail." The phallic symbolism of the tail is both universal and very old. Shakespeare utilizes it, for example, in act 2, scene 4 from *Romeo and Juliet* as has been observed by Conejero (55–56) and in other works (Partridge 200–201). Apollinaire uses it without ambiguity in *The Eleven Thousand Cocks* (35, 40).

The term cock is also found in León's *Dictionary of Spanish Slang*: "*Tail* (childhood slang) Cock" (54). As León indicates, the meaning of the word is even known by children. It appears, for example, in a scene among children in *Chronicle of Indifference* (Crónica del desamor) ("little tail" [colita]) (Montero 229). Martínez Nadal recalls some of the songs and poems he heard Lorca do. A particular habanera refers to the size of something that men have. *Tail* appears on two occasions in a poem (Martínez Nadal *Four Lessons* [Cuatro lecciones] 18–19). Although the author does not mention it, it is obvious that these are references to the phallus. The allusion is very clear in the habanera: "My father's 'cu-chu-cha' / is bigger than mine, / I saw it last night / At night when he was sleeping." The reference from the poems is somewhat more obscure. The poem deals with the tail of the peacock from the sky. In "Mediterráneo" the reference is clarified: "The sky's fat penis" (*CP* 305; *Suites* 133).

An unusual image from the lullaby is that the water is found "under" the branches (41; 577). It is possible that the branches have anthropomorphic traits similar to what was studied in chapter 3, "Symbols and Homosexual Intertextuality," where the branch was connected to the narrative and spermatic "cool of linen." It is somewhat significant that Lorca dedicates his "Waltz in the Branches" (Vals en las ramas) to Aleixandre. It may be recalled that meetings of homosexuals were celebrated in Aleixandre's home, and even dancing took place (Villena, *Cernuda recordado por Aleixandre* 84) (see "Lorquian Criticism," in chapter 1). The details from the dedication-homage to Aleixandre do not appear in the *Obras completas*, but they do appear in Eutimio Martín's critical edition. Martín indicates that Aleixandre, in turn, dedicated the second section from *Swords Like Lips* (Espadas como labios) to Lorca, which is headed by the poem "El Vals" (285).

It is very possible that the horse's resistance to drinking can symbolize the resistance to accepting homosexual inclinations. Water is presented as something terrible and desirable at the same time. It seems to enclose something very bad, but the horse or the most intimate and profound part of his being cannot do without water. One must drink although it may be while crying:

> WIFE. Carnation, sleep and dream,
> the horse is drinking from the stream.
> MOTHER-IN-LAW. My rose, asleep now lie,
> the horse is starting to cry [47; 586].

From "Dream" to "Verlaine."

In a 1918 letter to Adriano del Valle, Lorca compares himself "within" to Verlaine:

> I am a poor impassioned and silent fellow who, very nearly like the marvelous Verlaine, bears within a lily impossible to water, and to the foolish eyes of those who look upon me I seem to be a very red rose with the sexual tint of an April peony, which is not my heart's truth.... I see before me many problems, many entrapping eyes [*Selected Letters* 2; 1095].

Lorca names Verlaine in two passages from the first book he publishes, *Impressions and Landscapes* (883, 930). He also mentions him in his lecture on Góngora (1053) and in the poem "The Prayer of the Roses" (La oración de las rosas 724) and gives Verlaine's name to one of the poems from *Songs*. What can explain such an early and prolonged interest? What united both poets? The connections that existed had to be based only on the experience and knowledge Lorca had of the French poet since Verlaine died in 1896, two years before Lorca's birth.

In examining the passage in the letter, quoted above, Lorca defines himself as "impassioned and silent"; these adjectives have a direct connection to the central motif of the poem "Verlaine," which is a song that does not speak "filled with lips" (453, 321). This abundance of lips contrasts with the guarded silence and suggests, at the same time, the existence of a hidden passion.

Lorca gives the impression of knowing Verlaine well ("marvelous Verlaine") although the French poet was not read or appreciated very much. Manuel Machado published an anthology of translations of Verlaine in 1908, but the "complete" works of this poet did not begin to be published in Spain until 1921, three years after Lorca wrote his letter. In any case, however much or little Lorca knew about Verlaine as a person makes Lorca feel he has reached such a good understanding of Verlaine as to be able to state what the dead poet felt inside, something that "very nearly" coincides with what he himself feels within, something that is "impossible" to nourish. Lorca sees himself obliged to pretend a sexual shading that he does not feel ("which is not my heart's truth") because of social constrictions ("many entrapping eyes").

What the young Lorca knew or believed to know about the French poet surely would be based on observation and the study of the small amount published about him in Spain. More or less true information would also reach him by means of public opinion and through what was written about Verlaine at the end of the nineteenth century and beginning of the twentieth.

◆ ◆ ◆

In *Verlaine y los modernistas españoles*, R. Ferreres states that for Juan Valera "Verlaine's poetry seemed extravagant and unworthy of being read," and that in general, "Verlaine's poetry had less effect and was less admired among the Spanish poets who were his contemporaries. More than once it was indignation, as in the case of don Gaspar Núñez de Arce" (51, 55). It is fairly probable that Lorca knew of Núñez's indignation. If Verlaine interested Lorca, he, Lorca, would be interested in the opinion others had of Verlaine. Whatever the situation, Núñez de Arce does not appear to be Lorca's favorite person. Lorca calls him "insipid" in his lecture on Góngora (1031).

Towards the end of the nineteenth century, Rubén Darío asserts that Verlaine "in Spain is almost unknown and will be so for a long time" (*Los raros* 54). But why was Verlaine ignored? And what was the reason behind the indignation he provoked among those who read him? It is hard to know, but something might be deduced by analyzing what was maintained or insinuated about him. Darío's words are particularly interesting given his influence on Lorca (see "The Myths," in chapter 4), and also because Lorca joins Darío's name to Verlaine's in "The Prayer of the Roses" (724). We refer in particular to what Darío wrote in *Los raros*, a work that Lorca was familiar with, according to his brother's testimony (Gibson, *Federico García Lorca* 1:210, 637). The prologue is from 1905, but the essays were written previously. The one titled "Paul Verlaine" appears to have been edited soon after the French poet's death. In the first lines, Darío mentions "the malignant influence of Saturn" in Verlaine's life. E. Carrere, who translated Verlaine's *Poemas saturnianos*, also alludes to Saturn's influence in his poem "The Abyss" (Las simas).

What do Verlaine and his contemporaries associate with Saturn? Saturn is mentioned in "Poème saturnien." After this poem, "The Unrepentant" (L'impénitent) and "On a Statue of Ganymede" (Sur une statue de Ganymède) appear. The homosexual references are obvious, above all, in the last two. "Sodome et Gomorrhe" are mentioned in the last line of the poem that precedes "Saturnian," "The Last Elegant Feast" (La dernière fête galante) (*Obra poética* 270–81).[4]

The figure of Saturn brings together different myths associated with homosexuality: Saturn-son castrates Uranus. The castrated sky-Uranus is, nevertheless, ambiguously creative (see chapter 4, "Lorca's Billy Goat"). Saturn-father devours his deformed children, according to the well-known painting by Goya in the Prado museum (López Sancho 5). Verlaine was presented as deformed. In a certain sense, he was "spent" or "devoured" by the prevailing morality. In *My Imprisonment and Other Autobiographical Writings* (Mes prisons et autres écrits autobiographiques), Verlaine himself speaks of the humilliations and persecutions he suffered, at times alone, other times together with Rimbaud (231–86).

In "Prologue from a Book from Which Only the Abstracts Will Appear" (Prólogo de un libro del que no aparecerán más que los extractos) Verlaine's poetic "I" shows itself to be conscious that the reproaches for having "lost" his life will fall on him. He does not communicate to his readers what is the true bad "secret" of the heart from which he suffers. Suffice it to say that the author is a prisoner when he writes: "These sickly verses / were done in prison, in a word." It is made explicit that the poetic "I" was born a Saturnian: "I was truly born a Saturnian" (*Oeuvres poétiques* 497, 498).

According to Rivers, who bases himself on several examples taken from Proust, in those times "Saturnian" was a "code word for 'homosexual'" (72, 73, 323).

♦ ♦ ♦

> Panidas, yes Panidas;
> tragic Rubén
> in your poetry thus you called
> the languid Verlaine [Lorca, "Prayer of the Roses" 724].

"Panida," according to the dictionary *Pequeño Larousse*, is a "descendant of Pan" (762); "a follower of Pan," states Ricardo Gullón in his notes to Darío's *Selected Pages* (Páginas escogidas 81). One does not take away the other. Verlaine has this in common with Lorca's billy goat: his connection to "father Pan" (149). Darío calls Verlaine "Panida" (not "Panidas") in his "Responso a Verlaine," which is probably the Lorquian source of the noun qualifier changed into a proper noun: "Panida! You yourself Pan, what choirs you conducted...!" (81).

The poem ends with the wish for a cross to rise up and cover the horizon, "a brightness over the cross!" In the notes to this edition, Gullón states that it is understood that it is "a Christian rather than pagan cross," but arguments are not contributed which sustain the assertion, nor is it explained why the "Christian" cross has to be illuminated by a brightness rising on top of it. A.J. Carlos does not explain it either in the article he devotes to this cross, although he recognizes that its appearance in the last lines of the poem, in his opinion, "disturbs the unity of the entire poetic conception." He then asks himself: "After crowning the Greek god, is paganism forgiven and the protection of Christianity invoked?" (226).

Darío did indeed know what Verlaine's "religion" was, as he shows in mentioning his officiants or ministers: "One of my greatest wishes was to be able to speak to Verlaine. On a certain night in the D'Harcourt café, we found the Faun surrounded by equivocal acolytes" (*Selected Pages* 254).

Verlaine used the symbols of the Christian religion to express clearly homosexual activity. If this is taken into account, the connotations of the language that Verlaine uses to communicate with Rimbaud seem obvious, for example, when he asks: "When the devil do we begin the stations of the Cross — eh?"[5] (D'Eaubonne 103).

Associating Christianity with homosexuality is not something unique to Verlaine. Bush has shown that the Renaissance imagination merges the classical with the biblical. Pan adopts, among others, the form of Christ and the latter even appears as Ganymede, Zeus' lover (Bush 105, 168–69). Similar transformations are also observed in the work of Saint John of the Cross, as Nieto indicates, according to Gurméndez' review: "the Lover appears as a biblical Jesus, then is transformed into a Hellenic Orpheus, reappears as Dionysus and, lastly, changes into a Native-American." Dionysus, Bacchus' other name, is transformed into a billy goat, according to Lorca. For the homosexual connotation of the Lorquian Christ, see Semprún, "Cristo en Lorca" (23–24).

Darío refers to Pan or to the billy goat in alluding to Verlaine in *Los raros*: "One is surprised not to see two little horns above his forehead." What is not omitted here is the association with the Fall, or the reference to the sin-crime which is not stated but suggested through the adjective derived from "Olympus," the mansion of Zeus who abducted Ganymede: "fallen god, punished perhaps because of Olympian crimes" (50, 52). As we know, Lorca oversaw the edition of *Los raros* published in 1908 (Gibson, *Federico García Lorca* 1:210, 637). A manuscript in the Lorca family archives is related to a "religion" that evidently united Verlaine and Lorca: "In 'The Religion of the

Future' (January 16, 1918), the poet ... praises the 'heavenly religion' of 'warm Greece,' today a religion 'covered by fog' but whose resurgence is awaited" (*Federico García Lorca* 1:214).

◆ ◆ ◆

In *Los raros*, Darío twice names the Socratic nature of Verlaine, relating it to the "religion" of implicit homosexuality: "Surely, you have died surrounded by yours, by the sons of your spirit, by the young officiants of your church, by the students of your school, oh lyrical Socrates of an impossible time! ... a face with something of the Socratic" (49, 50).

Lorca associates Socrates with Jesus Christ in *Shadows* (Sombras), a work which, according to Eutimio Martín, "could well be considered as García Lorca's first dramatic text" ("*Sombras*" 51). Martín publishes some scenes and asks himself: "What kind of relationship might be established between the figure of the Greek philosopher and that of Jesus Christ...?" (53). In the previous section, the beginning of an answer to this question appeared. Martín is not very concise regarding what unites Socrates with Christ, but he recognizes "where Lorca's preferences are going" and states that, in regard to Lysis, Lorca, like Socrates, was "sensitive to the personal attractiveness of this adolescent" (54, 55).

Lorca associates the *duende* with Socrates and with Rimbaud: "The *duende* of which I speak, dark and shuddering, is a descendant of Socrates' very happy devil ... Rimbaud's delicate body dressed with a green suit of an acrobat" (1098, 1100).

The relationship between Verlaine and Rimbaud evokes Socrates and the pederasty of ancient Greece, among other things, because of the age difference between the "teacher" and the "student," although in this case the roles were interchangeable. In the last decades, it has been recognized that a major part of Rimbaud's works deals with homosexuality, and above all, his relationship with Verlaine. D'Eaubonne states in regard to *Hellish Night and Drunken Morning* (Nuit de l'Enfer y Matinée d'Ivresse): "It deals there with a precise account of the discovery of homosexuality in the company of Verlaine" (240).

It has been suggested that Plato was a disciple and lover of Socrates (Riess 19). Symonds called Socrates the Jesus Christ of Greece, and Clory states that while he was approaching death, Socrates freed himself of fear by thinking about Achilles (Jenkyns 229, 230).

◆ ◆ ◆

In "Prayer of the Roses," Verlaine appears as a "rose bloody / and yellow at the same time" (724). In "Double Poem of Lake Eden" it is Lorca's own poetic persona who appears as a rose:

> I want to cry saying my name,
> rose, child, and fir on the shore of this lake,
> to speak truly as a man of blood
> killing in myself the mockery and the suggestive power
> of the word [*PNY* 83; 490].

The speaker wants to say a word that identifies him, but it is clear that he does not dare to say it. "Rose," "child" and "fir" are not words which result in and of themselves in any kind of mockery. Nevertheless, let us apostrophize "rose!" to a male, to a "man of blood," and the word is transformed into mockery. The mockery is a reproach against the man who has something feminine within him. It suggests that this man-rose is a homosexual.

"Child" connotes a person who lives in a state of sexual neutrality that characterizes childhood, when feeling attracted to someone of the same sex as oneself is something normal and common. According to Freud, one can say that the child is *polymorphically perverse* (*Psychoanalysis* 186). This etiquette, like so many others, is inspired by the idea that in order to be "normal," one must be heterosexual and practice, first and foremost, coitus.

"Facing the sea I forget my sex," states Lorca in a letter. "I want to be a child, a child!" exclaims a character in *Once Five Years Pass*, a boy who does not see the difference between a male and a female cat (380, 384). In "Double Poem of Lake Eden," the connotation of "perverse" ambiguity of a *child* is sustained by the associative network of the third term that describes the poetic "I": "fir." In the poem "Idilio," this tree is placed in connection with what is secret, and with the possibility of many different byways:

> When it comes to secrets, I
> am exactly like the fir.
> A tree whose thousand little fingers
> point to a thousand byways [*CP* 497; 373].

This abundance of byways is contrary to God's designs. The fir indicates something contrary to what He orders "...Jehovah, that despot / who sends you packing / down the same old path" ("Song for the Moon" *CP* 73; 57).

God gave man a woman as a companion, and the Christian man's road goes towards the woman. But for Lorca's poetic "I" in "Little Infinite Poem" (Pequeño poema infinito), the road that leads to the woman is the wrong road: "To take the wrong road / is to arrive at woman" (*CP* 647; 547). The meaning of the road has been inverted.

◆ ◆ ◆

What the Lorquian rose evokes goes beyond what the poems connote that concern the figures of Verlaine and the Lorquian poetic voice. Its symbolism reaches the poet himself, intertwining the threads of his poetry with those of his life. According to what emerges from Claude Couffon's statement, the people of Granada interpreted the presence of a rose worn by Lorca as something shameful for a man: "His 'negligence' as an artist: black pants and a shirt of white silk on which he sported an enormous red rose, charming, but inappropriate — 'indecent' — I heard some say — [it] had provoked a scandal in Granada" (82).

The Fourth Laundress in *Yerma* suggests an association of ideas between roses and a man's sex: "In this world just a glance can be something. My mother always said that. A woman looking at roses isn't the same thing as a woman looking at a man's thighs" (act 2, scene 1, 122; 697).[6] The aesthetic relationship between roses and men's sexual organs is indicated with greater clarity in section V of "Themes," from *Impressions and Landscapes*, in evoking the friezes of a palace: "In these processions, muscled men go along naked, clutching rose garlands which cover their sex" (939). In "Ode to Walt Whitman," the association of ideas is transformed into an explicit connection between rose and phallus: "and the Jews sold to the river faun / the rose of circumcision" (*PNY* 155; 528). In the lines quoted above from *Impressions and Landscapes*, after alluding to men's sexual organs, Lorca mentions the "open mouths" of the women of the friezes, thus suggesting what these mouths that open "lustfully" might desire. To kiss roses is something so shameful that the poetic "I" of "The Prayer of the Roses" feels forced to hide and says, addressing the roses: "Sob for my hidden kisses / that my mouth gave to you" (727). In reality, it is not really a matter of roses but, rather, flesh, a flesh where fire burns: the roses are "carnal censers" (727). In "Little Stanton," they are associated with sulfur and with dreaded dawn (see chapter 4, "The Billy Goat"): "ten roses of powerless sulfur / on the shoulder of my dawn" (*PNY* 95; 496).

Catherine Nickel states that one of the principal themes of *Doña Rosita, the Spinster* is the fight between fertility and sterility (522). In contrast to the fruit trees, the rose, in addition to symbolizing sex, evokes the short but intense life of a beauty that does not bear fruit. Perhaps this is the reason why homosexuals frequently identify with it.[7] Gil-Albert cannot forget the afternoon in which he heard Lorca read his *Doña Rosita* by "playing her": "To my mind came Flaubert's expression: *Madame Bovary c'est moi*" (*OC en prosa* 2:249).

Songs contains a section called "Three Portraits with Shading" (Tres retratos con sombra) that consists of six poems. "Verlaine" and "Bacchus" (Baco) form the first portrait; "Juan Ramón Jiménez" and "Venus" form the second, and "Debussy" and "Narcissus" (Narciso) the third. The section begins and ends in a similar way, like a circle of silence: "I'll never speak" in the second line of "Verlaine" and "I shan't explain" in the last line of "Narcissus." Of great interest are "Verlaine" and "Bacchus," that is, the portrait of the

French poet and the shadow of the portrait. Nevertheless, first an examination of some details related to the motif of the rose, which has preceded this analysis, and that of silence, the central motif of "Verlaine," is appropriate.

In the myth, Narcissus falls in love with his own image reflected in the water and languishes from love because of not being able to embrace it. The myth has some implicit homosexual elements. Narcissus does not associate the image he sees with himself, but with something or someone external to him. Lorca introduces variations. Narcissus does not see his image, but he sees a rose. He informs us that he is inside the rose and he throws himself or falls into the water. The poem ends: "When he vanished into the water, I understood. / But I shan't explain" (*CP* 459; 326).

It is clear that something is hidden from the reader, something that needs an explanation that the poetic "I" who understands refuses to provide. Lorca reveals and subtracts at the same time and provokes his readers to look for what has been hidden in the text. He does the same thing in "Verlaine."

"Verlaine" and the Dream

> The song
> I'll never speak,
> on the tip of my tongue fell asleep.
> The song I'll never speak.
>
> On the honeysuckle
> a firefly blinked
> and the moon was pricking
> the water with a beam.
>
> It was then I dreamed
> the song
> I'll never speak.
> Song filled with lips,
> flowing from far away.
>
> Song filled with hours
> while away in the shade.
> song of stars alive
> In perpetual daytime skies [*CP* 453].

The poetic "I" of "Narcissus" will not explain what happened and that of "Verlaine" will never speak its song. In order to be explicit, "Three Portraits with Shading" opens and closes with a negative.

According to Cobb, Lorca had the feeling that Verlaine as well as he himself wanted to speak about sexual themes which society had prohibited (55). For Debicki, "Verlaine" deals with an "ideal and inexpressable" song.

The author perhaps does not pay the necessary attention to the nuances connoted by the verb tense. "I won't speak" does not necessarily imply that that which one won't speak is ideal and inexpressable. Andueza believes for his part that the refrain expresses "the unshakable decision of a firm will to be silent," with which we agree. Nevertheless, it is doubtful that the basic theme of the poem is "Verlaine's poetic art, the expression of the how of the lyrical creation of the French poet," as Andueza states (27). Rather, the principal motif of "Verlaine" is silence. The silenced song is mentioned six times in such a short space.

A speaker who talks incessantly about something that he refuses to say demonstrates an extremely ambiguous attitude towards what he silences. Rollo May, a psychoanalyst and writer, mentions the existence of two types of intentions: the voluntary and the unconscious. Both types would be based on intentionality or the cooperation of the will with unconscious impulses (233–35). The Lorquian poetic "I" states the intention of maintaining silence, but Lorca makes him speak in an indirect way. The poet writes inspired by unconscious impulses and creates the poem with the help of his conscious will. What the poetic "I" says/silences is the result of Lorca's intentionality.

Lorca and his poetic persona grant human traits to the song by writing/saying that it "fell asleep." Lorca's poetic "I" speaks through a voice that sleeps, that is, which has evaded the control of will. As a prelude or background to "Verlaine's" song, it states that "the moon was pricking / the water with a beam." The relationship of the moon and water to the unconscious and sexuality is something familiar. In a letter to Melchor Fernández Almagro, Lorca says "(Oh what a water obsession I suffer!)" having said previously: "You have no idea how much I suffer when I see myself portrayed in these poems" (*Selected Letters* 35, 36; 1125, 1126). The oneiric connotation of the moon and the water is reinforced in the poem by the downward movement of the moonbeam. According to psychoanalytic terminology of evolutionist origins, descent is a regression, a submersion into the shadows of instinct and a sexuality preceding one that is considered to be of a more mature nature, that is, heterosexual-genital (Freud, *Psychoanalysis* 177–89) (see chapter 6, note 8).

It is night, and the only lights from the poem are nocturnal, that of the moonbeam and the firefly. The phosphorescent light of this insect is of a green-white color as if announcing the arrival of Bacchus, the proximity of the "green sound" of the fig tree and the whiteness of the milk of the figs. Lorca refers to the abdominal part of the firefly, since the light that these insects spread emerges from there. The lunar light (which descends) as well as the light from the firefly orient themselves *downwards* and contrast with the type of light that Lorca mentions in his "Ode to Dalí," which "stays on the brow / not descending to the mouth or the heart of the man" (*CP* 591).

The vines of Bacchus "fear" that light which remains above, on the brow, the light that does not go beyond intellectual comprehension. The firefly is on the honeysuckle. In "Granada," from *Impressions and Landscapes,* Lorca connects this plant to wine and the billy goat (915).

The last lines of "Verlaine" form an incremental parallelism. Some traits emerge from the song, which was not to be spoken, and results in the revealing negative shadow of Verlaine's portrait. Rafael Bosch has mentioned several examples of these parallelisms in Lorca's work.

The song evokes "lips," love and words, lost in time and distance ("flowing far away"), vestiges of a culture immersed in "the shade," all that is hidden from us, our collective unconscious. After the song that will not be spoken, there are "stars alive" in the luminosity of "perpetual daytime skies," expressing a longing for a mythical Golden Age of homosexual love.[8] Or, as Cernuda expresses it in "El poeta y los mitos," "nostalgia for a spiritual and corporeal harmony broken and banished centuries ago among people (*Ocnos* 17).

In spite of being a portrait, "Verlaine" is characterized, in the first place, by the vagueness of the words and expressions that portray, or ought to portray, Verlaine. More than a portrait, it seems *the negative* of a portrait or photograph, in the double sense of the word: a negative that one must develop and a negative that denies or is denied: "I'll never speak," "I'll never speak," "I'll never speak." Paradoxically, the light comes from "Bacchus," that "shadow" of "Verlaine" towards which the poet wisely directs us. That is where the richer and more concrete symbols proliferate, such tasty fruits from the fig tree that symbolizes the god.

Lorca speaks of Bacchus in his "Ode to Dalí." In *Honey Is Sweeter Than Blood,* Santos Torroella includes a section titled "Federico's Dream and Shadow" (in the work of Dalí). Fourteen paintings are analyzed in which Lorca's figure appears more or less clearly. In chapter IX of his *Secret Life* Dalí states that Lorca "came and darkened the virginal originality of my spirit and of my flesh" (203).

"Bacchus." Shadow of "Verlaine."

Green sound intact.
the fig tree's arms open to me.

Its shadow, like a panther,
stalks my lyrical shadow.

The moon is counting dogs.
She slips and starts over.

> Yesterday, tomorrow, black and green,
> you haunt my laurel wreath.
> No one would love you like me
> if you'd only change my heart!
> ...And the fig tree shouts and comes at me
> in frightful proliferation [*CP* 453, 455].

◆ ◆ ◆

According to Camilo José Cela, "the whole world knows that the fig tree's shadow is propitious for sinning in peace." The author makes this commentary because Lázaro Codesal, one of the characters from *Mazurka for Two Dead Men* (Mazurca para dos muertos), was killed by a Moor "while he was jerking off under a fig tree" (9). In "Sale of Figs," Miguel Hernández mentions most of the lustful, sexual and sensual aspects of the fig tree and figs:

> The sun, without facing the branches, doesn't form a conspiracy with the wasps in places where sin hovers.... The delicious bowel movements from the fruity assholes, slow liqueurs, hold onto me as if pulled off the fingers in getting the fruit.... Figs ... long like female clappers, violated black Gothics... What an odor of lechery! [*The Bravest Bullfighter* (El torero más valiente) 193–94].

The fig tree is also mentioned in a letter that Hernández writes to Lorca on April 10, 1933, which has been published by Cano Ballesta. Although it may be after Lorca's poem, and although, from what we know, the two men did not have sexual relations with each other, it is interesting that Hernández talks about the "flesh" of his body ("my accordion flesh similar to a beheaded palm tree"). The poet tells Lorca that he is writing to him under a fig tree (*Bullfighter* 213).

Lorca indicates in his lecture on Góngora that Bacchus, after being a vine, was transformed into a fig tree "Out of love for his dancer Cyssus." The background or origin of the poem-shadow of "Verlaine" is a homosexual love.

In the mythology of ancient Rome, the fig tree was a sacred tree that was associated with Bacchus' virility. The statues of the phallic god Priapus were made of wood from the fig tree, and Dionysus himself had to allow himself be sodomized by a wood phallus from a fig tree before being able to go down to hell to rescue his mother Semele (Duché 108). The fig tree was called *ficus ruminalis*, associating it ambiguously with Jupiter-Ruminus and with Rumina, goddess of breasts (*Encyclopedia of World Mythology* 237).

In the Bible the fig tree is seen very differently. When Jesus leaves Bethany to go to Jerusalem, he is hungry and goes towards a fig tree. But the fig tree does not have any fruit; Jesus puts a curse on it and the fig tree and its roots dry up (St. Mark). Jesus takes the absence of fruit as a personal offense on the part of the fig tree, and the punishment he inflicts on it causes one to believe that for Jesus, not to bear fruit is an unpardonable sin. In an indirect but effective way, we are given an example of what can happen to someone who does not bear fruit when God comes to ask for accounts.

Frye has studied the Bible from the point of view of a literary critic who believes that "the Bible tells a story" and "the Bible is a myth" which are, in their essence, the same assertion, and that is necessary to clarify the social function of the Bible[9] (xi and 32–33). Frye has not analyzed the history of the barren fig tree, but it is obvious that, in this context, the social function of the Bible is to incite towards a procreative sexuality, by means of the veiled threat.

The fruits of the fig tree, when it has them, can have an offensive sexual symbolism. "Making" or "giving the fig" to someone is making a gesture with "the phallic hand," a finger representing the "membrum virile" and the others, folded, the testicles. The sign was made in ancient Greece to indicate one who was given to "unnatural vices" (Knight 126–29). Eric Partridge has pointed out the sexual allusion of the command "fig me, like The bragging Spaniard" uttered by Pistol in *King Henry the IV*, part 2, act 5, 3 (Partridge 112; Shakespeare, *Complete Works* 441). In Sweden, *ficus* is a synonym for homosexual.

Dalí did a painting with the appearance of Lorca's face on the beach in the form of a fruit basket with three figs (Romero 202). Apparently irrational, like so many of Dalí's paintings, the thematic content of it perhaps has more logic than it seems. One sees in it that the sea, "Lucifer of the blue" as Lorca would say (128), and an element of Dionysus-Bacchus, transformed into a fig tree, enters the poet's brain, a fruit basket that offers its fruits like a fig tree offering its figs. The figs of Lorca's brain are of an ambiguous sexuality. This fruit symbolizes the masculine and feminine sex (Cela, *Diccionario secreto* 313); the number three seems to indicate, nevertheless, a phallic predominance. According to Freud, three symbolizes the masculine genitals (*Psychoanalysis* 137, 146).

In "The Dispute" (Reyerta) from *The Gypsy Ballads*, the fig trees' madness causes the afternoon to fall over masculine thighs that ride:

> The afternoon, gone mad
> with figs and heated sounds,
> swoons and falls upon
> the riders' wounded thighs [*CP* 527; 399].

In comments on his own poem, Lorca had previously indicated that "every drama or dance is sustained by an intelligent needle of mockery or irony" (1116). He speaks to us afterwards of a fight: "In the ballad of young men *The Dispute* that sordid fight is expressed ... of groups which attack each other without knowing why, for mysterious causes, for a look, for a rose ... for a love from two centuries ago" (1117).

• • •

The fig tree does not have a voice but speaks through its sounds or murmurs. What the murmur communicates is prior to clear words, and belongs to another area, linked to intuition and premonition. The murmur of the poem has two addressees. It is directed towards the poetic "I," but also, indirectly, towards the reader. Murmurs have a bad reputation among those who can speak clearly, but because of their nature, the murmur cannot be said in a loud voice, although everyone may know what it is about.

In choosing the word "sound" (murmur) Lorca gives importance to what is not explicit. The adjective "intact" applied to the sound expresses that what is suggested has a potentiality that the established culture has not been able to destroy, nor order, nor sublimate, nor alienate. In *The Bacchants* by Euripides, Dionysus-Bacchus speaks in a different way from the dominant culture represented by Pentheus, who accuses him of not saying anything, while trying, at the same time, to silence this "nothing" that Dionysus says, according to Charles Segal in his detailed analysis of this work (281, 285–86). Pentheus, says Segal, is at times an example of savagery disguised as civility and discipline (36).

"Murmur" can have a profound meaning, the same as Dionysus' "nonsense." This is perhaps precisely what changes the murmur into something dangerous. Lorca's poetic "I" is afraid of mumurs; Lorca converts the murmur into a semiotic sign. The fig tree speaks of homosexuality as a whispering produced by the wind. "Bacchus" is a shadow, and the shadows dissolve when illuminated. The lovers of diaphanous clarity or those who fear the existence of shadows may say there are no conclusive proofs they exist. But what is repressed does not dissolve. The more darkness is repressed, the more it grows in the subconscious. At the end of "Bacchus," the fig tree has multiplied, but not in the sense desired by the Bible.

From his prison cell Oscar Wilde contemplates this era that "we call utilitarian" and states in "De Profundis": "our Art is of the Moon and plays with shadows, while Greek art is of the Sun and deals directly with things" (*Complete Works* 954).

• • •

The panther is associated with Bacchus in various ways: it was consecrated to Dionysus and likes the odor of wine (Detienne, *The Gardens of Adonis* 76). Like the fig tree, the panther emits a strong odor that serves to attract its victims. Like the dogs that are mentioned in the poem, the panther was used for the hunt, an activity reserved for men. The presents that were exchanged between lovers were often products of the hunt (Detienne, *Dionysos*

76). According to Jan Bremmer, it is important to point out that for a young man not to have a lover was a disgrace. To be hunted and captured by a lover was not only desirable, it was "a must" (286). In order to continue the ritual, one had to flee despite wanting to be hunted.

Lord Queensberry makes note of what Oscar Wilde stated in *De Profundis*, that by criminalizing homosexuality even in private life, the danger constituted half of the attraction. Having homosexual relationships became similar to celebrating "with panthers" (Queensberry 192).

Like the fig tree, Bacchus-Dionysus extends its arms-branches towards the poetic "I." Like a panther lying in wait, the shadow or what is hidden from Verlaine and his dream lies in wait for the "lyrical shadow" of the Lorquian character who fears being devoured by what is hidden-repressed, while at the same time feeling its attraction. In a letter to Melchor Fernández Almagro, Lorca states that his passions hound him "like a group of panthers" (1112). The internal passion is seen as something external. The "I" splits in two and projects its fear and desire onto the figure of Bacchus-fig tree-panther.

♦ ♦ ♦

In *Sociología contra psicoanálisis*, Mauron states that "Dreams exist in the spirit of the dreamer, and are later translated into verbal language.... They are the product not only of desire, but of desire and censorship that reality represents" (217–18).

The Generation of '27 was born and grew up in a culture that was an enemy of homosexuality. To discover this love within oneself is a traumatic experience when your whole life is spent learning that homosexuality is something dirty and detestable. The internal mechanisms of defense cause many to deny their feelings. What is desired is repressed and takes refuge in the subconscious. Nevertheless, we have the sensation that something or someone pursues us. The feeling of being persecuted or hating oneself is insufferable if it becomes too strong. The logical consequence is that this feeling is projected onto others and we think that someone hates and persecutes us. This can be the beginning of paranoia; Anna Freud has described in detail the paranoiac process in *Das Ich und die Abwehrmechanismen*.

Paranoia has two faces: the patient denies his internal persecution in saying that he finds himself in danger because someone persecutes him; society (parents, relatives, friends, doctors and various authorities) denies a persecution that is exercised within the (social) body itself. The expiatory victim is thus transformed into an object of treatment. R.D. Laing has dealt with this interaction in several books; particularly relevant is *Self and Others* (18, 24, 111, 127–28, etc.).

The poetic "I" of "Bacchus" does not want or cannot recognize that he feels attracted by what the fig tree represents. By saying that the fig tree has arms that open towards him, the protagonist is freed from the "guilt" of feeling attracted. The attraction is, at the same time, a persecution because the fig tree–panther is lying in wait, awaiting the moment to attack, when the defense mechanism of the "I" weakens. The "I" will then be hunted, and perhaps be broken up by what attracts him, that is, by what he feels internally, or as Lorca said in the quoted letter, by the "passions" which "hound" him. Contrary to the poetic "I," the biographical "I" knows that the panthers are a symbol of their own repressed passions.

Lorca was very familiar with the psychological phenomenon of projection, as shown in "Nocturno de marzo," a poem published by Eutimio Martín. The poet refers here principally to the "scapegoat" aspect of projection (see chapter 4, "Sociopsychological Function of the Scapegoats"). But homosexuality is also suggested through the reference to a "love impossible / to satisfy," that this "legendary ephebe" represented by the Devil has imbued into the "clay" of which we are made. Like the fig tree, the Devil-ephebe is presented before the poetic "I" "stretching his arms out" (the fig tree's "arms open"):

"Don't be afraid!"— he tells me —
...
The demons who dream
your brothers,
are they themselves their
own projections [*Federico García Lorca* 257, 258].

♦ ♦ ♦

Marie Delcourt relates that an Aphrodite who is identical to the moon is mentioned in *Saturnales*, and that the Aphrodite-moon is an androgynous or bisexual being (*Hermaphrodite* 43–44). According to P. Chalus, there was a moon-god named Wadd, a word that seems to mean "love" (250). In Plato's "Symposium," the author states: "man was originally the child of the sun, the woman of the earth, and the man-woman of the moon" (*Five Dialogues* 179).

Correa has indicated that Lorca grants the symbol of the moon "a semantic multivalence linked to its astral movements and to a complex cultural tradition" ("El simbolismo de la luna" 1075). This "multivalence" does not appear with much clarity. More than explaining, Correa divides, polarizes and classifies. He does not clarify why he considers some symbols negative and others positive. With respect to what do they have these values?: "*Asbestos* and *marble* also reveal a negative condition of the moon and are found associated with other negative symbols.... The lack of affirmative influence of the moon... The moon ... reveals itself in totally negative outlines ... a parade of negative signs..." (1068–71). (See also 1072, 1076, 1084.)

Saussure states that "in language there are only differences without positive terms. One considers the signifier or the signified; language does not imply either ideas or sounds which precede the linguistic system, but only conceptual differences and phonic differences ... *language is a form and not a substance*" (147, 149). Millet and Varin corroborate: "A language is a system of relationships and not a collection of terms; there are no positive terms which have value in and of themselves.... Ferdinand de Saussure already saw this" (11).

Alvarez de Miranda asks himself if stylistics, "too confident of the analysis of mere verbal and grammatical supports," does not create an abusive simplification on many occasions. Lorquian poetic objects and expressions "can reveal an intimate coherence, which comes forth from order; certainly not from logical and rational order, but from this 'other' order which presides over mythical intuitions, typical of the primitive and the poet" (59, 60). This "other" order which Alvarez names could be related to the otherness studied here in the middle sections of chapter 2 (from "The Accursed 'Breed'" through "'Everyone' and the Other"), and could be an order that at times is qualified as "homosexual." The "other" order appears very much in connection with the moon in the poem "Adán": "But a dark other Adam is dreaming / a neuter moon of seedless stone / where the child of light will burn" (*CP* 731; 264).

The Adam who dreams of "a child" nearby and the Adam who dreams of an absence of seed seem to symbolize two norms or two distinct orders: the heterosexual versus the homosexual. Thus has Mario Socrate understood it at least in his detailed study of "Adán," where he states that the Lorquian moon frequently represents "the infertile homosexual eros" (58). In "Sleep, Boy" (Duerme, muchacho), Cernuda evokes the symbol of the moon in an unmistakable way: "lust like moons" (*PC* 106).

Josette Blanquat states in her analysis of "Ballad of the Moon, Moon" that the abduction or ascent to the sky of the child, carried out by the moon, recalls the ascent to the sky of Ganymede, which only initiates recognize in looking at the vault of the Pythagorean Basilica of Rome's Porta Maggiore. Seen in this way, the ascent is a homosexual abduction (386). This abduction would then be related to the motif of the feared and desired hunt that we discussed in analyzing the symbol of the panther. Recall that the moon is named Diana, the huntress. Like the fig tree–shadow–panther, the moon represents something attractive and dangerous that seems to find itself as much outside as inside of people. Alvarez de Miranda recalls the words of Mircea Eliade: "in a certain sense man looks at himself and finds himself again in the life of the moon. Therefore, lunar symbolism and mythology are pathetic, but consoling" (47).

As Detienne indicates, felines of the "*panther*" type were used for hunting (91). For the moon, Artemis or Diana, the counting of their dogs does not turn out well. It can be because some of them are not as such, or rather that sometimes they appear as a dog, other times as a panther and other times as a fig tree. This dog–not dog could be the poetic "I" itself, with paranoic symptoms entering and leaving the different "I's." Chapter 4 discussed some of the different connotations of "dogs" and the contrary feelings associated with this word. As "dogs," homosexuals hunt "meat" and are, themselves, "bait." But "dogs" and "bait" are such because the spirituality of their carnal love has been denied and snatched from them. Persecuted and despised like dogs, they internalize persecution and persecute themselves. The poetic voice in "Bacchus" represses his homosexuality. He wants "the beast" to keep its distance but the fig tree "comes."

The connection between dogs and homosexuality appears clearly in the work of the Count of Lautréamont, whose influence on Lorca has been indicated by Higginbotham. In *Les chants de Maldoror*, the young Mervyn arranges to meet the stranger with whom he is madly in love. Upon arriving at the appointment, the adolescent is put in a sack and beaten. He groans in such a way that people think he is a mangy dog. They are going to kill him with blows, but they stop because what they believe to be the howls of a dog recall the shouts of pain of a child (Lautréamont 760).

In his first book, Lorca associates barking with crying and lamentations. He states that they have a "biblical accent" and "Dantesque chords" (877). Dante and the condemned of *The Divine Comedy* are, therefore, relevant to the understanding of the symbol of the dogs. The souls with whom Dante speaks in canto XVI are "illustrious fellow citizens" who were homosexuals. In *Impressions and Landscapes,* Lorca states that the "barks and lamentations" of the dogs are the "Crying of great souls ... apocalyptic shouts of the tortured" (877). Like homosexuals, dogs seem possessed by the devil: "there is a lot of fear, a lot of fear in the dog when it howls, ... it half closes its eyes with an expression of satanic spell" (878).

Lorca also associates dogs with something that is lying in wait (like the panther). Through the technique of complementary specifying parallelism in "Qasida of the Branches" (Casida de los ramos), the dogs become "children" who threaten, wait for or long for the "branches" of the poetic "I" (*the* becomes *my* in the last stanza):

> Through the groves at Tamarit
> the leaden dogs have come,
> to wait for the branches to fall,
> for the branches to break by themselves.
>
> ...
>
> Through the groves at Tamarit
> are many children with faces veiled

to wait for my branches to fall
for my branches to break by themselves [*CP* 671, 672; 591].

Nevertheless, in "Sonnet of the Sweet Complaint" (Soneto de la dulce queja), the poetic "I" presents itself like a dog or slave to love (see the beginning of chapter 4). The moon is mistaken because, under such circumstances, it is easy to be mistaken.

◆ ◆ ◆

In "Bacchus," the words "yesterday" and "black" evoke Antiquity, the ancient Greece of "The Billy Goat." Black is also the color of the panther, like the subconscious and the shadows in which the dominant culture has submerged homosexual love and its history. "Tomorrow" is "green" like hope, and like that terrible fig tree that opens its arms towards the poetic "I," offering him the green-lust of its dangerous love. Between that yesterday and that tomorrow are the today of laurels and the triumphs of the poetic "I" in society. Yesterday and tomorrow unite against that today ("haunt" is in the singular). The poetic "I" feels threatened and attracted at the same time. The verb haunt ("rondar" in Spanish), implies romantic courtship as well as the potential of danger. The laurel wreath is a protection and also a prison.

According to the *Dictionary of Symbols*, the crowning of the poet, the artist or the conqueror with laurel leaves "presupposes a series of inner victories over the negative and dissipative influence of the base forces" (173). The inner, the negative and the inferior are very close in the culture reflected in these words, which already has taken the side of Apollo against Dionysus. But the laurel does not crown the Lorquian poetic "I": it is rather a wreath around him. The "negative and dissipative influences" have not been conquered; they have been driven out from the redoubt of the established culture and have been silenced by the dominant sexual norm.

For the poetic voice of Lorca, the laurel does not symbolize the triumph of the word, but that of silence: "Tree that produces fruits of silence...!" exclaims the poetic "I" in "Invocación al laurel" (136). The myth of Daphne, transformed into a laurel to escape the (hetero)sexual pursuit of Apollo, is evoked here. Similarly, Lorca changes his work into a laurel which gives us "fruits of silence" to escape the attack or wreath of heterosexual culture.

Gil-Albert refers to the same wreath as Lorca in his poem "The Fig Tree" from *Las ilusiones*. Here is Apollo himself, personified by the sun, who puts a wreath around the "loving refuge" of the homosexual poet, the fig tree:

> Under your purple shadow
> I rested one day, happy,
> and in the warm odor of your existence
> I was drowning in desperation,
> because the acid sun,

                    put a wreath of mortality
                    around the loving refuge [*OPC* 1:189].

For Oscar Wilde's poetic "I" in the poem "Pan," the laurels did not suppose a victory, but rather, to the contrary, formed a barrier which impeded the vision of the billy goat's feet: "Nor through the laurels can one see / Thy soft brown limbs, thy beard of gold, / And what remains to us of thee?" (*Complete Works* 812). Wilde's use of the noun "limbs" can refer to parts (of your body) or to "branches" (of your tree).[10]

Charles Segal points to the city as a political and psychological entity in Euripides' *The Bacchants*, underscoring the use of landscape and road as metaphors or symbols. Nature outside the city is an actual landscape as well as a landscape of the soul (106). In "Bacchus," the "I" is hounded everywhere, spied upon by the savagery that threatens to destroy it (the panther) and stalked by civilization and the glory that traps its loving instinct (the "laurel wreath"). Segal shows that Pentheus, the "civilized" "I" of *The Bacchants*, sees his palace converted into a prison and the city into another prison on a larger scale (101). Pentheus intends to encircle and lock up Dionysus and his followers in towers in order to surround each tower with a fence, but it turns out to be he himself who is surrounded and ends up being destroyed by what he pursues (103).

Laurel or any other symbol should not be read, nevertheless, as if it had a meaning of fixed character in the culture of homosexuality or in any other culture. Prados, for example, uses laurel to refer to the glory of persecuted instinct in a poem from *The Written Stone*. Like Euripides in *The Bacchants* and Lorca in his letter, Prados uses the semiotic symbol-sign of the tower to evoke the proximity of a danger, fence or pursuit in the poem "Tower of Signs": "Gloria! Gloria! Is the laurel escaping? / (Stone and bird — inverted — ride it)" (*PC* 2:760). A poet can invert any form, and the substance can continue being the same.

♦ ♦ ♦

In the poem "Dream" the poetic "I" was obliged to abandon his heart, a heart that refused to continue riding the back of the billy goat. The same dichotomy appears in "Bacchus."

From childhood, the heart has been instructed to regard homosexuals as enemies. The feelings remain fixed in a world where values represented by family and heterosexuality predominate.[11] At the end, the "I" seems to realize that his instinct orients him towards Bacchus or homosexual love. But he sees that he will not be able to love "the fig tree" while his heart depends on people and a social order that pushes him to combat his own instinct and convert him into the enemy of a part of himself. His social being has been constructed year after year, during a whole life: his "Bacchic" being has just been discovered and still lacks roots to be able to affirm itself. The being would need to have a change of heart.

* * *

The *nomos*, that is, the power of the norms and restrictions of the dominant culture, invades texts and appropriates language. The oppressed is manifested subversively through signifiers and signs left by the poet who, in this way, creates, consciously or unconsciously, semiotic texts parallel to the linguistic ones. Sometimes the poet leaves trails; other times, without realizing it, he reveals situations and psychological and social mechanisms. "The fig tree" comes at the world of the speaker, having emerged previously in Lorca's mind, an unexpected and involuntary outbreak from a forgotten culture and from a smothered love that is not resigned to dying. The poet cultivates it, and the outbreak bears poetic fruits. The shout is the protest of the imprisoned voice. The shout is also the weapon or method that Pan uses to terrify the enemy and conquer him through *panic*, a term derived from this god's name.

Verlaine is "Panida"; he is "Pan" himself (Darío, *Selected Pages* 81). Verlaine screams through his shadow as later shouts will be heard from the Lorquian "sewers" of "Cry to Rome." There one has to scream, although it may be "with their heads filled with excrement" until knocking down the "prisons" in which one part of humanity has locked up another part, "because we demand that Earth's will be done, / that its fruits be offered to everyone" (*PNY* 153; 527).

Lorca's Unpublished Poetry of Youth

In 1994, Cátedra published the first edition of Lorca's youth poetry, *Unpublished Poetry of Youth* (Poesía inédita de juventud), edited by Christian de Paepe. The Lorquian veteran Marie Laffranque wrote the preface and highlights the importance of the 155 poems that appear in the book. Among other things, they are a "starting point," "a reference or resource" in the evolution of Lorca and his work, and a "principal key," as stated by Laffranque (9).

Because they are a "principal key" to Lorca's work and were published for the first time eight years after the appearance of my thesis, these poems of youth are of special importance. They can help us see if the vocabulary that appears there confirms or not the existence of a network of associations among groups of words that suggest homosexuality. Therefore, we will examine some concepts and techniques of suggestion that we studied before this poetry was published, for example: the bitter, the ancient, sterility, the rose, the secret, the comparison between Lorca and Verlaine, and the comparison between Lorca's poetic "I" and a woman.

The connection between the bitter and homosexuality was studied in chapter 2, "Lorca and the Sailors." In *Poetry of Youth*, the bitter appears in relation to other words and names of homosexual connotation. Poem 39, "Spiritual Twilight" (Crepuscular espiritual), suggests the existence of a relationship between Verlaine, the bitter and roses. Lorca evokes a cry that can be Verlaine's as well as that of the poetic voice. The poetic "I" predicts or knows the direction his life is going in, but does not wish to understand why. Evidently, he is afraid of that which, in reality, he understands without wanting to:

> Oh! Who sobs?
> Are they bitter, immortal specters?
> Oh! Who sobs?
> Perhaps Verlaine of the Saturnians
> touching his irises
> in an infinite rumor of rosebushes?
>
> ...
>
> We predict an end
> Which we do not wish to understand.
>
> ...
>
> Will they be opening my door?
> Oh! Who sobs?
> ... [140–42].

The house is the body, the soul and the sexuality of the poetic persona (see chapter 6, "Analysis of 'Suicide'"). The door that, perhaps, is opening, gives access to the house, that is, to the profound knowledge of the intimate aspects of the poetic "I." This knowledge transforms the person into a vulnerable being ("Oh!"), and probably will lead him to distance himself from family and/or society ("We predict an end"). The separation hurts, and the consequences that that end or separation may bring with it produce fear. This poem bears the date February 6, 1918. It is from the same year in which Lorca wrote a letter comparing himself to Verlaine ("From 'Dream' to 'Verlaine'".

Another example linked to the bitter may be found in poem 45, "Romance." Here the bitter is related to passion, as in several other Lorca poems, and also with another concept studied previously, the ancient (see chapter 4, "Lorca's Billy Goat"):

> An afternoon of sun in Castille.
> Passionate bitterness.
> A cascade of ancient gold
>
> ...
>
> *And here brave little bull*
> *And here gallant little bull.*

> *I'm the one from the other afternoon.*
> *Finish killing me* [158–60].

The italicized words evoked by Lorca belong to the richness of popular culture. The interesting thing here, nevertheless, is that the bull is presented as a "gallant fellow" and the poetic voice suggests that he has already encountered him before ("I'm the one from the other afternoon") and that it was "the other afternoon" when his "death" began. The image of this death, which occurs in stages, is found nearer to death as a metaphor for amorous encounters than the evocation of a real death. The cascade of gold in the poem probably refers to the ornamental richness of the bullfighter's tight-fitting suit. But one must observe that Lorca puts the ancient gold in relation to the passionate and to the bitter. In poem 43, Lorca makes a splendid defense of cypresses. The poet presents this tree in connection with the ancient and, at the same time, with a double sexuality: "Sun of ancient gold" ... "Virile and feminine tree" (151–52).

The great motifs of homosexual literature, silences and secrets, also appear in this book, linked to the bitter. For example, in poem 64, "May No One Ever Know My Secret" (Que nadie sepa nunca mi secreto), the poetic "I" again mentions the bitter and, at the same time, suggests that his way of loving is very similar to that of women:

> To love is such sweet bitterness
> Impossible and painful!
> Almost, almost like a woman
> ... [204].

The conjunction of several of the discussed themes and motifs also appear in poem 70, "Prayer" (Oración). The first line of the poem prays "May no one understand me" (264), and this verse is repeated in the last stanza of this lengthy poem:

> ...
> A tremendous anguish that I can't express
> Drowns my serene equilibrium from rhyming,
> A tremendous anguish of torment I suffer,
> An immense anguish as big as the sea.
> That I don't know what I'm saying, that I don't know what I feel
> Or if I know what I feel, I can't express it.
> ... [268].

In this book of poems, as well as in the poems we studied previously, it is obvious that one outstanding feature is expressed again and again. The poetic "I" feels desperation upon having to keep silent about the kind of love he feels. In poem 15, "Desolate Song" (Canción desolada), Lorca insists on the importance of this theme through the repetition of certain verses:

> One can't tell about love.
> Can't tell,
> Can't tell [79].

We end our observations with the same words used by Lorca in an interview and which also close the section from the introduction, "Lorca's Life and Letters: Silences and Secrets": "One cannot speak about whether man is a more suggestible object than a woman.... No, one can't speak about it."

Summary and Conclusions

In the poem "Dream," Lorca moved the thematics of "The Billy Goat" to the domain of the oneiric, showing with greater clarity the conflicted part of homosexual love. The conflict is born when homosexuals have to live in a reality in which there is no place for them. Love then necessarily has to take refuge in dreams and shadows.

As Freud already observed in *Delusions and Dreams in Jensen's "Gravida"* (El delirio and el sueño en "Gravida" de W. Jensen), literary dreams express the desires and fears that creators impute to their characters. They are also a reflection of the authors' conflicts with the reality imposed on them by the society in which they live. In "Dream" desire conquers. Lorca created a parable of the victory of instinct and the acceptance of homosexuality.

The theme again appears through the fantasy or "shadow" of "Verlaine," a poetic mirror of the referential character with the same name with whom Lorca identifies. Nevertheless, the resistance here is greater since the poetic "I" or the poet himself is surrounded-fortified by his "laurels." For the identity of the being in society, homosexual feelings are perceived as an attack. The protagonist tries to maintain them at a distance, but the more he suppresses his feelings, the bigger they grow, the more he tries to silence them, the more they shout. At the end, the fig tree "shouts and comes."

6
"Suicide": A Poem and Its Milieu, a Psyche and Its Circumstances

Despertar no es lucidez hallada,
es un terror dejado en las paredes,
es el día anterior que nos asalta
un desasido manantial que gruñe como lejos,
mundo hirviendo que manos estrangulan
    Gil-Albert, "Redada" *Obra poética completa* 1:59

Waking up is not a found lucidity,
its terror left on the walls,
it's the previous day that assaults us
a freed source that grunts from afar,
a seething world that hands strangle.
    Gil-Albert, "Raid," trans. Frouman-Smith

apuñalado en mis sueños
y estrangulado en mi sangre,
vuelo el cuerpo que me han dado
y el corazón que en él late;
vuelo el dolor que me toca,
que es más dolor que en mí cabe;
vuelo mis ojos sin lumbre
y el llanto que en ellos arde;
vuelo el luto de mi sombra,
sombra color de mi carne
    Prados, "La traición traicionada" *Poesías completas* 1:587

stabbed in my dreams
and strangled in my blood,
I blow up the body given to me
and the heart that beats in it;
I blow up the sorrow that touches me,
which is more sorrow than I can hold;
I blow up my eyes without light

and the weeping that burns in them;
I blow up the mourning of my shadow,
a shadow color of my flesh
   Prados, "The Betrayed Betrayal," trans. Frouman-Smith

Y el joven rígido, geométrico,
con una hacha rompió el espejo.
   Lorca, "Suicidio" 365

And the stiff, geometrical youth
smashed the mirror with a hatchet.
   Lorca, "Suicide" *Collected Poems* 491

Pero tronco y hachazo,
Placer, amor, mentira,
Beso, puñal, naufragio,
A la luz del recuerdo son heridas
De labios siempre ávidos;
Un deseo que no cesa,
Un grito que se pierde
Y clama al mundo sordo su verdad implacable.
   Cernuda, XVI *Donde habite el olvido* in *Poesía completa* 166

Trunk and ax-cut,
Pleasure, love, lies,
Kiss, dagger, disaster,
Are wounds from always greedy lips;
A desire that doesn't stop,
A yell that gets lost
And cries out its implacable truth to the deaf world.
   Cernuda, XVI *Where Oblivion Dwells* in *Young Sailor* 59

―――⊗⊗⊗―――

To be conscious in the world in which the poetic "I" of "Raid" lives is to have to accept the terror of a situation that renews itself each day "while the honorable leaders sell your life" (*OPC* 1:59). Very similar to the terrified awakening of Gil-Albert's poetic "I" is that of the homosexual protagonist of the novel by Christopher Isherwood, *A Single Man*. For the first one, waking up is an assault from the previous day; for the second one, a cold reminder of what awaits him. The novel begins with this awakening: "Waking up begins with saying *am* and *now*... But *now* isn't simply now. *Now* is also a cold reminder... A sickish shrinking from what waits, somewhere out there, dead ahead" (7).

For the moment readers do not know that the protagonist is homosexual, but they will know it soon. First, the dehumanization is presented. George is "that" or "it." He lives in a world that belongs to others and his conduct has to be acceptable to them: "it accepts its responsibilities to the others. It is even glad that it has a place among them. It knows what is expected of it. It knows its name. It is called George" (8).

If for Gil-Albert's poetic "I" in "Raid," waking up is a "seething world that hands strangle," the poetic voice of the quotation by Prados, "strangled" in his blood, finally blows up his body. Suicide is presented as a logical consequence of suffered oppression. The narrator kills himself, but in reality they have murdered him because they have "stabbed" his dreams and they have made his life impossible.

The quotation by Lorca is from "Suicide," a poem that will be examined in different stages throughout this chapter. The motif of the ax-cut serves as a connection to *Where Oblivion Dwells*. For Cernuda, the ax-cut represents the materialization of a desire and a wound that are also the shout of a truth that the world does not want to listen to. Like Prados, Cernuda presents an indirect murder: "Voices finally drowned in the voice of life, / ... / Like your eyes, your desires, your love" (*Young Sailor* 59).

Lorca suggests here a new way of approaching "reality": giving it an ax blow.

"Suicide" from the "Back of the World" Section of Songs

Suicide
(Maybe it was because you hadn't mastered geometry)

The lad was going blank.
It was ten in the morning.

His heart was growing full
of broken wings and rag flowers.

He noticed there remained
just one word on his lips.

and when he took off his gloves
a soft ash fell from his hands.

A tower showed through the balcony door.
He felt he was balcony and tower.

No doubt he saw how the clock,
stopped in its case, surveyed him.

He saw his shadow quiet and prone
on the while silk divan.

And the stiff, geometrical youth
smashed the mirror with a hatchet.

When it broke, a great burst of shadow
flooded the illusory room [*CP* 491].

Songs. *The Book and Its Critical Reception.*

The book *Songs* for the most part was written between 1921 and 1924, but Lorca was doing retouches and additions up until the moment of publication, in May 1927. *Songs* has received rather limited attention from the critics. In the bibliography of Lorca's *OC* from 1977, only eleven authors or critics are mentioned under the title of this book. In Colecchia's bibliography, which appeared two years later and is 313 pages long, *Songs* occupies only a little more than two pages, with only twelve mentions (Foster appears twice). In spite of being a select bibliography, the works mentioned in it are not always profound or extensive. Grass's work takes up only one half of a page and Schneider's, one page. Both authors analyze "Rider's Song" (Canción de jinete) (Colecchia 235–37).

Soon after the book's publication, Gerardo Diego published some of the most suggestive lines that have been written about it:

> Do not be fooled. There is a lot of calculation in these unexpected trills, in these smooth, fugitive glimmers ... the spontaneous subjected to the conscious.... But to a consciousness of another, external, not born of the same necessity as the work. The disciplined child, not for the child, but for a "grownup." ... Is this poetry, painting or is it music? Everything at once and everything seasoned, instrumentalized. With the ingenuity of a grownup. With corrupting, perverse rhetoric. One must insist on this because it is the greatest praise of and the supreme objection to Lorca's poetry [382, 383].

The poem that motivates Diego's question and subsequent responses is "Song of the Fairy" (Canción del mariquita). Not many critics have mentioned so clearly the stated perverse *corrupting rhetoric* of Lorca. The author does not explain in what sense the Lorquian language is perverse. Whom or what Lorca's rhetoric corrupts is also unclear.

In contrast or perhaps in opposition to what Diego believes about such rhetoric, G. Roberts states: "In reading the *Songs* of Federico García Lorca, what one most admires is finding a poetic world of such dense spiritual content with a minimum of rhetorical elaboration" (250). It is possible that each one of the recently cited authors means something different by the term "rhetoric," but since no one defines it, one can only observe the disparity of their judgments.

Several people maintain that Lorca was a "pure" poet. His brother mentions the purification of the lyric poetry from *Songs* (*Selected Poems* viii), and Angel del Río states that the poetry from *Songs* is the "product of the personality of a pure and exquisite poet ("La vida literaria" 126). Onís also names the "pure" poetry of the book that, in his opinion, is divorced from reality. The author refrains from saying what he understands by "reality." Neither does he explain what the "infantilism" consists of, something that, according to him, is always present in Lorca (31).

It seems that Francisco García Lorca was in agreement with the theory of infantilism in regard to Federico or his poetry. In his posthumous book he states that in *Songs* there is an "infantilized, arbitrary world" and, on some occasions, an "infantile" language. According to the poet's brother, it would be a question of "the elaboration of an infantile experience" (*Federico* 199–200).

A Literary History of Spain presents a point of view that contrasts sharply with the previous ones. The work shows that Lorca's interest in the folklore of childhood is a sophisticated, adult interest and that in many songs a sexual motif appears that is not infantile or playful. It also points out the assertion by many critics that in order to understand the most enigmatic images, they have turned their attention to Freud, Jung and Frazer, as well as to Andalusian folklore (G.G. Brown 86–87).

Onís states that the Lorca of *Songs* is heading towards a pure poetry, divorced from reality (31). This does not concur with what Debicki maintains, for whom the "vision of the poet's function" in *Songs* and *First Songs* is related to the way in which "the elements of reality interpenetrate with human and essential themes" (211). Both authors avoid entering into details about the theme of "reality" whose different aspects are very relevant to the study of Lorca, as was seen in the initial sections of chapter 5.

Bernard Sesé and Marie Laffranque have placed *Songs* in connection with Lorca's intimate private life but without shedding any particular concrete light on the matter. The critics suggest something, but they do not want to nor do they dare say what. For Sesé, the two poems entitled "Narcissus" betray some intimate aspects of Lorca's personality, and they show us his soul. The critic asks himself how one could not but be sensitive in the face of the moving sincerity of this "confession" ("PNY" 21). According to Laffranque, Lorca sees himself similar to "The Crazy Boy" in *Songs*, split from his shadow, from his past which was never lived, and from a present that is not of his measure, and that he cannot recognize any longer as his. Laffranque states that one can see how Lorca's personal drama expands (*Les idées* 90, 91).

The Grouping, Order and Background of the Poems

In a letter to Jorge Guillén dated February 14, 1927, Lorca mentions the importance of the order of his poems: "By now the presses are *groaning* with my book *Songs*. A book of surprises for many and of joy for a few... I've gone through veritable anguish arranging the songs" (*Selected Letters* 104; 1237).¹ In referring to the book's impression, Lorca uses the verb *groan*, which refers to the noise of machines. Given the poet's explicit anguish, it does not seem improbable that the verb can also have another meaning: perhaps the poet projects his feelings about the machines that "groan." Lorca's underscoring gives special importance to this groaning, and it is an indication that the function of the verb goes beyond the purely neutral-descriptive.

In the quoted letter, Lorca includes a fragment of the poem "Uncertain Solitude," some of whose lines express anguish as well as expectation: "While in the middle of the dark horror, / feigning song and awaiting fear / a shipwrecked sailor's disquieting voice rang out" (*CP* 105; 1238).

The poet seems to feel or senses beforehand a certain social antagonism since he believes that the book *Songs*, which is "of completely *noble* blood," as he says in his letter, will be "of joy for a few" (104; 1237). The group "Eros with a Cane" (Eros con bastón) precedes "Back of the World" (Trasmundo) where "Suicide" is found, both of which are of greatest interest.

There are seven poems in this group, and the majority deals with or seems to deal with heterosexual relationships, but these relationships are open to some questions.

The first poem of the series is called "Fright in the Dining Room" (Susto en el comedor). The fright is unjustified in regard to the sexual intention of the poetic "I" which makes explicit that he does not feel attracted to the woman who appears there, who is "rose color": "The apples I wanted were the green. / Not the rosy apples..." (*CP* 477; 349). This preference had made an impression already as a necessity in "The Moon Appears" (La luna asoma) from the preceding group, where the poetic "I" says that under the full moon, "Fruit must be eaten / green and ice-cold" (*CP* 471; 339).

The second poem, "Lucía Martínez," seems more erotic, but is it really? To use the last name of the person one is addressing does not express much intimacy, and to drag a woman by the hair suggests more the presence of a caricature of virility, or a wild macho dream of domination, than an erotic relationship, as metaphoric as the dragging may be. The true feelings of the masculine poetic "I" are hidden behind verbs of action and will: "I've come," "I want to" and "I can" (*CP* 479; 350). In the third poem, the unmarried woman is advised to give her breasts to the drone of the mass (479; 351), and in the fifth, "Nu," the woman of France is told twice how ugly she looked (481; 353).

Belamich calls these poems sarcastic gallantries (*Lorca* 139). Morris thinks that Lorca was being very playful when he felt incited to replace Eros's bow and the arrow with a cane (*Spanish Poets* 104). Is Lorca playing at playing or does he mean something with his game? Cobb thinks that the poet means either Eros is limping or that he is fiercely sexual (Cobb 56). One could conclude that the Eros that precedes "Back of the World" is somewhat lame.

"Back of the World"

In this ambiguous "Back of the World," or "other life," women have disappeared. In the first poem, "Escena," "the wedding ring" is offered to the poetic "I." The reaction of the character named "I" is clear and unequivocal: "I don't want it."

The same motif is repeated in the fifth poem of this group. The expression "throw that ring" appears in three of the nine lines of the poem (*CP* 489; 363). According to Martínez Nadal, in the first and fifth poems, the ancestors of the poet hope he perpetuates his name, but the poet refuses to do it. The conclusion in both poems is identical (*Federico García Lorca and the Public* 146–47). Years later the author will insist in another book: "the ring is a symbol of marriage; two rejections, two emphatic negations.... That is the ring that will go on reverberating throughout the poet's work" (*Cuatro lecciones* 109, 110). Since Martínez Nadal was a personal friend of Lorca, it is at times difficult to know if he is speaking about the poet or the poetic persona or both together.

The second poem of the group, "Disquiet and Night" (Malestar y noche), has been analyzed by María Andueza, who sees it as being difficult to understand logically: "one does not know what is occurring." The author states that "García Lorca probably did not know, either," which seems somewhat risky to us. Andueza continues:

> The poem refers to the surrealistic region of man's subconscious. The bee-eating bird nests there, an insect of long, pointed wings, a curved beak longer than the head and plumage of bright coloring where yellow, green and dark red dominate. This animal is abundant in the Andalusian region and is harmful to beehives because it eats bees. In another meaning the bee-eating bird is the newsmonger and gossip [36, 37].

The author asks herself, with good reason, what are the dark trees mentioned in the poem. With good reason because the bee-eating bird does not nest in trees, but under the earth. Like Lorca with his symbols, these birds construct long, subterranean galleries where they incubate. Bousoño has also studied this poem, but his method is based on certain suppositions that seem gratuitous.[2]

It is important to note that the motif of silence of "Disquiet and Night" is repeated in the poem that follows it, "The Voiceless Child" and later, in "Marriage Vow" (Desposorio): "Be still! / Ask me no questions" (*CP* 489;

363). The "voiceless" child does not speak, not because he does not have a voice, but because it was taken from him and it is "captive." After "The Voiceless Child" comes "The Crazy Boy," then "Marriage Vow," with the repudiation of the marriage ring, "Leave-taking" (Despedida) and, finally, "Suicide." This then is a sequence of great logic in which the order of the poems is matched by the evolution of a pressured and extremely divided psyche.

According to what R.D. Laing observes in *The Divided Self*, the schizophrenic who states that he has committed suicide can be perfectly conscious that he has not slit his throat nor has he thrown himself into a canal, in spite of being convinced that he has killed himself. That the body still lives is of little or no importance. The *I* and the *throat* can be felt as if they had only a tenuous and remote relationship: "sufficiently remote for what happens to the one to have little bearing on the other. That is, his self is virtually unembodied" (*The Divided Self* 149).

This is not to suggest that Lorca was schizophrenic. It is one thing to feel onself divided, as Lorca probably felt because of having to lead a double life, silent, hiding his loves, but, at the same time, utilizing this frustration as material or a poetic theme. It would be something very different to see this division as a fact, that is, to believe that one does not have a body, that one lives in two distinct bodies, or that the body's shadow is an autonomous being, as the young man seems to think in "Suicide."

Having repudiated the ring in "Marriage Vow," the poetic "I" in "Leave-taking" seems to be preparing himself for a possible death: "If I die / leave the balcony open" (*CP* 489; 364). It is notable that the protagonist in the poem does not say "when I die," but "if I die," as if he were about to carry out an action that could cost him his life, and not as if he were thinking about the arrangements to be made when in the future his day to die would come. "Suicide" perhaps does not lead him to death.

The balcony that is present in both "Leave-taking" and "Suicide" reinforces the relationship and continuity between the two poems whose connection was already apparent through the implicit "goodbye" in both titles.

"Suicide" and Criticism. The Refusal to Reproduce, and Death.

María Teresa Babín has dealt with this poem in two works (*Narciso y la esterilidad* and *El mundo poético de Federico García Lorca*) and presents the same idea in both. According to Babín, "the poem entitled 'Suicide' describes the nightmare of a young man on a white divan, absorbed in the contemplation of a balcony and a tower, accompanied by the tick tock of a clock 'stopped in its box,' unexpectedly surprised by his image reflected in the mirror in the room" (*El mundo poético* 267).

There are important differences between what Babín states and what Lorca wrote. Contrary to Babín's contention, Lorca does not present a person asleep, nor is that person having a nightmare. The critic believes that the young man is on a divan, but in the poem it is his shadow, and not the young man, who is on the divan. The character is not abstractedly contemplating a balcony and a tower. The text states: "A tower showed through a balcony door." Lorca does not refer to any tick tock; rather, a "stopped" clock evokes silence. Nor does it say that the young man was "surprised." Babín presents a very free interpretation of the poem, but what is missing are the arguments that support those views.

Vázquez Ocaña asks himself: "What does this poetry refer to? Does it not seem like the retrospection of a moment of anguish and failure in which the young man — perhaps Federico himself— sees himself 'prone and quiet' as the only possibility for escape?" (69–70). The author, who was a friend of Lorca's, does not provide the answer. His question implies that the young man, "perhaps Federico himself," is the object of a persecution, but Vázquez Ocaña does not follow up on this.

Emilia de Zuleta has a theory about the terrible harassment that pushes the young man to "suicide":

> To live among reflections, among mirrors, creates a profoundly disturbing situation.... Thus it is, in "Suicide," where from the first stanzas progressive indications of sterility and impotence accumulate. Towards the second half a split takes place: the young protagonist sees himself just as he is seen by others and, in order to end this anguished conscience, he breaks the mirror and then the shadow — death — inundates the room. Death as a rupture of one's own identity corroded by ambiguous perspectives [217].

Zuleta goes one step further towards the resolution of many underlying mysteries in Lorca's text. If the action of the young man is motivated by the "anguished conscience" from the looks of "others," this means that people despise or condemn the young man or something important in his life. If one accepts the connection between this young man from "Suicide" to the central character of the other poems from "Back of the World," then the disdainful looks of people and the surrounding pressure that frustrates the young man and leads him to "kill" the mirror, would be based on the rejection of the marriage ring and the homosexual feelings that take shape behind the refusal to reproduce, or the impossibility of doing it, alluded to by Martínez Nadal (*Federico García Lorca Public* 146–47).

The refusal of the poetic "I" to reproduce seems to be an echo of Lorca himself who would say: creator yes, procreator, no (Auclair 111).[3] The fact that several poems from "Back of the World" mention a boy could raise a question about the internal cohesion of the group of poems through a central poetic "I." The use of "could" raises a doubt based on the presence of the word "boy," something that is not relevant for the reader who knows that the Andalusians "call absolutely everbody a boy," according to Lorca's expression.[4] It is possible that the young man or Lorca's "boy" is saying goodbye to life because he cannot or does not want to reproduce and society will not pardon him.

For Binding, "Suicide," "The Voiceless Child" and "The Crazy Boy" are three poems that "constitute a presentation of Lorca's homosexual position" (112).

Analysis of "Suicide." Preliminaries.

At times it is forgotten that poetry is something more than lines, techniques and words. What animates "the poem itself," as a certain Anglo-American tradition would say, is not in the poem, but can be discovered through distancing oneself from the text. According to Kjell Espmark in his book *To Translate the Soul* (Att översätta själen), the "method" of translating the soul is one approach among many others that are important to use (13). In order to prevent possible orthodox objections to incursions into other fields from that of the analyzed text, what follows are Catherine Belsey's conclusions — who also quotes Wellek — concerning the limitations of the method used by the "New Criticism":

> New Criticism remained fundamentally non-theoretical and non-explanatory. Asserting that objective analysis of form is the task of criticism, it failed to pursue the theoretical implications of this position by developing an analysis of the relations between language and meaning. Cutting itself off from all discourse except the poetic, it increasingly isolated literary criticism from all other concerns.... by 1961 Renée Wellek ... observed that New Criticism had "not been able to avoid the dangers of ossification and mechanical imitation. There seems time for a change" [20].

Finally, a reflection by Robert Conquest about certain types of scientific or technical specialists of literary texts: "The man who only knows about literature does not even know about literature" (190).

♦ ♦ ♦

The title "Suicide" does not formally correspond to the content since the poem says only that the young man "smashed the mirror with a hatchet." This act appears like a suicide but it is not. In analyzing the symbol of the mirror, it is necessary to explain this apparent illogic.

❖ ❖ ❖

"(Maybe it was because you hadn't mastered geometry)"

It is not very common to find a parenthesis like this at the beginning of a poem. What relationship can geometry have with the feeling that life lacks meaning? But, in the first place, what purpose does the parenthesis serve? What is the author pursuing in using it? In his article about the function of the parenthesis in Lorca's poetry, Roberto Yahni states that the parenthesis means the "coexistence of planes marked by the disparity of registers." After presenting abundant examples, the author concludes: "To summarize, the parenthesis corroborates the at times antithetical duality of García Lorca's world, a world which because of caution or conflict isolates one from its parts" (218, 236).

In "Suicide" there is a world of conflicts, rather than caution. The clarifying parenthesis presents a vision distanced from what happens and offers a sign for identifying the causes of the duality and the push towards suicide. The distancing of the parenthesis removes the aspect of individual problem or private problematics from the drama. The young man has failed at something that society and family expects of him. The exorbitant importance given to what he has not yet learned, yet what he was expected to learn, is what pushes him towards suicide.

To whom does the voice of the parenthesis belong and to whom is it directed? Here is a situation analogous to the one described by Josipovici in "Text and Voice." Referring to the work of Muriel Spark, Josipovici observes that the narrator is converted into a part of the drama, without becoming a protagonist. It is only "that" which speaks. The voice that explains what has occurred liberates readers from the responsibility of choosing and deciding for themselves (21–22). The Lorquian voice does not seem to want to free us from this responsibility. What it does is suggest by pointing to a path or indication while, at the same time, it warns us that we could be mistaken in going there. One is dealing only with a "perhaps." Everything depends on what is understood by "Geometry."

Geometry is associated with exactness, with lines, surfaces and volume. But people do not kill themselves because of not understanding exactness, unless "Geometry" has deep emotional roots and may be associated with other areas. Therefore, the hypothesis is that Lorquian geometry possesses religious, philosophical and sexual connotations. The term is barely found documented in Lorca's work, and dictionaries do not explain what geometry can mean for a suicide. In order to verify our hypothesis and "translate the soul" one must investigate whether or not geometry exercises a psychic pressure on young people. Of special importance would be to observe the connections between geometric elements and the Generation of '27.

José R. de Armas has pointed out the influence of Valery on geometric concepts used in the poetry of the Generation of '27. In Salinas, geometry has religious and sexual connotations, for example, in his "use of the geometric figure *column*": "the identification of column with *soul* and *fire* is so absolute that he will use adjectives to describe the column which are characteristic of fire and soul.... The column, now changed into the body of the loved one..." (54, 55).

In *Les Métamorphoses du Cercle*, George Poulet treats the connection of light to spherical figures in the poetry of another member of this same group, Jorge Guillén. Parmenides, recalls Poulet, had compared the world to a sphere, and Guillén compares it to a dome, that is, a sphere perceived from the interior, or an exterior that *is internalized* (514). It is evident that the young man from "Suicide" perceives the exterior in the same way. Geometry, what was not mastered, finally manages to give him a geometric form.

The concepts relative to geometry and to exactness have been used to form humans and also, implicitly, to serve dominant religions and ideologies. Under the rubric "The geometrization of the soul," one reads in *The Mystical Geometry of the Soul in Spanish Literature of the Golden Age* (La geometría mística del alma en la literatura española del Siglo de Oro):

> The idea of the center includes within it a whole geometry of what surrounds it. Logically it evokes the existence of straight and curved lines, of radii and circumferences. Regarding these suppositions, since the most distant times, a spiritual, organic and structured configuration of man's interior was elaborated ... a geometry destined to imprint a godlike image on the spirit [Morales Borrero 24, 25].

In the first pages from the third part of his *Ethics*, Spinoza proposes "to deal with the vices of men and their illnesses in the manner of geometricians.... I will consider human actions and appetites as if I were dealing with lines, surfaces and solid bodies" (160, 161).

Geometric figures correspond to numbers, as Morales indicates: "In a kind of parallelism established by Plato between numbers and figures, two is equal to the line" (25). "But two has never been a number," states the Lorquian poetic "I" in "Little Infinite Poem" (Pequeño poema infinito) (*CP* 647; 547). In this same poem, parallel to the negation of the numerical character of the number two, it is implicitly denied that the road that leads to the woman be the straight or true road: "To take the wrong road / is to arrive at woman" (647; 547).

Lorca mixes the field of numbers with that of heterosexuality, morality, religion, semantics and geometry. The ideological assertions the poet faces did the same thing before; they invaded terrains that were not theirs and took love to desperation. The supposed number two "It is anguish and its shadow, /

it is the demonstration of something else's infinity" (647; 547). *Infinite* alludes to the ideological utilization of "exactness" and evokes Christian eternity and reproduction-multiplication. The poetic "I" feels anguished by the idea of a resurrection of the flesh that is like reproducing oneself infinitely, associated with the so-called number two which is described as "anguish and its shadow" ... "and the punishment of the new, unending resurrection" (647; 547, 548).

Lorca's associative net seems to have correspondences in Spanish society. In "Infinity Equal to Two" (Infinito igual a dos), Marqués relates two and geometry to the prescription for forming a heterosexual couple: "The number two, the couple... Geometry in support of the social formula" (34).

Geometry, supposedly neutral, changes with cultures, reflects people's loves and sexuality and is utilized for ideological as well as artistic ends. In Lorca's reading of *The Gypsy Ballads*, a conflict is profiled between "the poison ... of the Andalusian" and "geometry," which recalls the conflict between dreams or internal reality and "reality": "myth is mixed with the element we could call realist, although it is not, since once in contact with the magical plane it becomes even more mysterious and undecipherable, like the very soul of Andalusia, battle and drama of poison of the Orient of the Andalusian with geometry" (1116).

Poison is a word that, just like *dog*, can have many and very diverse connotations, diverse, but not disassociated. In the reading, *poison* evokes an internal creative force. In "Ode to Walt Whitman" poison is transformed into a destructive homosexuality. The "sleepless" faggots or homosexuals give boys a "bitter poison" or "drops of foul death" (*PNY* 161; 531). In connection with the "drama" of the Andalusian with "geometry" it is probably relevant to recall that Lorca associates the Andalusian with Bacchus and with purity. According to what he states in a letter to Jorge Zalamea, he himself goes in for "the style of a pure Andalusian, to a bacchanal of flesh and laughter" (*Selected Letters* 139; 1312).

In finalizing the fifth scene from *The Public*, the happy anarchism of the polymorphic-perverse hues of the students is suddenly cut off by the Prompter, who calls them to study geometric order: "Gentlemen, descriptive geometry class" (40; 524).

To a certain extent, this brief review of "geometry" verifies that the term has philosophical, religious and sexual connotations that, in the social domain, evoke the prescriptions of the established order. As one can observe, Lorca writes geometry with a capital letter in the original. It is a question of a "subject" that the young man has seen himself obliged to try to learn, without any success.

◆ ◆ ◆

The protagonist in the poem is a "lad," a lad who was going blank. The diminutive (in Spanish) indicates that the person finds himself at a critical age: he is no longer a child, but neither is he a complete man. Finding himself probably at puberty, the young man is in the most important period of life in terms of formation and consolidation of sexual identity. During this time, one has great need of a normative mirror in which to view oneself, a need for heroes with whom one can identify, intense and vivifying images of the responsible lives of adults which the adolescent can feel and copy. The young man in the poem lacks this mirror and these images. There is a mirror in the room, but it is not vivifying.

"The lad was going blank." Lorca writes the verb-predicate without the usual complement-object (in Spanish), emphasizing the reflexive nature of the verb (in Spanish). Like the enemy mirror, the action turns against the young man and paralyzes him ... "he was going blank." The life he lives is not his, it is barely life since he is going blank and his heart is growing full of "broken wings and rag flowers." In a letter to Sainz de la Maza, Lorca wrote, "*I haven't been born yet ... for a second I understood everything. I'm living on borrowed time, what I have within is not mine*" (*Selected Letters* 5; 1188–89).

The oblivion of living one's own life (the lad's and Lorca's) can be a mirror of the "oblivion" of society with respect to the education of homosexuals; the maturing homosexual is never offered a positive mirror in which to see himself. Herman van de Spijker points out the "significance" that "in most countries there is no official position, no official authority" where homosexuals or their parents can receive advice and opinions "of a scientifically irreproachable and humanly friendly kind" (83). In this repect, the family oftens reproduces the "oblivion" of society.

Family life appears as a background curtain of the non-existence of Lorca in the letter where the poet states he has not been born yet. In his "Elegía a María Blanchard," Lorca mentions a "dramatic dialogue" that took place during puberty: "when I sustained this dramatic dialogue of the burgeoning down with the family mirror" (1092).

Notice that "the mirror" is mentioned just as it is in "Suicide." The "burgeoning down" and its drama must be seen in connection with the poem "Childhood and Death," in which Federico is the protagonist (Martínez Nadal, "Prólogo" xxxv): "Child defeated in grade school and in the waltz of the wounded rose, / amazed by the dark dawning of the thighs' soft hair" (*CP* 643; 797).

The section in chapter 2, "Otherness, Homosexuality and Childhood," demonstrated the connection between this child's growth and the arrival of rats and sewers, that is, homosexuality. Puberty, marginalization and oblivion arrive at the same time: "Alone, here, I see they have closed the door on me. / The door has been closed on me" (643; 797).

♦ ♦ ♦

"It was ten in the morning." The mention of a specific hour indicates that the number ten ought to have a certain importance in this context. Lorca frequently uses numbers in a cabalistic, mysterious or surrealistic way, for example in "Suicidio en Alejandría" that, as the title indicates, has the same central motif as the poem under consideration, and is difficult to decipher. Semprún states "the most confusing aspect of the story are the numbers which begin every paragraph or sentence" and adds that he believes "the author uses these numbers like a daring hieroglyphic" (*Las narraciones* 4, 45–46).

To unearth the whole network of Lorquian numerical constructions would be a huge task, and this is not the moment to undertake it. In regard to the use of ten in "Suicidio," understanding the symbolic significance of the number ten is essential. According to Cirlot's *Dictionary of Symbols*, numbers are "idea-forces, each with a particular character of its own. The actual digits are, as it were, only the outer garments" (220). The number one is the symbol of being and "admit[s] neither two nor dualism" (221). Zero is non-being, "it symbolizes death as the state in which the life-forces are transformed" (221). This symbolism agrees in part with our theory that the suicide in the poem may represent a transformation.

Several authors have pointed out the presence of cabalistic elements in Lorca's work.[5] It can be relevant to observe what the Kabala states about the number ten. In *La Kábala. Una mística del lenguaje*, Marcos Ricardo Barnatan explains that the Yod, the tenth letter of the sacred cabalistic alphabet, corresponds to the letters J, Y, and I and to the number ten, meaning "hand." In a prediction, ten is an indication of "a confrontation with postponed duties" (127). In a letter addressed to Melchor Fernández Almagro, at the end of 1925, Lorca states: "*I am getting into problems* that I should have confronted long ago" (*Selected Letters* 63; 1142).

The number ten is also associated with a very important incident in the poet's life that Lorca relates to Adriano del Valle in the same letter in which he confesses that he has to feign a sexual hue that is not his heart's truth: "I was ten years old and I fell in love" (*Letters* 2; 1095–96).

Most likely, the young man in the poem and Lorca are in a similar situation. Ten or "it was ten" suggests that perhaps the moment is approaching of facing a deferred problem and accepting "the death" of a transformation. It is an age at which children often discover their sexual orientation: "We once compared notes on our sexual initiations, Rammelkamp's at the age of ten with a workman ... mine at the age of eleven with a teacher (Lambert 11).

♦ ♦ ♦

The broken wings that enter the lad's heart refer to the wings of symbolic birds. According to the *Dictionary of Ambiguous Spanish* of Manuel Criado de Val, homosexuals are associated with what flies in many Spanish-speaking countries: "bird: ambiguous name for homosexual in Costa Rica ... seagull: ambiguous name for homosexual in the Philippines ... bird: ambiguous name for masculine sexual organ in Argentina, Bolivia, Guatemala, Mexico. Ambiguous name for homosexual in the Dominican Republic, Panama, Costa Rica, Peru, El Salvador" (91, 102, 110). In his "Ode to Walt Whitman," Lorca shows that he is very well informed about the names given to homosexuals, not only in different countries but also in different cities. Among the quoted names is "pájaros" (*PNY* 161; 531).

The presence of "oxen" in "Blind Panorama of New York" suggests that "the birds" are going to be castrated: "the birds will soon become oxen" (*PNY* 73; 482). In the third of the "Four Ballads in Yellow" (Cuatro baladas amarillas) from *Suites* the change-castration has been consummated. The oxen have "eyes like a bird's," and it is quite explicit that previously they had wings. It is suggested that "the wings" were cut or ripped from their oxen bodies. For this reason, perhaps, they are always sighing: "think back to the wings / down their sides" (*CP* 209; 257).

According to Peter Tompkins, the castration of homosexuals and other "bothersome" or "dangerous" beings had been practiced in many so-called civilized countries until the middle of the twentieth century.[6] It is clear that the castration referred to by Lorca in "Suicide" is not a literal one, but rather metaphorically expresses the feeling of castration or frustration in regard to one's sexual life.

Like oxen, Lorca recalls the wings in a letter to Adolfo Salazar. He also mentions here his "yellow ballads," that is, the poems where the oxen–ex-birds appear: "my wings, what a pity! My dried-up childhood, what a pity!" (*Selected Letters* 19; 1183). The Second Friend in *Once Five Years Pass* longs for the wings he has lost or had stolen: "I'll go back for my wings, / I must be away! (act 1, 59; 391) The "I must be away" indicates that society or some powerful group intends to impede this person from recuperating his wings. In the same way, a repression or robbery of the personality of the Lorquian alter ego takes place: "But my face belongs to me, and it's being stolen from me" (61; 392).

The stolen or cut wings connote (homo)sexual frustration. The sexual symbolism of wings persists in other contexts that can be similar, but possess very different connotations. In "Ode to Salvador Dalí," Lorca's poetic "I" addresses the painter and states: "When you take up your palette, a bullet hole in its wing / you call on the light that brings the olive tree to life" (*CP* 591; 777). The bullet hole in "its wing" can refer to the hole in Dalí's wing-body and the hole in the palette. Santos Torroella refers to the vision that Lorca has of Dalí: "he sees him take up the palette, a palpitating bird that has 'a bullet hole in its wing' (the hole through which the painter passes his thumb, the latter changed afterwards into a phallic form, a frequent motif in his paintings from 1928)" (100).

In a portrait of Dalí that Lorca did in 1926, one sees the painter with his palette from which a clearly phallic cylindrical figure emerges. The palette has the shape of a heart, but it also can be seen as a pair of open wings, above all if one thinks about the Lorquian ode. These wings (or heart-palette) have a hole that contains a phallic-finger, a substitution for Cupid's arrow. The image is a symbolic or allusive compendium of five different ones: the palette, the heart, the testicles, the backside and the wings (see the reproduction in Romero, *Dalí* 220).

The movie *The Wings*, by Mauritz Stiller, was discovered by chance during the middle 1980s. Produced in 1916, the film was believed to have disappeared in a fire. According to Jon Voss in the headlines from the homosexual Swedish magazine *Reporter* (March 1987), it is the first homosexual picture in history. These headlines were also quoted in the Swedish daily *Aftonbladet*, June 18, 1987, 4–5, in the article from Innerspalten "Zeus as a Gay" (Zeus som gay). The script from *The Wings* is based on the novel *Michael* by the Danish homosexual writer Herman Bang, who was humiliated and persecuted through half of Europe at the end of the nineteenth and the beginning of the twentieth century. The persecutions and mockery the writer suffered were due primarily to the fact that Bang was a homosexual. Several writers have documented them, for example Knut Ahnlund, of the Nobel Institute of Sweden (151, 166–67, 173–78, 208–09).

◆ ◆ ◆

The winged "I" associated with a repressed or castrated sexuality is defined by Lorca in his article "Digression: The Rules of Music." There the poet resolutely opposes the rules of the established culture, using terms that imply much more than just music by what they connote as well as by what they explicitly say:

> Human passions are thousands in infinite tonality and thousands are the men, each one seeing things according to his soul; and if a corporation, or an academy writes a book in which it says what one must do and not do, those happy, tormented, religious or perverse spirits reject it with horrifying terror, like an eagle whose wings are to be cut.... As a general rule, these faultfinders, who do not know a word of feeling, and who grab onto rules like the hungry child onto the teat, are poor, unhappy individuals who believed that they had all the intellectual baggage in possessing a laudatory diploma from one of those awful corporations [1146–47].

Although Lorca's article is subtitled "The Rules of Music," the poet does not speak much of such rules. In their place he mentions those which are promoted to regulate "human passions" and lecture different spirits, among them the "perverse." The concert here is not musical but corporate: one group against another. In using the term "corporations," Lorca transcends the individual and the personal aspects of the problem and suggests that the oppressors are organized.

Homosexuality was and perhaps still is "the loathsome sin, as it was called" (Gil-Albert, *Heraclés* 45). The corporations Lorca designates as "awful" are those that try to regulate human passions, "academies" of censors that grab on to rules like onto a "teat." The Lorquian metaphor of comparing rules with a teat has several readings. It evokes in part the dependence on the rule-teat and also refers perhaps to the norm of grabbing on to the feminine body. It can even be a sign of what Lorca qualifies as childish, those "men" who try to impose their sexual norms. If that were the case, Lorca would be exchanging "awful" for "loathsome" and "childish" for "immature." It has been a common practice to refer to the supposed immaturity of homosexuals, departing from the starting point that in the lineal evolution of people's "normal" sexuality, homosexuals are detained halfway and do not reach genital, procreative heterosexuality, the sexuality considered mature. In the cases of a homosexuality that does not exclude heterosexuality, it is argued that the homosexual experience is backwards which, of course, is also seen as a sign of immaturity.[7]

◆ ◆ ◆

The heart of the young man was growing full of "broken wings and rag flowers." If one believes that the (homo)sexual wings have not been broken by themselves, the symbolic castration implies the existence of castrators, probably the corporations referred to by Lorca in mentioning the eagle that feared having his wings cut. In the same way, it may not be extravagant to think that a mechanism or some forces external to him drive the artificial flowers that are filling or occupying the heart of the young man. It is curious to observe that in Lorca's life a parallel incident of similar characteristics occurs. In the first of Lorca's letters to Regino Sainz de la Maza, which have been published, the poet states, "I'm sad now and bored by my false interior" (*Selected Letters* 5; 1189).

Taking into account the repressive cultural contexts studied previously, the situation evoked in "Suicide" has points in common with the colonization and castration of pagan eroticism and of the cultures and instincts called primitive.[8] As was seen in analyzing what geometry symbolizes and the allusions "The Rules of Music" contains, the poem does not only deal with the personal problems of an isolated individual.

Two other critics offer opinions on the utilization of the symbol of flowers and its implications. J. Alberish, who has studied the floral images and allusions in Lorquian theatre, is surprised to discover that, almost always, they refer "to men or boys, more than to women" (18–19). This is "the reverse of the normal situation in which the male pays compliments to the female by comparing her to a flower." In spite of his surprise from seeing that what Lorca does is "invert the direction," Alberich does not ask himself to what this may be attributed or what it could indicate. The author joins those who support the thesis that the only "signs" of "perverse" eroticism in Lorca's work are found in a fragment from *The Public*. Alberich does not believe that Lorca was homosexual (35).

In an essay about the aesthetic dimension of flowers in *Blood Wedding*, González del Valle indicates that flowers

> not only express concepts associated with life; there are many that are related to death. It often happens when flowers cease existing, they dry up. Examples of this are a plant called Jupiter with "red" flowers (the color of flesh and, therefore of life) which the father of the Bridegroom planted and which dried up after his death and the form in which the Mother describes her dead son ("an armful of dead flowers") [44].

The author does not seem very sure of the meaning of "the golden flower" that is mentioned on several occasions. He believes, nevertheless, that it is "the flower of life." In his *Dictionary of Symbols*, Cirlot names a "golden flower": "a non-existent flower that is also spoken of in alchemy; in the *Epistola ad Hermannum Arch. Coloniensem* (*Theatr. Chem.* 1622) it is given the name of the 'sapphire-blue flower of the Hermaphrodite'" (105).

In Lorca's poem "Madrigal," from the year 1919, Lorca's poetic "I" receives a kiss from someone whose sex is not specified, and compares his heart to a flower that, in opening up, shows its desire:

> And my heart opened
> like a flower under the sky,
> its petals of desire,
> its stamens of dreams [*CP* 31; 115].

Here the heart is associated with a living flower that is placed in connection with a powerful or extroverted sexuality and with the night or the subconscious. In contrast-opposition, in "Suicide" the heart appears below the light of day, in connection with lifeless flowers, broken sexuality and introverted feelings.

In "San Rafael" some boys with impassive faces undress and ironically ask a fish if it wants "wine flowers." That there is "Only one fish in the water" seems to indicate that the fish is rather symbolic or metaphoric. The "wine flowers" evoke the presence of Bacchus, and also that of a Ganymede-bartender or "cupbearer of Zeus." The nudity that precedes the offer suggests that the flower is found on the body of the "boys." This poem from *The Gypsy Ballads* forms part of a trilogy, "San Miguel," "San Rafael," and "San Gabriel" (*CP* 539–49; 410–16).

The purpose here is not to insinuate with this that each time that Lorca writes "flower" one should read "sex." Rather, what is affirmed is that in the poetry of Lorca and other poets studied here, the experiences and problems of homosexual love are frequently expressed by means of diverse floral symbols. If women are like flowers for heterosexual men, what is most natural for homosexuals is that men be like flowers. As one of Ruiz López's characters says: "Tell me, Ocaña, what flower is more beautiful than a man?" (*Ocaña* 35).

♦ ♦ ♦

"He noticed there remained / just one word on his lips."

The poem "The Billy Goat" states indirectly that one must understand something important that was not an explicit fact in the text: ("Ancient Greece / will understand you"). Something similar occurs in "Suicide." Lorca directs the reader's attention towards a word that is absent from the text. The importance of this silenced word is evident since it is, perhaps, the only thing the young man has left that is his own. The rest is artifice and frustration, a powerful and dictatorial form that takes hold of him and robs him of his idiosyncrasy and converts him into someone "geometrical."

The word is absent, but the context is present and because of it one can deduce what is missing. The previously analyzed oblivion is in connection with, and in contrast to, that word (he was *going blank*... but there *remained*). Oblivion was inevitable because of the situation in which the young man finds himself. The word, his own voice, fights to survive through the fire that burns the protagonist of the poem (notice the ash). The love that dares not speak its name is a "dense name" hidden by respect (Gil-Albert, *OPC* 1, 27).

Even in 1943 (and also many years later) it could be very difficult to get over "the horror of mentioning homosexuality by name," according to Gavin Lambert, quoting the film and theatre director Lindsay Anderson, who previously had written in his diary: "I can understand the mentality of a man who commits suicide" (26, 22).

♦ ♦ ♦

"And when he took off his gloves / a soft ash fell from his hands."

The hands of the young man are burnt since ash falls from them, and this ash seems to be connected to the silenced word (word on / his lips — ash from / his hands). The section "Lorca's Billy Goat" from chapter 4 spoke of the "burnt voice," and Walt Whitman's voice is "like a column of ash" (*PNY*

157; 529). With respect to the symbolism of gloves, hands and ashes, Cirlot states, "Gloves, since they are worn on the hands, derive their symbolism from them." Removing the right-hand glove "is a custom which suggests candor and the frank disclosure of one's mind" (114).

The young man in "Suicide" takes off his gloves and reveals his personality, which is disintegrating and burning. The gesture of removing gloves can also signify that the young man is preparing "to die," the equivalent of getting rid of his old personality or the false social "I" that had been imposed on him to hide the true one. This association of gloves with falseness or with what hides the truth appears in *The Public*. At the end of the play the public's arrival is announced again: this is the public that has killed the homosexuals from the work that was representing them and has prevented what the Director calls "the true drama" from being shown. Then, a slow shower of white gloves begins to fall. The young man from "Suicide" is "stiff." The gloves that fall at the appearance of the public are "rigid" (535). The theatre must continue. That rigid form, the only one that the author can use, hides, but it also insinuates the existence of another drama, "the true one."

In his book about the Lorquian and Freudian periods of Dalí, Santos Torroella says that the paintings "Honey Is Sweeter Than Blood" and "The Great Masturbator" mark the beginning and the end of an era in which how much Dalí may owe to his "tight friendship" with Lorca begins to be clearly acknowledged. In this period, he states, "over and over the theme of the hand is repeated: a hand that I dare to qualify as 'onanistic'" (71). The author also relates by way of an anecdote that "onanism, in reference to some of their most illustrious friends, gave rise to certain fairly frequent jokes for Lorca and Dalí during their time at the Student Residence" (85). (Lorca wrote "Suicide" during this period.)

In *The Forbidden Pleasures*, Luis Cernuda writes about the desert, a glove and a hand (*PC* 120). The forgotten glove asking for its hand is the visible poetic form of a love that has been falsified or poisoned by "pale history" (presented "with poisonous signs").

Once the symbolism of the glove and hands is seen, we may continue with the ashes and fire they evoke. According to Gil-Albert in *Heraclés*, the only alternative offered to homosexuals who aspired to form part of society was *to burn oneself*. Here the verb is used as a synonym of *to sublimate* or *to deny* homosexuality:

> "Burning ourselves," that is the only option suggested to us and at this price the homosexual can indeed enter into forming a passive part of a world that, if it does not grant him belligerency, is at least disposed to understand him and give him, in some sensitive cases, the signs of their commiseration which

can even turn out sincere.... For many, the cloister and the cell have constituted the only friendly refuge in which, checked by discipline, they have been able to give the deceptive virtuality of embers to their fire, from which some, the fewest, those of the most loving and sublime soul, succeeded in extracting, already changed from live embers into pure crystal, the erotic seeds of mysticism [49–50].

This definition of *to burn oneself* cannot be completely disassociated from others already seen that evoke equally the conditions of life of homosexuals. They already appear in the poetry of Quevedo, whom Lorca mentions several times in his lectures on Góngora and on the *duende*. In the sonnet "Women's Disillusion" (Desengaño de las mujeres), Quevedo's speaker exclaims, "As a fag may I die burned" (545). According to Crosby in the notes from his edition, several times Quevedo uses *mulatto* as "a metaphor for 'burned' homosexual" (314, 430, 547).

In "Blind Panorama of New York" the Lorquian poetic "I" says that he has lost himself "in order to find the burn that keeps everything awake" (*PNY* 73; 483). In this same poem are the now familiar birds "covered with ash." The stars, whose symbolism was analyzed in the section "Lorca's Billy Goat" from chapter 4, seem to have burned in "Landscape" (Paisaje): Ash falls from the stars just as it falls from the young man's hands in "Suicide": "The extinguished stars / fill the river with ash" (67). Through the word "nests," the presence of birds is evoked. Their hidden nests have been burned, or they themselves have burned: "Already the hidden nests / have been burned" (67). The poetic "I" finds himself near death, just as in "Suicide": "In my chest there is a depth / of the grave" (68). As in "Suicide," death is related to the love of the speaker, whose lips in "Landscape" are "stained / with sins": "The Lord's Prayer for my love...!" (68).

In the notes to his edition of *The Shoemaker's Prodigious Wife*, Joaquín Forradellas comments on an assertion by the Mayor in act 2, scene 3. Among the women the Mayor says he has known, there are "women whose hair smells of sweet oils and whose hands are always very warm" (*Five Plays* 87). The critic states the warm hands "are an indication of loving passion." Forradellas gives an example from *The Love Turned Doctor* (El amor médico) by Tirso de Molina. This example seems especially relevant to the context of "Suicide" because, more than warm hands, are hands of fire or hands that burn: "The palms of my hands / burn: as soon as they touch / they glow; touch, touch" (148).

◆ ◆ ◆

"A tower showed through the balcony door. / He felt he was balcony and tower."

Espmark points out that one must distinguish between landscape as real geography and landscape that is a projection of feelings (9–10). The young man from "Suicide" feels what he sees, projects his feeling onto the house's balcony and the tower. Jung states that if you ask doctors to speak about the course of an illness, they will use concepts like "infection" or "fever," while in dreams, the archetypal mind expresses itself in a more poetic way. The sick body is presented as a house being destroyed by fire (67).

In Freud's symbology, the places through which one enters or leaves rooms signify openings in the body (*Psychoanalysis* 141). Carlos Feal has done a Freudian analysis of *The Love of Don Perlimplín and Belisa in the Garden* and thinks that "it is significant that the lover's last letter has arrived through the balcony carried by a rock. A rather aggressive and direct way, in tune with the words of the writer. The balcony is, as on the wedding night, an opening penetrated by beings" (87).

The connection between weddings and openings in the house also appears in Lorquian poetry. "The cries beating against the windows of the wedding" appear in "Blind Panorama of New York" (*PNY* 73; 482). In the second of the "Nocturnes from the Window" (Nocturnos de la ventana) from *Songs*, an "arm" of the night enters the window of the poetic "I" who takes out or puts his head through the window, a symbolic head since it is the "eyeless head[s]" of its "desires" (*CP* 429, 431; 292, 293; for the phallic symbolism of "head," see Cela's *Diccionario secreto* 490–91).

The balcony and other openings in houses suggest receptiveness, not only sexual, but also emotional and spiritual. The image of a tower enters through the balcony and the young man feels as much balcony (that is, receptive and feminine) as tower. The latter's phallic symbolism is documented by Cela, who mentions, for example, the euphemism "inquiring tower" from another of the members of the Generation of '27, Rafael Alberti (463–64). In *Erotique du Surréalisme* a drawing by Dalí is reproduced of a tower and two balls — its phallic symbolism does not leave any doubts (Benayoun 225).

In a letter dated 1921 to Melchor Fernández Almagro, Lorca situates his passions in a tower by means of the psychological phenomenon of projection: "I laugh at my passions which in the tower of the city attack me" (*Selected Letters* 14; 1112). Lorca feels divided and identifies here with his conscious "I," perhaps because the passions that "are" in the tower are not assimilable into his daily life that seems to be the most important thing for him in these moments. In contrast, for the young man of the poem, daily life has turned out to be extremely frustrating and, perhaps, for that reason, he identifies with the tower and the balcony, for the double sexuality and double sensibility they symbolize. By not being able to live his own life himself, the young man lives, feels that of the tower through the balcony's opening and feels the balcony and its opening thanks to the tower that enters his eyes and feelings.

In "Earth and Moon," Lorca mentions a "tower of blood" and the already analyzed hands that burn. The poetic "I" explains that the kind of love that he is looking for is not what Diana's naked body can offer to him. He is searching for a "love that consumes itself," and not a love that procreates or reproduces itself (in the section "Mount..." of chapter 5, we saw that blood can be a symbol of semen). Diana is rejected with the following words:

> My love is a footstep, passage, long death that I relish,
> never the unharmed skin of your nakedness in flight.
> It's earth. My God! Earth, that I come looking for.
> Muffled horizon, heartbeat, and tomb.
> It's sorrow that runs out, love that consumes itself.
> Charred hands opening a tower of blood [*CP* 645; 809].

♦ ♦ ♦

"No doubt he saw how the clock, / stopped in its case, surveyed him."

Lorca humanizes the clock by saying that it "surveyed" the young man. The clock and the young man live parallel lives that are rather non-lives. The young man has been geometrized and the clock is enclosed in its case, "stopped," perhaps "dead." There is an analogous incident in *Once Five Years Pass*. The word "case" (the watch's in "Suicide") is used by Lorca as a synonym for coffin. A boy has been stopped and punished for something that is not clarified: "They tied my hands together" (act 1, 37; 379).

The verb "to work" (in Spanish), which is generally used to say that a watch is functioning (here, "going" is used), in this scene refers to the boy's heart:

> BOY: And I have a terrible pain in my heart.
> CAT: Oh why, boy, why?
> BOY: Because it doesn't go. Yesterday it ran down and it stopped [35, 37; 379].

The boy relates what happened when they tied his hands and put him in the box-coffin: "There was a man with a hammer who drove paper stars in my coffin in rows" (37; 379). (For the symbolism of Lorquian stars, see "Lorca's Billy Goat," chapter 4.)

It seems clear that the boy in the play shares the problems and fate of the clock and the young man in "Suicide": the boy is tied, the watch is "stopped" (detained). The young man has been geometrized, that is, he is a prisoner in a geometric form that is foreign to his nature. The word "stopped" (detained) leads one to think of the intervention of the police or a similar group. The young man is psychically detained and his heart is about to stop, like the clock. A proper understanding of the psychic situation evoked in the poem requires a continuous fluctuation, a pendulous movement that leads from the clock, seen as a humanized mechanism, to the young man, seen as a human being converted into a manipulated mechanism; from that which stops by himself to that which stops because he is detained, from suicide to indirect murder or castration of the potentials of the human being.

◆ ◆ ◆

> He saw his shadow quiet and prone
> on the white silk divan.
> And the stiff, geometrical youth
> smashed the mirror with a hatchet.
> When it broke, a great burst of shadow
> flooded the illusory room [365].

In Lorca's work in general and in "Suicide" in particular, light and shadows connote values that are the inverse of what these symbols ordinarily mean in the culture established upon Christian roots, and that the sources of this inversion come from homosexuals' (obligatory) necessity of living in the shadows.

In "Suicide," the mirror and the shadow have a relationship-interaction analogous to that of light and shadow: when the mirror-light "dies" the shadow enters. Some symbols with a high degree of interdependence should not be analyzed separately, nor should they be isolated from the rest of the Lorquian oeuvre.

According to Emilia de Zuleta, the young man "breaks the mirror and then the shadow — death — floods the room. Death as a rupture of one's own identity eroded by ambiguous perspectives" (217). Zuleta does not observe that the young man's identity was broken *before* the mirror broke. The supposition that shadow is equal to death is probably based on the popular idea that light is good and gives life, and shadow is evil and kills. In *Light and Darkness in Spanish Mysticism* (Luz y oscuridad en la mística española), M.J. Fernández indicates the following in relation to the work of St. Theresa: "The affective connotations of the sememe *light* obey two fundamental variants.... One of them constitutes a partially lexicalized connotation.... The semanteme *light* appears in a construction with the verb *to be*, with the sense of 'being good,' 'being convenient,' and synonymous expressions" (55).

"The second type of affective connotation" arises "in mystical or religious subjects, totally lexicalized today in expressions like 'may God enlighten us' or other similar ones" (56). Shadows and darkness do not appear equally lexicalized with the sense of "the good" or "the convenient," but not because they are lacking in history in our mysticism. M.J. Fernández observes:

> the mystic doctrine of St. John of the Cross is centralized in the static transcendence of inaccessible-absolute *God-night*. The mystic union of the soul with God takes place only after a total catharsis.... God-darkness becomes visible only when man has renounced himself.... Man must convert himself into *night* in order to find *Night* [60].

It may be relevant to recall here that the consciousness of oneself that a young man has, like the one in "Suicide," is what has been instilled by his family and by the society in which he lives. The construction of a proper identity begins in adolescence. To renounce "oneself" is, in this case, essential in order to be able to fulfill oneself.

In his article "Simbolismo ambiguo en la poesía de García Lorca," Richard L. Predmore presents an opinion similar to that of Zuleta about the symbolism of the shadow: "Among the symbols of death the shadow is one of the most obvious and persistent" (239). J.M. Aguirre sees the ambiguity of the Lorquian shadow better: "The symbolism of 'shadow' possesses negative connotations ... at the same time, it seems to affirm the loving existence, or rather, life in the shadow" (114).

Florence L. Yudin in her article "The Dark Silence in Lorca's Poetry" arrives at the conclusion that the "dark silences" trace a drama of fighting and survival that is intensely human (165). Light and shadow are also studied in J.F. Spencer's "El claroscuro en la trilogía lorquiana." Spencer shows a marked propensity to associate darkness and blackness with evil in different linguistic constructions. He mentions a "black and destructive" attitude and states that "what is darkness, evil" is "that parents contract the marriage of their children." "But the worst, the darkest..." and he continues further down: "Another dark and decadent custom that Lorca underscores is that of sinking into mourning." Further along it is stated: "The clarity of what could have been was changed into darkness." According to Spencer, Lorca points to "an obscure and antiquated custom.... Among the ancient norms that Lorca paints, one encounters the concept of the female peasant" (174–75, 178–79).

According to Huber, the shadow is not a symbol of importance in Lorca's work (150). In *A Concordance to the Plays and Poems of FEDERICO GARCÍA LORCA*, it can be verified that "shadow" is one of the words that Lorca uses most. It is found in the first column of "Indexed words in the poems in order of frequency" (Pollin 1141). Huber studies the symbols of light and the mirror in the poem "Caprice" and comments on the following lines:

> The mirror is the wellspring
> become mummy, closes
> like a shell of light
> at sunset [*CP* 173; 631].

The author indicates that what is seen in the Lorquian mirror is not the vivid and essential aspect of things but their "mummy" (152). It could be added that "Caprice," like "Suicide," deals with the enmity and incompatibility of the light-mirror with the shadow. The "shell of light" does not give life but mummifies. The wellspring, which is alive, remains free of its mummified image when night arrives and shadows fall. Note that in "Suicide," the shadow is described using terms that evoke the presence of a wellspring: it is "a great burst" that "inundates."

The young man who attacks the mirror-light is half mummified ("geometric" and with "rag flowers") and needs to free himself. The homosexual cannot live in the light, he is "stopped." This recalls the terror that the arrival of day brings with it for those who have to live in a society that belongs only to "the normal" (see the beginning of this chapter).

That the "I" that attacks the mirror seems or may be "geometric" has two readings or disparate interpretations, but which are perfectly compatible with the ambiguity inherent in poetry. Both have been suggested. The first: geometric=geometrized. The dominant "science" has imposed on the young man a form-formation. The young man, apparently "formed," wants to free himself from his artificial exterior. The second: the protagonist has his own geometry (homosexual) that differs from what "geometry" advocates, a subject of Christian society that the mirror reflects, reproduces and imposes. The young man has not mastered "geometry" (see the corresponding section above, in this chapter).

• • •

The next step after observing the importance of the role of shadow and light in the fight for life or death in "Suicide" is an examination of what this fight implies or reflects. The purpose is to show, first, the parallelism of light with the dominant culture(s) and with the sexuality institutionalized in marriage. Second, it is evident that Lorca and other members of the Generation of '27 demonstrate in their writings that they were conscious of what was going to happen to their works once they died: that the established culture, associated with light, was going to use them for their own benefit, obscuring or distorting the problematics of the love that has to live in the connotative shadows of the poems. These contexts seem essential to "translating" the soul and feelings that motivate "Suicide," and understanding the reason for the attack against the mirror.

The love and sexual connotations of the difference between light and shadow, between bright and dark, already appear in the first book of poems published by Lorca. In "Sad Ballad" the speaker states: "the *she* of the ballad plunged me / into light dreams" (28). The "she," that is, woman in the abstract, is associated with clarity. It is suggested that the poet's love can be listened to in the dark: "At night I would speak the sadness / of my unknown love" (28). This unknown love later would become the unknown "other half." Cernuda alludes to it in "If Only a Man Could Say" (Si el hombre pudiera decir): "the unknown truth" (*Young Sailor* 36; *PC* 125).

Ian Gibson states that unacceptable homosexual inclinations perhaps can be read in "Sad Ballad" ("Lorca's 'Balada triste'" 30). It is also possible to see in the poem that the speaker fails in his intent to enter the world of the woman and, implicitly, that of heterosexuality. Woman becomes realized when "el *ella*" (the *she* with a masculine definite article) becomes "la *ella*" (the *she* with a feminine definite article). She then becomes "inpenetrable": "the inpenetrable *she* of the ballad" ("Lorca's 'Balada triste'" 28). The word "penetrate" has additional meanings, apart from its sexual connotation. The ambiguity of Lorca's text suggests that there is an epistemological connection among the different penetrations.

According to Mircea Eliade, light is associated with procreation in different philosophies and religions (27, 48, 56). In "Autumn Song" (Canción otoñal), which, like "Sad Ballad," belongs to *Book of Poems*, Lorca presents light as an oppressor. The "I" is castrated symbolically, just as in "Suicide": "The light clips my wings" (*CP* 19; 15). In "Living Sky," from *PNY*, "the sun's duel with the creatures of flesh and blood" (85; 491) is mentioned.

The attacks of light against the central character from "Back of the World" already appear very advanced in "The Crazy Boy." The light plays "statue" with the boy, that is, it petrifies him. In R.D. Laing's *The Divided Self*, Laing indicates that *to petrify* others means, among other things, to deny their autonomy, ignore their feelings and to contemplate them as objects, killing the life they have within (46). In leaving, the light gives the boy the coup de grace, like someone playing "a trick": "It split the crazy boy from his shadow" (*CP* 489; 362).

In "Suicide" the young man already has been separated from his shadow that lies "quiet and prone / on the white silk divan." Here the luminous color white evokes the presence of a shroud that envelops or weakens the shadow. Silk conjures up softness and suggests that the young man's shadow is not being stifled through direct violence but through the quieting softness of the family surroundings. Silk is produced by certain worms and is also the viscous liquid in the form of a thread which caterpillars and spiders secrete. The young man's shadow has been trapped in a soft spider's web that is taking away his life.

In an earlier poem, "Invocación al laurel," one already foresees the problematics of the young man of the "quiet" shadow and invaded heart from "Suicide." Here the heart of the poetic "I" is being trapped as if in a "spiderweb" by the "silk threads" of the sweet words of others:

> Everyone spoke sweetly to my heart
> trembling on the threads of sonorous silk
> with which water envelopes standing things
> like a spiderweb of eternal harmony.
> ...

> You all overwhelm me with your songs;
> I only ask you about my uncertain one; [135, 136].

At times the Lorquian light is associated with something positive, in which case it is a different or persecuted light. "El diamante" presents the familiar symbol of the bird in connection with light ("bird of light"). This bird is a "prisoner" and wants "to escape" and flees "without knowing that he is wearing / a chain tied onto his neck" (47).

In "Dawn" (La aurora), from *PNY*, the poetic voice turns against a *rootless science* (emphasis added) that buries, that is, kills and hides García Lorca's New York light: "The light is buried under chains and noises / in an impudent challenge to rootless science" (11; 485). This "rootless science" seems to be in shameless alliance with the establishment. Doves, whose symbolism we already examined in chapter 2, splash here in "putrid waters," just as the first people to go out early in the light of this Lorquian dawn "know they will be mired in numbers and laws." The silk spiderweb of sweet words that previously enveloped the Lorquian "I" is not always sufficiently strong. On occasion, one must use "laws" and "chains."

The superficial theme of "Dawn" may be the technology and traffic of a great city like New York. The mention of frustrated love suggests, nevertheless, that the poem also or principally deals with other problematics of greater magnitude and profundity:

> Those who go out early know in their bones
> there will be no paradise or loves that bloom and die:
> they know they will be mired in numbers and laws,
> in mindless games, in fruitless labors [11; 485].

In Lorca's work, there are two opposing sciences: l) the "rootless science" of those who have the power to bury this light of the Lorquian dawn; and 2) the science mentioned in "Wounds of Love" (Llagas de amor) (*Sonetos* 47), the "bitter wisdom" of bitter love (see "Lorca and Sailors," chapter 2) which, contrary to the first, indeed has roots: "Love, my enemy, / bite your bitter root!" ("Ghazal of the Bitter Root" *CP* 660; 578).

The study of the other half revealed that homosexuals were "unredeemable" (chapter 2); in "Dawn," it is made explicit that "there will be no paradise." Lorca perhaps received inspiration from Nietzsche in writing "Dawn"; the German writer had authored a book with the same title, and both he and the Spanish writer had very similar ideas. According to López Castellón, Nietzsche's *Dawn* "consists of an inversion of all values" (9). Dalí read a lot of Nietzsche during the period in which he and Lorca were living together in the Residencia (Santos Torroella 102). Lorca expresses his admiration for Nietzsche's *Zarathustra* in an unpublished lecture quoted by Eutemio Martín (*Fed-*

erico García Lorca 104). Gil-Albert was also "very devoted" to Nietzsche (Simón 13).

In his prologue to *Dawn*, Nietzsche asks: "How can one explain that since Plato, all the creators of philosophy have built incorrectly?" The true answer, according to Nietzsche, is that "Kant as well as his predecessors have constructed their buildings on the seduction of morality; that their intention was directed towards only an appearance of truth and certainty; because what they were looking for in reality was the *majesty of morality's building*" (29).

It has been noted that Lorca's poetic voice in "Dawn" underscored being "mired in numbers and laws" that those who go out early encounter at the dawn of a new day. In similar fashion, Cernuda's poetic voice denounces the limits and laws that control his life and define his love. Like Nietzsche, Cernuda speaks in architectural terms of morality and the establishment, but where Nietzsche says "morality's building," Cernuda writes "building of sand":

> Hear them dictate the law to the world, define love,
> make a canon of inexpressible beauty,
> ...
> Contemplate their strange brains
> Trying to build, child by child, a complex building of sand
> ["The Poet's Glory," *Young Sailor* 68; *PC* 185].

Jacques Ancet in *Luis Cernuda* points to Cernuda's philosophical relationship with Nietzsche. The art of the poet is moral in that it obliges us to ask ourselves about our own existence, beyond the current values of a society that, like a new God, molds us in his image and likeness. For Ancet, the connection with Nietzsche is obvious (84). Both Nietzsche and Cernuda see the dominant morality as a construction; for Cernuda it is also a sexual construction. In the above poem, Cernuda associates the "building" with heterosexuality or, to be more precise, with the results of the practice of heterosexuality: the "building of sand" is constructed "child by child." In the same way, those who build this building dictate the laws that define or prohibit the love of others.

It seems one can deduce that Cernuda, or his poetic persona, believes that literary criticism has been placed at the service of the norms and values of heterosexuality. The "solemn intellectual" is presented as a product or sprouting of procreating "ghosts." The professor appears like a person who has sold out in his search for the applause and the prize of the establishment:

> Those are, brother mine,
> The beings for whom I die alone
> Ghosts from whom someday will bloom
> The solemn intellectual, an oracle of these my words before
> foreign students,

Becoming famous for this,
More a small country house... [68; 185].

The students are unfamiliar, but they are also made strange. The "oracle" perhaps hides the most important part of the text. In "El poeta y los mitos," from *Ocnos*, Cernuda refers to the homosexual origins of his poetry, through the connotations of the Hellenic: "whatever aspiration there may be in you towards poetry, those Hellenic myths were what provoked and directed it" (17). To keep quiet about these sources contributes to the students' alienation.

According to Cernuda, poetry is something whose cause remains "hidden": "by way of a very fleeting light among eternal darkness or sudden shadow between the demanding light" (*Crítica* 39). What inspires the poet has been condemned to "eternal darkness" by the dominant Christian culture and also by the majority of the "erudite" academic culture. The light of these cultures that marginalize homosexual love is an "oppressive" light. In evoking the work of Aleixandre, Cernuda reiterates his disdain: "It is well known that the greater the transcendence of a writer's work, the greater the difficulty of that work in being recognized and accepted. Let us not talk about critics because the history of literature gives us recurring proof of the habitual ignorance of professional critics and scholars" (*Crítica* 217).

Cernuda was not quite mistaken. According to Octavio Paz, at his death, poets and critics, "all one," covered "with the same gray cape of praise the work of a spirit who with admirable and inflexible obstinacy never ceased affirming his *dissent*.... There has been no lack of those who affirm that death has returned him to his country ('once the dog dies, the rage ceases')" (*Los signos* 128). "Do the dead hear what the living say about them?" inquires Cernuda in "Birds in the Night" (*Young Sailor* 124; *PC* 471). The question is motivated by what is said and written about Verlaine and Rimbaud, in general, and for the homage to them in the shape of a plaque in the house where they lived, in particular: "At its inauguration without doubt ambassador and mayor were in attendance, / All those who were enemies of Verlaine and Rimbaud while they lived." Alive, "even the black prostitute had a right to insult them." Dead, "France uses both their names and their work / For the greater glory of France and its logical art." For Cernuda, the official honors and homages that "Today" are paid to them are a "repugnant, eulogistic farce" (124; 471).

In general, it is believed and stated that the poets of the Generation of '27 represent the established culture. In *La cultura española y la cultura establecida*, Aranguren explains what is understood by *cultural establishment or established culture*: "the Royal Academies in their essential nucleus ... and even the 'children,' yet not the 'grandchildren,' of the Generation of '98. This for me is the established culture in Spain" (14).

Since homosexuality *is not* the established culture, one ought to refine a bit Aranguren's definition: the works of Lorca, Cernuda and others are representative of the established culture always and whenever depredation or expurgation of some of the most important aspects of their works is accepted. All these poets have marked in different ways the distance that separates them from the established culture in general and the Academy in particular. Cernuda, Prados, Gil-Albert and Lorca express themselves with sufficient clarity in this respect. In "Again with Feeling" (Otra vez con sentimiento), Cernuda refers to the silence Dámaso Alonso maintains about homosexuality in García Lorca's work. He is referring to what is written in Alonso's *Poetas españoles contemporáneos* (758–66). For Cernuda, "the stupidity" of Alonso's text is like a continuation of the crime committed against Lorca:

> Academic nonsense? Common nonsense leads
> to his writings. But his rhetorical fit
> does not clarify to our understanding
> The secret thing in your work, although they also call him
> A critic of our contemporary poetry.
> ...
> Now stupidity follows the crime [*PC* 486].

According to Villena, Cernuda's enmity towards Alonso was always crystal clear, perhaps due to the relative conservativeness of Dámaso Alonso or perhaps because of his "well-known mania against homosexuals" ("Cernuda recordado por Aleixandre" 86).

For his part, Lorca implicity compares the university to Calvary in "Lovers Slain by a Partridge": "I saw his cheeks tremble when the professors from the University would bring him honey and vinegar on a small sponge" (996). The scene is like an allusion to the thirst and anguish of Christ crucified, but Lorca's poem in prose does not deal with Jesus but with two lovers, "two disheartened men." The university professors incarnate the centurions of Rome in the ninth hour when Christ said: "My God! My God! Why have you abandoned me?" (St. Matthew 27:46–49, St. Mark 15:34–40). In the fifth scene from *The Public* it is insinuated that there is a relationship between the death-sacrifice of the Nude and the academic culture. Blood is being taken from the Nude, "crowned with thorns," at the door of a university, during people's applause. The public has already murdered the homosexuals, protagonists of the drama, and asks that "the poet be dragged off by his hair" like a dead bull-god. (In his lecture on the *duende*, Lorca affirms that "the liturgy of the bulls" is an "authentic religious drama in which, like the Mass, a god was worshipped and sacrificed to"; 1107.) An intimate connection is suggested between the sacrifice of the Naked Jesus Christ, the murder of homosexuals and the dragging-death of the poet-bull-god.

In "Cry to Rome," Lorca makes reference again to the sacrifice of Jesus and denounces the falseness or deceit of those in charge of education and learning. The man dressed in white "ignores the fact that Christ can still give water," and "The teachers show the children / a marvelous light coming from the mountain; / but what arrives is a junction of sewers" (*PNY* 151; 526).

Summary and Conclusions

Consistent with the first part of the subtitle of this chapter ("A Poem and Its Milieu"), "Suicide" has been situated in those contexts to which it belongs: the book *Songs* and the section "Back of the World." At the same time these contexts belong to Lorca's entire oeuvre.

The literary work should also be seen as a reflection of the vital situation of its creator and as a reflection of the society or societies from which it emerges and against which it takes shape. These factors are consistent with the second part of the chapter's subtitle: "A Psyche and Its Circumstances."

The different symbols that together constitute the formal and fundamental unity of the poem have been considered in detail, along with the viewpoints of other critics. The most important one, the mirror, symbolizes the invasion of the psyche of the young man by enemy projections that come from Christianity, obligatory heterosexuality and the lethal "scientific" light directed against homosexuals through the fields of medicine and academic analyses.

One could briefly summarize the poem by saying that "Suicide" deals with an adolescent who, pushed towards personal suicide, chooses social suicide. In "killing" the mirror and its projections, the young man "kills" the society that invades his psychic interior and tries to become embodied in his being. The "suicide" is a rite of passage. The young man assumes his destiny and, in this way, is born to his identity as an adult in the culture that society has condemned to living in the shadows: the culture of homosexuality. Through the ambiguity of the poetry, it is also suggested that under the prevailing circumstances, life in this culture can be equivalent to death, but that this "death" is life. Behind the shadow that inundates the poetic space of the symbolic suicide, in the illusory room, "Love" arrives "(with wings and arrows)"; that is, triumphant Eros emerges from the egg of night after floating in the waters of Chaos (Curtiss 40). On an erotic, mystical level there is reference to the dark night that takes us into the presence of Love.[9] On a religious-psychoanalytic level, the young man is the ego who refuses to bury the talents he has received from God. With his hatchet, he dies for society —

or the world — with the objective of being able to live for himself, that is, for God, or perhaps, for the authenticity of this being or homosexual feeling that the love creator (or the Creator-Love) has put in him.[10] The broken wings of pretense and of frustrated sexuality are thus transformed into the vivid wings of Love.

❖ ❖ ❖

The hypotheses formulated in the section of the introduction titled "Lorca's Life and Letters: Silences and Secrets" have been corroborated, although it is important to note that only some of the most important points of the complex Lorquian interweaving have been put forward. The study of what has been said and written about Lorca and his oeuvre has revealed that a part of literary criticism has participated in the process of the dispossession and objectification of the texts of homosexual culture.

In the second chapter the semantic dichotomies and points of view that exist between "our culture" and that which finds its expression in Lorca's texts have been made manifest. In the first culture, homosexuals are seen as "rats," while this poet consider himself to be "pure." It also has been verified that the symbols, "rats" and "pure ones" and the visions that imply their utilization coexist in the texts of homosexual culture. In Lorca's work, fear and guilt over homosexuality are evident mainly in the connection of love-sex with death and cancer. The liberation of the alienated point of view appears implicit after the Lorquian "robbery" of the symbol of the dove.

The analysis of the sonnet "I Know That My Profile Will Be Serene" in chapter 3 has revealed the rhetorical and revolutionary dimension of Lorquian poetry. The aesthetic symbolic-semiotic unity of the poem is inseparable from the unity in all of Lorca's work and is related to the crisis produced by the situation of the persecuted homosexual that the poet lived, according to Lorca's letters and the declarations of different friends of the poet. The concept "oppressed norms" that Lorca uses in the sonnet, and its implicit opposite, "oppressive norms," are testimony or indicators of a class consciousness deeply rooted in homosexual experience. In similar fashion, Lorca employed the term "corporation" to make reference to people, groups or classes that try to regiment human passions and intend to cut off the wings of dissidents.

The third chapter studied the connotations of *Mercury*. The fourth uncovered more evidence that Lorca searched for support and inspiration in the myths and symbols of ancient Greece, in particular, those that concern love and the transformations of Bacchus and Cyssus. This type of love and these myths have been degraded through the centuries in which homosexuals have lived under the domination and terror of the so-called Christian culture. The symbols that alluded to Bacchus were converted into symbols of the devil, while homosexuality was presented as a diabolical possession, and homosexuals were burned at the stake. The ambiguous "burning" love and the "burnt" and silenced voice are images that appear repeatedly in Lorca. The connection between these types of images and the role of scapegoat that has been assigned to homosexuals seems clear.

In chapter 5 Lorca associated poetic creation with oneiric activity. It has been demonstrated that Lorca's poetry is, in part, a product of a libidinous impulse that is against the restrictions imposed on homosexuality, and, in part, a product of the conscious work of the poet with motifs associated with dreams. This work reveals, at the same time that it hides, the homosexual origins of Lorca's inspiration.

The character of the billy goat, analyzed diachronically in chapter 4, has been studied synchronically in chapter 5, in the context of the aesthetic unity of "Dream" and also, indirectly, in analyzing "Bacchus," the poem that takes as its title the name of the god-"devil" symbolized by the above animal. The relationship between the homosexuality of "Verlaine" and that of Bacchus and the fear and desire of the Lorquian poetic "I" from the poem "Bacchus" has also been shown.

Finally, the intersection of diverse psychosociological isotopies in Lorca's words, poems and poetic groupings has been verified. The evolution of the theme of homosexuality implicit in the group of poems "Back of the World," which goes from the rejection of the matrimonial symbol of the ring to the breaking of the mirror of society-heterosexuality, has also been demonstrated.

Literature is often the mirror of society in a double sense: it reflects the society of its time and is a mirror constructed by the society of its time. The same can be stated about criticism in general. The attack against the mirror is the symbolic act of trying to free onself "by killing" the conventional "I" that is reproduced by, and which reproduces, the appearances and conventions that dominate the lives of people.

The intent here has been to interpret Lorca's work in such a way that the underlying psychic impulse of creativity becomes visible. The objective was to show the relationship between Lorquian feeling and the linguistic expressions that the poet uses and the aesthetic form he gives to his work.

Homosexuality did not cause Lorca to break with "our culture." It was "our culture" that broke with homosexuality and, indirectly, with Lorca and with one of the most important aspects of his work.

"I Know That My Profile Will Be Serene" affirmed the Lorquian voice in the poem examined in chapter 3. Once could add a serene and sharp profile in recalling Lorca's words about the dead in "The *Duende.*" One must allow the Lorquian profile, therefore, to cut through academic reflection:

> In every country, death comes as a finality. It comes, and the curtain comes down. But not in Spain! In Spain the curtain goes up. Many people live out

their lives between walls till the day they die and are brought out into the sun. In Spain, the dead are more alive than the dead of any other country of the world: their profile wounds like the edge of a barber's razor [Belitt, *PNY* 393; 1103].

Epilogue: The Centenary

Lorca's "Holy Year" arrived, proclaimed in the title of an article by Miguel Mora in *El País*, October 26, 1997. Two months before, plans for seven expositions, five movie and television projects, five conferences given by "specialists" and more than 40 musical and theatrical shows were already announced. When the National Commission for the Centenary of Federico García Lorca published its "Official Program of Activities," it consisted of 48 pages and included many more events.

It was impossible to attend every activity and read everything that was written. Nevertheless, I believe it is possible to say that the general trend was to present a popular Lorca, that is, someone embraceable and saleable. Shortly after the official beginning, the daily *El Mundo* published Pilar Ortega's article whose title is fairly symptomatic in this regard: "Lorca, Ambassador of Spanish Culture." Homosexuality, of course, is not something recommendable either for an ambassador of Spanish culture or for someone "holy." The article quotes producer Enrique Nicanor and "Lorca expert" John J. Healey, the director of a documentary budgeted at 60 million pesetas that TVE had programmed for 1998. Originally titled *Federico García Lorca*, its name was most likely changed due to the existence of another documentary, written by Healey and produced by Enrique Nicanor. The latter, *Portrait of a Family* (Retrato de una familia), appeared in many countries during 1998. Being more than just about Lorca, it deals with the acceptable and convenient image of Lorca and the opinions different members of his family have, whether they knew him or not. Christopher Maurer was the only Lorca scholar to participate, but his opinions did not differ greatly from the others presented.

The general attitude of Lorca's family in *Portrait*, expressed elsewhere, is to either ignore the poet's homosexuality or to try and minimize its importance. Lorca's sister, as usual, was completely silent on the issue. Others expressed themselves in the following way: "My feeling is that he had a very normal love life, that he was not especially uncomfortable with his homosexuality" (Laura García Lorca).

In *The Public*, Lorca suggests that only students could effect a radical change in society. Student 5 is ready to allow Student 1 to fall in love with him, and both are willing to destroy everything, including roofs and families (523–24). During the centenary in Spain, based on my own knowledge, students from a university group in Cáceres were the only ones who took action to hear a lecture about homosexuality in Lorca's life and works. The group's coordinator, Miguel Millán Chaparro, extended an invitation to me to come and stay in Cáceres, with the students arranging to pay my expenses. The group adopted a very poetic name that has multiple Lorquian resonances: "Dialogues with the Moon" (Diálogos con la luna). Although the title of this lecture did not appear in the "Official Program of Activities," news of it reached the journalist María Luisa Chamorro, from television's "Southern Channel." She, together with Jesús Vigorra, was preparing a program on the poet's homosexuality. Both wanted to include some aspects relating to my book, and, thanks to the students, they managed to do it. The program, bearing the title "Looking for Lorca" (Buscando a Lorca), appeared in the fall of 1998, with Ian Gibson as its advisor. This is merely an anecdote, but given the hopes embodied in the students from *The Public*, I believe it is relevant.

To sum up, García Lorca's family, the secretary of the Lorca Foundation and many experts or representatives of Lorquian criticism seemed satisfied with the results of the centenary. The daily *ABC* of January 21, 1999, states, "The García Lorca Foundation believes that the innumerable events that took place during the 1998 centenary of the poet's birth were a complete success." According to what is highlighted here, it seems that one of the reasons for the satisfaction of Manuel Fernández Montesinos, Lorca's nephew and secretary of the foundation, is that "The reductionist vision of the writer as a homosexual and a leftist has been overcome" (Ruiz Antón). Others seem less pleased with the celebration of this and other centenaries. The writer and columnist for *ABC*, Juan Manuel de Prada, expressed his dissatisfaction in the following way:

> Gigantic expositions are promoted, the specialists give the usual speech with wasted and itinerant saliva and the politicians recite some little poem, which sounds as sarcastic as a gob of spit, in front of the dead person's grave ... the organizers of the splendors trivialize the memory of the guests of honor, and even musical versions of Lorca's most characteristic poems become commercialized. And what remains after so much sound and fury? An empty hall, devastated by the rotten army, which will not be filled again until the next anniversary.

Chapter Notes

Introduction

1. The English word "unspeakable" is the translation used throughout the text as the most appropriate equivalent for "inconfesable" within the context of Sahuquillo's work.—*Trans.*

2. Following Greimas, F. Rastier defines isotopy as an iteration of a linguistic unity, which can perhaps be explained by saying it is the repeated appearance of words, sentences, etc., in relation to something concrete, which, in this case, would be homosexuality: "One calls all repetitions of a linguistic unity 'isotopy' ... the number of unities making up an isotopy is theoretically infinite" (82).

The linguistic sequence in which an isotopy is found can be a lower dimension, equal to or higher than that of the sentence (Rastier). In "La isopotía del discurso," from *Semántica estructural*, Greimas demonstrates the need to go beyond the semantic definition in order to analyze isotopies: "Semantic analysis, in search of criteria of judgment with a view to establishing isotopies, comes to use the concept of the 'hierarchy' of contexts which imbricate each other" (110).

Passing from the analysis of sentences to that of paragraphs, and from there to the analysis of passages, narratives, scenes, dialogues, chapters, works, etc., the difficulties gradually increase if we have to keep the contexts in mind. In these cases, says Greimas, the methods of semantic analysis "cannot be employed rigorously and formal criteria capable of being revealed are absolutely insufficient" (110). Similar to the observations of Greimas are those of Víctor Sánchez de Zavala in *Praxiologic Investigations* (Indagaciones praxiológicas): "the more semantic details and situational references are made explicit in the underlying structure, the more complex and debatable are the processes ... which connect the underlying structure with the superficial structure" (34–35).

As an example of the aforementioned processes, Sánchez de Zavala names the transformations and other rules defined in the whole of the structures assignable to speech (34–35).

3. The phenomenology referred to is, above all, existential. In "Foundations for a Science of Persons," from *The Divided Self*, Laing states that in existential phenomenology, the existence that we speak about can be one's own or that of another. When the other is a patient, existential phenomenology becomes an intent to reconstruct the patient's way of being, within the patient's own world (25). As far as what concerns us, it is a matter of reconstructing the homosexual existence of the "patient" of the text, and presenting it from the perspective of the conscious homosexual, that is, from a perspective which sees the homosexual situation within the context of the world from which it derives. One proceeds combining empathy with critical activity, the *view from within* with the analysis of the situation.

4. The concepts of *readerly* and *writerly* come from Barthes, who in turn owes them to Brecht, according to Belsey (125). Ann Jefferson explains the relationship of these concepts with that of intertextuality in her article "Intertextuality and the Poetics of Fiction" (236). The author also presents different points of view about this last concept. J. Lozano believes that the concept of textual competence "can be enriched with that of intertextual competence. With such a concept one implies that every reader in reading or hearing a text always has in mind the experience that he/she (as a reader) has of other texts" (21).

Chapter 1

1. "Rinconcillo" refers to a gathering of a group of intellectuals and artists from Granada that included Lorca. They would meet regularly at the Café Alameda in Granada during the period 1915–22. See Ian Gibson, *Federico García Lorca: A Life*. (New York: Pantheon Books, 1989).—*Trans.*

2. *Eros and Lorca* helps little in understanding Lorca's homosexuality. Feal Deibe's analysis in this regard is reduced to hardly more than citing some very debatable affirmations of Bergler, such as the following: "The homosexual frantically flees from women; unconsciously he feels toward them a panicky fear" (29–30). Some years later, Carlos Feal published a new book, *Lorca: tragedia y mito*, recognizing the importance of the "homosexual code" for the reorientation of Lorquian studies, but at the same time criticizing what Feal calls the "abusive use" of such a code (13). Nevertheless, the author does not point out the abusive use of psychoanalytic codes or the codes in other methods.

3. In a lecture presented in the Literary Journeys organized by the University of the Basque Country in 1988, I analyzed a variant reading of the "Christlike dimension of Lorquian homosexuality" mentioned by Eutimio Martín, as demonstrated in "After a Walk" (Vuelta de paseo), the first poem of *Poet in New York*. My work was published in 1990 in the proceedings of the above-mentioned Literary Journeys and was titled "The Assassination of 'After a Walk,' of Federico García Lorca." N.B.: Note correction, p. 497, from "Juliet was 'a girl' to 'a boy.'"

4. Often, "culture" is understood as the culture that openly disseminates the values of heterosexual love and represses the homosexual. The term "heterosexual culture" has only recently been used. I found it officially recognized for the first time in *Homosexuals in Society* (Homosexuella och samhället), a memoir of the investigations about the situation of homosexuals in society (*Betänkande av utredningen om homosexuellas situation i samhället*). The work was carried out under the auspices of the Swedish state by C. E. Sturkell, L. Ahlmark, B. Bjelle, E. Bohlin, L. Hansson, K. Israelsson, G. Jonäng, L. Malmgren and R. Sundgren, assisted by B. Ekdahl, S.A. Petersson and Wittorp. It began in 1978 and ended in 1984. The term cited appears, for example, in the index and on page 37.

5. The accusations of "immorality" made by the then minister of culture, Iñigo Cavero, were based, according to the minister, "on a morning program in which a man asked a doctor how he could perform homosexual acts, keeping in mind that he suffered from a definite illness," and the doctor "responded." According to Luis del Olmo, director of the program that was the object of the accusation, the minister probably listened to other broadcasts from Spain or abroad, but not National Radio. Luis de Olmo confessed to having dealt with the theme of homosexuals from different points of view, "but in no case have I given guidelines," he stated ("RTVE Answers the Critics of the Minister of Culture," *El País*, July 10, 1981).

6. Eutimio Martín was the first critic to publish the uncensored letter, in 1986, in his book *Federico García Lorca, heterodoxo y mártir* (86–88). Antonina Rodrigo had published the letter on various occasions, in *GL en Cataluña* (262–64) as well as in *Lorca-Dalí: A Friendship Betrayed* (Lorca-Dalí. Una amistad traicionada), where the text appears on two occasions (211–12, 219–33), invariably with the ending suppressed.

7. Eisenberg's quotation can also be found in Pablo Neruda's book *Para nacer he nacido* (Seix Barral: Barcelona, 1978, 107–108). Ian Gibson has also written about the publication of *Sonnets of Dark Love* and about the attacks on those who dare to mention Lorquian homosexuality:

I believe that those who silence Lorca's homosexuality are not really helping and thereby demonstrate that they are aligning themselves with the repressive people against whom Lorca had to struggle during his life.

In saying this, I am thinking not only of the usual bad critics, but also of certain Lorquian scholars who, I suppose in order not to have problems with the poet's family and out of fear of being excluded from the archive of the García Lorca Foundation, never say in public what they know or think about the poet's real problem. A symptom of this was the publication in *ABC* (March 17, 1984) of the famous *Sonnets of Dark Love*, surrounded by the respective articles of Fernando Lázaro Carreter, Miguel García-Posada and Miguel Hernández Montesinos, in which there is not a single mention of "homosexuality" or "homosexual" [*Federico García Lorca* 2, 87–88].

Chapter 2

1. Fernando de los Ríos, a teacher in Granada during Lorca's youth, was an important mentor to Lorca, in addition to being a leading intellectual in Spain. See Ian Gibson's comments about him in *Federico García Lorca: A Life* (44–46).—*Trans.*

2. "Raza," "race" in Spanish, can have additional meanings, e.g., an allusion to national origins.—*Trans.*

3. Note 17 of Christopher Maurer's translation of "Lecture: A Poet in New York" from *PNY* (Simon White, trans.) states that "This poem is erroneously titled 'Luna y panorama de insectos' in previous studies and editions of Lorca. The source of the error is that the rough draft of the poem in the Lorca archives was begun on a sheet of paper previously used for 'Luna y panorama de los insectos (poema de amor)'" (193).—*Trans.*

4. *Duende* is defined as a "mysterious communicative power" by Ian Gibson in *Federico García Lorca: A Life* 113.—*Trans.*

5. In "Arrival in Rome" (Aux abords de Rome), Louis Aragon uses words as the symbol of a phallic knife of homosexual desire:

> How can I be this rugby player,
> This bundle of violent meat,
> ...
> Like the knife for its lightning flash and
>   its ferocity, how can I penetrate him,
> Only with the unique marvel of words
> [15].

In the established culture it is customary to mention Aragon's love of Elsa, but, according to A. Prique, Aragon's old age knew only the consolation of masculine love: "Aragon's homosexuality is something other than an anecdote. Who will deny it among his intimates? Aragon's difficult, unhappy old age only knew one comfort: the love of boys, more precisely, of young men. He has said it; he has written it" (14).

6. At the beginning of "The Carthusian Monastery" (La cartuja) the allusions are quite guarded. Toward the middle and the end, they become more direct. The porch of the church is "strong and manly in configuration" (854). "The figure of the Redeemer" is spoken about later: "He is overflowing with passionate lust born of charity and sadness" (855). In "Cloister" (Clausura), the second part of the poem, Lorca alludes to the mediocrity of certain sculptors: "They reproduce ... they never create" (857). True art is "the infinite coupling of the artistic sentiment" (857). The poet associates the rooms of the cloister with "almost strangled passions" (858). While others see silence in the monastery, he sees "passion" ... "The soul feels loving desires, desires to love crazily, and desires for another soul which fuses with ours" (861). Along with the silence there is "a great sensuality." The silence and the solitude are "great aphrodisiacs" (861).

In the last page of the second part, "Cloister," "ivy" is named twice. In chapter 3 we will look at the connection between this plant and homosexuality.

7. The "head full of excrement" of those who shout toward Rome can allude to, among other things, the life of the sewers and the thought and the love of homosexuals, dirtied by the propaganda of Christian institutions. But it can also symbolize the result of a homosexual act that could not be carried out with the hygienic measures that might be desirable. In poetic imagery the phenomenon of compression is evident, such as occurs in dreams (Freud, *Interpretation* 22, 308–330). In "Freud and the Analysis of Poetry" K. Burke proposes "that we take key Freudian terms like 'compression' and displacement' as general categories for the analysis of the poem as dream" (194).

The connection of excrement with love, homosexual or not, is also found in W.B. Yeats and William Blake (Cowell 107). Juan Ramón Jiménez observed that connection in Yeats. J.C. Wilcox has commented on the impression it made on J.R. Jiménez (514).

In "Lyric as Performance: Lorca and Yeats," M. Baumgarten says, discussing Correa's critical text, that the rhythm forms the path of ejaculation. *Rhythm and path* are mixed in the same trajectory (333). The author's words seem to refer to the rhythm that precedes the launching of a shout, but they are somewhat ambiguous, like what Yeats thinks about the subject, and the meaning of the final crescendo of "Beheading the Baptist" noted in this chapter.

8. A comparative study of Wilde and Lorca would probably be quite fruitful. This is not the place for such an enterprise, but perhaps we can inspire other critics with a few examples that would lend support to such a study.

For Wilde's Salomé, the voice of the Baptist is like wine. Lorca's Baptist must do battle with "the roadhouse moon" (*CP* 627; 986). Wilde's Herod says that the moon is "like a mad woman, a mad woman who is seeking everywhere for lovers. She is naked, too. She is quite naked" (*Complete Works* 561). "The moon had become unbearable," states Lorca's narrator (626; 986). Wilde's young Sirius calls Salomé "a dove among doves," and asks her not to speak to John the Baptist as she was speaking to him (telling him that she desires his mouth). In Lorca's narration some doves "had remained silent," but now are "pounding on the door so furiously," as though wanting to enter with their voice and their organ or their homosexuality. Remember that the poetic phenomenon is one of compression of various images and experiences.

9. The past returns — transformed — when something in the present actualizes it. In *No Boundary* (La conciencia sin fronteras), Ken Wilber cites Alan Watts: "Do not look at all at the true past, but rather at a present vestige of the past." Wilber concludes: "Thus I can never know the true past, and I only know memories of the past, memories that exist only as a present experience" (94).

10. García-Posada, for example, a critic who dedicated a great deal of space and attention to the study of "Childhood and Death," states in an eponymous article: "The step from childhood to adolescence is commented upon with profound discontent" (192). Readers will perhaps ask themselves, only with discontent? Why then does Lorca write that his childhood-rat goes off "satisfied"? From what we understand, Lorca suggests that life as a rat is not totally lacking in attractions or satisfactions, however degraded this life appears.

On the same page García-Posada maintains:

"the rat into which childhood has been transformed, now debased, carries with it that last link that connected the adult with the dead child." Unlike García-Posada, we do not believe that adults can completely separate themselves from their childhood, nor do we think that Lorca might have suggested that. "Childhood and Death" is proof that those connections exist, however much one might want to forget the events that were most formative.

11. In Spanish, the word "cielo" can mean either "heaven" or "sky."—*Trans.*

12. Eduardo Naranjo's painting is dated 1986 and belongs to a book consisting of 12 color engravings, inspired by Lorca's *PNY*. For the history of the book and the reproduction of several of the paintings, among them one titled "Murdered by the Sky" (Asesinado por el cielo), see Fernando A. de Yraola's "Eduardo Naranjo: The Soul of Lorca" (Naranjo: El alma de Lorca) in *ABC*, 5 August 1990, 46–50 (*Blanco y negro* [supplement]).

13. Courage is a concept in which theological, sociological, and philosophical problems converge, according to Paul Tillich at the beginning of his book *The Courage to Be*. The author defines the courage to be, saying that it deals with an ethical act through which a human being affirms his own being, in spite of the elements of his existence which are in conflict with that essential affirmation of being (13, 15).

14. I want to thank Daniel Eisenberg for sending me Rivas Cherif's articles on Lorca. Lorca's words to Rivas Cherif confirm the hypothesis I presented in 1986, on the homosexual connotations of the concept of "the other half."

Chapter 3

1. The rites practiced by Alister Crowley are described in *Sexuality, Magic and Perversion* by F. King. I cite only the beginning of the ceremony, following Antonio Resines' translation:

Crowley began his work, as he himself said, "receiving the sacrament from a certain priest A.B."—which in this context means having sexual relations with him—and painting a pentagram (a symbol of design of Mercury)....

Crowley spent the greater part of the rest of the afternoon painting his mercurial pentagram until 11:30 pm, when he and Neuberg began the magic spell itself.

This spell began with the *Banishing Ceremony of the Pentagram*, of the golden dawn, which was *danced* by Neuberg, after which they invoked Toth-Hermes (Mercury)...

Jungitur in vati vates: rex inclyte rhabdou
Hermes tu venias, verba nefanda ferens.
(Magus with Magus united: Hermes,
 king of the rod,
appear, carrying the ineffable.) [King 152–53].

2. "Mercury" is the name of a Spanish group "for homosexual liberation," according to Soriano in *Homosexualidad y represión* (179).

3. "Hilo" can be translated as "thread" or "linen." Maurer uses "linen" in his translation of the poem. In Sahuquillo's analysis of the poem, "thread" seems to be the more appropriate word.—*Trans.*

4. The relationship between poetics and rhetoric is shown by Minguet in his article "From Rhetoric to Poetics." The author begins by reminding us that, historically, the object of rhetoric is far from stable. "The Art of Speaking" is one thing, says Minguet, but, how? and why? From the very first, we must confront the double problem of art and language, that is to say, the point of departure of aesthetics and philosophy. It is not true that rhetoric only concerns prose writers. Minguet points out, for example, that Domairon's French rhetoric manual takes the greater part of its examples from the utterances of the poets (330, 331, 334).

In "Literature and Semiotics" Todorov maintains that rhetoric is (and has always been) a semiotics of speech. This, in turn, becomes a type of knowledge that complements linguistics. Being conscious of the significant nature of many social phenomena—from literature to ritual, routine conversation to the poetic image—we will transform from within anthropology, art history, or literary studies (384, 385).

5. According to K.E. Read in *Other Voices: The Style of a Male Homosexual Tavern* (Novato, California: Chandler and Sharp Publishers, 1980), the sexuality of the group studied is "absolutely essential" to understanding its style, language being an integral part of it. The author maintains that methodologically it is essential to submerge oneself in the life of the people being studied (x, xii). The intention is to reach what Rossi and O'Higgins call the *view from within*: "In order to be objective, anthropologists must divest themselves of cultural prejudices and understand the culture they study as it is understood by those who live in its bosom. Only the *view from within* can permit the anthropologist to go beyond appearances that take the form of rules of interaction, customs and beliefs, in order to understand the meaning that these can have for the people who live them" (13). See Rossi and O'Higgins, *Teorías de la cultura y métodos antropológicos* (Barcelona: Anagrama, 1981).

6. In his critique of Whitman, Calvin Bedient states:

What is annoying today in "Calamus" is not its audacious homophilia (to which drama the series, giving itself courage, on top of the great valor it really implies, is entirely dedicated) but rather the presence of a repression that hungers for death. Homophilia itself is pure.... Whitman shows himself to be both proud and sagacious. He needs us, but he doesn't confide in us.... In the first poem, "there is no longer a reason to be ashamed." Whitman "publishes"—such is his wise promise—a new "norm" [202].

7. Andrés Ruiz López could be considered a follower of Lorca's invocation to the "Colleagues of the entire world." His work, *Ocaña*, is dedicated to the "proletariats of sex" who helped him to enter the roots of their souls. In scene 14, a declaration is made that alludes, perhaps, to Lorca's "men of flesh, with a violin and with dreams": "Because the revolution is not only asking for the plate of food or the eight-hour work day, comrades. The revolution is being able to vibrate with what one really feels" (135).

Chapter 4

1. Even in recent times there have been cases in which the members of some religious groups publicly accuse homosexuals of being allied with Satan. In Stockholm, on Sunday, April 21, 1985, a religious service for homosexuals was repeatedly interrupted with shouts of, "This is Satan's synagogue" (Steen-Johsson 6).

Some laws permit discrimination against, and even persecution of, homosexuals. Authorities of Christian congregations generally are opposed to changing these laws. Close to the root of the above-mentioned events in Stockholm, the deacon of a synod, G. Beijer, came out in favor of retaining the laws that permit open discrimination against homosexuality. According to what the synod said, homosexual acts are incompatible with faith and with Christian life (Jonasson 10). There is no reason to think that the attitude shown by this synod is at all unique. We already mentioned in chapter 1, "Lorquian Criticism," that Roig was secularized for having published a book about his life as a homosexual.

Let me make it clear that I do not think there must always be an opposition between the Christian and homosexual culture. I only indicate the incompatibility created and maintained by the representatives of Christian culture, or by the authorities who claim to represent it and who have the official and factual power to do it.

2. Even in 1981, Editions Gallimard continues deceiving those who buy a book called *Oeuvres poétiques complètes* by Verlaine (text established and annotated by Le Dantec; revised edition completed and presented by Jacques Borel). The poems of *Hombres* were sought in vain. They are not there. Trying to find an explanation, the reader will perhaps find a few words at the end in the "Avant-propos," and in the introduction to the *Album Zutique*. It was not judged "desirable" to include *Hombres*, says Borel. This is the only reason given: "In conformity with a pledge to the editor ... we had to avoid including *Femmes* and *Hombres* in the *Complete Poetic Works*" (164, xiii).

If Verlaine is censored in the deluxe editions of Gallimard, he is not in the homosexual magazines. *Blueboy* published a translation of some poems from *Hombres* in its July 1979 issue, pages 30–33. The poem "Even though" presents symbols of the Christian religion in a strongly homosexual context. From my point of view, the "solemn mass" in which male sexual organs participate should be borne in mind when one analyzes the role of religion in Verlaine's works, and probably also in those of Rimbaud and others:

But this God of a cock will seek
to go to a solemn high Mass
in my hands, my mouth, and my ass,
it is an idol quite unique [33].

Obscene? Conquest has some thoughts about the meaning of this adjective, starting with two definitions from Webster's dictionary ("foul," "disgusting"). The author finds it much easier to apply these expressions to some of the scenes in the halls of Justice, about the judgment against *Lady Chatterley's Lover*. According to Conquest, Lawrence (like other authors we studied), "preached the religion of sex" (81, 82).

3. The data on where the manuscript of *Hombres* is located can be found in the *Encyclopedia Erotica*, the Swedish edition of the *Dictionnaire de Sexologie* (1967, 737). The Spanish edition does not publish it (*Enciclopedia Ilustrada de Sexología y Erotismo* 1979, 1224).

4. According to Sartre, if the novelist is given the right to describe those individuals that society calls "ill-fated," it is on condition that they be considered from the outside, as though they were a species separated from us by an abyss. This is equivalent to prohibiting the thief from talking about robbery and the homosexual from speaking about his loves. They are only allowed expression if they agree to represent the role of repentant sinners, separated from the "vice" by disgust and remorse of conscience. Genet refuses. He does not speak to us about the thief or the pederast. He speaks as a thief and as a pederast. The reader then reacts with surprise in the face of this perspective from within, to which he is not accustomed, "That thing *exists*, a pederast?

That thing? That thing judges, judges us, *sees us*?" (538, 539).

5. On the proper name, Derrida thinks: "When in the consciousness, the name *is called* 'proper,' it is already classified and obliterated in being *named*. It is nothing more than a *so-called* proper name" (161).

Derrida cites Lévi-Strauss, who distinguishes two types of proper names: the name that marks the identification, which confirms the individual's membership in a class, group or system, and the name that is a creation, which expresses the subjectivity of the person who does the naming. In reality, Derrida affirms, one is never "named." One classifies someone or classifies oneself. Often both things occur (160).

Among the journals dedicated to studying the importance of names, one could mention *Names*, which had already published some thirty volumes in 1990–91 and *Beiträge zur Namenforschung*, which was verging on twenty.

6. Grace Alvarez-Altman has specialized in the study of Lorquian names. In "Nihilismo sexual en *La casa de Bernarda Alba*" she makes a short presentation of the onomastics and formulates various questions: "Literary onomastics is a new focus in the criticism of any literary genre, a focus in which the names of characters, symbols and places are exclusively studied. Why does only one of the eighteen characters of *Blood Wedding* have a name (Leonardo-Félix)? What onomastic virtuosity produced the invented name YERMA?" (67).

In "*Blood Wedding*: A Literary Onomastic Interpretation," Alvarez-Altman affirms that the onomastic concepts cannot be disassociated from their respective philosophies, and that the legacy of García Lorca reflects an onomastic mix from different cultures and philosophies that the author describes over a few pages (62–71).

Another study is dedicated to the proper names in *The House of Bernarda Alba*. Alvarez-Altman analyzes, for example, the name *Angustias*, keeping in mind its religious and Freudian aspects (6–10).

7. I thank my opponent, Poul Rasmussen, who reminded me of the relevance and importance of the Danaids' killing their husbands.

Chapter 5

1. This is a reference to the Golden Age playwrights of Spain: Lope de Vega, Tirso de Molina and Antonio de Zamora.— *Trans*.

2. In "Ortega as Translator," Juan Rof Carballo speaks, among other things, of what the established culture represses or expels from its body. He explains why "expulsion" seems better to him than "repression" as a translation of the concept of "VerdrÄngung," which he writes as "VerdrÁngung": "The translation of Ortega y Gasset, who was familiar with German, is correct. 'VerdrÁngung' comes to mean removal, displacement, and expulsion. But 'repression' is the universally accepted word" (3).

3. Antonina Rodrigo published an undated letter from Dalí to Lorca in which Dalí makes remarks about the *Gypsy Ballads* in general, and the concepts of horse and rider in particular:

You speak of a rider and this presumes that he is on top of a horse and that the horse gallops, *this is saying a lot*, because in reality *it would be useful to determine* if it is really the rider who is on top. If the reins are not an organic continuation of the hands themselves, if in reality the little hairs of the rider's testicles prove faster than the horse and if the horse is precisely something attached to the earth for good reasons, etc., etc.... Imagine what it is to arrive as you do at the concept of a Guardia Civil.... Poetically a Guardia Civil does not in reality exist... [232].

From Dalí's words one can see the outline of three essential Freudian psychoanalytical concepts: the social ego (rider), the id or instinct (horse), and the superego that censors, which has its immovable roots in the ground of fixed norms of the dominant culture.

4. Saturn continues to be associated with homosexuality and with unconventional virtues. As stated in *Paradiso*, "the anus" is "Saturn's ring" (Lezama Lima 373). *In Front of the Mirror* (Ante el espejo), memories of "a forbidden adolescence," would have been published with the title *Born Under the Sign of Saturn* (Nacido bajo el signo de Saturno) if a book by that title had not already existed (see Villena *Ante el espejo* and "Luis Antonio de Villena publica *Ante el espejo*..."). In his analysis of *Las criaturas saturnianas* of Sender, Ressot states that it deals with a book about instinct, what is fundamental, anti-virtue and anti-rationalism (47).

5. Riess cites a love poem that Verlaine dedicates to Rimbaud, in which the cross is also mentioned:

My love is the ember that burns forever in lascivious flesh...
...
so that one day the cross on which I die will rise up like a miracle arising from good and you will be mine, trembling and ashamed [Riess 169–70].

6. Psychologically, to deny the relation of two expressive unities can be an artifice to induce the reader to associate them consciously or unconsciously. It is improbable that a man's thighs and roses would be associated without the falsely disassociative observation of the Fourth Laun-

dress. The First Laundress has just affirmed: "Speaking is not a sin," (697) but the reader knows that it is so that Yerma should not speak with Victor. The message is ambiguous: no, but yes.

7. One of the most famous books whose theme is primarily homosexual is *Miracle de la rose* (Genet 1967) (for "rose" see especially pages 370 and 452–462). Yukio Mishima posed for an album of photographs where he appears naked and in "extraordinary poses," according to Henry Scott-Stokes. The album is entitled *Barake*: (*Tortured by Roses*), and, like the "indecent" rose of Lorca, it caused a certain scandal, ("gave Mishima a bad reputation in some quarters") (Scott-Stokes 1975, photography and text between pp. 172 and 173).

8. The Golden Age is a constant in the dream of homosexual culture. According to Vernant's introduction to Detienne's *The Garden of Adonis*, in this mythologized age there were only men: "In a way the Phoenix's mode of existence recalls that of men in the Golden Age ... before the creation of women and marriage, when mankind — exclusively male — still led a pure life" (xxv).

The mecca of homosexuals in the twenties was a Berlin cabaret called Eldorado, a name that evidently evokes the Golden Age of homosexuals. In 1983 a great exposition of this cabaret was put on, together with "One hundred years of history, daily life and homosexual culture in Berlin" (Ocón 40, 41).

9. J.L. Aranguren is of the same opinion as Frye. In *The Job of the Intellectual and Criticism of Criticism* (El oficio de intelectual y la crítica de la crítica) he states: "The problems of *reading and interpretation* are established, have to be established also with respect to texts not considered strictly literary, or considered much more than strictly literary. It is the case of the Bible and its translation-interpretation" (89).

10. In "A Moment of Green Laurel," one of the short novels from *A Thirsty Devil* by Vidal, the narrator meets a young man loaded down with laurels who seems to be his adolescent self. He then remembers with terror the old garlands or funeral wreaths: "'What are you going to do with these?' I asked, touching a branch of laurel, 'Make wreaths the way the Roman did?.'.. He looked at me with surprise; then he smiled. 'Yes, I do that sometimes.' 'Nothing has changed,' I thought, and the terror began" (41).

A voice calls-shouts a name that makes them jump when the adolescent leaves the circle of light. The narrator sees him going away along the unpaved road (41).

11A. The "sentimental education" of the senses in bourgeois society has been analyzed by Peter Gay in *Education of the Senses*, the first part of *The Bourgeois Experience: Victoria to Freud*. Carl Rudbeck comments on the book in "Privata delar av borgarnas liv" (Private parts of bourgeois life).

11B. In the article "The Sexism of the Ministry of Health" (El sexismo del Ministerio de Sanidad), in the name of "diverse groups of the Feminist Movement of Madrid," Concha Lorenzana, Justa Montero and Montserrat Oliván protest the fact that heterosexuality in general, and coitus in particular, continue to be presented and promoted as "normal" sexuality: "The feminist movement — and, together with it, a considerable number of sexologists and psychologists — have affirmed for more than a decade that exalting coitus, calling it 'the sexual act,' assumes a patriarchal imposition upon women.... Could it be that in your ministry you haven't read anything about people who are sexual beings but not exclusively heterosexuals? Our attention is called to the fact that you don't know that it is society that orients sexual desire towards exclusive heterosexuality and that it does it with clear political intentionality" (*El País*, May 29, 1986, 36).

Chapter 6

1. As far as the order and unity of the poems of *Songs* is concerned, opinions vary and are not always supported with consistent arguments. Cirre states that "*Songs* do not emerge from a deliberate, unified purpose. They are born from independent, spontaneous intuitions which, occasionally, are connected or related, but without offering a genuine sequence" (207).

In contrast, Marie Laffranque says that the poems of *Songs* are frequently found grouped in suggestive suites (*Les idées* 91). Cobb appears to agree: "In the last half of the book, which has puzzled and disturbed critics, Lorca is projecting his turbulent state of mind and as a group the poems reveal much about the poet" (51).

2. Bousoño's primary arguments in his "Concerning 'Disquiet and Night' by García Lorca" are mostly based on what the author thinks everyone feels about a poem. A couple of examples: the poem "moves and drags up, without our, in another sense, understanding it" (306). "What did we feel upon reading it? A serious emotion of something artful, turbid, sinister?" (308). For a criticism of such a method, see Celaya, *Inquisición de la poesía* 199–201.

More commonly, we don't all feel the same about a poem or a poetic image. As Hansson states in his thesis: as a general rule, different readers have totally different experiences with the same text (19). The same can be said of concepts. Words like shadows and darkness will awaken very different feelings in different people, according to the experiences each has had, and according to the degree of maturity of each individual. The person who fears his shadow will never feel the same as the one who lives at peace with it.

3. The refusal to reproduce is also associated with dying for Hjalmar Bergman, a homosexual Swedish author. According to Erik Hjalmar Linder, H. Bergman declared symbolically that he was ready to say goodbye to life to avoid reproducing, and he had also protested in a letter the brutal way society has of coupling people and asking them to reproduce (30–31).

4. Sáenz de la Calzada tells the following anecdote about Lorca: "I was very timid in those days; Federico only referred to me as 'this boy,' and making a supreme effort I dared to say to him that I was twenty, and he said to me that I should not be offended, that in Andalusia they call absolutely everybody a boy, even if they are more than 50" (30).

5. According to Vázquez Ocaña, Lorca was quite influenced by the Kabala at one time in his life, even though the author doesn't specify: "The track of the confessional Kabala and of the repressions occasioned to Lorca's spirit was being erased by a juvenile and sarcastic humor" (69).

In the second chapter of his thesis, "A Mystic Way to Love and Power," H.C. Arrington mentions Lorca's reputation of sexual inversion and states that, in the poet, the masculine and feminine principles were gloriously united within his own being that, "in the alchemical and occult tradition," represented a synthesis (120–21).

6. According to Peter Tompkins in the last pages of *The Eunuch and the Virgin*:

In Norway, during the Nazi occupation, anyone declared demented could be castrated, with the ability "to ask for police support" to carry out the operation in case of resistance on the part of the victim. That operations carried out in countries like Denmark, Norway, Iceland, Finland, Sweden and Nazi Germany were "voluntary" is denied by the Swiss psychiatrist Charles Wolf. He explains that when confronted with "on the one side detention and, on the other, castration followed by liberty ... almost invariably the victims chose castration simply to recover their liberty," and the Swedish doctor Olaf Kinberg adds significantly, "It is doubtful that there would be another penalty, apart from capital punishment and life in prison, that would be as effective as castration in the prevention of crime."

In these penal codes, castration is triggered for the offense of "indecent coitus" or for "indecent acts and conduct." It must be noted that, in these cases, indecent coitus is that practiced *interfemora* or *in anum* [312, 313].

García Valdés tells that "surgical castration," "lobotomy" and "cerebral surgery" are among the "treatment techniques" used against homosexuality in exceptional cases (328).

7. Even though Freud tries to be objective, his ideology in favor of a sexuality of lineal evolution in the service of reproduction implicitly underlies many of his assertions, for example in naming the "danger" of "regression":

the libido function goes through an extensive development before it can enter the service of reproduction...

I think that it will be in agreement with the doctrines of general pathology to assume that such a development involves two dangers; first that of *inhibition*, and secondly, that of *regression* [*Psychoanalysis* 297].

D.J. West is convinced that the passionate embraces of a grown man are not compatible with a sexuality other than that which takes place within the framework of matrimony, the only redoubt for the healthy sexual appetite. The author, a known psychiatrist, doesn't take the trouble to hide his antihomosexual ideology. Like incest, homosexuality should be prevented "at all costs" "in the interests of family and social institutions" (115).

The hidden ideological dimension of the concept of "maturity" is shown by Berger and Kellner in "Le mariage et la construction de la réalité." According to the authors, the preparation for marriage takes place in an ideological picture strictly defined in advance, imposed on the individual in the adolescent phase (9). It is frequently stated that married people have a superior emotional stability and are more "mature" than single people. In response, Berger and Kellner state that it is true if one wants to say that married people live in a narrower, more closed world in conformity with what society expects of them (29).

8. According to Tompkins, it can be stated that Christians, to a certain extent, have been the greatest castrators, from having removed 100,000 phalluses from a pantheon of pagan statues, without leaving a single whole penis (144).

Homosexuality was an integral part of the indigenous cultures the Spaniards found when they "discovered" America. *The True History of the Conquest of New Spain* is very informative in this respect, even though it probably was not the author's intention to discuss the state of normality of homosexual practices in "New Spain." It was understood that even "Popes" engaged in this "service." Wherever they went, the Spaniards prohibited homosexuality in the name of their own god. They destroyed the idols and the "evil figures" that other cultures would probably appreciate as works of religious or sexual art" (Díaz del Castillo 30–31, 107, 108–9, 110, 124–5, 184).

9. For the "erotic sexual level" of *The Dark Night* (La noche oscura) see the section that bears that title in chapter III of J.C. Nieto's book, *Místico, poeta, rebelde, santo: en torno a San Juan de la Cruz*. According to Nieto, "the most important and obvious aspect of this poem (*La noche oscura*) is the erotic element.... This is not said with the intention of defaming the ethical purity of John or his integrity or sincerity, but because it is the only way this poem expresses its whole vital feeling" (71, 72).

10. Not all Christians see that there is an opposition between love or homosexual practice and Christianity. There are priests who live openly as homosexuals (see "Reverend Troy Perry" in *The Gay Crusaders* by Tobin & Wicker (13–27). In the United States, Holland and Denmark, ministers of the church exist who are willing to bless a union between two men (or two women).

The Vatican remains more or less the same as when Lorca wrote his "Cry to Rome." The theologian and priest Charles Curran, known among other things for his breadth of vision with respect to homosexuality, was separated from his post by order of the Vatican "as a reprisal for his refusal to recant his points of view in matters of sexual morality" (*El País* August 21, 1986, 17). Nevertheless and as the theologian Gianni Gennari indicates upon criticizing the document of Cardinal Ratzinger, now Pope Benedict, on homosexuals, in "An Immoral Condemnation" (*El País*, Nov. 6, 1986, 13):

There has been an increase in the number of Catholics who are homosexuals and show it and, at the same time, want to continue declaring themselves Catholics. The true novelty, it is clear, is not the existence of observant homosexuals, but the fact that they make explicit declaration of both realities: their homosexuality and their faith.

11. Although the texts commented upon in this study were written about 77 years ago, unfortunately they are still relevant in 2007. An article by Emilio de Benito from the Spanish newspaper *El País*, March 10, 2007, with the title "It's Luck Not to BE Hit for Being Gay" shows how homosexual children continue to be persecuted and humiliated in school today: "They insultd me, spit on me and hit me many times. It's constant harassment at school" (38).

Bibliography

Adams, Mildred. *García Lorca: Playwright and Poet.* New York: George Braziller, 1977.
Aguirre, J.M. "El sonambulismo de Federico García Lorca." In *El escritor y la crítica.* Ed. I.M. Gil. N.p.: Taurus, 1975. 97–119.
Ahnlund, Knut. *Diktarliv i Norden.* Estocolmo: n.p., 1981.
Alberich, J. "El erotismo femenino en el teatro de García Lorca." *Papeles de Son Armadans* 34 (1965): 9–36.
Alfaya, Javier. "El rostro oculto de Lorca." *La Calle* 132 (1980): 51–53.
Allen, Rupert. *Psyche and Symbol in the Theatre of Federico García Lorca.* Austin: University of Texas Press, 1974.
———. *The Symbolic World of Federico García Lorca.* Albuquerque: University of New Mexico Press, 1972.
Almodóvar, Pedro. *Carne trémula. El guión.* Barcelona: Plaza and Janés, 1997.
Alvarez-Altman, Grace. "*Blood Wedding*: A Literary Onomastic Interpretation." *García Lorca Review* 8 (1980): 60–72.
———. "Charactonyms in García Lorca's *House of Bernada Alba*." *Onomástica Canadiana* Winnipeg (1972).
———. "Nihilismo sexual en *La casa de Bernarda Alba*." *García Lorca Review* 3 (1975): 67–69.
Alvarez de Miranda, Angel. *La metáfora y el mito.* Madrid: Taurus, 1963.
Amis, Martin. "Return of the Male." *London Review of Books.* December 5, 1991, 3–5.
Ancet, Jacques. *Luis Cernuda: Poètes d'aujourd'hui.* Paris: Seghers, 1972.
Anderson, Andrew A. "¿De qué trata *Bodas de sangre*?" *Hommage à Federico García Lorca.* Toulouse: Université de Toulouse-Le Mirail, 1982. 53–64.
———. "García Lorca como poeta petrarquista." *Cuadernos Hispanoamericanos* 435–436 (1986): 495–518.

———. "García Lorca en Montevideo: un testimonio desconocido y más evidencia sobre la evolución de *Poeta en Nueva York.*" *Bulletin Hispanique* 83 (1981): 145–53.
Anderson, Sherwood. *Winesburg, Ohio.* Ed. J.H. Ferres. New York: The Viking Critical Library, 1976.
Andrade, Raul. "García Lorca: alegoría de la España yaciente." *El perfil de la quimera.* Quito: Casa de la cultura ecuatoriana, 1977.
Andueza, María. *Once poemas comentados de Federico García Lorca.* Mexico: Universidad Nacional Autónoma, 1978.
Anson, Luis María. *La negritud.* Madrid: Castilla, 1971.
Apollinaire, Gillaume. *Las once mil vergas.* Barcelona: Icaria, 1977.
Aragon, Louis. "Aux abords de Rome." *Gai Pied* 50 (1983): 15.
Arango, Manuel Antonio. *Símbolo y simbología en la obra de Federico García Lorca.* Madrid: Fundamentos, Espiral Hispanoamericana, 1995.
Aranguren, José Luis. *La cultura española y la cultura establecida.* Madrid: Taurus, 1975.
———. *El oficio del intelectual y la crítica de la crítica.* Madrid: Vox, 1979.
Arias, Jesús. "Si Lorca volviera a nacer en Granada, volverían a matarlo." Entrevista con Nicolás López. *El País,* 21 August 1998, 16.
Armas, José R. de "La columna, el círculo y sus variantes en la poesía primera de Pedro Salinas." *Hispania* 53 (1970): 53–58.
Armiño, Mauro. "Una interpretación modélica." *El País,* 30 May 1982, 8.
Arrington, Hilda Cowan. "A Study of Federico García Lorca and Surrealism." Diss., University of California, 1975.
Auclair, Marcelle. *Enfances et mort de García Lorca.* Paris: Seuil, 1968.

Avila, Pablo Luis. "Lo redondo y lo punzante en la poesía de Miguel Hernández." *Quaderni Ibero-americani* 34–35 (1966–70): 150–59.

Ayala, Francisco. "Unisex in excelsis." *El País*, 15 November 1983, Opinión.

Azancot, Leopoldo. "Singularidad de Gil-Albert." *Cuadernos Hispanoamericanos* 324 (1977): 523–32.

Babín, María Teresa. *El mundo poético de Federico García Lorca*. San Juan, Puerto Rico: Biblioteca de autores puertorriqueños, 1954.

———. "Narciso y la esterilidad en la obra de García Lorca." *Revista Hispánica Moderna* 11 (1945): 48–51.

Balakian, Anna. *El movimiento simbolista*. Madrid: Guadarrama, 1969.

Baldwin, James. *Giovanni's Room* and *Another Country*. (Quoted by Sarotte.)

Barbachano, Carlos J. "Hacia una lectura consecuente de Jean-Arthur Rimbaud." *Cuadernos Hispanoamericanos* 355 (1980): 154–67.

Barea, Arturo. *Lorca: The Poet and His People*. London: Faber and Faber, 1944.

Barnard, Mary E. "The Grotesque and Courtly in Garcilaso's 'Apollo and Daphne.'" *Romanic Review* 72 (1981): 253–73.

Barnatan, Marcos Ricardo. *La Kábala: Una mística del lenguaje*. Barcelona: Barral, 1974.

Barthes, Roland. *Le degré zéro de l'écriture*, suivi de *Nouveaux essais critiques*. Paris: Seuil, 1972.

———. Preface. *Tricks*. By R. Camus. Paris: Mazarine, 1979. 13–22.

Baudrillard, Jean. "El maligno genio de la pasión." *Revista de Occidente* 15–16 (1982): 17–35.

Baumgarten, Murray. "Lyric as Performance: Lorca and Yeats." *Comparative Literature* 29 (1977): 328–50.

Beauvoir, Simone de. *Pour une morale de l'ambigüité*. Paris: Gallimard, 1972.

Bedient, Calvin. "Walt Whitman, anulado." *Homosexualidad: literatura y política*. Madrid: Alianza, 1985. 192–219.

Belamich, André. *Lorca*. Paris: Gallimard, 1962.

Bell, Alan, and Martin Weinberg. *Homosexualities: A Study of Diversity Among Men and Women*. New York: Simon and Schuster, 1978.

Belsey, Catherine. *Critical Practice*. London, New York: Methuen, 1980.

Benayoun, Robert. *Erotique du surréalisme*. Paris: Pauvert, 1965.

Benedetti, Mario. "La paz o la aceptación del otro." *El País*, 5 October 1986, 16–17 (Sunday).

Bergamín, José. "He sido tan sentimental que tengo el corazón hecho un trapo." *El País*, 4 September 1983, 1, 8.

Berger, Peter L. and Hansfried Kellner. "Le mariage et la construction de la réalité" *Diogène, Revue Internationale des Sciences Humaines*. Paris: Conseil International de la Philosophie et des Sciences Humaines; No.46 (April-June 1964): 3–32.

———, and T. Luckmann. *The Social Construction of Reality*. New York: Anchor Books, 1966.

Bergh, Steinar, Birgit Bjerck and Elin Lund. *Homofila/Myter och verklighet*. Estocolmo: Natur och Kultur, 1981.

The Bible for Students of Literature and Art. New York: Anchor Books, 1964.

Binding, Paul. *Lorca: The Gay Imagination*. London: GMP Publishers, 1985.

Blanco Aguinaga, Carlos. *En voz continua*. Madrid: Alfaguara, 1997.

Blanco Aguinaga, Carlos, and A. Carreira. Prólogo. *Poesías completas de Emilio Prados*. xi–lxviii. Mexico: Aguilar, 1975.

Blanco-Amor, Eduardo. "Federico, otra vez; la misma vez." *El País*, 1 October 1978, I, VI and VII.

Blanquat, Josette. "La Lune Manichéenne dans la Mythologie du *Romancero Gitano*." *Revue de Littérature Comparée* 38 (1964): 376–99.

Bleiberg, Germán. "Sobre una comedia perdida de Luis Cernuda." *Revista de Occidente* 19 (1977): 20–24.

Booth, Wayne C. *Critical Understanding*. Chicago: University of Chicago Press, 1979.

Bordier, Roger. "Whitman et Lorca." *Europe* 483–84 (1969): 188–91.

Bosch, Rafael. "El choque de imágenes como principio creador de García Lorca." *Revista Hispánica Moderna* 30 (1964): 35–44.

———. "Los poemas paralelísticos de García Lorca." *Revista Hispánica Moderna* 28 (1962): 36–44.

Bousoño, Carlos. "En torno a 'Malestar y noche' de García Lorca." *El comentario de textos*. Vol. 1. Madrid: Castalia, 1978. 305–42.

———. *Superrealismo poético y simbolización*. Madrid: Gredos, 1979.

Boutet, F. *Dictionnaire des Sciences Occultes*. Westmount: Desclec, 1979.

Bremmer, Jan. "An Enigmatic Indo-European Rite: Paederasty." *Arethusa* 13 (1980): 279–98.

Brines, Franciso. *Escritos sobre poesía española*. Valencia: Pre-Textos, 1995.

———. "La justicia de un homenaje tardío." *El País*, 3 December 1982.

———. "La voluntaria jubilación de un escritor." *El País*, 16 June 1981.

Brown, G.G. *The Twentieth Century. A Literary History of Spain*. London: Benn; New York: Barnes and Noble, 1972.

Brown, Norman O. *Love's Body*. New York: Random House, 1966.

Brown, Phil. "Civilization and Its Dispossessed: Wihelm Reich's Correlation of Sexual and Political Repression." *The Radical Therapist*. The Radical Therapist Collective. Middlesex: Penguin Books, 1974. 45–53.

Buñuel, Luis. *Mi último suspiro*. Barcelona: Plaza and Janés, 1982.

Burke, Kenneth. "Freud y el análisis de la poesía." *Psicoanálisis y literatura*. Ed. H.M. Ruitenbeek. Mexico: Fondo de Cultura Económica, 1975. 174–210.

Bush, Douglas. *Mythology and the Renaissance Tradition in English Poetry*. New York: Norton and Company, 1963.

Bussell Thomson, B. and J.K. Walsh. "Un encuentro de Lorca y Hart Crane en Nueva York." *Insula* 479 (October 1986). N.p.

Buxán, Xosé M., ed. *ConCiencia de un singular deseo*. Barcelona: Laertes, 1997.

Byrd, Suzanne. "*La destrucción de Sodoma*: A Reconstruction of Federico García Lorca's Lost Drama." *García Lorca Review* 4.2 (1976): n.p.

———. "Paneroticism: A Progressive Concept in the Final Trilogy of García Lorca. *García Lorca Review* 3 (1975): 53–56.

Caballero, José. "García Lorca y Cuba: algunas rectificaciones." *García Lorca Review* 6 (1978): 43–54.

Cachin, Francoise. "Monsieur Vénus et l'ange de Sodome." *Nouvelle Revue de Psychanalyse* 7 (1973): 63–69.

Campos, P.M. "Se crea el Instituto de Estudios Juan Gil-Albert en Alicante." *El País*, 7 January 1984.

Cano, José Luis. *García Lorca: Bibliografía ilustrada*. Barcelona: Destino, 1962.

Cano Ballesta, Juan. "Peripecias de una amistad: Lorca y Miguel Hernández." *Cuadernos Hispanoamericanos* 433–34 (1986): 210–20.

Carlavilla, Mauricio. *Sodomitas*. Madrid: Nos, 1956.

Carlos, A.J. "La cruz en el 'Responso a Verlaine.'" *Hispania* 48 (1965): 226–29.

Caro Baroja, Julio. *Las brujas y su mundo*. Madrid: Alianza, 1982.

———. *Teatro popular y magia*. Madrid: Revista de Occidente, 1974.

Carrere, Emilio. Qtd. by Ferreres.

Casares, Julio. *Diccionario ideológico de la lengua española*. Barcelona: Gustavo Gili, 1984.

Cavendish, Richard. *The Black Arts*. 1967. London: Pan Books, 1977.

Cela, Camilo José. *Diccionario secreto*. 1971. Vol. 2. Madrid: Alianza, 1975.

———. *Mazurca para dos muertos*. Barcelona: Seix Barral, 1984.

———. Prólogo. *El triángulo de las verduras*. Barcelona: Plaza and Janés, 1981. 9–10.

Celaya, Gabriel. *Inquisición de la poesía*. Madrid: Taurus, 1972.

Cernuda, Luis. "Carta a Gregorio Prieto." *El País*, 15 November 1981, no. 240, weekly.

———. *Crítica, ensayo y evocaciones*. Barcelona: Seix Barral, 1970.

———. *Estudios sobre poesía española contemporánea*. Madrid: Guadarrama, 1957.

———. "Morir como un fénix." *El País*, 4 July 1987, 27.

———. *Ocnos. Variaciones sobre un tema mexicano*. Madrid: Taurus, 1979.

———. *Poesía completa*. Barcelona: Barral, 1977.

———. *Selected Poems*. Trans. Reginald Gibbons. Berkeley: University of California Press, 1978.

———. *The Young Sailor and Other Poems*. Trans. Rick Lipinski. San Francisco: Gay Sunshine Press, 1986.

Chalus, P. *L'homme et la religion. Recherches sur les sources psychologique des croyances*. Paris: Albin Michel, 1963.

Chauncey, G., Jr. "De la inversión sexual a la homosexualidad: la medicina y la evolución de la conceptualización de la desviación de la mujer." *Homosexualidad: literatura y política*. Eds. G. Steiner and R. Boyers. Madrid: Alianza, 1985.

Cirlot, J.E. *A Dictionary of Symbols*. Trans. Jack Sage. New York: Philosophical Library, 1962.

Cirre, José Francisco. "Algunos aspectos del 'jardín cerrado' en las *Canciones* de Federico García Lorca." *Cuadernos Americanos* 132 (1964): 206–17.

Clason, S. "Litteraturen i feministiskt perspektiv." *Svenska Dagbladet*, 20 February 1986, 12.

Claudel, Paul and André Gide. *Correspondance*. Paris: Gallimard, 1949.

_____. *The Correspondence between Paul Claudel and André Gide*. Trans. John Russell. New York: Pantheon Books, 1952.

Cobb, Carl W. *Federico García Lorca*. New York: Twayne, 1967.

Cocteau, Jean. *Le livre blanc. Quatorze textes érotiques inédits*. Paris: Persona, 1981.

Colecchia, Francesca. *García Lorca: A Selective Annotated Bibliography of Criticism*. New York: Garland Press, 1979.

Colinas, A. "El silencio de Vicente Aleixandre." *El País*, 3 April 1984, 11–12.

Coll, José Luis. *El eroticall: Diccionario exótico*. Madrid: Ediciones Temas de Hoy, 1991.

Conejero, Manuel Angel. *Eros adolescente*. Barcelona: Península, 1980.

Conquest, Robert. *The Abomination of the Moab*. London: Temple Smith, 1979.

Córdoba Montoya, Pedro. "Lorca teórico del lenguaje o el origen sentimental de las palabras." In *Hommage à Federico García Lorca*. Toulouse: University of Toulouse, 1982.

Corliss, Richard. "The Final Frontier." *Time*, March 1996, 47–48.

Corominas, J. *Breve Diccionario Etimológico de la Lengua Castellana*. Madrid: Gredos, 1967.

Correa, Gustavo. *La poesía mítica de Federico García Lorca*. Portland: University of Oregon, 1957.

_____. "El significado de *Poeta en Nueva York* de Federico García Lorca." *Cuadernos Americanos* 18 (1959): 224–33.

_____. "El simbolismo de la luna en la poesía de Federico García Lorca." *PMLA* 72 (1957): 1060–84.

_____. "El simbolismo religioso en la poesía de Federico García Lorca." *Hispania* 39 (1956): 41–48.

Cortázar, Julio. "El destino del hombre era ... '1984.'" *El País*, 9 October 1983, 8–10.

Couffon, Claude. *En Granada, tras las huellas de Federico García Lorca*. La Habana: Revolución, n.d. (original French edition pub. in 1951).

Cowell, R. *W.B. Yeats*. New York: Arco, 1970.

Craige, Betty Jean. *Lorca's Poet in New York: The Fall into Consciousness*. Lexington: University Press of Kentucky, 1977.

Crane, Hart. *The Complete Poems and Selected Prose*. New York: Oxford University Press, 1968.

Criado de Val, Manuel. *Diccionario del español equívoco*. Madrid: EDI-6, 1981.

Crisp, Quentin. *How to Become a Virgin*. Glasgow: Fontana, 1981.

Crosby, J.O. Edición y notas de *Poesía varia* de Francisco Quevedo. Madrid: Cátedra, 1981.

Crowley, Aleister. Qtd. by King.

Cullhed, A. *Tiden Söker sin rost. Studier Kring Erik Lindegrens Mannen utan väg*. Estocolmo: Bonniers, 1982.

Cummings, Philip. Qtd. by Eisenberg in "Poeta en Nueva York."

Curtiss, H.A., and F.H. Curtiss. *The Key to the Universe*. California: Newcastle, 1983.

Dalí, Salvador. "La conquista de lo irracional." *Escritos de arte de vanguardia*. Barcelona: Turner, 1979. 417–25.

_____. "Dos poemas de Salvador Dalí." In Appendix B from Santos Torroella.

_____. *Hidden Faces*. New York: William Morrow and Company, Inc., 1974.

_____. *El mito trágico del "Angelus" de Millet*. Barcelona: Tusquets, 1983.

_____. "Nuevas consideraciones generales sobre el mecanismo del fenómeno paranoico desde el punto de vista surrealista." *Escritos de vanguardia*. Barcelona: Turner, n.d. 389–93.

_____. *Salvador Dalí escribe a Federico García Lorca*. *Poesía* 27–28. Madrid: Ministerio de Cultura, 1987.

_____. *The Secret Life of Salvador Dalí*. Trans. Haakow M. Chevalier. New York: Dover, 1993.

Daniel, M., and A. Baudry. *Los homosexuales*. Barcelona: Sagitario, 1975.

Dante Alighieri. *The Divine Comedy*. Trans. H.R. Huse. New York: Holt, Rinehart and Winston, 1964.

Darío, Rubén. Ricardo Gullón, ed. *Páginas escogidas*. Madrid: Cátedra, 1979.

_____. *Los raros. Obras Completas*. Vol. VI. Madrid: Mundo Latino, 1920.

The Dartmouth Bible. Boston: Houghton Mifflin Co., 1961.

D'Eaubonne, Françoise. *Verlaine et Rimbaud*. Paris: Albin Michel, 1960.

Debicki, A.P. *Estudios sobre poesía española contemporánea. La generación de 1924–25*. Madrid: Gredos, 1968.

Del goce y de la dicha. Introducción. Rafael Pérez Estrada. Torremolinos: Litoral, 1985.

Delcourt, Marie. *Hermafrodita*. Barcelona: Seix Barral, 1970.

_____. *Hermaphrodite*. Paris: Presses Universitaires de France, 1958.

Delgado, Fernando G. "Juan Gil-Albert, después del silencio." *Insula* 350 (1976): 4–5.

Derrida, Jacques. *De la grammatologie*. Paris: Les Editions de Minuit, 1967.

Detienne, Marcel. *Dionysos mis à mort*. Paris: Gallimard, 1977.
———. *The Gardens of Adonis: Spices in Greek Mythology*. Sussex: The Harvester Press, 1977.
Díaz del Castillo, Bernal. *Historia verdadera de la Nueva España*. Madrid: Espasa Calpe, 1975.
Díaz Plaja, Guillermo. *Federico García Lorca*. Buenos Aires: Austral, 1954.
Diccionario de la Mitología Mundial. Madrid: EDAF, 1971.
Diego, Gerardo. "Federico García Lorca: *Canciones*, Suplementos de *Litoral*." *Revista de Occidente* 51 (1927): 380–84.
Doménech, Ricardo. "Sobre la 'Nana del caballo' en *Bodas de sangre*." *Trece de nieve* 1–2 (1976): 202–09.
Dover, K.J. *Greek Homosexuality*. Qtd. by Knox.
Duché, Jean. *La mytholgie racontée à Juliette*. Paris: Robert Laffont, 1977.
Eaubonne, Françoise D'. *Verlaine et Rimbaud*. Paris: Robert Laffont, 1977.
Eisenberg, Daniel. "Dos textos primitivos de *Poeta en Nueva York*." *Papeles de Son Armadens* 74.221–222 (1974): 169–74.
———. *"Poeta en Nueva York": Historia y problemas de un texto de Lorca*. Barcelona: Ariel, 1976.
———. "Reaction to the Publication of the *Sonetos del amor oscuro*." *Bulletin of Hispanic Studies* 65 (1988): 261–71.
———. Revs. of *Lorca: The Gay Imagination*, by Paul Binding, and *Federico García Lorca y la cultura de la homosexualidad*, by Ángel Sahuquillo. *Bulletin of Hispanic Studies* 65 (1988): 415–16.
El Gamoun, Ahmed. *Lorca y la cultura popular marroquí*. Madrid: Libertarias/Prodhufi, 1995.
Eliade, Mircea. *Méphistophélès et l'androgyne*. Paris: Gallimard, 1962.
Ellis, P.J. *The Poetry of Emilio Prados: A Progression Towards Fertility*. Cardiff: University of Wales Press, 1981.
Enciclopedia Erótica. Ed. Lo Duca. Estocolmo: Spegeln, 1967.
Enciclopedia Ilustrada de Sexología y Erotismo. Ed. J.M. Lo Duca. Mexico: Daimom, 1979.
Encyclopedia of World Mythology. London: Octopus, 1975.
Engels, F. Qtd. by Vovelles.
Epps, Bradley S. *La epopeya bíblica*. Madrid: Aguilar, 1957.
———. *Significant Violence, Oppression and Resistance in the Narratives of Juan Goytisolo 1970–1990*. Oxford: Clarendon Books, 1996.
Espmark, Kjell. *Att översätta Själen*. Estocolmo: Norstedt and Söners, 1975.
Estévez Molinero, Angel. *Federico García Lorca o poética de la libertad*. Córdoba: Ayuntamiento de Córdoba en España, 1987.
Estraton de Sardes, et al. *La musa de los muchachos*. Madrid: Hiperión, 1980.
Feal Deibe, Carlos. *Eros y Lorca*. Barcelona: EDHASA, 1973.
———. *Lorca: tragedia y mito*. Ottawa Hispanic Studies 4. Canada: Dovehouse Editions, 1989.
Fernández, Dominique. *Le Rapt de Ganymède*. Paris: Grasset, 1989.
Fernández, Jean and Patrick Kobuz. "Conversación con Louis Aragon." *Poesía* 9 (1980): 81–90.
Fernández-Galiano, Manuel. "Amor y deseo en el mundo clásico." *Revista de Occidente* 15–16 (1982): 77–99.
———. "Los dioses de Federico." *Cuadernos Hispanoamericanos* 217 (1968): 30–43.
Fernández Leborans, María Jesús. *Campo semántico y connotación*. Madrid: Cupsa, 1977.
———. *Luz y oscuridad en la mística española*. Madrid: Cupsa, 1978.
Ferreiro, Alfredo Mario. "García Lorca en Montevideo." *Bulletin Hispanique* 83 (1981): 154–61.
Ferrer, Esther. "Todorov encuentra al 'otro' en la conquista de América." *El País*, 3 October 1982, 1, 11.
Ferreres, Rafael. *Verlaine y los modernistas españoles*. Madrid: Gredos, 1975.
Fierro, A. "Creencias y esquemas cognitivos." *Insula* 440–41 (1983): 12.
Finkelstein, Haim. "Dali's Paranoia — Criticism or the Exercise of Freedom." *Twentieth Century Literature* 21 (1975): n.p.
Flys, Jonathan. *El lenguaje poético de Federico García Lorca*. Madrid: Gredos, 1955.
———. "*Poeta en Nueva York*: la obra incomprendida de Federico García Lorca." *Arbor* 114 (1955): 247–57.
Fonvieille-Alquier, François. *André Gide*. Paris: Pierre Charron, 1972.
Forberg, Friedrich-Karl. *Manuel d'érotologie classique*. Mónaco: Editorial du Rocher, 1979.
Ford, Clellan and Frank A. Beach. *Patterns of Sexual Behavior*. New York: Harper and Row, 1972.
Forradellas, Joaquín. "Introducción, edición

y notas" de *La zapatera prodigiosa* de García Lorca. Salamanca: Almar, 1978.
Foster, David William. *Gay and Lesbian Themes in Latin American Writing*. Austin: University of Texas Press, 1991.
Foucault, Michel. "Opción sexual y actos sexuales: una entrevista con Michel Foucault." With J. O'Higgins. *Homosexualidad: literatura y política*. Madrid: Alianza, 1985. 16–37.
———. *Teatrum Philosophicum* and *Repetición y diferencia* by G. Deleuze. Barcelona: Anagrama, 1981.
———. *Un diálogo sobre el poder y otras conversaciones*. Madrid: Alianza, 1981.
Franz, Marie Louise von. "The Process of Individuation." *Man and His Symbols*. New York: Dell, 1978.
Frazer, James G. *The Golden Bough: A Study in Magic and Religion*. London: The MacMillan Press, 1974.
Freedman, Mark. "Homosexuals May Be Healthier Than Straights." *Psychology Today* 8.10 (1975): 29–33.
Freud, Anna. *Jaget och dess försvarsmekanismer*. Estocolmo: Natur och Kultur, 1976.
Freud, Sigmund. *El delirio y los sueños en la "Gradiva" de W. Jensen*. Barcelona: Grijalbo, 1977.
———. *A General Introduction to Psychoanalysis*. New York: Simon and Schuster, 1963.
———. *La interpretación de los sueños*. Barcelona: Planeta-Agostini, 1985.
Front Homosexuel d'Action Révolutionaire. *Rapport contre la normalité*. Paris: Champ Libre, 1971.
Frye, Northrop. *The Great Code: The Bible and Literature*. Surrey: Gresham, 1982.
Galán, Lola. "Cincuenta años después de la rebelión." *El País*, 19 October 1980 (weekly): 41–46.
Gallego Morell, Antonio. Prólogo y edición. *Teatro*. By Ignacio Sánchez Mejías. Madrid: Espasa-Calpe, 1988.
García Calvo, A. "Los dos sexos y el sexo: las razones de la irracionalidad." *Filosofía y sexualidad*. Barcelona: Anagrama, 1988. 29–54.
García Lorca, Federico. *The Billy Club Puppets*. *Five Plays*. 13–55.
———. *The Butterfly's Evil Spell*. *Five Plays*. 191–236.
———. *Collected Poems*. Ed. Christopher Maurer. Trans. Christopher Maurer, et al. Vol. 2. New York: Farrar, Straus & Giroux, 1991.
———. *Diván del Tamarit, Llanto por Ignacio Sanchez Mejías y Sonetos*. Madrid: Alianza, 1981.
———. *Doña Rosita, the Spinster*. *Five Plays*. 131–90.
———. "The Duende: Theory and Divertissement." *Poet in New York*. Trans. Ben Belitt. 154–166.
———. *Five Plays*. Trans. James Graham-Luján and Richard L. O'Connell. New York: New Directions, 1963.
———. *Four Puppet Plays. Divan Poems and Other Poems. Prose Poems and Dramatic Pieces. Play without a Title*. Trans. Edwin Honig. New York: The Sheep Meadow Press, 1990.
———. "In the Frame of Don Cristóbal: A Farce." *Four Puppet Plays*. 17–31.
———. "La muerte de la madre de Charlot." *El País*, 3 December 1989, supplement "Domingo": 14–15.
———. *The Love of Don Perlimplín and Belisa in the Garden*. *Five Plays*. 105–30.
———. "Lovers Slain by a Partridge." *Poet in New York*. Trans. Ben Belitt. 152–53.
———. *Obras completas*. Madrid: Aguilar, 1977.
———. *Oda y burla de Sesostris y Sardanápalo*. Ed. García-Posada. Ferrol: Sociedad de Cultura Valle-Inclán, 1985.
———. *Once Five Years Pass*. Trans. William Bryant Logan and Angel Gill Orrios. Barrytown, New York: Station Hill Press, 1989.
———. *Poesía inédita de juventud*. Ed. Christian de Paepe. Madrid: Cátedra: 1994.
———. *Poeta en Nueva York. Tierra y luna*. Edición crítica de Eutimio Martín. Barcelona: Ariel, 1981.
———. *Poet in New York*. Trans. Ben Belitt. New York: Grove Press, 1955.
———. *Poet in New York*. Trans. Greg Simon and Steven F. White. New York: Farrar, Straus & Giroux, 1988.
———. "The Poetic Image in Don Luis de Góngora." *Poet in New York*. Trans. Ben Belitt. 167–177.
———. *The Public and Play Without a Title*. Trans. Carlos Bauer. New York: New Directions, 1983.
———. *El público y Comedia sin título*. Barcelona: Seix Barral, 1978.
———. *Selected Letters*. Ed. and trans. David Gershator. New York: New Directions, 1983.
———. *The Shoemaker's Prodigious Wife*. *Five Plays*. 57–104.
———. *Sonetos de amor (Sonetos del amor oscuro)*. *ABC*, 17 March 1984, 45–66.

———. *Suites*. Ed. A. Belamich. Barcelona: Ariel, 1983.
———. *Teatro inconcluso*. Granada: Universidad de Granada, 1987.
———. *Textos inéditos*. *Cuadernos Hispanoamericanos* 433–34 (1986): n.p.
———. *Three Tragedies of Federico García Lorca: Blood Wedding, Yerma, Bernarda Alba*. Trans. James Graham-Luján and Richard L. O'Connell. New York: New Directions, 1947.
García Lorca, Francisco. *Federico y su mundo*. Madrid: Alianza, 1981.
———. Prefacio. *The Selected Poems of Federico García Lorca*. New York: New Directions, 1961. viii–xi.
García-Posada, Miguel. "Cernuda y Garcilaso. Ecos garcilasianos en la elegía 'A un poeta muerto.'" *Insula* 455 (1984): 1, 3.
———. "Comentarios de una carta de Lorca a su familia." *Trece de Nieve* 1–2 (1976): 62–64.
———. "Importantes manuscritos de Lorca serán subastados el lunes en Madrid." *El País*, 18 February 1995, 31.
———. "Infancia y muerte." *Lecciones sobre Federico García Lorca*. Various authors. Granada: Editorial del Cincuentenario, 1986. 179–93.
———. *Lorca. Interpretación de* Poeta en Nueva York. Madrid: Akal: 1981.
———. "Un monumento al amor." *ABC*, 17 March 1984, 43.
———. "Nota previa" y "Estudio." *García Lorca*. Madrid: EDAF, 1979. 11–154.
García Valdés, Alberto. *Historia y presente de la homosexualidad*. Madrid: Akal, 1981.
Garrigues Díaz-Cañabate, Emilio. "Al teatro con Federico García Lorca." *Cuadernos Hispanoamericanos* 340 (1978): 99–117.
Garro, Elena. "No me gusta hablar de Luis Cernuda." *Nueva Estafeta* 2 (1979): 111–116.
Gauthier, Xavière. *Surrealismo y sexualidad*. Buenos Aires: Corregidor, 1976.
Gay Left Collective. *Homosexuality: Power and Politics*. London: Allison-Busby, 1980.
Geist, Anthony L. "Las mariposas en la barba: una lectura de *Poeta en Nueva York*." *Cuadernos Hispanoamericanos* 435–36 (1986): 547–565.
Genet, Jean. *Miracle de la rose*. Paris: Gallimard, 1967.
Gennari, Gianni. "Una condena inmoral." *El País*, 6 November 1986, 13.
Gérard, A. "Origines historiques et destin littéraire de la négritude." *Diogene* 48 (1964): 14–37.

Gershator, David. "Federico García Lorca's *Trip to the Moon*." *Romance Notes* 9 (1968): 213–20.
Gibbons, Reginald, ed. and trans. *Selected Poems of Luis Cernuda*. Berkeley: University of California Press, 1978.
Gibson, Ian. "Una biografía de García Lorca que pretende ser definitiva." Interview with J. Cruz. *El País*, 24 March 1985, 1–2.
———. "Con Lorca y Dalí en Figueras." *El País*, 26 January 1986, 10–11.
———. *The Death of Lorca*. Suffolk: Paladin/Chaucer Press, 1974.
———. "En torno a Lorca hoy." *Cuadernos de Música y Teatro* 1987, 81–92.
———. *Federico García Lorca 1: De Fuente Vaqueros a Nueva York*. Barcelona: Grijalbo, 1985.
———. *Federico García Lorca 2: De Nueva York a Fuente Grande*. Barcelona: Grijalbo, 1987.
———. *Guía a la Granada de Frderico García Lorca*. Barcelona: Plaza y Janés, 1989.
———. "Lorca's 'Balada triste': Children's Songs and the Theme of Sexual Disharmony in *Libro de Poemas*." *Bulletin of Hispanic Studies* 46 (1969): 21–38.
———. *La vida desaforada de Salvador Dalí*. Barcelona: Anagrama, 1998.
———. "Les vies multiples de Federico García Lorca." Interview with J.F. Fogel. *Magazine Littéraire*, January 1988, 16–23.
———. *Lorca-Dalí. El amor que no pudo ser*. Barcelona: Plaza y Janés, 2000.
Gide, André. *Corydon*. Paris: Gallimard, 1951.
———. *Les nourritures terrestres*. Paris: Le livre de poche, 1966.
———. *Le voyage d'Urien*. Paris: Gallimard, 1950.
———. *Si le grain ne meurt*. Paris: Le livre de poche, 1966.
Gil-Albert, Juan. *Los Arcángeles*. Barcelona: Laia, 1981.
———. *Fuentes de la constancia*. Barcelona: Llibres de Sincera, 1972.
———. *Heraclés. Sobre una manera de ser*. Madrid: Josefina Betancor, 1975.
———. *Obra completa en prosa*. Vol. 2. Valencia: Institución Alfonso el Magnánimo, 1982.
———. *Obra poética completa*. 3 vols. Valencia: Institución Alfonso el Magnánimo, 1981.
———. "La poesía en la muerte de Federico García Lorca." *Hora de España* 15 (March 1938): 90–94.
———. "Realidad y deseo en Luis Cernuda."

Luis Cernuda. Sevilla: University de Sevilla, 1977. 35–107.

Ginsberg, Allen. *Antología poética*. Buenos Aires: Editorial del Mediodía, 1969.

———. *Entrevista*. With A. Young. *Cónsules de Sodoma*. Barcelona: Tusquets, 1982.

———. *Howl and Other Poems*. San Francisco: City Light Books, 1968.

Girard, René. *Le bouc émissaire*. Paris: Grasset and Fasquelle, 1982.

Goldman, Lucien, et al. *Sociología contra psicoanálisis*. Barcelona: Martín Roca, 1974.

Gómez Beneyto, Manuel. "Algunos aspectos médicos, psicólogicos y jurídicos de la homosexualidad." *Los marginados en España*. Madrid: Fundamentos, 1978. 141–54.

Gómez Lanch, Betty Rita. "Muerte y vida en el drama de Federico García Lorca." *Hispania* 43 (1960): 376–77.

González Cruz, Luis F. "Muertes del Amargo: El 'Romance del Emplazado.'" *García Lorca Review* 7 (1979): 25–35.

González del Valle, Luis T. "La dimensión estética de las flores en *Bodas de sangre*." *El teatro de Federico García Lorca y otros ensayos sobre literatura*. Nebraska: Society of Spanish-American Studies, 1980. 35–60.

González Espina, Carlos. "La otra cara de la luna." *A Federico García Lorca*. Gijón: Ateneo Obrero, 1987. 65–67.

Goytisolo, José Agustín. Introducción. *Posible imagen de José Lezama Lima*. Barcelona: Llibres de Sinera, 1972.

Goytisolo, Juan. "Homenaje a Luis Cernuda." *Luis Cernuda: El escritor y la crítica*. Madrid: Taurus, 1977.

———. *Juan sin tierra*. Barcelona: Seix Barral, 1977.

———. *Juan the Landless*. Trans. Helen R. Lane. New York: Viking Press, 1977.

Grass, R. "Lorca's 'Canción de jinete.'" *Explicator* 19 (1960): 19.

Green, Julien. *Partir avant le jour*. Paris: Le livre de poche, 1972.

Greenfield, Sumner M. "Lorca's Theatre: A Synthetic Reexamination." *Journal of Spanish Studies* (spring 1977): 31–46.

Greimas, A.J. *Semántica structural: Investigación metodológica*. Madrid: Gredos, 1976.

Guerin, Daniel. *Le feu du sang. Autobiographie politique et charnelle*. Paris: Grasset, 1977.

Gurméndez, Carlos. "Una interpretación audaz de San Juan de la Cruz." *El País*, 21 November 1982, n.p.

Hahn, Pierre. *Nos ancêtres les pervers. La vie des homosexuels sous le second empire*. Paris: Olivier Orban, 1979.

Halliburton, Charles Lloyd. "García Lorca's Rejection of Mechanical Civilization." Diss., Louisiana State University, 1970.

Hamon, Philippe. "Pour un statut sémiologique du personnage." *Poétique du récit*. Paris: Seuil, 1977. 115–80.

Hansson, Gunnar. "Dikten och läsaren." (The poem and the reader.) Diss., Estocolmo: Prisma, 1970.

Harris, Derek. *García Lorca: "Poeta en Nueva York."* London: Grant and Cutler, 1978.

———. *Luis Cernuda: A Study of the Poetry*. London: Tamesis, 1973.

Harris, D.R. "The Religious Theme in Lorca's *Poeta en Nueva York*." *Bulletin of Hispanic Studies* 54 (1977): 315–26.

Hernández, Mario. Prólogo. *Federico y su mundo*. De Francisco García Lorca. Madrid: Alianza, 1980. i–xxxvii.

———. Introducción y notas. *Diván del Tamarit de Federico García Lorca*. Madrid: Alianza, 1981. 9–50.

Hernández, Miguel. *Cartas a Lorca*. See Cano Ballesta.

———. *Obra poética completa*. Introducción, estudios y notas: Leopoldo de Luis y Jorge Urrutia. Bilbao: Zero, 1979.

———. *El torero más valiente. La tragedia de Calisto y Otras prosas*. Madrid: Alianza Tres, 1986.

Herrero, Javier. "Lo social y su contenido en la sociología de Ortega y Gasset." *Arbor* 83 (1972): 5–30.

Hesse, Carlota. "Dadaísmo y surrealismo." *Cuadernos Hispanoamericanos* 350 (1979): 349–64.

Hierro, José S.P. *Principios de filosofía del lenguaje I*. Madrid: Alianza, 1980.

———. *Problemas del análisis del lenguaje moral*. Madrid: Tecnos, 1970.

Higginbotham, Virginia. "García Lorca and Hart Crane: Two Views from the Bridge." *Neophilologus* 66 (1982): 219–26.

———. "Lorca's Apprenticeship in Surrealism." *Romanic Review* 61 (1970): 109–22.

———. "Reflejos de Lautréamont en *Poeta en Nueva York*." *Federico García Lorca: El poeta y la crítica*. Madrid: Taurus, 1975. 299–310.

Higuera Rojas, Eulalia-Dolores de la. *Mujeres en la vida de García Lorca*. Granada: Nacional, 1980.

Hinostroza, Rodolfo. *El sistema astrológico*. Barcelona: Seix Barral, 1973.

Hobson, Laura Z. *Consenting Adult*. New York: Warner Books, 1982.
Houston, John Porter. "The Symbolic Structure of Rimbaud's Hell." *Modern Language Quarterly* 1960: 69–72.
Huber, Egon. *García Lorca*. München: Wilhelm Fink Verlag, 1967.
Humbert, Juan. *Mitología griega y romana*. México: G. Gili, 1982.
Infantes, Víctor. "Lo 'oscuro' de los '*Sonetos del amor oscuro* de Federico García Lorca." *Federico García Lorca*. Schena, Italia: Saggi Critici, 1988.
Iser, Wolfgang. "The Indeterminacy of the Text: A Critical Reply." *Comparative Criticism* 2 (1980): 27–47.
Isherwood, Christopher. *A Single Man*. London: Mathuen, 1981.
Jakobson, Roman. "Lingüística y poética en *El lenguaje y los problemas del conocimiento*." Buenos Aires: Rodolfo Alonso, 1971. 7–47.
———. "Qu'est-ce que la poésie?" *Huit questions de poétique*. Paris: Seuil, 1977. 31–49.
Janssen-Jurreit, Marie Louise. *Sexism: The Male Monopoly on History and Thought*. New York: Pluto Press, 1982.
"Jean Genet's Sailors Through the Eyes of Jean Cocteau." *In Touch*, May/June 1976: 58–61.
Jean, Marcel. *Histoire de la peinture surréaliste*. Paris: Seuil, 1959.
Jefferson, A. "Intertextuality and the Poetics of Fiction." *Comparative Criticism: A Yearbook*. Vol II. New York: Cambridge University Press, 1980.
Jenkyns, Richard. *The Victorians and Ancient Greece*. Oxford: Basil Blackwell, 1981.
Jiménez, José. *El ángel caído*. Barcelona: Anagrama, 1982.
Jonasson, Curt. "Synoden ger sitt stöd till Werkström." *Svenska Dagbladet*, 23 April 1985: 10.
Josipovici, Gabriel. "Text and Voice." *Comparative Criticism*. Vol. 2. New York: Cambridge University Press, 1980.
Jung, Carl. "Approaching the Unconscious." *Man and His Symbols*. New York: Dell, 1978. 1–94.
Kamen, Henry. *The Spanish Inquisition*. New York: New American Library, 1971.
Kaplan, J. *Walt Whitman: A Life*. New York: Bantam, 1982.
King, Francis. *Sexo, magia y perversión*. Madrid: Felmar, 1978.
Klein, Dennis A. "*El maleficio de la mariposa*: The Cornerstone of García Lorca's Theatre." *García Lorca Review* 2.2 (fall 1974): n.p.
Kleinberg, Seymor. Introduction. *The Other Persuasion*. Suffolk: Picador, 1978. vii–xx.
Knight, Payne. *El culto a Priapo y sus Relaciones con la Teología Mística de los Antiguos. Un ensayo sobre el Culto de los Poderes Generadores durante la Edad Media*. Madrid: Tres, Catorce, Diecisiete, 1980.
Kolakowski, Leszek. *The Key to Heaven and Conversations with the Devil*. New York: Grove Press, 1972.
Knox B. "The Socratic Method." *The New York Review*, 25 January 1979, 5–8.
Koning, Frederik. *Bajo el signo de Venus*. Barcelona: Bruguera, 1976.
Kristeva, Julia. *Semiótica I*. Madrid: Fundamentos, 1981.
Laclau, Ernesto. Qtd. by Paramaio.
Laffranque, Marie. "Estudio y notas." *Teatro inconcluso de Federico García Lorca*. Granada: University de Granada, 1987.
———. *Les idées esthetiques de Federico García Lorca*. Paris: Centre de Recherches Hispaniques, 1967.
———. "Puertas abiertas y cerradas en la poesía y el teatro de García Lorca." *Federico García Lorca: El escritor y la crítica*. Madrid: Taurus, 1975. 73–93.
Laguardia, Gari. "The Butterflies in Walt Whitman's Beard: Lorca's Naming of Whitman." *Neophilologus* 62 (1978): 540–54.
Laing, R.D. *The Divided Self*. Middlesex: Pelican, 1971.
———. *Self and Others*. Middlesex: Pelican, 1971.
Lambert, Gavin. *Mainly About Lindsay Anderson: A Memoriam*. London: Faber and Faber Ltd., 2000.
Landell, Nils Erik. "Förakta icke mossigheten." *Svenska Dagbladet*, 20 November 1988, 14.
Landerson, Louis. "Psychiatry and Homosexuality: New 'Cures.'" *The Radical Therapist*. Middlesex: Penguin, 1974.
Larrea, Juan. "Asesinado por el cielo." *Trece de nieve* 1–2 (December 1976): 117–24.
———. "Ingreso a una transfiguración." *Poesías completas de Emilio Prados*. Mexico: Aguilar, 1976. 9–24.
Laubenthal, Penne Jones. *Prometheus, Prophet, and Priest: An Interpretation of García Lorca's Poet in New York in Relationship to Walt Whitman's Leaves of Grass*. Diss., George Peabody College for Teachers. Ann Arbor: University of Michigan, 1972.
Lautréamont, Comte de. *Oeuvres Poétiques Compltes*. Paris: Robert Laffont, 1980.

León, Victor. *Diccionario del argot español.* Madrid: Alianza, 1980.

Lévi-Strauss, Claude. Qtd. by Derrida.

Lewis, Wyndham. *The Childermass.* London: John Calder Publishers Ltd., 1965.

Lezama Lima, José. *Paradiso.* Rev. ed. México: Biblioteca Era, 1976.

———. *Posible imagen de José Lezama Lima.* Barcelona: Llibres de Sinera, 1972.

Lima, Robert. *The Theatre of García Lorca.* New York: Las Américas, 1963.

Lindegreen, E. Qtd. by Cullhed.

Linder, Erik Hjalmar. *Kärlek och fadershus farväl.* Estocolmo: Bonniers, 1973.

Lindkvist, Kent and Karin Moritz. "Förtryck och homosexuell försvarskamp under 1900-talet." *Zenit* 5 (1975): 15–33.

Lindström, J. "Den nya spetälskan." *Expressen,* 19 May 1983, 10.

Lipinski, Rick, trans. *The Young Sailor and Other Poems.* By Luis Cernuda. San Francisco: Gay Sunshine Press, 1986.

Litvak, Lily. *Erotismo fin de siglo.* Barcelona: Bosch, 1979.

Llamas, A. "Un demi-siècle de silence." *Magazine Littéraire,* January 1988: 51–52.

Llamas, Ricardo. *Teoría torcida: Prejuicios y discursos en torno a "la homosexualidad."* Madrid: Siglo XXI, 1998.

López Castellón, Enrique. "El comienzo de la campaña nietzscheana contra la moral." *Aurora.* Madrid: Busma, 1984.

———. *Federico García Lorca: El poeta y la muerte.* Madrid: Felmar, 1981.

López Sancho, Lorenzo. "Los siete velos de Saturno." *ABC,* 6 September 1981, suplemento dominical: 5.

Loren, Victoriano Domingo. *Los homosexuales frente a la ley.* Barcelona: Plaza and Janés, 1978.

Loughran, David K. *Federico García Lorca: The Poetry of Limits.* London: Tamesis Books, 1978.

Lozano, Jorge, Cristina Peña Marín and Gonzalo Abril. *Análisis del discurso: Hacia una semiótica de la interacción textual.* Madrid: Cátedra, 1982.

Maffesoli, Michel. "La rebelión del cuerpo." *El País,* 28 August 1983, n.p.

Marais, Jean. *Historias de mi vida.* Madrid: AQ, 1976.

Marañón, Gregorio. Qtd. by García Valdés.

Marcial. *Epigrams of Marcial.* New York: The New American Library, 1970.

Marcilly, Charles. "Enfin la verité sur Lorca?" *Les langues néo-latines* 140 (1957): 21–28.

Marful, Inés. "Pasión y muerte en el drama lorquiano." *A Federico García Lorca.* Gijón: Ateneo, 1987.

Marín, K. "Seminario de investigación interdisciplinaria sobre la mujer." *El País,* 22 April 1982, n.p.

Marinello, Juan. *García Lorca en Cuba.* La Habana: Colección Ediciones Especiales, 1965.

Marqués, Josef Vicent. "Infinito igual a dos." *El País,* 10 February 1985 (weekly), 34.

Marquina, Eduardo. Qtd by Ferreres.

Martín, Eutimio. *Federico García Lorca, heterodoxo y mártir.* Madrid: Siglo XXI, 1986.

———, ed. Introducción. *Poeta en Nueva York. Tierra y luna.* Barcelona: Ariel, 1981.

———. "L'utopie messianique (christo-qui chottesque) de Federico García Lorca: *Amor de don Perlimplín con Belisa en su jardín.*" *Las utopías.* Madrid: Casa de Velázquez, 1990. 271–290.

———. "Sombras. Una obra inédita de García Lorca." *Quimera* 36 (1984): 51–55.

Martínez Nadal, Rafael. "Baco y Ciso." *Cuadernos del Sur* (1972): 228–40.

———. *Cuatro lecciones sobre Federico García Lorca.* Madrid: Cátedra, 1980.

———. *Españoles en la Gran Bretaña. Luis Cernuda.* Madrid: Libros Hiperión, 1983.

———. *Federico García Lorca and The Public.* New York: Schocken Books, 1974.

———. "Guía al lector de *El público.*" *El público y Comedia sin título.* Barcelona: Seix Barral, 1978.

———. Prólogo. *Federico García Lorca. Autógrafos.* Oxford: The Dolphin Book, 1975.

———. *El público. Amor, teatro y caballos en la obra de Lorca.* Oxford: The Dolphin Book, 1970.

Masters, William, and Virginia Johnson. *Homosexuality in Perspective.* New York: Bantam Books, 1982.

Maurer, Christopher, ed. *Federico García Lorca: Collected Poems.* Trans. Christopher Maurer, et al. Vol. II. New York: Farrar Straus Giroux, 1991.

———. "Millonario de lágrimas." *El País,* 3 December 1989, Sunday supplement, 15.

Mauron, Charles, et al. *Sociología contra psicoanálisis.* Barcelona: Martínez Roca, 1974.

May, Rollo. *Love and Will.* London: Souvenir Press, 1969.

Mayer, Hans. *Historia maldita de la literatura: La mujer, el homosexual, el judío.* Madrid: Taurus, 1977.

Méndez, José. "Semprún: *Poeta en Nueva York,* de Lorca, es comparable a *Las iluminaciones* de Rimbaud y 'Homosexualidad.'" *El País,* 3 April 1990, 36.

Merlau-Ponty, Maurice. *Fenomenología de la percepción*. Barcelona: Planeta Agostini, 1984.
Meschonnic Henri. "Pour la poétique." *Langue Française* 3 (1969): 14–31.
Meyer, Eva. Qtd. in Clason.
Mieli, M. *Elementos de crítica homosexual*. Barcelona: Anagrama, 1979.
Millán, María Clementa. "Líneas de una biografía en 'Dibujos.'" Madrid: Ministerio de Cultura, 1986. 55–62.
———. Introducción. *Poeta en Nueva York*. Madrid: Cátedra, 1988. 11–105.
———. Introducción. *El público*. Madrid: Cátedra, 1991. 9–115.
———. "Voces poéticas de un *Poeta en Nueva York*." *Nueva Estafeta* 9–10 (1979): 98–106.
Miller, H. Qtd. by Pérez Estrada.
Miller, Norman C. *García Lorca's Poema del cante jondo*. London: Tamesis Books, 1978.
Millet, Louis and Madeleine Varin d'Ainvelle. *El estructuralismo como método*. Barcelona: LAIA, 1975.
Milorad. Introducción. *Le livre blanc*. By Jean Cocteau. Paris: Persona, 1981. 9–23.
Minguet, P.H. "Du rhétorique au poétique." *Vers un esthétique sans entrave*. Paris: Union Genérales d'Editions, 1957. 329–44.
Mirabet i Mullol, Antoni. *Homosexualidad Hoy*. Barcelona: Herder, 1985.
Moix, Terenci. Prólogo. *Salomé*. By Oscar Wilde. Barcelona: AYMA, 1979. 7–18.
Monegal, Antonio. "Un-Masking the Masculine: Transvestism and Tragedy in García Lorca's *El público*." *MLN* 109 (1994): 204–16.
Montaner, Carlos Alberto. "Lorca y el orgullo gay." *ABC*, 7 July 1998, 62.
Montero, Rosa. *Crónica del desamor*. Madrid: Debate, 1982.
Mora, Miguel. "Llega el 'año santo' de Lorca." *El País*, 26 October 1997, 36.
Mora Guarnido, José. *Federico García Lorca y su mundo*. Buenos Aires: Losada, 1958.
Morales Borrero, Manuel. *La geometría mística del alma en la literatura española del Siglo de Oro*. Madrid: Fundación Universitaria Española, 1975.
Morand, Paul. Qtd. by Viers.
Morris, C. Brian. *A Generation of Spanish Poets 1920–1936*. New York: Cambridge University Press, 1969.
———. *Surrealism and Spain 1920–1936*. New York: Cambridge University Press, 1972.
———. *This Loving Darkness: The Cinema and Spanish Writers 1920–1936*. New York: Oxford University Press, 1980.

Muñoz, M.L. "Fascinación y resistencia." *El País*, 1 June 1989, "Temas de nuestra época," 8.
Neruda, Pablo. *Para nacer he nacido*. Barcelona: Seix Barral, 1978.
Newton, Candelas S. "Nostalgia del paraíso infantil en *Libro de poemas*: el poeta sobre su Pegaso." *García Lorca Review* 8 (1980): 73–81.
Newton, Huey P. *To Die for the People*. New York: Vintage Books, 1972.
Nickel, Catherine. "The Function of Language in García Lorca's *Doña Rosita la soltera*." *Hispania* 66 (1983): 522–31.
Nieto, José C. *Místico, poeta rebelde, santo: en torno a San Juan de la Cruz*. México: Fondo de Cultura Económica, 1982.
Nietzsche, Friedrich. *Aurora*. Madrid: Busma, 1984.
Norton Anthology of English Literature. Vol. 1. New York: Norton and Co., 1974.
Ocón, M. "Los dorados homosexuales de Berlín." *El País*, 23 September 1984, 40–41.
Olano, A.D. "75 años siendo Dalí." *Gaceta ilustrada*. June 17, 1979:16.
Onís, Federico de. "Federico García Lorca." *Writers of Our Years*. Ed. A.M.I. Fiskin. Denver: University of Denver Press, 1950. 24–35.
Ortega, José. "*Poeta en Nueva York*: Alienación social y surrealismo." *Nueva Estafeta* 18 (1980): 45–54.
———. "Surrealismo y eroticismo: Así que pasen cinco años de García Lorca." *García Lorca Review* 10 (1982): 75–93.
Ortega y Gasset. Qtd. by Rof Carballo.
———. *El espectador*. Madrid: Salvat, 1969.
Panebianco, Candido. *Simbolo e "pathos" nel "Diván del Tamarit" di F. García Lorca*. Rome: Bulzoni, 1981.
Paramaio, L. "Ernesto Laclau: 'A través del peronismo llegué a Gramsci.'" *El País*, 6 September 1983, n.p.
Parr, James A. "La escena final de *Yerma*." *Duquesne Hispanic Review* 1 (1971): 23–29.
Partridge, Eric. *Shakespeare's Bawdy: A Literary and Psychological Essay and a Comprehensive Glossary*. New York: Dutton and Co., 1948.
Pasolini, Pier Paolo. *Actos impuros. Amado mío*. Barcelona: Seix Barral, 1984.
Paz, Octavio. *Conjunctions and Disjunctions*. Trans. Helen R. Lane. New York: Viking Press, 1974.
———. "Octavio Paz rescata casualmente una obra inédita de teatro de Luis Cernuda." *El País*, 10 November 1985, 30.

———. *Los signos en rotación y otros ensayos.* Madrid: Alianza, 1971.
Penón, Agustín. *Diario de una búsqueda.* Ed. Ian Gibson. Barcelona: Plaza and Janés, 1990.
Pequeño Larousse Ilustrado. Paris: Larousse, 1969.
Pérez Estrada, Rafael. "Introducción a *Del goce y de la dicha.*" *Del goce y de la dicha.* Torremolinos: Litoral, 1985. 7–19.
Peyre, Henri. "The Legacy of Proust." *Proust: A Collection of Critical Essays.* Ed. R. Girard. New Jersey: Prentice Hall, 1962.
Plato. *Five Great Dialogues.* Trans. B. Jowett. Ed. Louise Ropes Loomis. Princeton: D. Van Nostrand Co., 1942.
Plaza Molina, Gabriel. *El triángulo de las verduras.* Barcelona: Plaza y Janés, 1981.
Pollak, Michael. "L'homosexualité masculine, ou: le bonheur dans le ghetto?" *Communications* 35 (1982): 37–55.
Pollin, A.M., ed. *A Concordance to the Plays and Poems of Federico García Lorca.* Play programmer D.C. Weinberger. Poetry programmer P.H. Smith, Jr. Ithaca: Cornell University Press, 1975.
Pons, Esther Bartolomé. "Tiempo, amor y muerte en el lenguage poético de Luis Cernuda." *Insula* 36 (1981): 1.
Porché, François. *L'Amour qui n'ose pas dire son nom.* Paris: Grasset, 1927.
Poulet, Georges. *Les métamorphoses du cercle.* Paris: Librairie Plon, 1961.
Prada, Juan Manuel de. "Centenarios." *ABC,* 5 June 1998, 20.
Prados, Emilio. *La piedra escrita.* Ed. J. Sanchis-Banús. Madrid: Clásicos Castalia, 1979.
———. *Poesías completas I.* Mexico: Aguilar, 1975.
———. *Poesías completas II.* Mexico, Aguilar, 1976.
Predmore, Richard L. *Lorca's New York Poetry: Social Injustice, Dark Love, Lost Faith.* Durham, North Carolina: Duke University Press, 1980.
———. "Nueva York y la conciencia social de Federico García Lorca." *Revista Hispánica Moderna.* 36 (1970–71): 32–40.
———. "Simbolismo ambigüo en la poesía de García Lorca." *Papeles de San Armadens* 189 (1971): 229–40.
Prieto, Gregorio. "Gregorio Prieto, entre carne y carne, fresas." With J.M. Ullán. *El País* 240 (15 November 1981) (weekly): 11–16.
———. *Lorca y su mundo angélico.* Madrid: Organización, 1972.
Prique, A. "Aragon surpris par le soleil." *Gai Pied* 50 (1–7 January 1983): 14–15.
Proust, Marcel. *Sodome et Gomorrhe.* Paris: Gallimard, 1969.
Queensberry, Lord and P. Colson. *Oscar Wilde et le Clan Douglas.* Paris: Arts et Métiers Graphiques, 1950.
Quevedo, Francisco de. *Poesía varia.* Madrid: Cátedra, 1981.
Racionero, L. "Dalí o el principio del placer." *Revista de Occidente* 5 (1981): 103–11.
Ramond, Michéle. "El otro (o la letra viva)." *Cuadernos Hispanoamericanos* 435–36 (1986): 431–37.
Ramos Gil, Carlos. *Ecos antiguos, estructuras nuevas y mundo primario en la lírica de Lorca.* Bahía Blanca: Cuadernos del Sur, 1967.
———. "Hacia una revisión del teatro lorquiano." *Revista de Literatura* 42.83 (1980): 131–57.
Rastier, F. "Systématique des isotopies." *Essais de sémiotique poétique.* Paris: Librairie Larousse, 1972. 80–106.
Ressot, J.P. "Par-dela-le-bien et le mal: *Las criaturas saturnianas* de Ramón J. Sender." *Les langues néo-latines* 188–89 (1969): 43–51.
Ricoeur, Paul. "On Interpretation." *Philosophy in France.* Ed. A. Montefiiore. Cambridge: The Press Syndicate, University of Cambridge, 1983: 175–97.
———. "Psicoanálisis y cultura." *Sociología contra psicoanálisis.* Barcelona: Martínez Roca, 1974. 208–22.
Rieff, Philipp. "La cultura imposible: Wilde, profeta moderno." *Homosexualidad: literatura y política.* Eds. G. Steiner and R. Boyers. Madrid: Alianza, 1985. 301–29.
———. Introduction. *Sexuality and the Psychology of Love.* By Sigmund Freud. New York: Collier Books, 1974. 7–10.
Riess, Curt. *¿También tú, César...? La homosexualidad como destino.* Barcelona: Argos Vergara, 1984.
Riffaterre, Michael. "La métaphore filée dans la poésie surréaliste." *Langue Française* September 1969: 46–60.
Rimbaud, Arthur. *Oeuvres Poétiques Complètes.* Paris: Robert Laffont, 1980.
Río, Angel del. "*Poet in New York*: Twenty-five Years After." *Poet in New York.* New York: Grove Press, 1955. ix–xxxix.
———. "La vida literaria en España." *Revista de estudios hispánicos* 1 (1928): 176–80.
Rivas Cherif, Cipriano. "La muerte y la pasión de Federico García Lorca." *Excelsior,* 27 January 1957, n.p.

———. Letter published by Rodrigo in *García Lorca en Cataluña*.
Rivers, J.E. *Proust and the Art of Love*. New York: Columbia University Press, 1980.
Roberts, Gemma. "La intuición poética del tiempo finito en las *Canciones* de Federico García Lorca." *Revista Hispánica Moderna* 33 (1967): 250–61.
Rodrigo, Antonina. *García Lorca en Cataluña*. Barcelona: Planeta, 1975.
———. *Lorca-Dalí: Una amistad traicionada*. Barcelona: Planeta, 1981.
———. *Memoria de Granada: Manuel Angeles Ortiz, Federico García Lorca*. Barcelona: Plaza and Janés, 1984.
Rof Carballo, Juan. "Ortega como traductor." *ABC*, 24 June 1983, 3.
Roig, Antonio. *Todos los parques no son un paraíso*. Barcelona: Planeta, 1977.
Rojas, Carlos. *El ingenioso hidalgo y poeta Federico García Lorca asciende a los infiernos*. Barcelona: Destino, 1980.
———. *El mundo mítico y mágico de Salvador Dalí*. Barcelona: Plaza and Janés, 1985.
———. "A Salvador Dalí." "Cartas abiertas a los vivos y a los muertos." *El País*, 1 August 1981, 7.
Romero, Luis. *Dalí*. New Jersey: Chartwell, 1979.
Rosselló, Ramón. *L'homosexualitat a Mallorca a l'Edat Mitjana*. Barcelona: Calamvs Scriptorivs, 1978.
Rowse, A.L. *Homosexuals in History: A Study of Ambivalence in Society, Literature and the Arts*. London: Weindenfeld and Nicolson, 1977.
Rudbeck, Carl. "Privata delar av borgarnas liv." *Svenska Dagbladet*, 19 February 1984, n.p.
Ruiz Antón, Francisco. "La Fundación Lorca cree que el Centenario sirvió para cumplir el deseo del poeta de llevar la cultura al pueblo." *ABC*, 21 January 1999, 46.
Ruiz López, Andrés. *Ocaña, el fuego infinito. El público*. Madrid: Ministerio de Cultura, 1989.
Ruiz Silva, Carlos. *Arte, amor y otras soledades en Luis Cernuda*. Madrid: Editorial de la Torre, 1979.
Rupert de Ventós Xavier. *Los metopías. Metodologías y utopías de nuestro tiempo*. Barcelona: Montesinos, 1984.
Sábato, Ernesto. "Reflexiones sobre la obra de arte (y II)." *ABC*, 16 August 1986, 18.
Sáenz de la Calzada, Luis. "*La Barraca.*" *Federico García Lorca y su teatro universitario*. Madrid: Biblioteca de la Rev. de Occidente, 1976.

Sagaseta, S. "Electrochoques contra la homosexualidad." *El País*, 30 November 1979, "Tribuna libre," n.p.
Sahuquillo, Ángel. "El asesinato de 'Vuelta de paseo,' de Federico García Lorca." *Ensayos de literatura europea e hispanoamericana*. San Sebastián: Universidad del País Vasco, 1990, 493–504.
———. "Juan Goytisolo, Severo Sarduy, and San Juan de la Cruz: Birds, Passion, Homosexuality, AIDS, and Sainthood." *Readerly/Writerly Texts* 5.1, 2 (1997, 1998): 223–50.
———. "¿Qué hace un burro podrido encima de un piano? Homosexualidad, actividad paranoico-crítica, surrealismo y carnaval en la vida y la obra de Salvador Dalí." *La nueva literatura hispánica* 8–9 (2004–05): 149–204.
Salinas, Pedro. "Lorca and the Poetry of Death." *Lorca*. Ed. Manuel Durán. New Jersey: Prentice Hall, 1965. 100–07.
Salvador, Gregorio. *Glosas al "Romance sonámbulo" de García Lorca*. Granada: University of Granada, 1980.
Sánchez de Zavala, Víctor. *Indagaciones Praxiológicas. Sobre la actividad lingüística*. Madrid: Siglo Veintiuno, 1973.
Sánchez Mejías, Ignacio. *Sin razón* (qtd. by Morris in *Surrealism and Spain 1920–1936*).
———. *Teatro*. Madrid: Espasa Calpe, 1988.
Sánchez Vidal, Agustín. *Buñuel, Lorca, Dalí: El enigma sin fin*. Barcelona: Planeta, 1988.
———. Introduccción, notas. *Luis Buñuel*. Aragón: Heraldo de Aragón, 1982.
———. "Algunas notas sobre *Perito en lunas*." *Documenta Miguel Hernández* 1985: 37–45.
Sanchis Banús, José. "La amistad entre Federico García Lorca y Emilio Prados." *Revista de la Universidad Complutense de Madrid* 26 (1977): 281–92.
Santos Torroella, Rafael. *La miel es más dulce que la sangre: Las épocas lorquiana y freudiana de Salvador Dalí*. Barcelona: Seix Barral, 1984.
Sarotte, Georges Michel. "Le thème de l'homsexualité masculine dans le roman et le théatre américains de Herman Melville James Baldwin." Diss., University de Lille, 1975.
Sartre, Jean Paul. *Saint Genet: Comédien et martyr*. Paris: Gallimard, 1967.
———. "Sartre: Entretien exclusif. Sartre et les homosexuels." With Jean Le Bitoux. *Gai Pied* 13 (1980): 1, 11–14.
Satué, Francisco. "Anotaciones para un retrato de Lorca." *Cuadernos Hispanoamericanos* 433–34 (1986): 45–53.

Saussure, Ferdinand de. *Curso de lingüística general.* Barcelona: Planeta-Agostini, 1985.
Savater, Fernando. "Lo inconfesable." *El País,* 3 March 1983, 11.
Sbarbi, J. *Florilegio o ramillete alfabético de refranes y modismos.* Madrid: Atlas, 1980.
Schneider, Franz. "Lorca's 'Canción de jinete.'" *Explicator* 20 (1962): 74.
Schonberg, Jean-Louis. *A la recherche de Lorca.* Suiza: Neuchtel, 1966.
Schwartz, Kessel. *Vicente Aleixandre.* New York: Twayne, 1970.
Scott-Stokes, H. *The Life and Death of Yukio Mishima.* New York: Dell, 1975.
Sebastián, Santiago. *Arte y humanismo.* Madrid: Cátedra, 1981.
Segal, Charles. *Dionysiac Poetics and Euripides' Bacchae.* New Jersey: Princeton University Press, 1982.
Sémolué, J. *Julien Green o la obsesión del mal.* Madrid: Ibérica Europa, 1970.
Semprún Donahue, Moraima. "Cristo en Lorca." *Explicación de Textos Literarios* 4 (1975): 23–34.
———. "Una franca interpretación de 'Poemas del lago Edem Mills' de García Lorca." *García Lorca Review* 33 (1975): 79–90.
———. *Las narraciones de Federico García Lorca: un franco enfoque.* Barcelona: Hispam, 1975.
———. "Nuevos indicios en la interpretación de 'Romance sonámulo.'" *Cuadernos Americanos* 194 (1974): 257–60.
Sesé, Bernard. "A propos de *Poeta en Nueva York*" and "Les yeux et le regard." *Les langues Néo-Latines* 160 (1962): 2–35.
———. "Les valeurs de la bouche dans l'univers imaginaire de Federico García Lorca." *Les langues Néo-Latines* 182 (1967): 29–53.
Shakespeare, William. *The Complete Works of Shakespeare.* London: Spring Books, n.d.
Shamblin, Donald Gray. *Erotic Frustration and Its Causes in the Drama of Federico García Lorca.* Diss., University of Minnesota, 1966. Ann Arbor: University of Michigan.
Sheklin Davis, Barbara. "El teatro surrealista español." *Revista Hispánica Moderna* 33 (1967): 309–29.
Shephard, Esther. "Possible sources of Some of Whitman's Ideas and Symbols in *Hermes Mercurius Trismegistus.*" *Modern Language Quarterly* 14 (1953): 60–81.
Silver, Philip. *"Et in Arcadia Ego": A Study of the Poetry of Luis Cernuda.* London: Tamesis Books, 1965.
———. *De la mano de Cernuda: Invitación a la poesía.* Madrid: Cátedra, 1989.
Simón, César. *Juan Gil-Albert: de su vida y obra.* Alicante: Diputación Provincial, 1984.
Singer, June. *Androgyny: Towards a New Theory of Sexuality.* New York: Anchor Press/Doubleday, 1977.
Socrate, Mario. "L'Adán di Lorca e la simultaneit del punto di vista." *Strumenti Critici* 44 (1981): 46–67.
Sollers, Philippe. *La escritura y la experiencia de los límites.* Valencia: Pre-textos, 1978.
Sontag, Susan. "Entrevista con Susan Sontag." With R. Boyers and M. Bernstein. *Revista de Occidente,* July 1976: 36–45.
Sorel, Andrés. *Yo, García Lorca.* Bilbao: Zero, 1977.
Soriano Gil, Manuel. *Homosexualidad y represión.* Bilbao: Zero, 1978.
Sou. Homosexuella och Samhället. Estocolmo: Liber, 1984.
Soufas, C. Christopher, Jr. "Cernuda and Daimonic Power." *Hispania* 66 (1983): 167–75.
Sousa, Ronald de. "Norms and the Normal." *Freud: A Collection of Critical Essays.* Various authors. New York: Anchor Books, 1974. 196–221.
Spencer, Janes Frances. "El claroscuro en la trilogía lorquiana." *Cuadernos Americanos* 4 (171–87): 1979.
Spijker, Herman van de. *Homotropía: Inclinación hacia el mismo sexo.* Madrid: Sociedad de Educación Ateneas, 1976.
Spinoza, Benito. *Etica.* Buenos Aires: Aguilar, 1982.
Steakley, J.D. "Love Between Women and Love Between Men: Interview with Charlotte Wolff." *New German Critique* 23 (1981): 73–81.
Steen-Johsson, C. "Demonstranter släpades ut." *Dagen Nyheter,* 22 April 1985, 6.
Tasker, Yvonne. *Spectacular Bodies: Gender, Genre and the Action Cinema.* London: Routledge, 1993.
Taylor, Carl L., Jr. "Mexican Gaylife in Historical Perspective." *Gay Sunshine* 26–27 (1975–76): 1–3.
Tijeras, Eduardo. "Hacia García Lorca por las imágenes del agua." *Cuadernos Hispanoamericanos* 433–34 (1986): 89–102.
Tillich, Paul. *The Courage to Be.* Glasgow: Fontana, 1979.
Tobin, Kay and Randy Wicker. *The Gay Crusaders.* New York: Paperback Library, 1972.
Todorov, Tzvetan. "Littérature et semio-

tique." *Vers un esthétique sans entrave.* Paris: Unión Genérale D'Editions, 1975.

Tompkins, Peter. *El eunuco y la doncella.* Barcelona: Luis de Caralt, 1976.

Torre, Guillermo de. *Carta a Eduardo Blanco Amor.* 31 de V. 1938. Archivo de la Biblioteca de la Diputación Provincial de Orense.

———. "Presencia de Federico García Lorca." *La aventura estética de nuestra edad.* Barcelona: Seix Barral, 1962. 265–88.

———. "Reverso y anverso de André Gide." *La metamorfosis de Proteo.* Buenos Aires: Losada, 1956. 155–76.

———. "Tres retratos de Rubén Darío." *Papeles de Son Armadans* 137–38 (1967): 121–40.

Tripp, C.A. *The Homosexual Matrix.* New York: Signet Book, 1976.

Tripp, Edward. *The Meridian Handbook of Classical Mythology.* New York: New American Library, 1974.

Ullán, José-Miguel. "El primitivo Serrat." *El País,* 9 May 1982, n.p.

Umbral, Francisco. "Análisis y síntesis de Lorca." *Revista de Occidente* 32 (1971): 221–29.

———. *Lorca, poeta maldito.* Madrid: Biblioteca Nueva, 1975.

———. "Mémories d'un enfant du sicle." *Magazine Littéraire,* January 1988: 26–27.

———. "Sexo y muerte en García Lorca." *La Estafeta Literaria* 387 (1968): 16–17.

Utrera, Rafael. *García Lorca y el cinema.* Sevilla: EDISUR, 1982.

Van der Meersch, Maxence. *La máscara de carne.* Barcelona: Libro Plaza, 1961.

Valle-Inclán, Ramón. *Sonata de estío.* Madrid: Espasa-Calpe, 1963.

Valls, Manuel. *La música en el abrazo de Eros.* Barcelona: Tusquets, 1982.

Varderi, Alejandro. *Severo Sarduy y Pedro Almodóvar: del barroco al kitsch en la narrativa y el cine postmodernos.* Madrid: Pliegos, 1996.

Vázquez Ocaña, Fernando. *García Lorca: vida, cántico y muerte.* Paris: Ruedo Ibérico, 1962.

Velasco, Joseph. "La poesía erótica del primer Lorca." *Hommage Jean-Louis Flecniakoska.* Various authors. Montpellier: University Paul Valery, 1980. 445–61.

Velázquez Cueto, Gerardo. "Para una lectura de *Un río, un amor* de Luis Cernuda." *Insula* 455 (1984): 3, 7.

Verlaine, Paul. "*Hombres.*" "The Erotic Poetry of Paul Verlaine." *Blueboy,* July 1979: 30–33.

———. *Mes prisons.* Paris: Le Livre de Poche, 1973.

———. *Obra poética completa.* Vol. 2. Bilingual ed. Barcelona: Libros Río Nuevo, 1980.

———. *Oeuvres poétiques complètes.* Ed. Jacques Borel. Paris: Gallimard, 1981.

Vidal, Gore. *A Thirsty Devil.* London: Panther Books, 1974.

Viera, David J. "El caballo negro en Antero de Quental y en García Lorca, y el tema amor-muerte." *Thesaurus* 36 (1981): 71–89.

Viers, Rina. "Evolution et sexualité des plantes dan *Sodome et Gomorrhe.*" *Europe* 502–03 (1971): 100–13.

Villegas, Juan. "El leitmotiv del caballo en *Bodas de sangre.*" *Hispanófila* 29 (1967): 21–36.

Villena, Luis Antonio de. *Ante el espejo.* Barcelona: Argos Vergara, 1982.

———. "Cernuda recordado por Aleixandre." *A una verdad.* Various authors. Sevilla: University Internacional Menéndez Pelayo, 1988.

———. Qtd. in "Luis Antonio de Villena publica *Ante el espejo*: el libro de una adolescencia prohibida." *El País,* 15 December 1982.

———. Prólogo. *La musa de los muchachos.* By Estraton de Sardes, et al. Trans. L.A. Villena. Madrid: Hiperión, 1980.

———. *El razonamiento inagotable de Juan Gil-Albert.* Madrid: Anjana, 1984.

———. "La rebeldía del dandy." *3 Luis Cernuda.* Various authors. Seville: University of Seville, 1977. 109–55.

Vivanco, Luis Felipe. "Federico García Lorca, poeta dramático de copla y estribillo." *Introducción a la poesía española contemporánea.* Vol. 2. Madrid: Guadarrama, 1974. 9–79.

Voltaire, François M.A. *Dictionnaire Philosophique Portatif.* Rev. ed. London: By the author, 1765.

Voss, Jon. "Upphittad: världens första gayfilm!" *Reporter,* June–July 1987: 16.

Vovelles, Michel. "Ideologies and mentalities." *Culture and Politics.* London: Routledge and Kegan Paul, 1982. 2–11.

Walsh, John K. "'Las cintas del vals': Three Dance-Poems from Lorca's *Poet in New York.*" *Romanic Review* 79 (1988): 502–16.

Weimer, Christopher Brian. "Journeys from Frustration to Empowerment: *Cat on a Hot Tin Roof* and Its Debt to García Lorca's *Yerma.*" *Modern Drama* 35 (1992): 520–29.

Welles, M.L. "Lorca's *Así que pasen cinco años.*" *Romance Notes* 17 (1976): 137–44.
Wells, C. Michael. "The Natural Norm in the Plays of Federico García Lorca." *Hispanic Review* 38 (1970): 299–313.
West, Donald J. *Homosexuality.* Middlesex: Pelican Books, 1963.
Whitman, Walt. *Leaves of Grass.* New York: New American Library, 1954.
Wilber, Ken. *La conciencia sin fronteras.* Barcelona: Kairós, 1987.
Wilcox, J.C. "'Naked' versus 'Pure' Poetry in Juan Ramón Jiménez, with Remarks on the Impact of W.B. Yeats." *Hispania* 66 (1983): 511–21.
Wilde, Oscar. *The Complete Works of Oscar Wilde.* New York: Harper and Row, 1989.
———. *Salomé.* Barcelona: AYMA, 1979.
Wildgans. Qtd. by Vázquez Ocaña.
Wizelius, Tore. "Homosexuella sjukskriver sig i protest." *Dagens Nyheter,* 30 August 1979.
Wolff, Charlotte. *Bisexualidad.* Barcelona: Plaza and Janés, 1978.
———. Interview with Steakley. *New German Critique* 23(1981):73–81.
Yanhi, Roberto. "Algunos rasgos formales en la lírica de García Lorca: función del paréntesis." *Federico García Lorca: El escritor y la crítica.* Various authors. Madrid: Taurus, 1975. 217–36.
Yeats, W.B. Qtd. by Cowell.
Yourcenar, Marguerite. *Mishima o la visión del vacío.* Barcelona: Seix Barral, 1988.
Yudin, Florence L. "The Dark Silence in Lorca's Poetry." *García Lorca Review* 6 (1978): 151–67.
Zardoya, Concha. "Los espejos de Federico García Lorca." *Asomante* 18.1 (1962): 14–45.
Zubiri, Xavier. *Inteligencia y logos.* Madrid: Alianza Editorial, 1982.
Zuleta, Emilia de. *Cinco poetas españoles.* Madrid: Editorial Gredos, 1971.

Index

ABC 236
"accursed breed or race" 75, 104
"Adam" (Adán) 125, 191
Adams, Mildred 47, 79, 147, 167
"After a Walk" 101, 238n.3(chapter 1)
Aftonbladet 100, 215
Aguilar, *Complete Works* 14, 90
Aguirre, J.M. 49, 224
Ahnlund, Knut 215
Akelarre 135
Aladrén Perojo, Emilio 72
Alberish, J. 217
Alberti, Rafael 18, 221
Aleixandre, Vicente 54, 127, 229; and "El Vals" (*Swords Like Lips*) 176
Alfaya, Javier 48
Alfonso X, "the Wise": and *The Royal Code of Spain* 136
Allen, Rupert 45, 174
Almodóvar, Pedro 62; and films by 61
Alonso, Dámaso 18, 230
Altmann, Werner 60
Alvarez de Miranda, Angel 173, 191
Alvarez-Altman, Grace 158, 242n.6
Ancient Greece 31, 232; and homosexual love 143
Andalusia (Andalusians) 208, 211
Anderson, Andrew 51, 86, 173
Anderson, Sherwood, *Hands* 137
Andrade, Raúl 47
Andueza, María 184, 205
angels 150
Anset, Jacques 228
Apollinaire, Guillaume 175
Apollo 113, 193
Aragón, Luis 19, 239n.5
Arango, Manuel Antonio 59
Aranguren, José Luis 229, 230, 243n.9
Armas, José R. de 210
Armiño, Mauro 41
Arrington, Hilda Cown 168, 244n.5
Auclair, Marcelle 23, 36, 41, 67, 127, 141, 157
"Autumn Song" 226

"¡Ay!" 24
Azancot, Leopoldo 18

Babín, María Teresa 206, 207
bacchanal 71–72, 73
Bacchus 113, 114, 131, 132, 185, 211, 218, 232; and Dionysus 189; symbols of: billy goat, fig tree, ivy, vine 131; panther 188
"Bacchus" 63, 182, 183, 185, 189, 193, 194, 233
"Back of the World" 204, 205, 208, 226, 231, 233
"The Ballad of Back Pain" 64
"Ballad of the Moon, Moon" 191
Barbachano, Carlos: and Rimbaud and Christianity 139
Bardem, Javier 52
Barea, Arturo 37
Barnard, Mary E.: and Garcilaso's Apollo and Daphne 157
Barnatan, Marcos Ricardo, *La Kábala. Una mística del lenguaje* 213
Baroja, Pío 166
La Barraca 157
Barthes, Roland 158
Bartolomé Pons, Esther 165
Baudrillard, Jean 143
Baumgarten, Murray 239n.7
Beauvoir, Simone de 120
Bedient, Calvin 240–41n.6
The Beheading of the Innocents 91; and bees, flowers, sword 92
"Beheading the Baptist": doves 99; knife 89; neck 90, 92
Belamich, André 141, 204
Bello, Pepín 22
Belsey, Catherine 208
Benito, Emilio de 245n.11
Bergamín, José 36
Berger and Kellner 244n.7
Berger and Luckman 16
Bergman, Hjalmar 244n.3
Bible 135
billy goat 31, 75, 113, 131, 134, 150, 157, 160,

263

171, 178, 233; "The Billy Goat" 141; diabolical image 134, 141, 142, 155; "Dream" 141; Leviticus 134; "mute devil" 141, 149; orgies and perversions 135; satanism 142; sexuality 142
"The Billy Goat" 24, 130, 140, 156, 169, 174, 193, 198, 218, 233; and homosexual love 144
birds 102, 214
"The Birth of Christ" 46
Binding, Paul 208; and *Lorca: The Gay Imagination* 50, 57
The Black Ball 44, 118
Blanco Aguinaga, Carlos 15–16
Blanco Amor, Eduardo 18, 50
Blanquet, Josette 191
"Blind Panorama of New York" 47, 214, 220, 221; and death 97
blood 172–73; and animal blood, "sailor blood" 76, 77, 104
Blood Wedding 45, 69; blood 172, 173; branches 175; green 175; horses 172, 174; horse's lullaby 174; horse's tail 175; movie of 173
Book of Poems 18, 109, 113, 130–31, 157, 226
Bordier, Roger 47
Borel, Jacques 140
Bosch, Rafael 185
Bosquet, Alain 19
Bousoño, Carlos 205, 243n.2
Boutet, F., *Dictionnaire des sciences occultes* 134
"breed" 75
Bremmer, Jan 189
Bretón, André 153
Brines, Francisco 17, 18, 59
Brown, Norman O. 29
Brown, Phil 168
bunches of grapes 131–32; "Ode to Walt Whitman 132; and Prados, "If I Could..." 132
Buñel, Luis 51, 166; and *My Last Sigh* 123
Bush, Douglas 179
Busoño, Carlos 167
Bussell Thomson, B.: and J.K. Walsh, García Lorca and Hart Crane 79
butterfly 102, 122, 156
The Butterfly's Evil Spell 102, 121, 156; and Alacranito, Butterfly 89; Boybeetle 121, 122, 156; Sylvia 121
Buxán Bran, Xosé M. 60
Byrd, Suzanne 46, 147

Caballero, José 41
Cáceres, Spain 236
Cadaqués, Spain, and Dalí 58
Calvo, García 86
Campos, Pere Miquel 18
Cano, José Luis 41
Cano Ballesta, Juan: and García Lorca and Miguel Hernández 81 186

"Caprice" 224
Carlavilla del Barrio, Mauricio, and *Sodomitas* 138–39
Carlos, A.J. 179
Caro Baroja, Julio 134, 158, 165, 169
Carreira, Antonio 15–16
Carrere, Emilio 178
"The Carthusian Monastery" 239n.6
"caste" 76
Cátedra 195
Catholic Church 69
Catholic Monarchs 136
Cavendish, Richard 171
Cavero, Iñigo 52, 238n.5
Cela, Camilo José: *Diccionario secreto* 81 88, 221; *Mazurka for Two Dead Men* 186
Cernuda, Luis 15–17, 18, 26, 59–60, 94; "Again with Feeling" 230; "Apologia pro vita sua" 65, 165; "Birds in the Night" 229; *Estudios sobre poesía contemporánea* 20; "The Forbidden Pleasures" 107, 219; "La gloria del poeta" 107, 228; "If Only a Man Could Say" 132, 225; "Lightkeeper's Soliloquy" 143; Lorca 20, 117; Nietzsche 228; "El poeta y los mitos" 185, 229; *Reality and Desire* 164; "River" 175; sea, use of 155; "Seated Bellys" 68; "Sleep, Boy" 191; "Spanish Diptych" 65; "Speaking of Flowers" 116; *What a Pity It Was My Land* 27; *Where Oblivion Dwells* 155, 201
Cerón, Miguel 45
Chalus, P. 190
Chamorro, María Luisa 236
"Childhood and Death" 42, 55, 94–95, 212, 239n.10; "blood of sailors" 97; childhood as otherness, as rat, fish and rats, fish as phallic symbol 95; childhood and rats 97, 232; childhood and sexuality 96; Fuente Vaqueros 96; "the other half" 97; sailor suit 96–97; sewers 97, 104
"Children's Cradle Songs" 72
"Children's Lullaby" 174, 175
Christ 180, 231; and fig tree 186; homosexual passion 100–03; Lorca's oeuvre 58, 102
"Christmas on the Hudson": and accursed "race," beheading of sailors 92
Chronicle of Indifference 175
"cielo" ("heaven," "sky"): 240n.11
Cirlot, *Dictionary of Symbols*: and alchemy 173; billy goat 133; flowers 125; gloves 219; golden flower 173 217; laurel leaves 193; Mercury 112–13; numbers 213; pilgrim 169; rats, mice 95; serpent 171
"Cloister" 239n.6
Cobb, Carl W. 98, 183, 204
Cocteau, Jean 58; sailors 78; sea, ass 154; *The White Book* 78
Colecchia, Francesca 202
ConCiencia de un singular deseo 60
Conquest, Robert 208

Córdoba, Pedro 140, 141, 150,
Cordobilla González, Angelina 56
Corominas, J. 134
"corporations" 216, 232
Correa, Gustavo 68, 174, 190
Corsés, Dr. Valentín 166
Coseriu 117
Couffon, Claude 182
Councils of Toledo 135
Craige, Betty Jean 68, 71, 98
Crane, Hart: drinking 80; García Lorca 79 84; homosexuality 79; "Reply" 35; sailors 80
"The Crazy Boy" 24, 97, 203, 206, 208, 226
Criado de Val, Manuel, *Dictionary of Ambiguous Spanish* 81, 214
Cronus (Saturn, Time) 153
Crosby, J.O. 220
"Crucifixión" 101, 147, 160
"Cry to Rome" 75 104, 127, 139, 145, 148, 231, 245n.10; dove 98; "head full of excrement" 239n.7; "man dressed in white" 75; Pope and Rome 100–01; sewers 96, 195
Cuadernos El Público 52–53
"Cueva" 145
Cummings, Philip 43; and García Lorca 82; and Daniel Eisenberg 82
"Cut Down by the Sky" 101, 150
Cyssus 131, 132, 232

Dadaism 166
Dagger: as penis 86; and plowing, sowing 87
Dalí, Salvador 15, 25, 53, 70, 75, 86, 133, 172, 185, 187, 227; and Freud 167; Lorca's head 90; "Reality and Superrealism" 35; relationship with Lorca 19, 36, 58, 97, 215, 219
"Dance of Death" 125
Daniel, M., and A. Baudry, *Los homosexuales* 144, 151
Dante Alighieri, *The Divine Comedy* 148, 153
Daphne 157, 193
Darío, Rubén 141; "Responso a Verlaine" 178, 179; "Verlaine"and *Los raros* 177, 180
"dark love" 27 42, 46
"Dawn" 227, 228
death, as Lorquian motif 84, 233
D'Eaubonne, Françoise
Debicki, A. P. 183, 203
"Debussy" 182
Delcourt, Marie 190
Démeron, Pierre 146
Derrida, Jacques 158, 242n.5(chapter 4)
"Desolate Song" 197
La destrucción de Sodoma 44, 46, 119, 147, 150
Detienne, Marcel 191
"Dialogue of Amargo, the Bitter One": Alvarez de Miranda on 85; Carl Cobb on 85; González Cruz on 85; L.F. Vivanco on 85; Loughran on 85; plot of 85; Rider and Amargo 88; Rider as death 87
"Dialogues with the Moon" 236
"El diamante" 227
Diana, and moon 191
Díaz Plaja, Guillermo 130
Dictionary of Spanish Slang 102, 175
Dictionary of World Mythology 112, 158
Diego, Gerardo 18, 202
"Digression: The Rules of Music" 215; and "corporations" 216, 232
Dionysus 179, 187, 193, 194
Dionysus-Bacchus 187
"Dispute" (*Gypsy Ballads*) 187
"Disquiet and Night" 205
dogs 192; and Count of Lautréamount 192; and Dante's *Divine Comedy* 192; and homosexuality 192; *Impressions and Landscapes* 192; "Qasida of the Branches" 192; "Sonnet of the Sweet Complaint" 193
Domínguez, Antonio José 63
Doña Rosita the Spinster 126, 182; and dahlias 126
"Double Poem of Lake Eden" 63, 110, 145, 180, 181
Douché, Jean 112
Douglas, Lord Alfred: and Oscar Wilde 144
Dove 232; and "Cry to Rome" 98, 104; Holy Spirit 98, 104; Lorca's lecture on Góngora 99; Lorquian dove 98, 115; "mouse traps" 99; "the other half" 104; paloma 99; purity sexuality 99, 104; Yerma 99
"Dream" (1919) 129–30, 169, 194, 198, 233; and demonic 171; grandfather 70; horse's lullaby 174; shadow 170; swan 170–71
dreams 31, 232
"The Drunken Sailor" 75; and Church of Rome 75
Duchamp 166
duende 81, 110, 114, 180, 220, 238n.4(chapter 2)
"The *Duende*: Theory and Divertissement" 110, 152, 233–34

"Earth and Moon" 86, 222
"Ecce Homo" 100–01; and Rome and Pope 100
Eisenberg, Daniel 26, 37, 44, 46, 50, 55, 82, 99, 238n.7, 240n.14
"Elegía" 23
"Elegía a María Blanchard" 212
"Elegía del silencio" 24
El Gamoun, Ahmed 58
Eliade, Mircea 191, 226
Ellis, P.J.: and *The Poetry of Emilio Prados* 15; Prados 154; *The Three Nights of Man* 164
Enciclopedia Ilustrada de Sexología y Erotismo 70, 73
"The Encounters of an Adventurous Snail" 158–59

Encyclopedia of World Mythology: and billy goat 134
Engels, Frederick 106
Epps, Bradley S. 61
Eros 204
"Eros with a Cane" 204
Erotique du Surréalisme 221
"Escena" 205
Espmark, Kjell, *To Translate the Soul* 208, 220
Estévez Molinero, Angel 122, 123
Estrella 157–58
Euripides and *The Bacchants* 188
Exile 15

fags 71
Farrel, J.T. 77
Faulkner, William 77
Feal Delibe, Carlos 45, 145, 221, 238n.2(chapter 1)
Fernández Almagro, Melchor 24; and Lorca's letters to 21, 22, 25, 38, 184, 189, 213, 221
Fernández-Galiano, Manuel 141
Fernández Leborans, María Jesús, and *Light and Darkness in Spanish Mysticism* 223
Fernández Montesinos, Manuel 236
Fernández Retama, Roberto 14
Ferreiro, Alfredo Mark 111
Ferrer, Esther 93
Ferreres, Rafael 177; and *Verlaine y los modernistas españoles* 177
Fierro, A. 165
fig tree 186, 189, 190, 195, 198; and ancient Rome 186; and Bible 186, 188; and mumurs 188; and mythology 186; and sexual symbolism 187
First Songs 24
"Flesh" 81–82, 175; and "blood" of the "rigid heart" 125; "conquers and shines" 125; "I Know That My Profile Will Be Serene" 124–25; "rhythm" 125; "shines," "sound" 125; "the sky's inhuman blush" 125; "veins" 81–82
Flight 70–71; and birds 70; and poetic flight 70
Flores, Angel 79
Flys, Jonathan M. 38
Fonville-Alquier, François 152
Forberg, Friedrich-Karl 74
Ford, Clellan, and Frank S. Beach 118
Forradellas, Joaquín 220
Foster, David William 62
Foucault, Michel 106–07; and *A Dialogue on Power* 107
"Four Ballads in Yellow" 214
Franco, Francisco 18
Fray Antonio 131
Freud, Anna 189
Freud, Sigmund 49, 163, 166, 167, 181, 187, 221, 244n.7; and *Delusions and Dreams in Jensen's "Gravida"* 198; and phallic symbols 85; plow as phallus 86
Freudian ego, superego, id 70
"Fright in the Dining Room" 204
Frye, Northrup 187
Fuller, Henry, *Bertram Cope's Year* 152

Galán, Lola 166
Gallego Morell, Antonio 167
Ganymede 178, 191
Garaudy, Roger 59
García Carrillo, Francisco 72,
García Lorca, Federico: and asexuality 52; Christ 103; drinking 79; *duende* 84; fiftieth anniversary of Lorca's death 50; first love 94; "flesh" 81; Góngora, lecture on 72 114; internal crisis 22, 110; *juvenilia* 51; messianism 103; nervous breakdown 67; New York 23; Proust, and lecture on Góngora 76, 220; rose sailors 84; sea 21; sexuality and singing 92; silences 23, 25; trip to United States 22; Walt Whitman 73, 113; writings of *see* individual titles
García Lorca, Francisco 35, 48, 131, 202, 203; and *Federico y su mundo* 67
García-Posada, Miguel 41, 42, 55, 56, 68–69, 239n.10; and bacchanal 71; *Book of Poems* 130; "Cry to Rome" 98–99; Lorca and sailors 78, 84; "Your Childhood in Menton" 122
García Valdés, Alberto 28, 123, 136
Garro, Elena 16
Gauthier, Xavier, and surrealism, surrealists 85
Gay, Peter 243n.11A
Geist, Anthony L. 51
Gellrich, Michelle 57
Generation of '27 14, 16–17, 18, 28, 167, 189, 208, 210, 221, 229
Genesis 19 147
Genet, Jean 146, 241n.4, 243n.6
"Geometry" 209
Gershator, David 167
"Ghazal of Desperate Love" 96, 116, 147, 149
"Ghazal of the Bitter Root" 58, 84
Gibson, Ian 42, 50, 53, 54, 56, 69, 112, 225, 236, 238n.7; Aladrén, Lorca and Proust 92; billy goat 141; *The Death of Lorca* 45; *Federico García Lorca* (3 vols.) 49, 52; *Guía a la Granada de Federico García Lorca* 62; homosexual relationship between Lorca and Dalí 20; Lorca's death 36; Lorca's homosexuality 53–54, "Sad Ballad" 131
Gide, André 34, 94, 138, 145–46, 151, 168; and *Corydon* 145–46; and *Le voyage d'Urien* 151
Gil-Albert, Juan 15–18; 20, 26, 30, 59–60, 109, 143, 182, 228, 230; and "Before the Sea" 155; *Bíblica* 74; "Didático" 148; "The Fig Tree" 193; *Heraclés* 219; Lorca 21; "Once

Autumn" 131; *Origins of Evidence* 132; "Raid" 200–01; "Shattered Culture" 68; "To an Andalusian Boy" 155; "veins" and *Presencia misteriosa* 81; "Your Lies" 163
Ginsberg, Allen: and Hart Crane 81; *Howl and Other Poems* 81; sailors 81
Girard, René 120, 133
Glossary of Obscenities 102
Golden Age 243n.8
Goldman, Lucién 122
Gómez, Betty Rita: and death, García Lorca 84
Gómez Beneyeto, Manuel 28
Gómez Contreras, Cristina 42
González Cruz, F., and death 85
González del Valle, Luis T. 217
González Espina, Carlos 53
González Ruano, Cesár 53
Goytisolo, José Agustín 16; and *Posible imagen de Lezama Lima* 14
Goytisolo, Juan 16; and Arabs, homosexuality, Morocco, works by 60–61; *Juan the Landless* 116
Granada 45, 56, 62, 88, 120, 182
"Granada" 185
Greece, and young men 74
Greek mythology 112
Green, Julian 94, 137, 167
Guerenabarrera, Juanjo 53
Guillén, Jorge 18, 203, 210
Gullón, Ricardo 178, 179
The Gypsy Ballads 53, 70, 211
"The Gypsy Nun" 64

Hahn, Pierre 144
Halliburton, Charles Lloyd 68
Hammar, Karl Gustav 100
Hamon, Philippe 142
Harris, Derek 47, 68; and "Cry to Rome" 98; *Luis Cernuda: A Study of the Poetry* 17, 107
"head full of excrement" 239n.7
Healey, John 235
Hellenism 43
Hermes 113
Hernández, Mario 48, 55, 108–09
Hernández, Miguel 81, 186
Hernández Castenado, Francisco 102
Hess, Carlota 166
heterosexual culture 52
Hierro, José S.P. 117
Higginbotham, Virginia 80
Higuera Rojas, Eulalia-Dolores de la, and *Women in the Life of García Lorca* 42
"hilo" ("thread," "linen") 240n.3
"Holy Year" 235
Homosexuality and Christian culture 104, 161, 241n.1, 245n.10; crucifixion 102; "culture" 238n.4(chapter 1); "the established culture" 65, 229, 230; homoeroticism 14; homosexual culture 15, 25, 26, 27, 63, 65, 106;

homosexual love 14, 25, 26, 28, 29, 149; literary criticism 14; norms 118; oppressed class 106; otherness 93, 94; "our culture" 65, 232, 233; silence 24
Homosexuals in Society 238n.4(chapter 1)
Horses, symbolism of 172
Houston, John Porter 139
Huber, Egon 224

"I Know That My Profile Will Be Serene" 31, 106, 108, 119, 126, 232, 233; and blush, crocodile's blush 115; broom, bitter like broom 116; dahlias 125, 126; death 109; desert 116; dove 115; "Hermes-Mercury" 125, 126; Holy Spirit, flame, dove 115; "ivy" 114, 127; "neck" 109; "north" 109; oppressed norms 117, 127, 232; "profile" 110; profile in the sand 116; "pulse" 110, 113; "sky" 109; "stiff" 109, 124; ivy, thread 114; tongue 109; tongue of fire 115
"Idilio" 145, 181
"Imaginación, inspiración, evasion" 163, 168
Impressions and Landscapes 87, 144, 176, 182, 185
impure 72, 74; and women 74
"In the Frame of Don Cristóbal: A Farce" 89
Infántes, Victor 54–55
"International" 127
inverse, inverted 71, 160
"Invocación al laurel" 24, 113, 147, 193, 226
Isherwood, Christopher, *A Single Man* 200–01

Jacobson, Roman 117
James, Henry, *The Turn of the Screw* 94
Jammes, F. 34
Janssen-Jurreit, Marie Louise 106
"Jardines" 143
Jenkyns, Richard 74
Jiménez, José 150
Jiménez, Juan Ramón 182
"Joke About Don Pedro on Horseback" 145
Josipovici, Gabriel 209
Judeo-Christian culture 73
Juvenilia 69, 70

Kamen, Henry 136, 159
King, Francis 135, 172, 240n.1
King Flavio Egica 136
King Flavio Rescindo 136
"King of Harlem" 116
Kinsey, William, and Kinsey's studies 38, 40
"kisses" 82
Klein, Dennis A. 122
Kleinberg, Seymour 77
knife, symbolism of 86, 88
Kolakowski, Ledzek, and *libido sciendi, libido sentiendi* 150, 155–56

Laclau, Ernest 106
Laffranque, Marie 42, 118, 147, 168, 195, 203

Laguardia, Gari 47
Laing, R.D., *The Divided Self* 206, 226, 237n.3; *Self and Others* 133, 189
Lambert, Gavin 218
Landell, Nils-Erik 111
"Landscape" 220
"Landscape of a Vomiting Multitude" 80
Lapesa, Soriano 67
Larrea, Juan 15, 37, 107
Laubenthal: *Leaves of* Grass and *PNY* 73; Penne Jones 47
"Leave Taking" 206
Legal Code 135
Lenson, David 57
León, Victor 102
Lévi-Strauss, Claude 158
Lezama Lima, José 14
"Literary Conversations" (and Lorca) 23
A Literary History of Spain 203
"Little Infinite Poem" 181, 210
"Little Stanton" 99, 113, 124, 182
"Little Viennese Waltz" 55
"Living Sky" 115, 226
Llamas, Ricardo 60
"lo inconfesable" 14
"Looking for Lorca" 236
López Calera, Nicolás 56
López Castellón 72, 227
Lorca, the Death of a Poet 52
Loren, Victoriano Domingo, *Homosexuals Before the Law* 135
Lorquian criticism 40, 65, 140
Loughran, David, and sailors 78
"love in the taverns" 131; and *The Public* 131
The Love of Don Perlimplín and Belissa in the Garden 221; and penis as sun-fish 95
"Lovers Slain by a Partridge" 114, 230
Lozano, Jorge 30
"Lucía Martínez" 204
Lucifer 150, 151, 160
Lucifer-Venus 174

Machado, Manuel 177
"Madrigal" 217
Magazine Littéraire 53
Mallo, Maruja 72
Marañón, Dr. Gregorio 75, 123
"March Nocturne" 133–34, 148
Marcial 81
Marcilly, Charles 40
Marful, Inés 53
marginalization 16
Marinello, Juan 108, 110, 111
Marqués, Josef Vicent, "Infinity Is Equal to Two" 211
"The Marriage Vow" 63, 205, 206
Martín, Eutimio 51, 101, 102, 176, 180, 227, 238n.3(chapter 1); 238n.6; and "The Billy Goat" 131, 142; *The Love of Don Perlimplín and Belissa in the Garden* 103; and Marcolfa 103
Martínez, Nadal Rafael 44, 45, 46, 48, 112, 115, 153, 175, 205, 207; and "Childhood and Death" 94, 96; death and García Lorca 84–85
"Martyrdom of St. Eulalia" 159
Marx, Karl 106; and Marxism 106
Masters, William: and Virginia Johnson 28
Mateos Miera, Eladio 60
Maurer, Christopher 103, 235, 238n.3(chapter 2); and Chaplin 103
Mauron, Charles 189
May, Rollo 184
"May No One Ever Know My Secret" 197; the bitter 197
Mayer, Hans 146
"Meditation Under the Rain" 174
"Mediterranean" 111, 175
Melville, Herman 137
Mendicutti, Eduardo 60
Mercury 109, 111, 112, 113, 114, 232, 240n.2
Meridian Handbook of Classical Mythology 112
Merlau-Ponty, Maurice 29
Michael, and Herman Bang 215
Millán, María Clementa 57–58, 68, 101
Millán Chaparro, Miguel 236
Miller, Norman 87
Milorad, and Cocteau, sailors 78
Minguet, P.H. 240n.4
Mira, Alberto 3, 9, 60
Mirror (as metaphor) 23
"Mirror That Does Not End" 164
"Mística" 81
Moix, Terenci 60; and Oscar Wilde's *Salomé* 90–91
Monegal, Antonio 57
moon 190, 191
"Moon and Panorama of the Insects" 113
"Moon Appears" 204
Mora, Miguel 235
Mora Guarnido, José 29, 34, 40, 141
Morand, Paul, and homosexuals and the plague 95
Morla, Carlos 34
"Morning" 174
Morris, C. Brian 166
moss 111
mounting, as symbol 87
El Mundo 235
Murcia, J.I. 164
"My Shadow's Soul" 156
The Mystical Geometry of the Soul in Spanish Literature of the Golden Age 210
Mysticism That Treats the Curbs Society Places on the Nature of Our Body and Souls 140
Myth 140, 169
Mythology of the Renaissance Tradition 158

Naranjo, Eduardo 101
"Narciso" 24, 182, 183, 203
Narcissus 183
"Native Moments" 112
Neruda, Pablo 55, 238n.7
"Nest" 24
New Spain 244n.8
"New York (Office and Denunciation)" 68, 69, 75, 113, 123
Newton, Candela S. 131
Nicanor, Enrique 235
Nickel, Catherine 182
Nieto, José C. 179, 245n.9
Nietzsche, Friedrich 59; and *Dawn* 227, 228
"The Night Sings Naked" 92
"Nocturne of the Void" 115, 153
"Nocturnes from the Window" 221
"Nocturno de marzo" 190
nomos 203
"Nu" 204
Nuñez de Arce, Gaspar 177

"O secret voice of dark love" 75
O'Brian, Justin 165
Ocaña, the Infinite Fire 50, 63–64, 94, 149, 155; and "little branch" 125
"Ocean" 150–51, 157
"Ode to Savador Dalí" 147–48, 184, 214
"Ode to Walt Whitman" 24, 46, 55, 71–72, 88, 92, 111, 174, 182, 211, 214; and butterflies 102; faggots 102; faggots as rats 96; purity of "the other half" 93; sewers 99, 101
Ohlson, Elizabeth, and "Ecce Homo" 100–01
Once Five Years Pass 46, 47, 159, 214, 222; and Boy-Cat, Girl-Cat 181; child 181
Onís, Federico de 202, 203
"oppressed norms" 31, 107, 109, 122; and oppressive norms 107
orality, and aggression and eroticism 69
Ortega, José 47, 49
Ortega y Gasset 29, 166
Other, otherness 93; and homosexuality 93; 163
"the other half" 67–69, 70, 71, 76, 79, 109, 113, 138; and sexuality 99
Our Perverse Ancestors 95–96

Paepe, Christian de 195
Painter, George 49
El País 236
Palencia, Benjamín 21
"Palimpsestos" 24
Panebianco, Candido 87
"Panida" (Pan) 178, 195
Parr, J.A. 82
Partridge, Eric 14, 88
Pasolini, Pier Pablo 146
Pater, Walter 74
Pavano, Pastora 110

Paz, Octavio 16, 29; and Cernuda 229; *Graces and Disgraces of the Eye of an Ass* 114
Pearson, Hesketh 14
Pederasts 14
Penón, Augustín 56
Pérez Rodá, Ramón
Peyre, Henri 119
Plato 45, 180, 210; *Dialogues* 67; Platonic myth of Venus 150; *Symposium* 190
Poem of the Deep Song 24
Poesía 53
"The Poet Asks His Love to Write Him" 64; and "veins," "waist" 82
Poet in New York 23, 37, 47, 57; and alcohol, sailors 80
"The Poet Prays to the Virgin for Help" 76
poison 211
Porché, François 144
Portrait of a Family 235
Poulet, George 210
Prada, Juan Manuel de 236
Prados, Emilio 14–16, 18, 26, 230; "Ascención" 173; "The Betrayed Betrayal" 210; "Cross of the Sea" 154; *The Daily Heart and Other Songs* 154; *Diario íntimo* 21; *En voz continua* 16; "Hour of Birth" 150; "If I Could..." 154; Lorca 14, 20; "Naked Angel" 154–55; *Persecuted Body* 148; "Return to the Shadow" 148; *Semi-Darkness I* 71; *Signos de ser* 70–71; "Solitudes" 154; *Time* 154; "Tower of Signs" 164, 194; "Underground Weeping" 68; *The Written Stone* 194
"Prayer" 197
"The Prayer of the Roses" 176, 177, 180, 182
"Preciosa and the Wind" 145
Predmore, Richard 68, 115, 122, 224
"Premonition" 156–57
Prieto, Gregorio: Cernuda 84; *The Drawings of Lorca* 83; García Lorca, sailors 84; *Lorca y su mundo angélico* 83; sailors 83; St. Eulalia 159
"Prologue" 160
Proust, Marcel 14, 49; and persecution of homosexuals 76; *Sodome et Gomorrhe* 76, 118, 119, 125, 146, 147
Proust and the Art of Love 14
The Public 23, 44, 45, 52, 57, 63–64, 69, 77, 89, 91, 92–93, 97, 101, 115, 133, 148, 153, 173, 211, 219, 230, 236; and Christ 103; sea and ass 154
purity 22, 23, 67, 71–72, 75, 232; and Roman Centurion 75; Roman Centurion as a rat 95

Queensberry, Lord 189
"queer with the bowtie" 60, 63
queers 71, 72
Querelle de Brest: and Cocteau, Genet, Fassbinder 78
Quevedo, Francisco de 220

Racionero, Luis 168
Ramos, Carlos 48
Rasmussen, Poul 143, 242n.7
"raza," "race" 238n.2(chapter 2)
Read, K.E. 240n.5
Real Academia de la Lengua 18
Residencia de Estudiantes 20, 227
"Rhythm of Autumn" 75
Ricoeur, Paul 30, 106
"Rider's Song" 202
Rimbaud, Arthur 15, 180, 229; and "The Drunken Boat" 154; *A Season in Hell* 138, 139, 152
"Rinconcillo" 34, 237n.1(chapter 1)
Río, Angel del 37, 43, 79, 202
Ríos, Fernando de los 67, 238n.1
Ríos, Laura de los 48
Rivas Cherif, Cipriano 38, 39, 40, 104
Rivers, J.E. 14, 165, 178
Roberts, Gemma 202
Rodrigo, Antonina 238n.6, 242n.3; and *García Lorca en Cataluña* 46; *Lorca-Dalí: A Betrayed Friendship* 19, 38; *Memoria de Granada: Manuel Angeles Ortiz, Federico García Lorca* 49
Rof Caballo, Juan 166, 242n.2
Rojas, Carlos 19, 49
"Romance" 196; bull, death 197
Romeo and Juliet 175
Rosales, Luis 18
rose 181, 182, 183
Rosselló, Ramón 136
Rowse, A.L. 80
Rubert de Ventós, Xavier 32
Ruiz Alonso, Ramón 36
Ruiz Castillo 166
Ruiz López, Andrés 63, 218, 241n.7

Sábato, Ernest 25
Sabbat 134; and witches' Sabbat 134, 135
"Sad Ballad" 225, 226
Saénz de la Calzada, Luis 41, 147, 157, 244n.4
Sahuquillo, Angel 102
Sailors 80; and Cocteau, Jean 78; García Lorca's drawings of 79; García-Posada 78; homosexuality 77; Loughran, David 78;"sailor blood" 76, 77, 79
Saint Augustine 150
Sainz de la Maza, Regino, Lorca's letter to 170, 212, 216
Salazar, Adolfo 214
Salinas, Pedro 210; and death, García Lorca 84
Salvador, Gregorio 49
"San Gabriel" (*Gypsy Ballads*) 218
"San Miguel" (*Gypsy Ballads*) 39, 218
"San Rafael" (*Gypsy Ballads*) 217, 218
San Vicente Orchard 56
Sánchez Mejías, Ignacio 169
Sánchez Vidal, Agustín 54

Sanchis Barnús, José 20, 164
Santos Torroella, Rafael 19, 89, 111, 167, 215, 219; and *Honey Is Sweeter Than Blood* 185
Sarotte, Georges Michel 77, 94, 136, 152
Sartre, Jean Paul 241n.4; and *Saint Genet* 133
Satan, and homosexuals 241n.1
Satué, Francisco J. 51
Saturn 178, 242n.4
Savater, Fernando
Schonberg, Jean-Louis 40, 41, 42, 50, 131, 157
Sebastián, Santiago 149
Segal, Charles 73; and Euripides' *The Bacchants* 132, 188, 194
Sémolué, J. 137
Semprún, Jorge 55
Semprún Donahue, Moraima de 46, 213; and Lorca, beheadings, *Salomé* 91
"Serenade" 92
Sesé, Bernard 69, 203
Seville 17
"The Sexism of the Ministry of Health" 243n.11B
Shadows 170, 180, 244n.2
Shakespeare, William 14; and *Measure for Measure* 88; *Romeo and Juliet*, and beheading 89
Shamblin, Donald Gray 44
Sheklin, Barbara 44
Shepherd, Esther 112
Shephard, Matthew 102
The Shoemaker's Prodigious Wife 220
Sierra Nevada, Spain 86
Las siete partidas 136
Silvanus 158
Silver, Philip 107; and *From Cernuda's Hand* 17; *The Poetry of Luis Cernuda* 16; Six Galician Poems 18
"The Silver Poplars" 155
Singer, June, *Androgyny* 76, 150
"Sketch for an Ode" 114
sky 150, 240n.11; in "Mediterranean" 111; "Ode to Walt Whitman" 111
"Sleepless City" 81, 82–83
"Sleepwalking Ballad" 46, 49
Socrate, Mario 191
Socrates 180
Sodome et Gomorrhe 76, 118, 119
Sodomy, sodomites 118–119
Sollers, Philippe 148–149,
"Some Souls" 146
"Song for the Moon" 160
"Song of the Fairy" 92, 202
"Song of the Seven-Hearted Boy" 25
Songs 24, 202, 203, 231
"Sonnet of the Sweet Complaint" 132–33
Sonnets of Dark Love 41, 42, 54
Sorel, Andrés 36, 51
Soriano Gil, Manuel 138

Spain 56; and democracy 17, 23; homophobia 51; homosexual culture 14
Spanish Civil War 15, 18
Spencer, Janes Frances 224
Spijker, Herman van de 212
Spinoza, Benito 210
"Spiritual Twilight" 196
Soufas, Christopher
Sousa, Ronald de 168, 171
"Spring" 157
"Star(s)" 158, 159, 163
"Stone" 164
"Suicide" 31 147, 201, 206, 208, 231; and ashes and fire 219, 220, 233; balcony and tower 220, 221; broken wings 214; broken wings and rag flowers 216; clock 222; geometry 209; gloves 218, 219; lad 212; mirror-shadow 223, 225; ten 213; white silk divan 226
"Suicidio en Alejandría" 213
"Summer Madrigal," and Estrella 157–158
Surrealism 166
Svenning, Olle 100

Teatro inconcluso 118, 147
thread 114 116
"Three Portraits with Shading" 182
Tijeras, Eduardo 51
Tirso de Molina 220
toads 149
Todorov, Tzvetan 240n.4; and other 93
"The Tombs of Burgos" 144
Tomkins, Peter 214, 244n.6, 244n.8
Torre, Guillermo de 18, 43, 120, 144
Torre, Dr. Luis de la 36
Trescastro, Juan Luis 36–37, 51
"Trip to the Moon" 166, 167
Tripp, C.A. 77, 145
"Two Sailors Ashore" 24, 115
"Two Views from the Bridge" 80

Ullán, José Miguel 15
Umbral, Francisco 45, 46, 54, 141
Unamuno, Miguel de, *The Life of Don Quixote and Sancho* 103
"Uncertain Solitude" 151, 204
Unpublished Poetry of Youth 195; the bitter 196 "unredeemable" 67 69
"unspeakable" 17, 327n.1(Introduction)
Uppsala 100
Uranism 151, 152
Uranus 113, 178; and the sea 154; and the sky 151
Uribe, Imanol, and "The Death of Mikel" 61
Utrea, Rafael, *García Lorca y el cinema* 173

Valera, Juan 177
Valle, Adriano del 21, 176, 213
Valle-Inclán, Ramón 143, 144
Valls, Manuel 92

Van der Meersch, Maxence 138
Vásquez Ocaña, Fernando 34, 39, 40, 95, 131, 144, 244n.5
Velasco, Joseph 48, 49, 157
"Venus" 182
"Verlaine" 24 176, 177, 182, 183, 184, 189, 195, 198, 233; and parallelism 185
Verlaine, Paul 176, 179, 180, 183, 203, 229, 241n.2, 242n.5; and "The Abyss" 178; child 181; Christianity 178; fir 181; "fresh veins" as "kissed" penises 83; "The Last Elegant Feast" 178; "Luxures" 139; *Men* 140; *My Imprisonment and Other Autobiographical Writings* 178; Poème saturnien" 178; "Prologue from a Book from Which Only the Abstracts Will Appear" 178; relationship with Rimbaud 139, 178; rose 181; Saturn 178; "The Unrepentant" 178; "vein" and cock, symbol of 81
Victorian period, and homosexual purity 74; white 74; women 74
Vidal, Gore 243n.10
Viers, Rina, and Proust's *Sodome et Gomorrhe* 92
view from within 117, 237n.3
Vigorra, Jesús 236
Villa, Moreno 167
Villegas, Juan 172
Villena, Luis Antonio de 60; and "Cernuda recordado por Aleixandre" 54, 230; *The Inexhaustible Reasoning of Juan Gil-Albert* 17
"Visión" 154
"The Voiceless Child" 24, 145, 205, 208

"Wake Up, Ring Out" 24
Walsh, John K. 55
"Waltz in the Branches" 175
Weimer, Christopher Brian: and Lorca and Tennessee Williams 56–57
Welles, M.L. 47
Wells, C. Michael 121, 122
West, Donald J. 38, 244n.7
Whitman, Walt 80, 112, 120, 127, 147; "In Paths Untrodden" 119; *Leaves of Grass* 47, 119; purity 73; "Songs of Myself 73, 76
Wilber, Ken 239n.9
Wilde, Oscar 34, 149, 168, 239n.8; "The Ballad of Reading Gaol" 35; "De Profundis" 188; Lord Alfred Douglas 144; "Pan" 194; *The Portrait of Dorian Gray* 146; *Salomé* 90–91; Tennessee Williams, *Cat on a Hot Tin Roof* and *Yerma* 56–57
The Wings, and Mauritz Stiller 215
Withoutreason 167, 169
Wolf, Charlotte 118
"Women's Disillusion" 220
"Wounds of Love" 88, 227

Yahni, Roberto 209
Yeats, W.B. 170

Yerma 82, 87, 115, 116, 145, 182, 242–43n.6; and "branch" 125; and dahlias 126
Yermo 87
"Your Childhood in Menton" 71, 117, 153, 154
Yourcenar, Marguerite 121
Yudin, Florence L. 224

Zalamea, Jorge 22; Lorca's letter to 72, 211
Zeus 170
Zola, Émile 137
Zuleta, Emila de 43, 141, 207, 223, 224

www.ingramcontent.com/pod-product-compliance
Ingram Content Group UK Ltd.
Pitfield, Milton Keynes, MK11 3LW, UK
UKHW041930140426
5217IPUK00014B/407